Using

QuickBooks Pro®
FOR ACCOUNTING
2010

Using QuickBooks Pro® FOR ACCOUNTING 2010

Glenn Owen

Allan Hancock College

University of California at Santa Barbara

SOUTH-WESTERN
CENGAGE Learning™

Australia · Brazil · Japan · Korea · Mexico · Singapore · Spain · United Kingdom · United States

**Using QuickBooks Pro
for Accounting 2010**

Glenn Owen

VP/Editorial Director: Jack W. Calhoun

Editor-in-Chief: Rob Dewey

Acquisition Editor: Sharon Oblinger

Developmental Editor: Ted Knight

Editorial Assistant: Julie Warwick

Senior Marketing Manager: Kristen Hurd

Content Project Manager: Sathyabama Kumaran,
PreMediaGlobal

Media Editor: Bryan England

Production Technology Analyst: Adam Graffa

Senior Manufacturing Coordinator: Doug Wike

Production House/Compositor: PreMediaGlobal

Senior Art Director: Stacy Shirley

Permissions Acquisition Manager/
Photo: Deanna Ettinger

Permissions Acquisition Manager/
Text: Mardell Glinski Schultz

Cover and Internal Designer: cmiller design

Cover Image: © iStock Photo

For product information and technology assistance, contact us at
Cengage Learning Customer & Sales Support, 1-800-354-9706

For permission to use material from this text or product,
submit all requests online at **www.cengage.com/permissions**
Further permissions questions can be emailed to
permissionrequest@cengage.com

Library of Congress Control Number: 2010926285

Student Edition ISBN 13: 978-0-538-47587-7
Student Edition ISBN 10: 0-538-47587-0
Student Edition with CD ISBN 13: 978-0-538-47585-3
Student Edition with CD ISBN 10: 0-538-47585-4

South-Western Cengage Learning
5191 Natorp Boulevard
Mason, OH 45040
USA

Cengage Learning products are represented in Canada by
Nelson Education, Ltd.

For your course and learning solutions, visit **www.cengage.com**
Purchase any of our products at your local college store or at our
preferred online store **www.cengagebrain.com**

Printed in the United States of America
1 2 3 4 5 6 7 13 12 11 10

Brief Contents

Part 1 Getting Started with QuickBooks   1

Chapter   1   **An Interactive Tour of QuickBooks**   2

Chapter   2   **Preparing a Balance Sheet Using QuickBooks**   28

Chapter   3   **Preparing an Income Statement Using QuickBooks**   45

Chapter   4   **Preparing a Statement of Cash Flows Using QuickBooks**   67

Chapter   5   **Creating Supporting Reports to Help Make Business Decisions**   76

Part 2 Creating a QuickBooks File to Record and Analyze Business Events   95

Chapter   6   **Setting Up Your Business's Accounting System**   96

Chapter   7   **Cash-Oriented Business Activities**   149

Chapter   8   **Additional Business Activities**   218

Chapter   9   **Adjusting Entries**   261

Chapter 10   **Budgeting**   289

Chapter 11   **Reporting Business Activities**   312

Appendix 1   **Payroll Taxes**   348

Appendix 2   **Traditional Accounting: Debits and Credits**   358

Index   369

Contents

Preface xi
Note to the Student and Instructor xix

Part 1 Getting Started with QuickBooks 1

Chapter 1 An Interactive Tour of QuickBooks 2

Case: Century Kitchens 2
Using This Text Effectively 3
QuickBooks Application Installation CD 3
Data Files CD 4
What Is QuickBooks? 4
Lists 4
Forms 5
Registers 5
Reports and Graphs 5
Launching QuickBooks 8
Restoring and Opening a QuickBooks File 8
The QuickBooks Window 9
Backing Up and Closing a QuickBooks File 11
QuickBooks's Menus and Shortcut List 12
Using QuickBooks to Make Business Decisions:
    An Example at Century Kitchens 12
Printing in QuickBooks 15
Using QuickBooks Help 16
The QuickBooks Home Page 17
QuickBooks Coach and Tutorials 21
Exiting QuickBooks 24
End Note 24
Chapter 1 Practice 25
Questions 25
Matching 25
Assignments 26

Chapter 2 Preparing a Balance Sheet Using QuickBooks 28

Case: Century Kitchens 28
Creating a Balance Sheet 28
Creating a Comparative Balance Sheet 30
Creating a Summary Balance Sheet 31
Investigating the Balance Sheet Using
    QuickZoom 32
Modifying Balance Sheet Reports 35
Memorizing a Report in QuickBooks 38
Printing the Balance Sheet 40
Chapter 2 Practice 41
Questions 41
Matching 41
Assignments 42
Case Problem 1: Sierra Marina 43
Case Problem 2: Jennings & Associates 44

Chapter 3 Preparing an Income Statement Using QuickBooks 45

Case: Century Kitchens 45
Date Formats 45
Creating an Income Statement 46
Modifying an Income Statement 47
Creating a Comparative Income Statement 50
Using QuickZoom with the Income Statement 52
Modifying the Income Statement Report 53
Printing the Income Statement 57
Chapter 3 Practice 63
Questions 63
Matching 63
Assignments 64
Case Problem 1: Sierra Marina 65
Case Problem 2: Jennings & Associates 65

Chapter 4 Preparing a Statement of Cash Flows Using QuickBooks 67

Case: Century Kitchens 67
Creating a Statement of Cash Flows 67
Using QuickZoom with the Statement
    of Cash Flows 71

Formatting and Printing the Statement
 of Cash Flows   72
Chapter 4 Practice   73
Questions   *73*
Matching   *73*
Assignment   *74*
Case Problem 1: Sierra Marina   *74*
Case Problem 2: Jennings & Associates   *75*

Chapter 5 Creating Supporting Reports to Help Make Business Decisions   76

Case: Century Kitchens   76
Creating and Printing an Accounts Receivable
 Aging Report   76
Creating and Printing a Customer Balance Summary   80
Creating and Printing an Inventory Valuation
 Summary Report   81
Creating, Printing, and Analyzing an Accounts
 Payable Aging Report   83
Creating and Printing a Vendor Balance Summary   85
End Note   89
Chapter 5 Practice   90
Questions   *90*
Matching   *90*
Assignments   *91*
Case Problem 1: Sierra Marina   *92*
Case Problem 2: Jennings & Associates   *92*

Part 2 Creating a QuickBooks File to Record and Analyze Business Events   95

Chapter 6 Setting Up Your Business's Accounting System   96

Case: Wild Water Sports, Inc.   96
Creating a New Company File Using the EasyStep
 Interview   97
Set Up Company Preferences   101
Set Up Company Items   104
Set Up Customers, Vendors, and Accounts   110
Set Up Payroll and Employees   120

Backing Up Your Company File   127
End Note   129
Chapter 6 Practice   131
Questions   *131*
Matching   *131*
Exercise 1: Create a New Company   *132*
Exercise 2: Add Customers   *133*
Exercise 3: Add Vendors   *134*
Exercise 4: Add Items   *134*
Exercise 5: Add Employees   *135*
*Exercise 6: Add Accounts and Set Opening
  Balances*   *135*
Assignment 1: Wild Water Sports   *136*
Assignment 2: Central Coast Cellular   *137*
Assignment 3: Santa Barbara Sailing   *139*
Case 1: Forever Young   *142*
Case 2: Ocean View Flowers   *144*
Case 3: Aloha Properties   *146*

Chapter 7 Cash-Oriented Business Activities   149

Case: Wild Water Sports, Inc.   149
Recording Cash-Oriented Financing Activities   150
Recording Cash-Oriented Investing Activities   152
Recording Cash-Oriented Operating Activities   155
Evaluate a Firm's Performance and Financial
 Position   184
End Note   188
Chapter 7 Practice   190
Questions   *190*
Matching   *190*
Exercise 1: Cash-Oriented Financing Activities   *191*
Exercise 2: Cash-Oriented Investing Activities   *191*
*Exercise 3: Cash-Oriented Operating
  Activities – Sales*   *192*
*Exercise 4: Cash-Oriented Operating
  Activities – Purchases*   *192*
*Exercise 5: Cash-Oriented Operating
  Activities – Expenses*   *193*
Assignment 1: Wild Water Sports   *194*
Assignment 2: Central Coast Cellular   *197*
Assignment 3: Santa Barbara Sailing   *198*
Case 1: Forever Young   *200*
Case 2: Ocean View Flowers   *202*
Case 3: Aloha Properties   *204*

Comprehensive Problem 1: Sarah Duncan, CPA   206
Comprehensive Problem 2: Pacific Brew   210
Comprehensive Problem 3: Sunset Spas   213

Chapter 8 Additional Business Activities   **218**

Case: Wild Water Sports, Inc.   218
Recording Additional Financing Activities   219
Recording Additional Investing Activities   222
Recording Additional Operating Activities   223
Recording Noncash Investing and Financing Activities   240
Evaluate a Firm's Performance and Financial Position   241
End Note   244
Chapter 8 Practice   246
Questions   246
Matching   246
Exercise 1: Financing Activities   247
Exercise 2: Investing Activities   247
Exercise 3: Operating Activities – Purchases and Payments from/to Vendors   248
Exercise 4: Operating Activities – Expenses & Sales   248
Assignment 1: Wild Water Sports   249
Assignment 2: Central Coast Cellular   252
Assignment 3: Santa Barbara Sailing   253
Case 1: Forever Young   254
Case 2: Ocean View Flowers   256
Case 3: Aloha Properties   259

Chapter 9 Adjusting Entries   **261**

Case: Wild Water Sports, Inc.   261
Accruing Expenses   261
Accruing Revenue   264
Recording Expenses Incurred but Previously Deferred   268
Adjusting for Unearned Revenues   272
Preparing a Bank Reconciliation and Recording Related Adjustments   276
End Note   278
Chapter 9 Practice   280
Questions   280
Matching   280

Exercise 1: Accruing Expenses   281
Exercise 2: Accruing Revenue   282
Exercise 3: Recording Expenses Incurred but Previously Deferred   282
Exercise 4: Preparing Bank Reconciliation   283
Assignment 1: Wild Water Sports   283
Assignment 2: Central Coast Cellular   284
Assignment 3: Santa Barbara Sailing   285
Case 1: Forever Young   286
Case 2: Ocean View Flowers   287
Case 3: Aloha Properties   288

Chapter 10 Budgeting   **289**

Case: Wild Water Sports, Inc.   289
Budgeting Revenues   290
Budgeting Expenses   293
Budgeted Income Statement   294
Budgeting Assets, Liabilities, and Equities   297
Budgeted Balance Sheet   299
End Note   303
Chapter 10 Practice   304
Questions   304
Matching   304
Exercise 1: Budgeting Revenues and Expenses   305
Exercise 2: Budgeting Assets, Liabilities, and Equities   305
Assignment 1: Wild Water Sports   306
Assignment 2: Central Coast Cellular   306
Assignment 3: Santa Barbara Sailing   307
Case 1: Forever Young   308
Case 2: Ocean View Flowers   309
Case 3: Aloha Properties   310

Chapter 11 Reporting Business Activities   **312**

Case: Wild Water Sports, Inc.   312
Creating and Memorizing a Customized Income Statement   313
Creating and Memorizing a Customized Balance Sheet   317
Creating Graphs to Illustrate Financial Information   319
Create Additional Detail Reports   324
Exporting Reports to Excel   328

End Note   332
Chapter 11 Practice   333
Questions   *333*
Matching   *333*
Exercise 1: Graphs   *334*
Exercise 2: Additional Reports   *334*
Exercise 3: Export to Excel   *334*
Assignment 1: Wild Water Sports   *335*
Assignment 2: Central Coast Cellular   *335*
Assignment 3: Santa Barbara Sailing   *336*
Case 1: Forever Young   *337*
Case 2: Ocean View Flowers   *337*
Case 3: Aloha Properties   *338*
Comprehensive Problem 1: Sports City   *339*
Comprehensive Problem 2: Pacific Brew   *341*
Comprehensive Problem 3: Sunset Spas   *344*

Appendix 1 Payroll Taxes   **348**

Overview   348
Federal Income Tax Withholding   348
Social Security and Medicare Taxes   351
Federal Unemployment Taxes   353

State Income Tax Withholding and
    Unemployment Taxes   355
Appendix 1 Practice   356
Questions   *356*
Assignments   *356*

**Appendix 2 Traditional
              Accounting: Debits
              and Credits**   **358**

Case: Wild Water Sports, Inc.   358
Trial Balance   359
General Ledger   361
General Journal   364
End Note   366
Appendix 2 Practice   367
Questions   *367*
Assignments   *367*
Case Problems   *368*

Index   **369**

What if you could integrate a popular computerized accounting program into your classroom without using complicated and confusing manuals? What if your students could use this program and reinforce basic accounting concepts in an online and interactive case setting? What if you could accomplish both without spending a fortune and a vast amount of time preparing examples, cases, and illustrations? In fact, *Using QuickBooks® Pro 2010 for Accounting* by Owen is a textbook that fulfills and expands upon all three of these "what ifs."

Why Is This Textbook Needed?

The first course in accounting has evolved significantly over the last several years. Educators are responding to the demand of accounting and nonaccounting faculty who rely on this course to lay a foundation for other courses. Moreover, the accounting profession relies on this course to attract the "best and the brightest" to become accounting majors. The evolution of this course has also put pressure on instructors to integrate computers into the classroom and, in so doing, develop students' skills in intelligently using and interpreting accounting information.

Faculty often want to incorporate computerized accounting into the first course but are reluctant to invest the time and effort necessary to accomplish this laudable goal. Existing materials are often "preparer" driven in that they focus on the creation of financial reports only. Students are often discouraged in their use of computers in the first accounting course because of the confusing and complicated accounting software manuals that concentrate on accounting mechanics.

This text responds to all of these needs. It provides a self-paced, step-by-step environment in which students use *QuickBooks® Pro 2010* or *QuickBooks® Basic 2010* to create financial statements and other financial reports, to reinforce the concepts they learn in their first course, and to see how computer software can be used to make business decisions.

Notable New Features in the 2010 Version of QuickBooks

QuickBooks Pro 2010 has several new features from the previous edition. Most notable, and incorporated into this text, are the ability to add or edit multiple entries in QuickBooks lists from one spreadsheet view and the new user interface in the Report Center.

The software now allows you to add or edit multiple inventory items, customers, vendors, etc. at one time. A spreadsheet-like interface allows you to customize columns for all lists, which will help you make new entries. The software also allows for the import of Excel spreadsheet data into these lists.

In addition, the Report Center now contains four tabs: Standard, Memorized, Favorites, and Recent to allow quick access to reports you want to view. Within each of these tabs you can now select reports in a Carousel, List, or Grid view. The Carousel View lets you specify a date range for the report and illustrates what the report might look like. You can flip through these options easily with a simple mouse click to the left or right. The List View provides the standard list of reports by functional area: Company & Financial, Customers & Receivables, etc. with no illustration of what the report might look like. The Grid View again provides reports by functional area but includes an illustration of what the report might look like.

Video Demonstration

New Features in This Edition of the Textbook?

In this Edition, QuickBooks Pro 2010 for Accounting, we have created two new resources, one for students, and one for instructors. The author has created many student demonstration videos throughout the text to help students visualize QuickBooks processes. These demonstrations are referenced by a demonstration video Icon in the margin (see example icon in the margin). These demonstrations are stand alone full action videos with audio showing step by step illustrations of business processes explained in this text. All of these are available via the text's Companion web site located at http://www.academic.cengage.com. The second resource are rubrics for instructors to grade all cases in the end of chapter material. These rubrics link each case requirement and events to a specific student learning outcome. These rubrics are available on the instructor companion web site to this text.

In our last edition, we added two important features. The first was a business events summary, which appears at the end of Chapters 6 through 11. This table identifies the various business events addressed in the chapter, the process steps to record this business event, and a page reference in the text where these steps are explained.

Secondly, we added a series of short exercises at the end of each chapter for Chapters 6–11. These exercises require students to make small changes to a company file. The new company, which is created in Chapter 6, is Boston Catering, a catering firm located in Cambridge, Massachusetts, that provides catering services to businesses in the Cambridge and Boston area. Each exercise stands by itself and is not cumulative except exercise 1 in Chapter 6. In that exercise, the student creates a new file. The exercises that follow in Chapter 6 require the use of the file created in exercise 1 but do not rely on any previous exercise. Thus students and instructors can focus on specific tasks. For example, in Chapter 6 exercise 2, students add customers. In exercise 3 they add vendors, in exercise 4 they add items, and in exercise 5 they add employees. Students can complete all or just some of the exercises as each is independent of the other.

In each successive chapter, a beginning student file is provided and each exercise adds business events. For example, Chapter 7 exercise 1 requires the student to add some cash-oriented financing activities, exercise 2 requires the student to add some cash-oriented investing activities, exercise 3 requires the student to add some cash-oriented operating activities like sales, etc. Once again, students can complete all or just some of the exercises as each is independent of the other.

What Are the Goals of This Textbook?

This textbook takes a user perspective by illustrating how accounting information is both used and created. QuickBooks is extremely user friendly and provides point-and-click simplicity with excellent and sophisticated accounting reporting and analysis tools. The textbook uses a proven and successful pedagogy to demonstrate the software's features and elicit student interaction.

The text's first and foremost goal is to help students learn or review fundamental accounting concepts and principles through the use of QuickBooks and the analysis of business events. The content complements the first course in accounting and thus should be used in conjunction with a core text on accounting.

A second goal is to enable students to view financial statements from a user perspective. After an initial tour of QuickBooks, students learn how to use QuickBooks to understand and interpret financial statements.

A third goal of the text is to provide students a means to investigate the underlying source documents that generate most financial accounting information, such as purchase orders, sales invoices, and so on. Students will experience this process by entering a few business events for later inclusion in financial reports.

A fourth goal is to provide students a means of exploring some managerial aspects of accounting by performing financial analysis and comparisons. Budgets are created and compared to actual operating results, and receivables and payables are aged for the purpose of analyzing cash management and cash flow projections.

A fifth goal of this text is to reduce the administrative burdens of accounting faculty by providing a self-paced environment, data sets, cases, and a correlation table describing how this book might be used with a variety of popular accounting texts.

What Are the Key Features of This Textbook?

This text is designed to work with *QuickBooks*® *Pro 2010*. It can be used with other versions of QuickBooks, but the screen shots and instructions are based entirely on *QuickBooks*® *Pro 2010*.

The text is divided into two parts. Part 1 is designed to help you navigate through QuickBooks. It provides a foundation for Part 2, which will show you how to create a new QuickBooks files and to record a variety of operating, investing, and financing transactions. Part 2 consists of five chapters, each with its own set of questions, assignments, and case problems. All chapters in Part 1 revolve around Century Kitchens, a remodeling contractor. Century specializes in remodeling existing homes and is well known in town for its high-quality construction and timely completion of projects. You've answered an ad for a part-time administrative assistant and are about to learn more about what QuickBooks can do for a business. Chapter 1 gives you a quick interactive tour of QuickBooks, in which you will restore data files and become familiar with QuickBooks's essential features. Chapters 2, 3, 4, and 5 introduce you to creating and preparing the balance sheet, the income statement, the statement of cash flows, and supporting reports.

Part 2 is designed to teach you how to use QuickBooks and the accounting methods and concepts you've learned in your introductory accounting course. This part is divided into six chapters, each with its own set of questions, assignments, and case problems. You will follow the adventures of Donna and Karen at Wild Water Sports, who have hired you to help them set up their business in QuickBooks, capture various business transactions, make adjusting entries, set up and use budgets, and generate key business reports. You will utilize QuickBooks EasyStep Interview to establish accounts, customers, vendors, items, and employees and then record business transactions using key source documents like sales receipts, invoices, bills, deposit forms, and checks. You will learn how to create journal entries in QuickBooks to accrue revenues and expenses, adjust deferred assets and liabilities, and record depreciation of long-lived assets. Finally, you will learn how QuickBooks's budgeting and reporting process can help Wild Water Sports plan and control their business activities.

A tested, proven, step-by-step methodology keeps students on track. Students enter data, analyze information, and make decisions all within the context of the case. The text constantly guides students, letting them know where they are in the course of completing their accounting tasks.

Numerous screen shots include callouts that direct students' attention to what they should look at on the screen. On almost every page in the book, you will find examples of how steps, screen shots, and callouts work together.

Trouble? paragraphs anticipate the mistakes that students are likely to make—or problems they might encounter—and then help them recover and continue with the chapter. This feature facilitates independent learning and frees you to focus on accounting concepts rather than on computer skills.

With very few exceptions, QuickBooks does not require the user to record journal entries to record business events. An appendix on traditional accounting records gives you the flexibility to teach journal entries at your discretion. It provides the information necessary for students to make journal entries to record the events described in Chapters 6 through 11.

Questions begin the end-of-chapter material. They are intended to test students' recall of what they learned in the chapter.

Matching exercises follow the questions. Each matching exercise lists 10 key concepts/terms used or introduced in each chapter, terms that the student must match with the appropriate definition. This helps reinforce the student's grasp of the accounting and QuickBooks concepts.

Assignments follow the matching exercises. In the first five chapters, the assignments involve continuing the students' exploration of QuickBooks by viewing Century Kitchens's information. Two additional cases are used to extend their practice and exploration of QuickBooks files. The first is Sierra Marina, a sole proprietorship renting boats in the Sierra Mountains. The second is Kelly Jennings, an advertising agency doing business as a corporation.

In Chapters 6–11, exercises follow the matching exercises. Each exercise revolves around Boston Catering where students are asked to add customers, vendors, items, employees, and operating, investing, and financing activities. Each exercise stands alone and does not require completion of the previous exercise.

In Chapters 6–11, three assignments follow the exercises. Each assignment in Chapters 7–11 includes a beginning backup data file, which is used to get the student started. This includes an extension of the Wild Water Sports continuing business problem used in the chapter, followed by the Central Coast Cellular and Santa Barbara Sailing assignments. Three additional cases follow these assignments. None of these cases include a beginning data file; students continue the case from the previous chapter. These include the Forever Young, Ocean View Flowers, and Aloha Properties cases.

Three comprehensive problems appear at the end of Chapters 7 and 11. These problems provide an opportunity for students to demonstrate their comprehensive understanding of QuickBooks procedures and accounting knowledge.

The Student version of the text Web site includes multiple-choice quizzes and PowerPoint slides for each chapter. All beginning data files for each chapter and for each assignment are also provided for downloading.

The Instructor's Manual includes solutions to all questions, matching exercises, assignments, cases, and comprehensive problems. Completed QuickBooks backup files are provided for the assignments, cases, and comprehensive problems to enable instructors to see what the student completed data file should look like after each chapter. The instructor's section of the text Web site includes PowerPoint slides, multiple-choice questions, student data files, and instructor completed data files. The text Web site is located at **www.cengage.com/accounting/owen.**

Dates

QuickBooks, like all accounting programs, is extremely date sensitive. This follows from the accounting periodicity concept, which requires accounting information to be organized by accounting periods such as months, quarters, or years. It is most important that, when using this text, you enter the proper dates to record business transactions or view business reports. For example, if you are using this book in 2010 (and thus your computer has a system date of 10/1/10, for example) then you will need to adjust the date references. In the Employee Center, for instance, the concept of "The Calendar Year" means 2010. However, if you are using this book in 2011 (and thus your computer has a system date of 2/1/11, for example) then the reference to "The Calendar Year" refers to 2011, so you would need to change the date reference to "Custom" and then change the From date to 1/1/09 and the To date to 12/31/09 because all of Century Kitchens's transactions are recorded in 2009.

The end-of-chapter assignments, cases, and comprehensive problems often have dates that differ from the date you might be entering business transactions. For example, the Central Coast Cellular assignment is dated 2009. When entering dates for transactions, QuickBooks automatically warns you of transactions being recorded more than 30 days into the future or more than 90 days in the past as shown by the following windows:

Figure P.1

Future Transactions
Warning

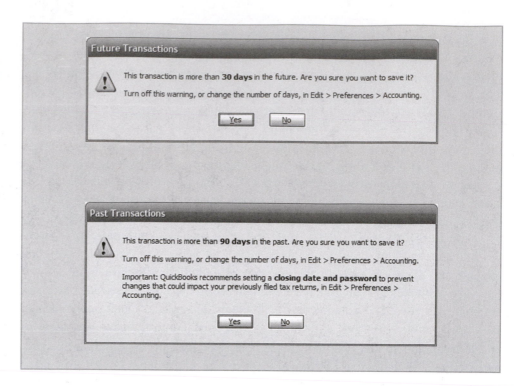

Figure P.2

Past Transactions Warning

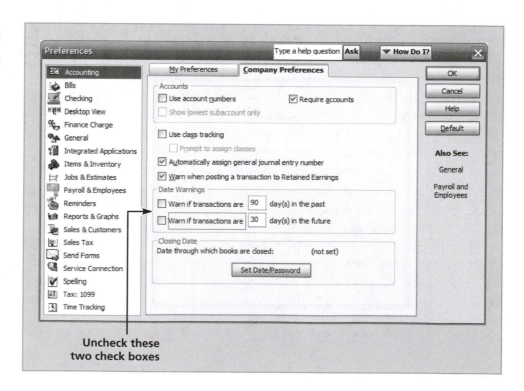

Click the **Yes** button when this occurs and then go to the Edit menu, click **Preferences,** click **Accounting,** and then click the **Company Preferences** tab. Uncheck the two check boxes located in the Date Warnings section as shown below.

Figure P.3

Turning Off Date Warnings

About the Author

Glenn Owen is a tenured member of Allan Hancock College's Accounting and Business faculty, where he has lectured on accounting and information systems since 1995. In addition, he is a lecturer at the University of California at Santa Barbara, where he has been teaching accounting and information systems courses since 1980. He has also been a lecturer at the Orfala College of Business at Cal Poly San Luis Obispo teaching financial and managerial accounting courses. His professional experience includes five years at Deloitte & Touche as well as vice president of finance positions at Westpac Resources, Inc., and Expertelligence, Inc. He has authored many Internet-related books and accounting course supplements and is currently developing online accounting instruction modules for his Internet-based financial accounting courses. Mr. Owen has released a new 2008 edition of his Excel and Access in Accounting text, which gives accounting students specific, self-paced instruction on the use of spreadsheets (Excel 2007) and database applications (Access 2007) in accounting. His innovative teaching style emphasizes the decision maker's perspective and encourages students to think creatively. His graduate studies in educational psychology and his 35 years of business experience yield a balanced blend of theory and practice.

Dedication

I would like to thank my wife Kelly for her support and assistance during the creation of this and previous editions of this text. While our boys are now out of the house and pursuing their own interests she continues to listen to my often crazy ideas for new cases and experiences with college students, providing an excellent sounding board and reality check. You and the boys continue to be what life is all about.

Note to the Student and Instructor

QuickBooks Version and Payroll Tax Tables

The text and related data files created for this book were constructed using *QuickBooks® Pro 2010* release R5P. To check your release number, open *QuickBooks® Pro 2010* and type **Ctrl 1.** If your release is less than number R5P, use the QuickBooks Update Service under the Online menu to update your version. This is a free service to version 2010 Pro users and requires an Internet connection. The files accompanying this text can be used in any *QuickBooks® Pro 2010* release R5P or higher. If you are using a higher release number, QuickBooks will automatically offer to update your file when you try and restore from the Data Files CD. Click **Yes** in the corresponding Update Company window.

In this version of QuickBooks, Intuit continues its use of a basic payroll service. This is a requirement in order to use the QuickBooks payroll features that automatically calculate taxes due to federal or state agencies. QuickBooks initially comes with the current tax tables; however, these tables soon become outdated, and the payroll feature is disabled unless the user subscribes to the payroll service.

Some previous versions of this text applied whatever tax tables were in effect at the time of publication. Users who had different tax tables often noted differences in solutions as a result. This new requirement solves that problem. The author decided to use the manual payroll tax feature, which requires that students manually enter the tax deductions. This alleviates the discrepancies between the solutions manual and the students' data entry and removes the burden of having to purchase the tax table service for each copy of QuickBooks installed in a lab environment. Instructions on how to set up payroll for manual calculation of payroll taxes are provided in the text. For more information, see your QuickBooks documentation.

All reports have a default feature that identifies the basis in which the report was created (e.g., accrual or cash) and the date and time the report was printed. The date and time shown on your report will, of course, be different from that shown in this text.

Getting Started
with QuickBooks

In this part, you will:

- **Take an interactive tour of QuickBooks**
- **Create a balance sheet and modify its presentation**
- **Create an income statement and modify its presentation**
- **Create a statement of cash flows and modify its presentation**
- **Create supporting reports and modify their presentation**

Part 1 is designed to help you navigate through QuickBooks. It provides a foundation for Part 2, which will show you how to create a new QuickBooks file and record a variety of operating, investing, and financing transactions.

This part is divided into five chapters—each with its own set of questions, assignments, and case problems. Chapter 1 gives you a quick interactive tour of QuickBooks, in which you will become familiar with the essential features of QuickBooks. Chapters 2, 3, 4, and 5 introduce you to creating and preparing the balance sheet, the income statement, the statement of cash flows, and supporting reports.

1

An Interactive Tour of QuickBooks

Learning Objectives

In this chapter, you will:

- Learn QuickBook's basic features
- Restore, open, backup, and close a QuickBooks file
- Identify the components and menus available in the QuickBooks window
- Use QuickBooks Help resources
- Examine a few forms and reports available in QuickBooks

Case: Century Kitchens

You've been working in a part-time job at a restaurant, and today you decide that you've served your last hamburger. You want a new part-time job—one that's more directly related to your future career in business. As you skim the want ads, you see an ad for an administrative assistant at Century Kitchens, a remodeling contractor. Century specializes in remodeling existing homes and is well known in town for its high-quality construction and timely completion of projects. The ad says that job candidates must have earned or be earning a business degree, have some computer skills, and be willing to learn on the job. This looks promising. And then you see the line "Send a résumé to Scott Montalvo." You know Scott! He was in one of your marketing classes two years ago; he graduated last year with a degree in business. You decide to send your résumé to Scott right away.

A few days later you're delighted to hear Scott's voice on the phone. He remembers you well. He explains that he wants to hire someone to help him with clerical and other administrative tasks in support of his new company, Century Kitchens. He asks if you could start right away. When you say yes, he offers you the job on the spot! You start next Monday.

When you arrive Monday morning, Scott explains that the first thing he needs you to learn is how to use a software package called QuickBooks. You quickly remind Scott that you're not an accounting major. Scott laughs as he assures you that you'll have no problem with QuickBooks because it is so user oriented. He chose QuickBooks exactly for that reason and has been using it for about three months. Scott wants accurate, useful, and timely financial information to help him make sound business decisions—and he's not an accountant, either.

Scott explains that the company incorporated on January 1, 2007, and he's been using QuickBooks since then, entering each transaction. However, he's become so busy at Century that he needs someone else in the office who can enter transactions, generate reports for the managers, and so on. So he says that today he will give you a tour of QuickBooks and teach you some of the basic features and functions of this package. You tell him that you're familiar with Windows and you're ready to start.

Using This Text Effectively

Before you begin the tour of QuickBooks, note that this textbook assumes you are familiar with the basics of Windows: how to control windows, how to choose menu commands, how to complete dialog boxes, and how to select directories, drives, and files. If you do not understand these concepts, please consult your instructor. Also note that this book is designed to be used with your instructor's and/or another textbook's discussion of essential accounting concepts.

The best way to work through this textbook is to read the text carefully and complete the numbered steps, which appear on a shaded background, as you work at your computer. Read each step carefully and completely before you try it.

As you work, compare your screen with the figures in the chapter to verify your results. You can use QuickBooks with any Windows operating system. The screen shots used in this book were captured in a Windows XP Professional environment. So if you are using a prior version of Windows you may see some minor differences between your screens and the screens in this book. Any significant differences that result from using QuickBooks within different operating systems will be explained.

Don't worry about making mistakes—that's part of the learning process. The *Trouble?* paragraphs identify common problems and explain how to correct them or get back on track. Follow those suggestions *only* if you are having the specific problem described.

After completing a chapter, you may do the questions, assignments, and case problems found at the end of each chapter. They are carefully structured so that you will review what you have learned and then apply your knowledge to new situations.

Demonstrations

Video Demonstration

Demonstrations are available throughout this text and are referenced by a Video Demonstration Icon in the margin. These demonstrations are stand alone full action videos with audio showing step by step illustrations of business processes explained in this text.

All of these are available via the text's Companion web site located at http://www. academic.cengage.com. Select Accounting from the Business & Economics listing and then select QuickBooks from the Accounting Information Systems section.

QuickBooks Application Installation CD

To complete the chapters and exercises in this book, you must have access to the QuickBooks application. Your instructor might make the application available in a lab environment or you may already own the software. Alternatively, the CD located in the inside back cover of this text, labeled "QuickBooks Accounting Pro 2010" from Intuit contains all the files you need to run QuickBooks on your own computer. Insert the CD in your computer and the setup installation program should begin automatically. Follow the instructions provided to install the QuickBooks application onto your computer. If it does not start automatically, use Windows Explorer to open the CD and double-click the setup application.

Data Files CD

To complete the chapters and exercises in this book, you must have access to data files. The CD located inside the back cover of this book, labeled "Files to Accompany QuickBooks Pro 2010 for Accounting", contains backups of all the practice files you need for the chapters, assignments, and case problems. If the CD becomes unusable or misplaced, you can download the data files from the text's companion site at http:// www.cengage.com/highered/. Select Accounting from the Business & Economics listing and then select QuickBooks from the Accounting Information Systems section. Data files can be found on the Companion Site of your text.

You will need to restore the backup files to their original format. The files on your Data Files CD are named to correspond to chapters and sessions in this book.

Working from your computer's hard drive is the most efficient way to use the QuickBooks program. However, if you are in a lab environment and want to take your file with you when you leave, you'll need to copy that file to a removable disk (ideally a portable USB drive). More on this later.

What Is QuickBooks?

Scott is excited about using QuickBooks because it is the best-selling small business accounting software on the market today. He explains that QuickBooks is an automated accounting information system that describes an entity's financial position and operating results and that helps managers make more effective business decisions. He also likes the QuickBooks reports and graphs, which quickly and easily organize and summarize all the data he enters.

Video Demonstration

DEMO 1A - Overview and introduction

Scott says he especially likes QuickBooks because it can handle all of Century Kitchens' needs to invoice customers and maintain receivables and can also be used to pay bills and maintain payables. It can track inventory and create purchase orders using Century Kitchens' on-screen forms—all without calculating, posting, or closing. Scott can correct any previously recorded transaction, and an "audit trail" automatically keeps a record of any changes he makes.

Scott explains further that QuickBooks has four basic features that, when combined, help manage the financial activity of a company. The four features—lists, forms, registers, and reports and graphs—work together to create an accounting information system. Let's take a closer look at each of these four features. Don't start the QuickBooks program yet. Just read through the following to better understand QuickBooks's features.

Lists

Lists are groups of names—such as customers, vendors, employees, inventory items, and accounts—and information about those names. Lists are created and edited from a list window or while completing a form, such as an invoice, bill, or time sheet. Figure 1.1 shows a list of Century Kitchens' customer names with jobs for each of these customers, balances owed for each job, and any explanatory notes.

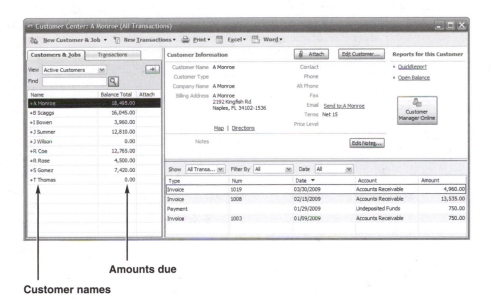

Figure 1.1

A Customer List from Century Kitchens

Amounts due

Customer names

Forms

Forms are QuickBooks's electronic representations of the paper documents used to record business activities, such as customer invoices, a vendor's bill for goods purchased, or a check written to a vendor. The customer invoice form in Figure 1.2 contains many **fields**, or areas on the form that you can fill in.

If you fill in a field, such as the Customer: Job field, QuickBooks often automatically fills in several other fields with relevant information to speed up data entry. In Figure 1.2, for example, the Bill To, Terms, and Invoice # fields are filled in as soon as the Customer: Job field is entered.

Also, filling in a field is made easier through the use of drop-down lists. Whenever you see an arrow next to or in a field, that field is a drop-down list.

Registers

A QuickBooks **register** contains all financial activity for a specified balance sheet account. Examples of registers include checking (cash), accounts receivable, inventory, and accounts payable. The checking register in Figure 1.3 shows some of Century Kitchens' cash payments and cash receipts; it also provides cash balances after each transaction.

The financial effects of business transactions may be entered directly into the register or into the forms that automatically record the effects of these transactions in the relevant register. For example, if an owner's cash contribution is recorded on a Deposit form, the increases in both the checking account and relevant owner's equity account are simultaneously recorded in the Checking register and Contributed Capital register.

Reports and Graphs

QuickBooks **reports** and **graphs** present the financial position and the operating results of a company in a way that makes business decision making easier. The Profit and Loss report in Figure 1.4 shows the revenues and expenses of Century Kitchens

Figure 1.2

An Invoice Form for Century Kitchens

Your screen may show the words Print, Send, Ship, and Find if your Create Invoices window is expanded. QuickBooks automatically removes words to save space when the window size is reduced.

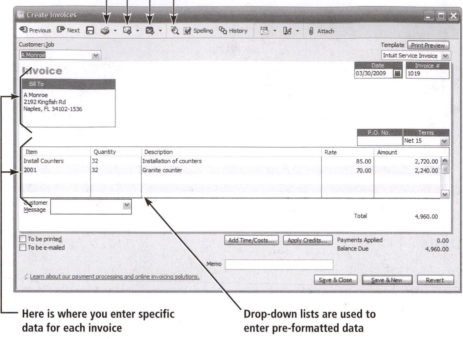

Here is where you enter specific data for each invoice

Drop-down lists are used to enter pre-formatted data

Figure 1.3

A Section of the Checking Register from Century Kitchens

Note the four-digit year   Cash payments   Cash receipts

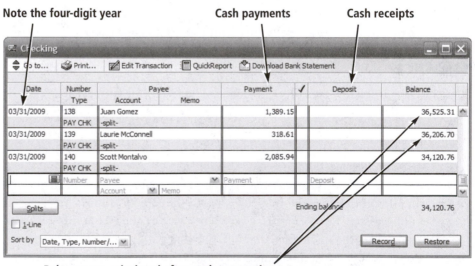

Balances are calculated after each transaction

for a specific period of time. Note that QuickBooks uses the title "Profit & Loss," but the generally accepted accounting title for this report is "Income Statement." Titles for this and other reports are all changeable using QuickBooks's Header/Footer tab. You can modify reports in many other ways, such as by comparing monthly periods, comparing this year with prior years, or examining year-to-date activity.

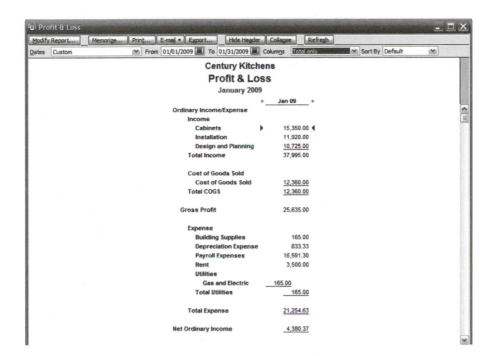

Figure 1.4

A Profit and Loss Report (Income Statement) from Century Kitchens

Income Statement

QuickBooks can also graph data to illustrate a company's financial position and operating results. For example, the bar chart in Figure 1.5 illustrates sales by month, and the pie chart illustrates sales by construction category.

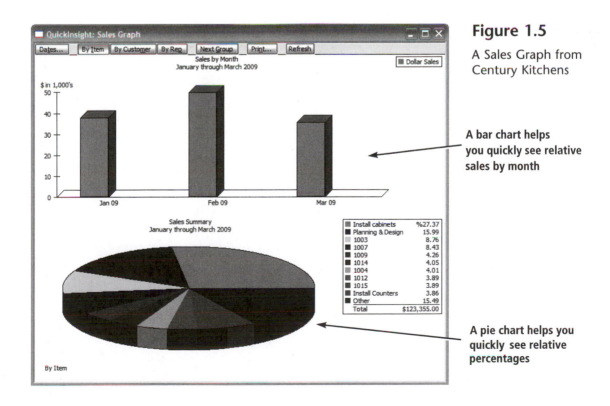

Figure 1.5

A Sales Graph from Century Kitchens

A bar chart helps you quickly see relative sales by month

A pie chart helps you quickly see relative percentages

Launching QuickBooks

Now that you know about lists, forms, registers, and reports and graphs, you are ready to launch QuickBooks. Scott invites you to join him in his office and use his large-screen monitor to start your tour. You open Windows, and Scott tells you how to launch QuickBooks.

To launch QuickBooks in Windows:

1 Click the **Start** button.

2 Select the **Programs** menu and look down the list for QuickBooks.

3 Once you've located the QuickBooks program, click and release the QuickBooks icon or name.

   Trouble? If, when QuickBooks was last used, the file being worked on was closed, you will see a No Company Open window. If, however, a QuickBooks file is open, click **File**, and then click **Close Company**. Be sure to close any open files before you proceed to the next set of steps.

Now that you have launched QuickBooks, you can begin to learn how to use it.

Video Demonstration

DEMO 1C - Restoring and backing up a file

Restoring and Opening a QuickBooks File

Scott hands you a disk and tells you to open a file called Century Kitchens.qbw. (You will find a backup of this file included on your Data Files CD.)

To restore a backup file to its original format:

1 Insert your Data Files CD into your CD drive (or download the data files from the textbook's Web site).

2 Launch QuickBooks if you closed it above.

3 Click **File** and then click **Open or Restore Company.**

4 Choose the **Restore a backup copy** option button and then click **Next.**

5 Choose the **Local backup** option button and then click **Next.**

6 Locate the Century Kitchens (Backup) file on either your Data Files CD or wherever you downloaded the file from the textbook's Web site. Select it and then click **Open.**

7 Click **Next** in the Restore Backup: To Location window which appears next.

8 Navigate the Save Company File as window to the location where you want the file to be restored on your computer's hard drive. Be sure to note its location for future use. In the example shown in Figure 1.6, we chose to save the restored file in a folder called "Restored QuickBooks files."

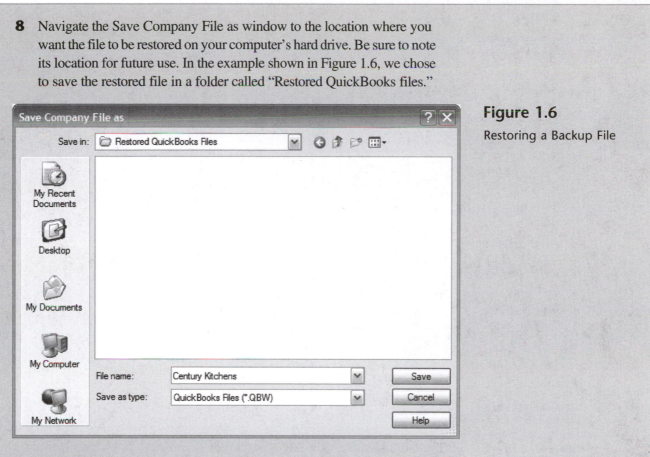

Figure 1.6

Restoring a Backup File

9 Click **Save.**

10 Click **OK** in the QuickBooks Information window, indicating that the file has been successfully restored.

11 Click the **Begin Using QuickBooks** button if presented.

Later, you can continue this process for all the backup files on your Data Files CD as you need them. As mentioned before, you may be working in a lab environment where files you work on today may be erased tomorrow. To preserve your work, you should backup your files to removable data storage (e.g., a USB drive).

The QuickBooks Window

Scott explains that QuickBooks operates like most other Windows programs, so most of the QuickBooks window controls should be familiar to you. He reaches for the mouse and quickly clicks a few times until his screen looks like Figure 1.7. The main components of the QuickBooks window are shown in this figure. Let's take a look at these components so that you can become familiar with their location and use.

The **title bar** at the top of the window tells you that you are in the QuickBooks program and identifies the company file currently open. The **menu bar** contains the **command menus**, which open windows within QuickBooks. The File, Edit,

Figure 1.7

Components of the
QuickBooks Window

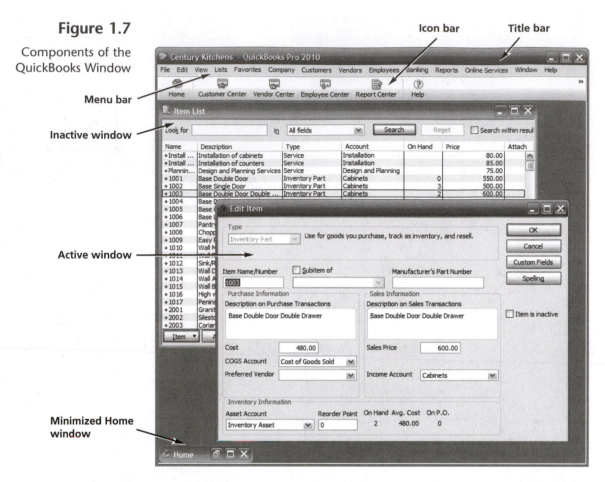

View, and Help menus are similar to other Windows programs in that they allow you to perform such common tasks as open, save, copy, paste, find, and get help.

The Lists menu gives you access to all lists, including the chart of accounts, customers, vendors, employees, and inventory items. The Company, Customers, Vendors, Employees, and Banking menus provide easy access to QuickBooks Centers as well as common tasks unique to that menu. For instance, in the Customers menu you can create invoices, enter cash sales, create credit memos, receive payments, and so forth. The Reports menu will give you quick access to common reports and graphs for easy creation. The Window menu allows you to choose the format for window displays, such as cascade or tile vertically. Finally, the Help menu will give you immediate access to an index of help topics.

The **icon bar** gives you one-click access to the QuickBook Centers and Home page. From time to time, you may want to hide the icon bar so you can have more horizontal space for the customizable icon bar.

The icon bar includes icons representing tasks you do every day, such as entering and paying bills, creating invoices, and receiving payments. If you use QuickBooks's payroll system, you might consider adding icons for your payroll forms. Icons can be added, removed, or reordered to fit your needs. Use the View menu to hide or display the icon bar and make any changes.

The **active window** is the window in which you can enter or edit data, and it is identified by a solid window title bar. Only one window can be active at a time. Other windows may be open, but they are inactive. If the active window is closed, or if a window behind it is selected, it becomes **inactive**, and the newly selected window becomes active.

Backing Up and Closing a QuickBooks File

Now that you have seen the components of the QuickBooks screen, Scott wants to show you how to backup and close a file so that you will always be able to save your work and exit QuickBooks.

"Maintaining backups is important just in case your original file is somehow damaged or lost," Scott explains.

To create a backup file for later use and then close the file:

1 In Windows Explorer, create a folder on your USB or other external drive called "My QuickBooks Backups."

2 In QuickBooks, click **File** and then click **Save Copy or Backup.**

3 Choose the **Backup copy** option button and then click **Next.**

4 Choose the **Local backup** option button and then click **Next.**

5 Identify the location where you want to backup your file for later use. (In this example, the backup location is K:\My QuickBooks Backups\, where K is the drive letter assigned by the Windows operating system for the USB drive; your drive letter may be different. The My QuickBooks Backups is the folder created in Step 1.) Uncheck the **Add the date and time of the backup to the file name** check box and then uncheck the **Remind me to back up when I close my company file** check box. Then click **OK.**

6 Click **Next.**

7 Your screen should look like Figure 1.8. Click **Save.**

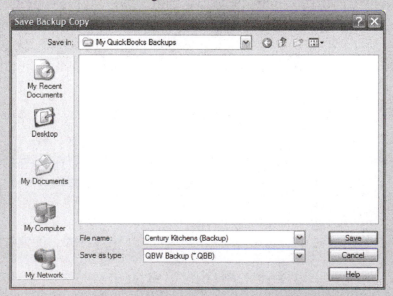

Figure 1.8

Backing Up a Data File

8 Click **OK** in the QuickBooks Information window, which indicates your backup was successful. Keep this QuickBooks file open.

Then Scott tells you something very unusual. He says that, unlike other Windows programs, QuickBooks *does not have a Save command*. In other words, in Quick-Books you cannot save a file whenever you want. You stare at Scott in disbelief and ask how that can be possible. Scott explains that *QuickBooks automatically saves all of the data you input and the changes you make as soon as you make them and click OK*. Scott admits that, when he first used QuickBooks, he was uneasy about exiting the program until he could find a way to save his work. But he discovered that there are no Save or Save As commands on the QuickBooks File menu as there are on most other Windows programs. He reassures you that, as unsettling as this is, you'll get used to it once you become more familiar with QuickBooks.

QuickBooks's Menus and Shortcut List

Scott explains that to enter sales receipts, create invoices, pay bills, receive payments, and so on, you use QuickBooks menu commands. Some of these functions are also available from buttons on the QuickBooks icon bar.

Some QuickBooks menus are dynamic; in other words, the options on the menu change depending upon the form, list, register, or report with which you are working. For instance, when you enter sales receipts information, the File and Edit menus change to include menu commands to print the sales receipts or to edit, delete, memorize, or void the sales receipts, as shown in Figure 1.9.

Because this is all new to you, Scott suggests that you first become familiar with how managers at Century Kitchens use QuickBooks to make business decisions.

Figure 1.9

Dynamic Menu Example

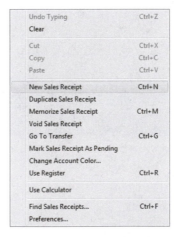

Using QuickBooks to Make Business Decisions: An Example at Century Kitchens

Once transactions are entered into the QuickBooks accounting information system, they can be accessed, revised, organized, and reported in many ways to aid business decision making. This capability is what makes a computerized accounting information system so valuable to managers.

While you're sitting with Scott, he receives a phone call from Laurie McConnell. Laurie needs some information on whether any accounts are past due. You know from your accounting course that Laurie is really asking for information about Century Kitchens' **accounts receivable**, or amounts due from customers from previously recorded sales. Laurie wants to know how much is due from customers and how current those receivables are; specifically, which customers owe Century Kitchens and when their payments are due. Scott tells Laurie he'll look into this immediately and call her right back.

Be aware that dates are critical to retrieving relevant information in QuickBooks. In most cases when you ask for a report, QuickBooks will give you that report as of the system date (today's date, whatever that might be). For example, if you are working on this assignment on January 5, 2011, and you request a report on receivables, QuickBooks will give you a report of receivables as of January 5, 2011. If you want a report as of March 31, 2009, you will need to change the date on the report and then refresh the report to see that information.

To identify the customers who owe Century Kitchens money and the total amount of receivables due from these customers:

1 Click **Reports**, click **Customers & Receivables**, and then click **A/ R Aging Detail**. Change the report date to **3/31/2009**; then click the **Refresh** button. The report in Figure 1.10 will appear.

Trouble? The report you see might be slightly different from the one shown in Figure 1.10. Some column widths have been altered. Use the scroll bars to view this report both vertically and horizontally.

Figure 1.10

Accounts Receivable Detail

Change the report date here

Click here to refresh the report for the change you make in the report date

Purchase order column; resized to view the entire width of the report

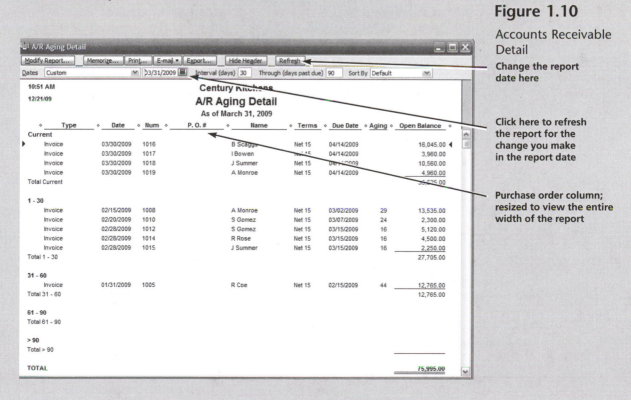

2 Note that customers owe Century Kitchens a total of $75,995.00.

3 Scott wants to see a graphic illustration of this information. From the Menu bar, click **Reports**, click **Customers & Receivables**, and then click **Accounts Receivable Graph**. Change the report date to 3/31/2009. The graph in Figure 1.11 will appear.

Figure 1.11

Accounts Receivable by Aging Period and Customer

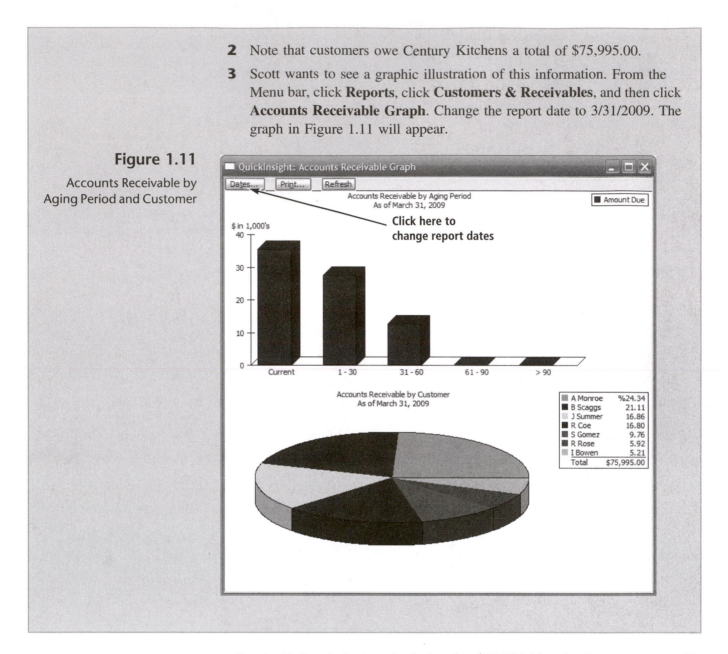

Scott calls Laurie back and tells her that $75,995.00 is due from customers. He explains that only the R Coe account is past due. Laurie would like to know specifically what invoices were sent to R Coe, when payments were made, and in what amounts. Scott knows he can easily get this information by accessing the Customer Balance Detail report for R Coe.

To access the Customer Balance Detail for R Coe:

1 From the Menu bar, click **Reports**, click **Customers & Receivables**, and then click **Customer Balance Detail.**

2 Scroll down the report to **R Coe's** detailed information shown in Figure 1.12. This report describes the two invoices that billed R Coe for services rendered. It also shows the cash payment received to date from R Coe.

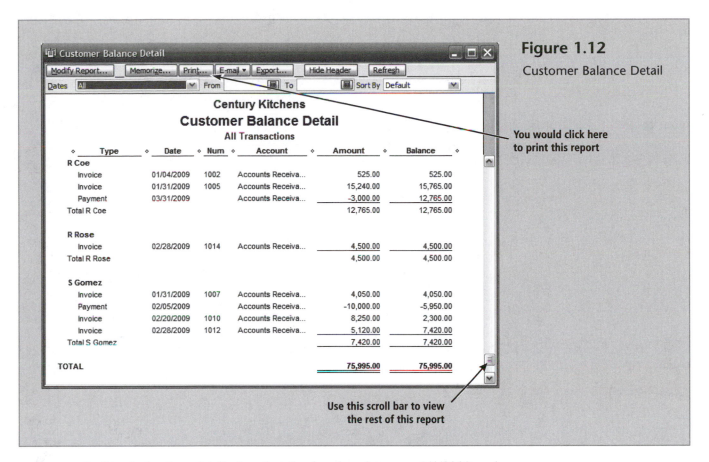

Figure 1.12

Customer Balance Detail

Scott calls Laurie back and tells her that the invoice dates are 1/4/2009 and 1/31/2009 and that a payment was made on 3/31/2009. He has quickly and easily accessed financial information from the company's QuickBooks data file, and Laurie thanks him. She is grateful for his quick response so she can make her decision. She asks if, before the end of the day, he would print out a copy of this information and leave it on her desk. Scott is happy to oblige.

Printing in QuickBooks

Scott suddenly remembers a meeting he must attend. But before exiting QuickBooks, you remind him that he promised to print a Customer Balance Detail report for Laurie.

To print a Customer Balance Detail report:

1 If you have closed the Customer Balance Detail report, click **Reports**, click **Customers & Receivables**, and then click **Customer Balance Detail.**

2 Click the **Print** button located on the button bar. See Figure 1.12.

3 Click **Print** in the Print Reports dialog box. The report prints out.

   Trouble? You might have to set up a printer before printing. If necessary, click **Cancel** in the Print Report dialog box. Then select **Printer Setup** from the File menu. QuickBooks allows you to set up different printers for different functions. Click the **Settings** tab and select the printer you would like to use from the printer name drop-down list.

> **4** You've opened several windows and not closed them. Click **Window** in the menu bar, and then click **Close All** to close all open windows and return to the QuickBooks opening window.
>
> Since you may have modified the settings for one or more reports, a Memorized Reports window may appear. Since we don't plan to use this report again, click **No.**

Scott asks you to drop off this report at Laurie's desk sometime after lunch.

Using QuickBooks Help

Scott suggests you explore QuickBooks's Help features while he is at his meeting. He tells you that QuickBooks Help has the standard features and functions of Windows Help and also has other help features specific to QuickBooks. These other features are listed in the main Help menu shown in Figure 1.13.

As with other Windows programs, you can access Help by clicking on the Help menu or pressing **F1**. In QuickBooks, pressing F1 opens a Have a Question window. QuickBooks Help is context sensitive—that is, different help screens appear depending on where you are in the program. You can get help for a specific topic by choosing the Help Index menu item.

You decide to follow up on Scott's suggestion to look at a help feature he finds very useful, the Help Index. You are specifically interested in how QuickBooks uses accounts.

Figure 1.13

The Help Menu

> **To use the Help Index:**
>
> **1** Click **Help** from the menu bar. Then click **QuickBooks Help** on the menu. Click the **Search** tab.
>
> **2** Type the phrase **add a new account** in the text box and then click the start search arrow.

3 Click the text **add a new account (select the account type)**. Your screen should look like Figure 1.14.

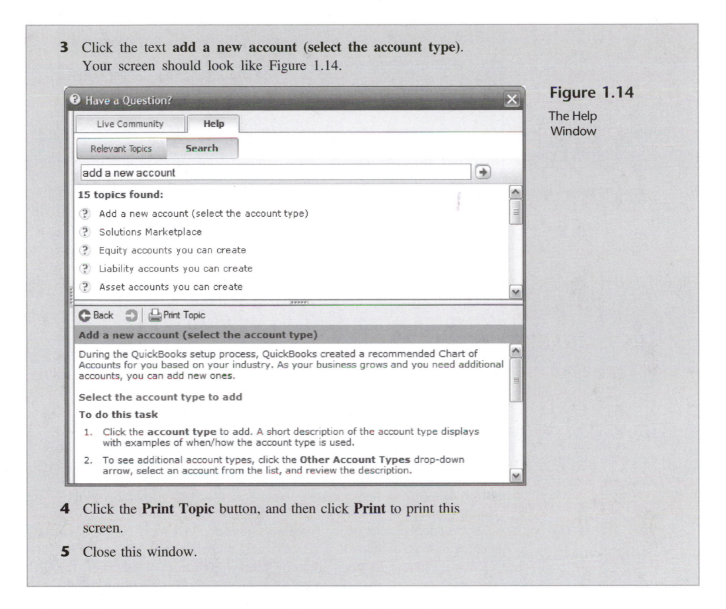

Figure 1.14

The Help Window

4 Click the **Print Topic** button, and then click **Print** to print this screen.

5 Close this window.

You will have an opportunity to use most of these options in this and later chapters.

The QuickBooks Home Page

Scott reminds you that another feature he previously mentioned was the QuickBooks home page, shown again in Figure 1.15. The QuickBooks home page provides a big picture of how your essential business tasks fit together. Tasks are organized into logical groups (Customers, Vendors, Employees, Company, and Banking) with workflow arrows to help you learn how tasks relate to each other and to help you decide what to do next.

The workflow arrows indicate a logical progression of business tasks in QuickBooks. However, these arrows do not restrict you from doing tasks in a different order or in an order that works better for your business needs.

The Customers portion of the home page includes two main activities: invoicing and receiving payments. Note, however, that invoices may receive input from

Figure 1.15

The QuickBooks Home Page

Video Demonstration

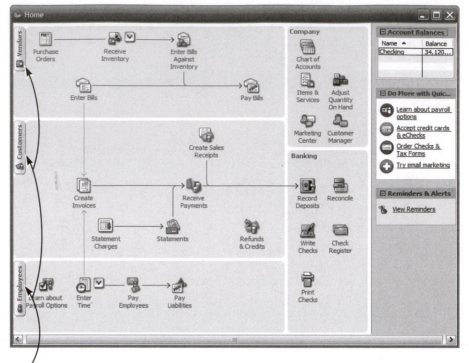

DEMO 1B - Using navigation centers

Click here to access the Vendor, Customer, or Employee Center

the vendor section (when we're billing customers for parts purchased from a vendor) as well as the employee section (when we're billing customers for employee time).

The Vendors portion of the home page includes four main activities: creating purchase orders, receiving items, establishing a liability, and paying that liability. QuickBooks provides you the means of managing all of these tasks with the click of an icon.

The Employees portion of the home page includes two main activities: recording employee time and paying employees and tax authorities. The work flow here does require sequential input, in that employee time must be entered *before* employees and tax authorities can be paid.

The Banking and Company portions of the home page are generic to the whole company and aren't necessarily business processes requiring workflow steps. The Company section allows you to update your chart of accounts, items, services, and physical quantities of items on hand. The Banking section allows you to record deposits, write checks, and reconcile your bank accounts.

The home page also provides you access to lists of customers, vendors, and employees via the Customer, Vendor, and Employee Centers, respectively. In these Centers, QuickBooks provides easy access to managing customers, vendors, and employees and allows entering transactions for each. For example, in the Employee Center you can view an employee's recent paychecks, edit that employee's information, enter a new employee, enter time worked, and write a new paycheck.

Scott reminds you that the home page is one of many ways to access the core features of any accounting information system like QuickBooks. There are menus, icons, centers, and workflow diagrams, all of which eventually take you to the same place to edit, enter, or process business events.

After you have learned the basics about QuickBooks in this course, you might decide to use QuickBooks Centers and workflow diagrams more often. But for now, follow the steps as they are written in this text.

To view and explore the home page:

1 Click **Home** from the icon bar.

2 Click the **Enter Bills** icon in the Vendors section to view the Enter Bills window, where later you'll enter bills received from vendors.

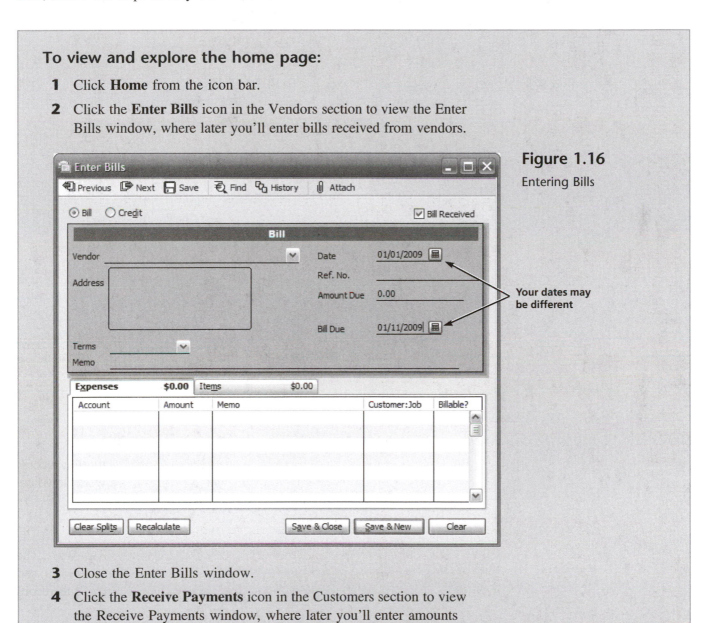

Figure 1.16

Entering Bills

3 Close the Enter Bills window.

4 Click the **Receive Payments** icon in the Customers section to view the Receive Payments window, where later you'll enter amounts received from customers. Click **No Thanks** if a Get More From QuickBooks window appears.

Figure 1.17

Receive Payments

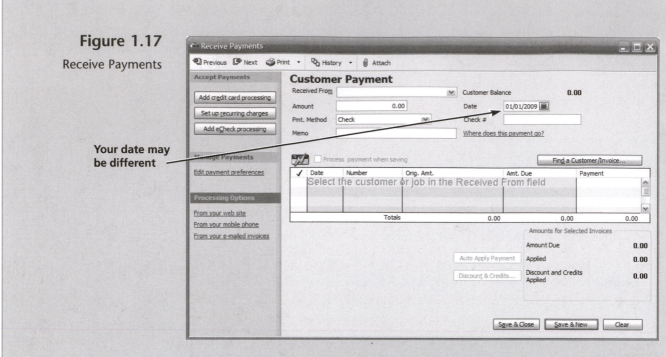

Your date may be different

5 Close the Receive Payments window.

6 Click **Employees** to view the Employee Center and then change the date to All as shown in Figure 1.18.

Figure 1.18

Employee Center

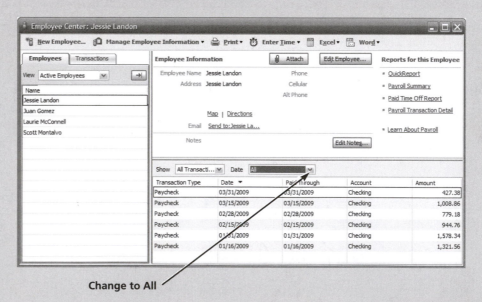

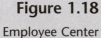
Change to All

7 Close this window.

QuickBooks Coach and Tutorials

The QuickBooks Coach is designed to guide you through the business flows on your home page. It also uses spotlights and tips to explain when and why to do each task. The QuickBooks Coach is available when you first create a new QuickBooks file. It can be turned on and off using Preferences.

After Scott returned from his meeting, he asks if you've tried the Coach. He's found this to be an effective way of learning about key business tasks in QuickBooks.

To experience the QuickBooks Coach:

1 Click the **Edit** menu and then click **Preferences.**

2 Click **Desktop View** and check the **Show Coach window and features** check box.

3 Click **OK** to close the Preferences window and then click the **Start Working** button in the QuickBooks Coach window.

4 Your window should look like Figure 1.19.

Trouble? If your screen does not match Figure 1.19 it could be that someone before you clicked one of the **i** buttons. Just continue on and eventually you will see the screens as expected.

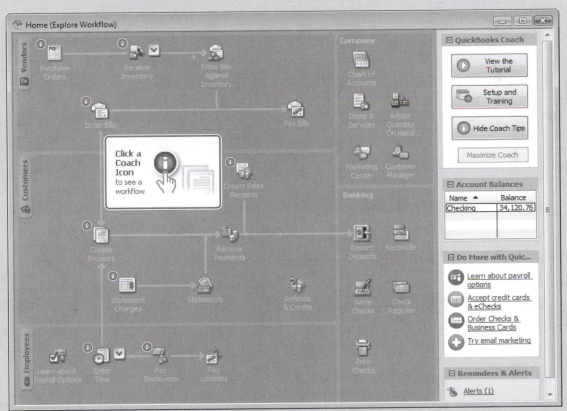

Figure 1.19

Home Page with Coach Tips Showing

5   Place your mouse over the blue **i** above the Receive Inventory task (but don't click it yet) to access the "spotlight this workflow" as shown in Figure 1.20.

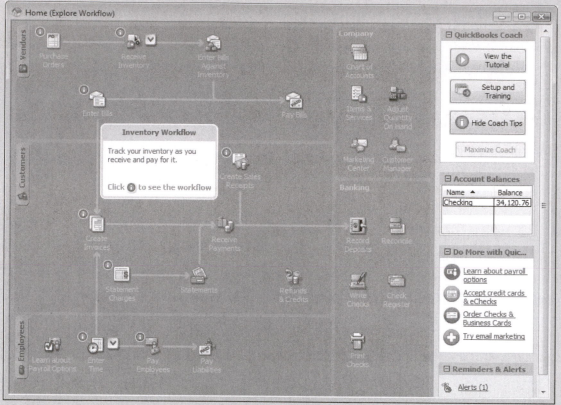

Figure 1.20

Accessing the Spotlighting the Inventory Workflow

6   Now click the **i** over the Receive Inventory task to view the inventory workflow as shown in Figure 1.21.

7   Click the **Hide Coach Tips** button to remove the coach tips from the home page.

8   Click **View Tutorial**s from the QuickBooks Coach window. (Note: you must be connected to the Internet to view these tutorials.)

9   Click **Customers and Sales** and then click **Create an invoice** from the list of tutorials available in this section.

10 The QuickBooks tutorial on how to create and invoice should begin immediately. Be sure you can hear the presentation. After a few seconds, the tutorial should look like Figure 1.22.

11 When you're done, close the Tutorial and QuickBooks Learning Center windows.

12 Click the **Edit** menu and then click **Preferences.**

13 Click Desktop View and uncheck the **Show Coach window and features** check box.

14 Click **OK** to close the Preferences window.

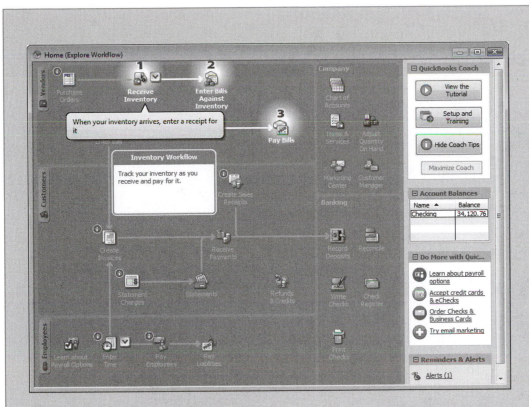

Figure 1.21

Spotlighting the Inventory Workflow

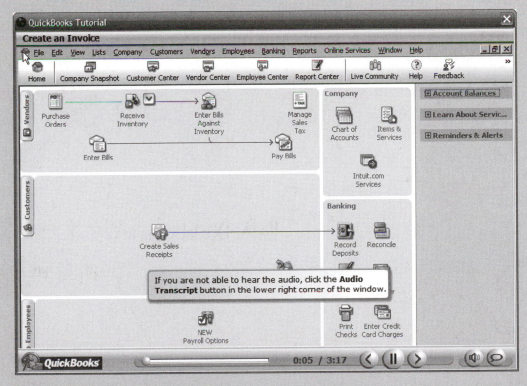

Figure 1.22

QuickBooks Tutorial Example

Exiting QuickBooks

You thank Scott for taking the time to introduce you to QuickBooks as he rushes off to yet another meeting. You know you can probably exit QuickBooks on your own, using standard Windows commands. You choose to use the Exit command on the File menu.

To exit QuickBooks:

1 Click **File** on the QuickBooks menu bar to display the File menu.

2 Click **Exit**. Once again, a dialog box might display the message "Intuit highly recommends backing up your data to avoid any accidental data loss. Would you like to backup now?"

3 Click **No** to exit QuickBooks and return to Windows. Good accounting practice encourages backing up data files, but backup is not necessary now with these sample files.

End Note

Scott has shown you some of the features of QuickBooks, how to navigate these features, and how business decisions can be aided by the reporting and analysis of accounting information afforded by QuickBooks. You are impressed by the speed at which information is made available and are anxious to learn more.

Chapter 1 Questions

1 Describe, in your own words, the various uses of QuickBooks.

2 List the four basic features of QuickBooks.

3 Describe how lists are used in QuickBooks.

4 Describe how forms are used in QuickBooks.

5 Name three forms used in QuickBooks.

6 Describe how registers are used in QuickBooks.

7 Describe how reports and graphs are used in QuickBooks.

8 Describe the function of the navigators in QuickBooks.

9 Describe how to print a report in QuickBooks.

10 Describe two of the Help features available in QuickBooks.

Chapter 1 Matching

Select the letter of the item below that best matches the definitions that follow. Use the text or QuickBooks Help to complete this assignment.

a. Data Files CD   _____ A repository for all financial activity for a specific balance sheet account.

b. Lists   _____ A means of presenting the financial position and the operating results of a company in a way that makes business decision making easier.

c. Forms   _____ The process of creating a copy of a QuickBooks file for safekeeping or transporting to a different computer.

d. Registers   _____ Contains backups of all the practice files needed for chapter work and completion of assignments.

e. Reports and graphs   _____ Groups of names such as customers, vendors, employees, items, and accounts.

f. Restoring a backup   _____ A big-picture approach of how your essential business tasks fit together organized by logical groups such as customers, vendors, and employees.

g. Icon bar   _____ Electronic representations of paper documents used to record business activities such as customer invoices, vendor bills, and checks.

h. Home page   _____ The process of rebuilding a backup file to a full QuickBooks file ready for additional input.

i. Backing up a file   _____ One click access to QuickBooks Centers and Home page.

Chapter 1 Assignments

1 *Working with Files*

Use the Century Kitchens file to practice opening, closing, and printing. Create a report of Open Invoices as of 3/31/2009 from the Customers & Receivables menu item on the Reports menu. Print the resulting Open Invoices report.

2 *Practice Using the QuickBooks Help Menu*

Use the QuickBooks Help menu to learn more about QuickBooks's features.

a. Search on printing reports and print this topic.

b. Search on add a customer. Print this topic.

c. Search on calculating payroll taxes manually. Print this topic.

d. Click **Chart of Accounts** from the Company menu. Press **F1** (which will open QuickBooks's Help window) and then print the topic.

3 *Using the QuickBooks Learning Center Tutorials*

From the Help menu, select **Learning Center Tutorials**. Click **Inventory**, and then watch the tutorial on using reports to manage inventory. Explain what information is provided on the Inventory Valuation Summary report.

4 *Accessing Century Kitchens Inventory Data*

Scott Montalvo wants to know the amount and nature of inventory on hand as of January 31, 2009. Use Century Kitchens.qbw to obtain this inventory information. Open Century Kitchens.qbw. Open an Inventory Valuation Summary report as of January 31, 2009. Write your responses to questions below and print the Inventory Valuation Summary report.

a. What is Item 1003?   *Base Double Door*

b. How many of this item were on hand on that date?   *3*

c. What was the average cost of this item on that date?   *$480.00*

d. Print the Inventory Valuation Summary report in landscape orientation.

5 *Accessing Century Kitchens Sales Data*

Scott also wants to know the company's sales for the period January 1 through January 31, 2009. Use Century Kitchens.qbw to obtain this sales information. Open Century Kitchens.qbw. Open the Sales by Customer Detail report for the period January 1 through January 31, 2009. Write your responses to the following questions.

a. How much was J Wilson billed this period? $12,480.00

b. What was S Gomez billed for this period? $4,050.00

c. What was the total amount billed during this period?

$37,995.00

2

Preparing a Balance Sheet Using QuickBooks

Case: Century Kitchens

It's your second day at your new job, and you arrive early. Scott is already hard at work at the computer. He tells you he is preparing for Century Kitchens' quarter year-end on March 31, 2009. Since this is the first time he will prepare financial statements using QuickBooks, he's a little nervous.

You recall from your accounting course that a balance sheet reports the assets, liabilities, and owners' equity of a company at a specific point in time. As part of your continued training on QuickBooks, Scott asks you to watch what he does while he prepares the balance sheet. He explains that his immediate goals are to familiarize himself with how to prepare a balance sheet using QuickBooks and to examine some of the valuable features that QuickBooks provides for helping managers analyze and interpret financial information.

Video Demonstration

DEMO 2A - Creating a balance sheet

Creating a Balance Sheet

You know from your business courses that the information on a balance sheet can be presented in many ways. Scott tells you that QuickBooks provides four preset ways to present a balance sheet; QuickBooks also allows him to customize the way he presents the information. He decides to examine one of the preset balance sheets first. He chooses what QuickBooks calls the Standard Balance Sheet report.

Scott is amazed at how rapidly QuickBooks creates this balance sheet compared to how long it has taken him to create one manually in the past. As you both look over this balance sheet, Scott comments that—because he generated this information so quickly and with so little effort—he might now be able to add information to balance sheets that he didn't have time to include before. For example, he has always wanted to include comparative information on balance sheets to help him make better business decisions.

To create a Standard Balance Sheet report:

1   Open Century Kitchens.qbw.

2   Click **Report Center** from the navigation bar. Click **Company & Financial** on the left (if it is not already selected) Scroll. Click the **Standard** tab at the top of the Report Center window. In the upper right hand corner of the Report Center window, click the **List View** icon (place your mouse over the three icons shown noting that the List View is the middle icon). Scroll down the window, and then double-click **Balance Sheet Standard** under the heading **Balance Sheet & Net Worth**. Change the As of date to **3/31/2009**. Click the **Modify Report** button on the button bar, click the **Header/Footer** tab, uncheck the **Date Prepared, Time Prepared**, and **Report Basis** check boxes, and then click **OK.** Then click **Refresh.** QuickBooks's Standard Balance Sheet appears. See Figure 2.1.

Change As of date here

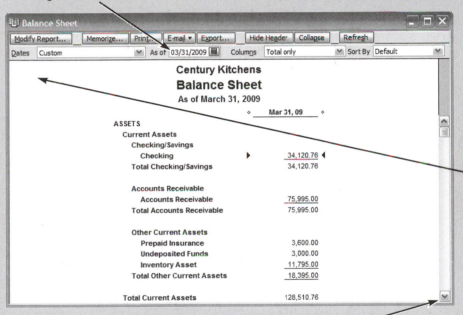

Scroll down to see the rest of the Balance Sheet

Figure 2.1

Century Kitchens' Balance Sheet as of March 31, 2009, in QuickBooks's Standard Preset Report

Note there is no reference to Date Prepared, Time Prepared, or Report Basis

3   Scroll down the Balance Sheet. Notice that this report shows the balance in each account, with subtotals for assets, liabilities, and owners' equity. Unlike standard accounting practice, QuickBooks displays net income for the year to date as part of owners' equity. In particular, take note of the current assets, fixed assets, current liabilities, long-term liabilities, and owners' equity. Observe that QuickBooks refers to "owners' equity" as simply "equity."

4   Do not close this window.

Trouble? On many of these reports, when you change the size of a column and then close the window, a "Memorized Report" window pops up asking if you want to memorize these new settings ("Would you like to memorize this report?"). I suggest that at this point you just click **No.**

Creating a Comparative Balance Sheet

By using the help function of QuickBooks, Scott discovers how easy it is to create a comparative balance sheet. He learns that he can modify the existing standard balance sheet by creating one that compares each month of the quarter just ended. When Scott sees how easily it is to create a comparative balance sheet, he decides to create one comparing the balance sheets of January, February, and March 2009.

To create a comparative balance sheet report for January, February, and March 2009:

1 Modify the standard balance sheet you just created by clicking the **Modify Report** button. (*Note:* If you have already closed the standard balance sheet window, follow the previous steps to re-create it.)

2 Change the From date to **1/1/2009**. (*Note:* The To date should already be 3/31/2009.)

3 Change the Columns text box from Total Only to **Month**, and then click **OK.**

4 Click the **Refresh** button to view the comparative balance sheet, shown in Figure 2.2.

Figure 2.2

QuickBooks's Comparison Balance Sheet Report for Century Kitchens for January, February, and March 2009

Drag to adjust column widths

Check here to change columns to months

Note the significance of these two columns

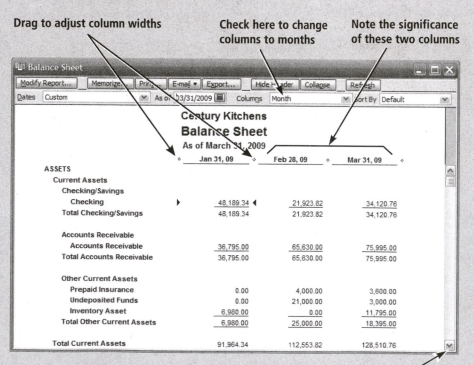

Scroll down to see more of this balance sheet

5 Scroll down and across this balance sheet. Note that this report is similar to the Standard report except that the columns compare the amounts by month for a three-month period as compared to just one date.

Trouble? The balance sheet on your screen might not look the same as Figure 2.1 because the column widths are different. To change the column widths on any QuickBooks report, click and hold the mouse over the small diamond-shaped symbols to the right or left of any column. Drag to the right or left to increase or decrease each column's width. A dialog box might appear asking if you want to make all columns the same width. You may answer yes or no.

6 Close this window.

Creating a Summary Balance Sheet

Scott wonders if QuickBooks has a preset report that summarizes balance sheet information—in other words, one that provides no detail, only totals. In annual reports, such a summary is useful to external financial statement users, who usually do not have much interest in detailed balance sheet information. Scott again consults Help and learns that QuickBooks has a Summary Balance Sheet preset report.

To create a Summary Balance Sheet report:

1 From the Report Center, click **Company & Financial**, if it is not already selected, and then click **Balance Sheet Summary**. (*Note:* This is not clicking the Reports menu item; it's clicking **Company & Financial** from the Report Center.) Remove the Date Prepared, Time Prepared, and Report Basis as you did in the previous balance sheet.

2 Change the As of date to **3/31/2009**, and then click **Refresh**. See Figure 2.3.

3 Scroll down the summary balance sheet if necessary. Note that it is a brief version of the Standard Balance Sheet; it shows amounts for each account type, such as Other Current Assets, but not for individual accounts within each account type.

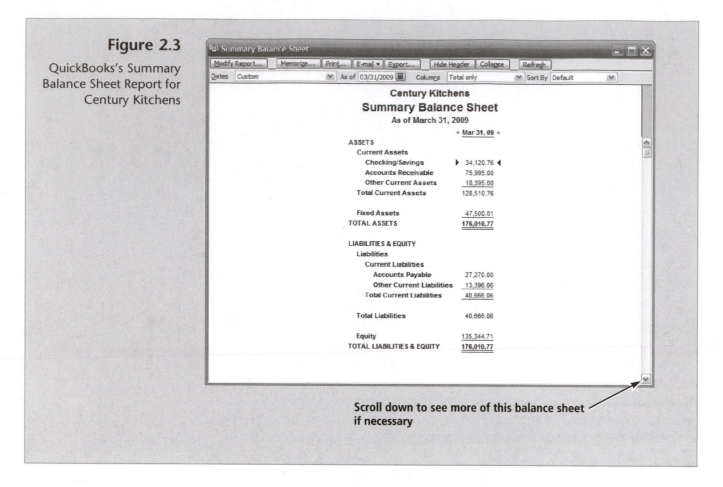

Figure 2.3

QuickBooks's Summary Balance Sheet Report for Century Kitchens

Scroll down to see more of this balance sheet if necessary

Investigating the Balance Sheet Using QuickZoom

Now that Scott knows he can generate the type of reports he wants, he decides to investigate QuickZoom—a feature he has heard QuickBooks provides for most reports. He tells you that QuickZoom shows you what transaction or transactions underlie any amount found in a report. You know that this is a helpful feature because managers must often explain report balances quickly; thus, knowledge of the underlying detailed transactions is essential.

Scott decides to practice using QuickZoom by analyzing the transactions that make up the Accounts Receivable balance.

To use QuickZoom:

1 Place the cursor over the Accounts Receivable balance of **$75,995.00.**
A cursor shaped like a magnifying glass and containing a "Z" appears. This cursor indicates that a QuickZoom report is available for this amount. See Figure 2.4.

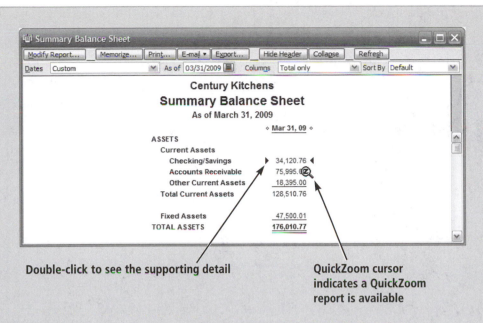

Figure 2.4

Using QuickZoom

Double-click to see the supporting detail

QuickZoom cursor indicates a QuickZoom report is available

2 Double-click the amount **$75,995.00**. The Transactions by Account report appears but lists only one item. That's because this report is showing only the events that took place on 3/31/2009.

3 Change the From date to **3/1/2009** and leave the To date at 3/31/2009, and then click **Refresh.** Remove the Date Prepared, Time Prepared, and Report Basis items as you did previously. The resulting Transactions by Account report now appears with all changes to Accounts Receivable occurring during the month of March, as shown in Figure 2.5.

Transactions are listed for 3/1/09 to 3/31/09

Figure 2.5

Viewing Transactions by Account

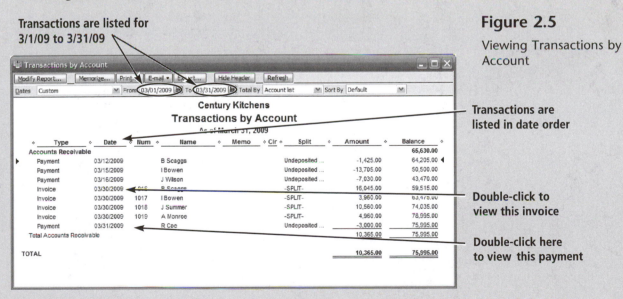

Transactions are listed in date order

Double-click to view this invoice

Double-click here to view this payment

4 Double-click invoice **1016** in the Num column to examine one of the actual invoices that increased accounts receivable during March. See Figure 2.6.

Figure 2.6

Examining Invoice Number 1016 for B Scaggs

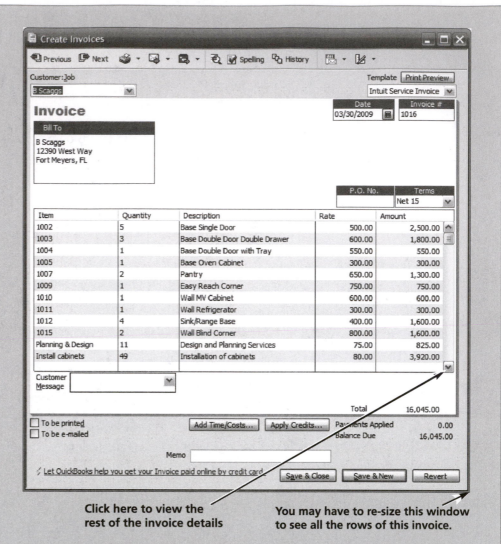

Click here to view the rest of the invoice details

You may have to re-size this window to see all the rows of this invoice.

5 Close the Create Invoices window. The Transactions by Account report, which was hidden while you examined invoice 1016, reappears.

> *Trouble?* If the transactions report does not reappear, activate the Transactions by Account report by clicking **Transactions by Account** on the Window menu; or, if you closed the window, repeat Steps 1 through 4 as necessary.

6 Double-click anywhere on the row containing the payment made by R Coe posted 3/31/2009. A Receive Payments window appears (see Figure 2.7). Note that this payment was a payment on account and was applied to invoices 1002 and 1005.

7 Close the Receive Payments window.

8 Close the Transactions by Account window.

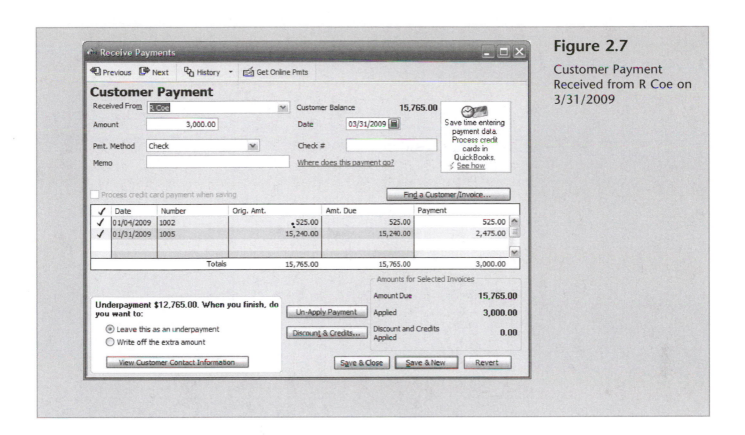

Figure 2.7

Customer Payment Received from R Coe on 3/31/2009

Scott is pleased with the QuickZoom feature of QuickBooks because it allows him to quickly and easily investigate any of the balances reported.

Modifying Balance Sheet Reports

The balance sheet report, like all other reports created in QuickBooks, can be modified using the report button bar located on the menu bar. Scott decides that since this summary balance sheet is for internal use, he wants to change the heading, include the previous month's balances, report the numbers in thousands, and make a few other appropriate cosmetic changes.

To modify the Summary Balance Sheet report:

1   Click the **Modify Report** button on the report button bar. (*Note:* The summary balance sheet should still be open. If not, re-create it.)

2   Click the **Display** tab if it is not already active; then change the From date to **2/1/2009**, change Display columns by setting to **Month**, and check the **% of Column** check box, as shown in Figure 2.8.

3   Click the **Fonts & Numbers** tab as shown in Figure 2.8.

Figure 2.8

The Modify Report
Dialog Box Display Tab

**Click the
Fonts & Numbers
tab**

**Change From
date here**

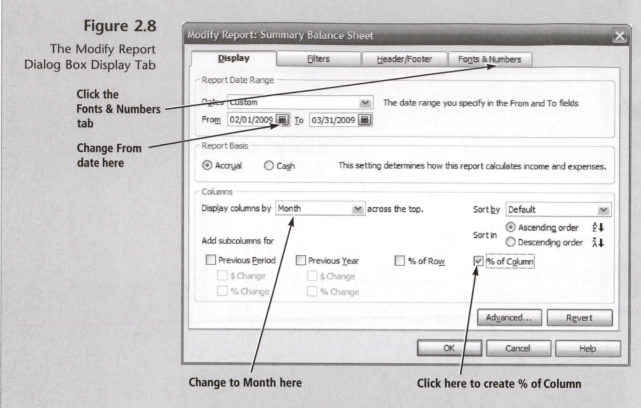

Change to Month here   **Click here to create % of Column**

4 Click the **Divided By 1000** and **Without Cents** check boxes under
the Show All Numbers section of the Modify Report dialog box. See
Figure 2.9.

Figure 2.9

The Modify Report
Dialog Box Fonts &
Numbers Tab

**When selecting Without
Cents, QuickBooks rounds
to the nearest whole dollar.
Be aware that resulting
column totals may be
off by $1.**

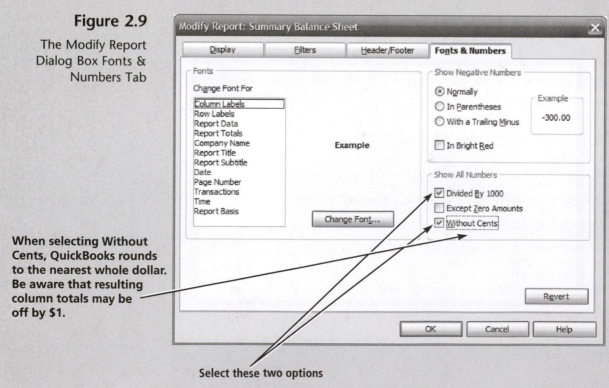

Select these two options

5 Click the **Header/Footer** tab.

6 Click inside the Report Title edit box. Change the name of the report from Summary Balance Sheet to Comparative Summary Balance Sheet by adding the word **Comparative** as shown in Figure 2.10. (*Note:* To properly identify this report as yours, you may want to type your name in the Extra Footer Line of the Header/Footer tab.)

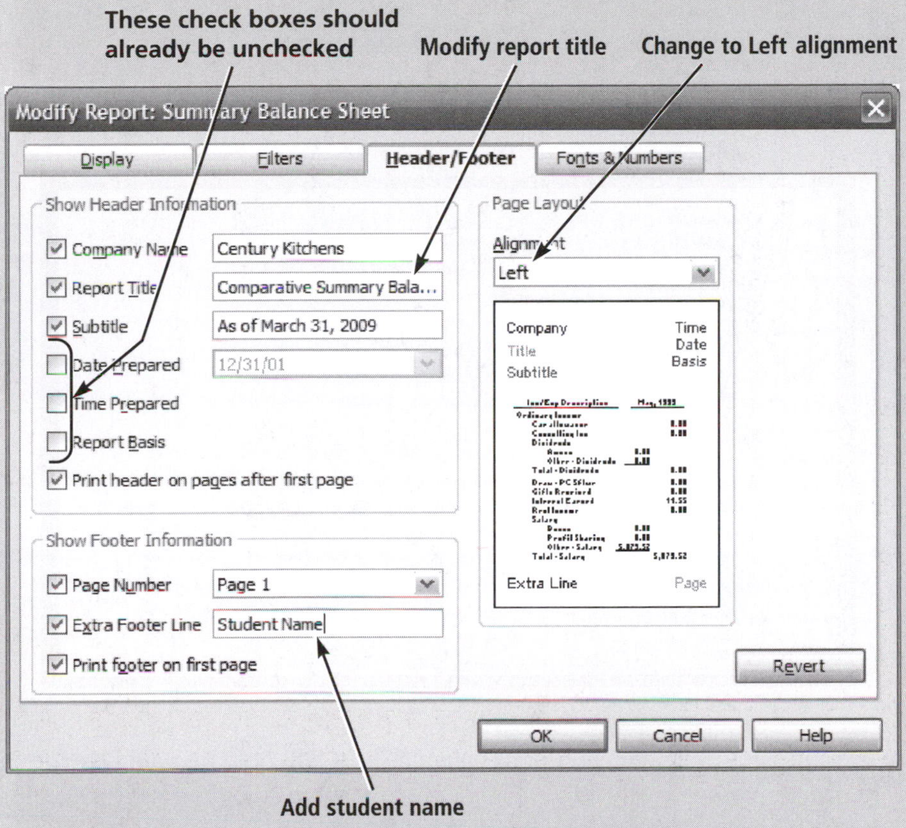

Figure 2.10

The Header/Footer Tab

These check boxes should already be unchecked   **Modify report title**   **Change to Left alignment**

Modify Report: Summary Balance Sheet

| Display | Filters | Header/Footer | Fonts & Numbers |

Show Header Information

☑ Company Name   Century Kitchens
☑ Report Title   Comparative Summary Bala...
☑ Subtitle   As of March 31, 2009
☐ Date Prepared   12/31/01
☐ Time Prepared
☐ Report Basis
☑ Print header on pages after first page

Page Layout

Alignment
Left

Company   Time
Title   Date
Subtitle   Basis

Extra Line   Page

Show Footer Information

☑ Page Number   Page 1
☑ Extra Footer Line   Student Name
☑ Print footer on first page

Revert

OK   Cancel   Help

Add student name

7 Change the alignment by clicking the **Down Arrow** in the Page Layout section and clicking **Left.** This changes the alignment of the title text to a left alignment.

8 Click **OK** to close the Modify Report window. The resulting report is shown in Figure 2.11.

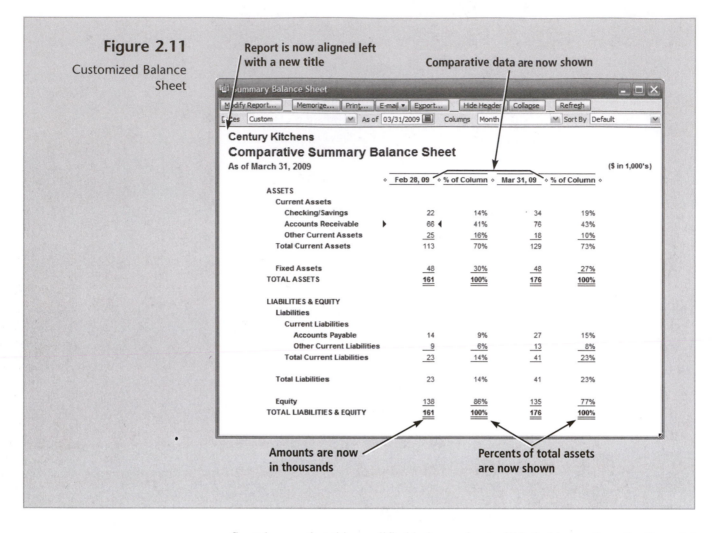

Figure 2.11

Customized Balance Sheet

Scott knows that this modified balance sheet will help him analyze the financial information more easily and quickly. You will have an opportunity to explore other report modification features available in QuickBooks in the chapter assignments.

Memorizing a Report in QuickBooks

Scott, knowing that he wants you to be an efficient QuickBooks user, suggests that you learn how to memorize the report just created so it can be produced again. He explains that, while standard reports are always available, unique reports like the one you just created should be memorized. Later they can be accessed, dates changed if necessary, and then re-created.

"How will I know where they are when I need them?" you ask.

Scott explains that he will create a memorized report group for you using your name. That way, when you need them again, they will be easy to find.

To memorize the comparative balance sheet just prepared:

1 Open the Report Center.

2 Click the Memorized tab at the top of the Report Center and then click **Edit Memorized List.**

3 Click the **Memorized Report** button at the bottom of the Memorized Report List window, and then click **New Group.**

4 Type your name as the new group, and then click **OK.** (For illustration purposes, the list will show "Student Name" as your name.)

5 Go to the Summary Balance Sheet still open in QuickBooks by clicking its name from the Open Windows List.

Trouble? If the Open Windows List is not present, click the **View** menu and then click **Open Windows List.**

6 Click the **Memorize . . .** button at the top of the report.

7 Check the **Saved in Memorized Report Group** check box, and select your name from the drop-down list.

8 Click **OK** to memorize the report accepting the default report title provided.

9 Click the Memorized Report List window, which should look similar to that shown in Figure 2.12. Then close the Memorized Report List.

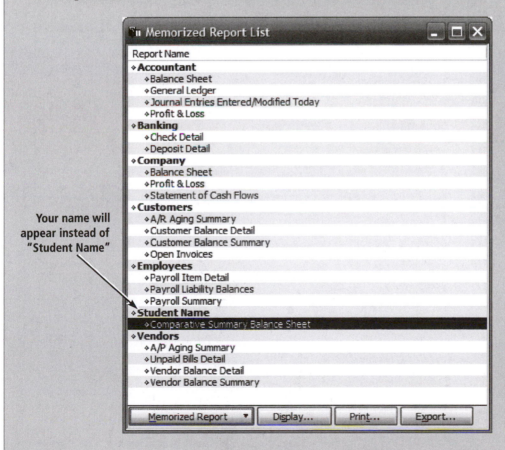

Figure 2.12
Memorized Report List

Your name will appear instead of "Student Name"

Printing the Balance Sheet

Scott receives a phone call from Frances Wu, an accountant with Century's CPA firm of Stoddard & Wong. Frances says she needs a printed copy of the company's balance sheet as of 3/31/2009 to analyze the need for an allowance for uncollectible accounts. Scott knows that printing the balance sheet he just created will provide her with the information she needs. He also knows that printing a balance sheet is just like printing any other report in QuickBooks.

To print the Comparative Summary Balance Sheet report:

1 Click **Print** on the report button bar.

2 Click **Preview** in the Print Reports dialog box to preview the report.

3 Click the **Zoom In** button to see what the report will look like when printed. (Alternatively, you could have clicked anywhere on the screen to zoom in on the report.) See Figure 2.13.

Figure 2.13

Preview the Balance Sheet

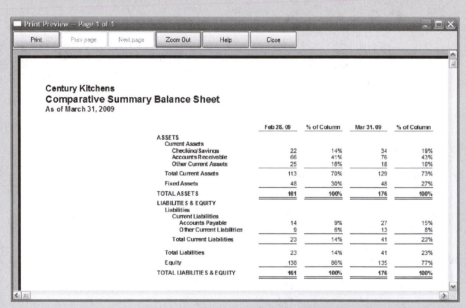

4 Click the **Print** button if you would like to print the report.

5 Close all windows and, if you are not proceeding to Chapter 3, exit QuickBooks. If a Memorized Report window appears, click in the check box next to Do not display this message in the future, and then click **No.**

Scott feels much more confident about using QuickBooks. You are quickly becoming more comfortable with QuickBooks as well.

In the next chapter, you will expand your QuickBooks knowledge to include the creation, modification, and printing of another useful financial statement—the income statement.

Chapter 2 Questions

1 List the preset ways in which QuickBooks can present a balance sheet.

2 What time period alternatives does QuickBooks provide for a balance sheet?

3 List the steps you would take to create a balance sheet for a date other than the current system date.

4 Describe the steps to generate a balance sheet in QuickBooks.

5 Describe the steps to resize the columns of a comparative balance sheet.

6 Describe the different types of transactions you might find in a Transactions by Account report on accounts receivable.

7 Describe how QuickZoom gives you more information about a balance sheet.

8 How might a manager use QuickZoom to analyze a business's financial position as reported in a balance sheet?

9 List five ways you can customize a QuickBooks report.

10 Suppose you wanted to include a column in a balance sheet that described what percentage each asset, liability, and owners' equity account was of the total assets amount. How would you do this in QuickBooks?

Chapter 2 Matching

Select the letter of the item below that best matches the definitions that follow. Use the text or QuickBooks Help to complete this assignment.

a. Balance Sheet Standard report

_____ When selected in the Modify Report window, this check box requires QuickBooks to add a column representing the percentage of each item compared to total assets.

b. To date

_____ When selected in the Modify Report window, this check box requires QuickBooks to round amounts to the nearest whole dollar.

c. Summary Balance Sheet report

_____ The start of the reporting period.

d. QuickZoom

_____ A financial statement reporting in detail the assets, liabilities, and equities of a business as of a certain date.

e. Transactions by Account report

_____ A process by which modified reports are saved for later use.

f. % of Column

_____ When selected in the Modify Report window, this check box requires QuickBooks to report amounts in thousands.

g. Memorizing a report   _____ The end of the reporting period.

h. Divided by 1000   _____ A QuickBooks feature that allows you to view the transaction details underlying amounts in a report.

i. Without Cents   _____ A report generated when using QuickZoom.

j. From date   _____ A financial statement reporting in summary form the assets, liabilities, and equities of a business as of a certain date.

Chapter 2 Assignments

corporation   merchandising

1 *Creating a Balance Sheet for Century Kitchens*

Scott asks you to help him prepare a balance sheet. (Be sure to type your name in the Extra Footer Line of this report.)

a. He asks you to prepare and print a summary balance sheet as of January 31, 2009. He wants the amounts represented in thousands without cents and with no date prepared, time prepared, or report basis shown. Memorize this report, and save it in your report group.

b. Scott also asks you to prepare and print a standard balance sheet as of January 31, 2009. He wants amounts to be displayed in thousands, without cents, and with the page layout left-aligned but with no date prepared, time prepared, or report basis shown. Memorize this report, and save it in your report group.

2 *Investigating the Balance Sheet Using QuickZoom*

Scott asks you to help him investigate the Accounts Receivable balance as of January 31, 2009. Create a summary balance sheet as of January 31, 2009, and then investigate the Accounts Receivable balance.

a. Print the resulting Transactions by Account report.

b. Examine and print a copy of invoice 1005.

3 *Customizing a Balance Sheet*

Modify the balance sheet you created in Assignment 1a (remember, you memorized it, so it is easy to recall) to include January and February amounts with a % of column. Change the report title and format the page as shown in Figure 2.14. (*Hint:* Use the Modify Report button.) Print the report with your name in the Extra Footer Line in portrait orientation.

Century Kitchens
Comparative Balance Sheet
As of February 28, 2009   ($ in 1,000's)

	Jan 31, 09	% of Column	Feb 28, 09	% of Column
ASSETS				
Current Assets				
Checking/Savings	48	34%	22	14%
Accounts Receivable	37	26%	66	41%
Other Current Assets	7	5%	25	16%
Total Current Assets	92	65%	113	70%
Fixed Assets	49	35%	48	30%
TOTAL ASSETS	141	100%	161	100%
LIABILITIES & EQUITY				
Liabilities				
Current Liabilities				
Accounts Payable	7	5%	14	9%
Other Current Liabilities	5	3%	9	6%
Total Current Liabilities	12	8%	23	14%
Total Liabilities	12	8%	23	14%
Equity	129	92%	138	86%
TOTAL LIABILITIES & EQUITY	141	100%	161	100%

Figure 2.14

Comparative Balance Sheet

Chapter 2 Case Problem 1:
SIERRA MARINA

Meagan Casey is the sole proprietor and owner of Sierra Marina, located at the north end of Shaver Lake in the California Sierra Mountains. She has been in business for a few years and decided on July 1, 2007, to automate her accounting using QuickBooks. Meagan has already entered the June 30, 2007, ending balances from her previous accounting system as well as all transactions for July and August 2007, and she has asked you to help her prepare some basic financial reports related to the company's assets, liabilities, and equities.

sole proprietorship   *service*

Requirements:

Prepare, memorize, and print the following reports using Meagan's Sierra Marina QuickBooks file. (Remember, you'll have to restore this file from the Data Files CD. Be sure to include your name in the Extra Footer Line of each report where possible.)

1 A standard balance sheet as of July 31, 2007.

2 A summary balance sheet as of July 31, 2007.

3 A comparative summary balance sheet for June and July 2007 without cents, with a % of column, and in a left alignment. Be sure to change the report title to include the word "comparative."

4 A report of those transactions recorded in July 2007 that affected accounts receivable. (***Hint:*** From your summary balance sheet created in Step 2, double-click **Accounts Receivable** and make sure the From date is 7/1/07 and the To date is 7/31/07.)

Chapter 2 Case Problem 2:
JENNINGS & ASSOCIATES

corporation   *service*

Kelly Jennings has just started working full time in her new business, an advertising agency named Jennings & Associates and located in San Martin, California. Like many eager entrepreneurs, she started her business while working full time for another firm. At first, her billings were quite small. But as her client base and her billings grew, she decided to leave her job and set out on her own. Two of her colleagues and friends—Cheryl Boudreau and Diane Murphy—see Kelly's eagerness and dedication, and they decide the time is right for them, too. Cheryl and Diane ask Kelly if they can join her sole proprietorship as employees, and so together they leave the traditional corporate agency environment.

Kelly knows that one of the first tasks she must accomplish is setting up an accounting system for Jennings & Associates. Also, she has just received a request from her banker to submit a balance sheet as documentation for a business loan. As a close friend you recommend she use QuickBooks, and you volunteer to help her get started.

Kelly tells you that in 2007 she borrowed $5,000 to start the business. Now she is applying for a loan to help expand the business. She also reminds you that, although she did conduct some business in 2007, her first full-time month was January 2008.

Requirements:

Prepare and print the following reports using Kelly Jennings.qbw (include your name in the Extra Footer Line of each report where possible). Remember, you'll need to restore this file from your Data Files CD.

1 A standard balance sheet as of December 31, 2007.

2 A standard balance sheet as of January 31, 2008.

3 A Transactions List by Date report for the month of January 2008 in landscape orientation. (**Hint:** This report is listed in the Report menu section labeled Accountant & Taxes.)

4 A summary balance sheet as of January 31, 2008, formatted in thousands and without cents and without the date prepared, time prepared, or report basis included.

5 A report of those transactions recorded in January 2008 that affected accounts payable. (**Hint:** Create a summary balance sheet and double-click **accounts payable**.)

Preparing an Income Statement Using QuickBooks

Learning Objectives

In this chapter, you will:

- Change the way dates are formatted in QuickBooks
- Create income statements for different time periods
- Create an income statement with year-to-date comparative information
- Investigate the detail underlying income statement items
- Use the Income Statement Report button bars
- Print an income statement

Case: Century Kitchens

Now that Scott has created a balance sheet, he is ready to create an income statement for the period January 1, 2009, through March 31, 2009. You recall from your accounting course that the income statement reports revenues and expenses for a specific period.

Again, as part of your training with QuickBooks, Scott asks you to watch how he prepares the income statement. He expects to use many of the same functions and features to prepare an income statement that he used to prepare the balance sheet.

Date Formats

You mention to Scott that the default four-digit year format in QuickBooks (12/15/2009) seems a bit excessive, and perhaps they should return to the more standard date format (12/15/09). Scott agrees and decides to show you the steps necessary to change the date preferences.

> **To change date preferences:**
>
> 1 Open the Century Kitchens.qbw file, click **Edit**, and then click **Preferences.**
>
> 2 Click the **General** icon on the left of the Preferences window, and then click the **Company Preferences** tab.

> **3** Uncheck the **Always show years as 4 digits (1999)** check box.
>
> **4** Click **OK** to save the changes, and close the Preferences window.
>
> **5** To restore the home page, click **Home** in the Navigation bar.

Scott confirms that all dates in QuickBooks registers, report windows, and so forth will now be in the standard format of a two-digit year (12/15/09).

Video Demonstration

DEMO 3A - Creating an income statement

Creating an Income Statement

As with the balance sheet and other reports available in QuickBooks, the income statement can be presented in preset ways and can also be customized. Scott decides to examine one of the preset income statement formats first—the format called Standard.

Before doing so he mentions that QuickBooks does not use the traditional name for this report. Instead of calling it the income statement, QuickBooks refers to it as the "Profit & Loss" report. Scott prefers "income statement" because it is really the most accurate name for this report. Although the report title on the menu cannot be changed, Scott will show you how you can change the title on the report.

To create a standard income statement:

1 Open the Report Center, click the Standard tab, and then click **Company & Financial**, and then double-click **Profit & Loss Standard**. Change the From date to **3/1/09** and the To date to **3/31/09.** Then click **Refresh.**

2 Click **Modify Report**, click the **Header/Footer** tab, and then uncheck the **Date Prepared, Time Prepared**, and **Report Basis** check boxes. The report shown in Figure 3.1 should appear.

3 Scroll down the Century Kitchens income statement. This report summarizes revenues and expenses for this month-to-date. Notice that QuickBooks does not use the standard accounting term "revenue" but instead uses the term "income." Subtotals are included for revenues and expenses. Observe also the period specified for this particular report is March 1–31, 2009, the span of this report period.

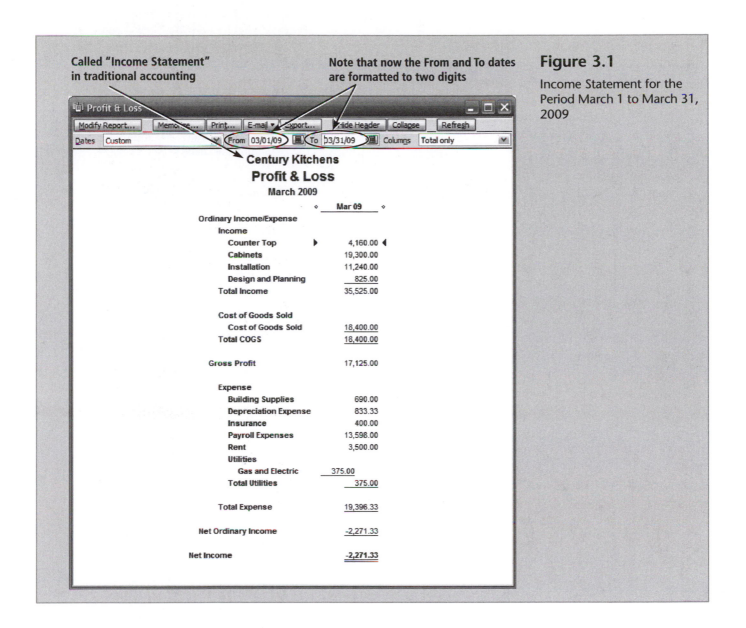

Figure 3.1

Income Statement for the Period March 1 to March 31, 2009

Scott changes his mind and wants a year-to-date statement for his preliminary income statement.

Modifying an Income Statement

Scott decides to revise the previously created income statement to make it a year-to-date statement for the period January 1, 2009, through March 31, 2009. He also wants to show you how to change the report title from "Profit & Loss" to the more accurate "Income Statement." For this title change you will modify the header, a task you learned how to perform previously with the balance sheet.

To revise the period of time and the report title:

1 Change the From date on the previously created income statement to **1/1/09.** Click **Refresh.** The revised report appears as in Figure 3.2.

Figure 3.2

Revised Income Statement for the Period January 1 to March 31, 2009

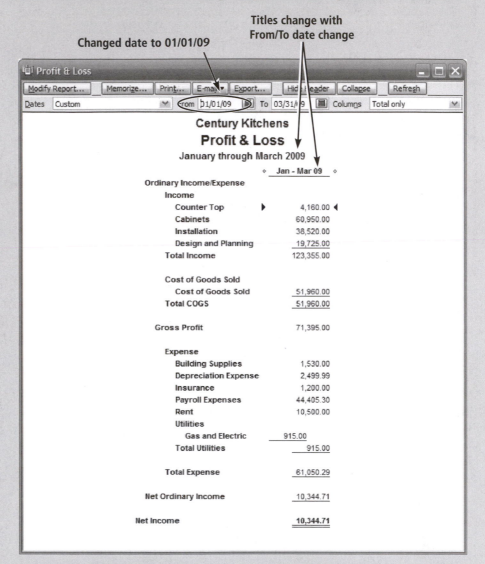

2 To change the report title, click **Modify Report**, and then click **Header/Footer.** The Header/Footer tab appears (see Figure 3.3).

3 Move the cursor to the Report Title edit box and delete Profit and Loss. Type **Income Statement.** (*Note:* To properly identify this report as yours, you may want to type your name in the Extra Footer Line of the Header/Footer tab.)

4 Click **OK** to view the revised report. See Figure 3.4.

5 When you have finished viewing the revised report, close this window.

6 This time, if the Memorized Report window appears, click **Yes** to memorize this report. If not, click the **Memorize** button.

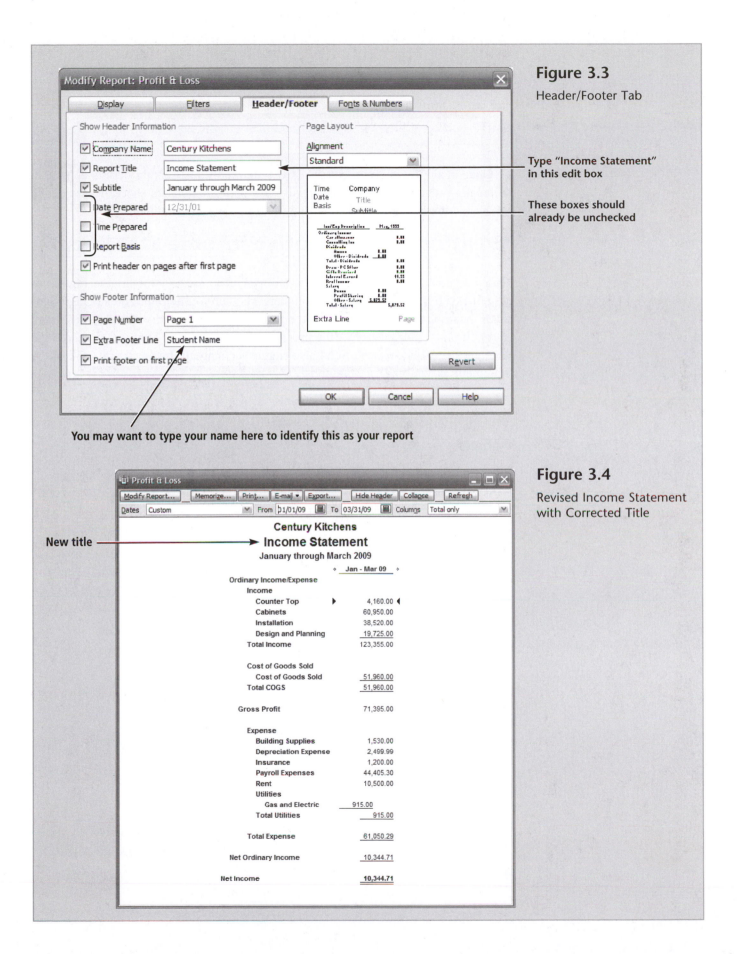

Figure 3.3

Header/Footer Tab

Type "Income Statement" in this edit box

These boxes should already be unchecked

You may want to type your name here to identify this as your report

Figure 3.4

Revised Income Statement with Corrected Title

New title

7   Click **New** if asked whether you want to replace the old standard income statement.

8   Save this report as Income Statement in the Memorized Report Group you created in the last chapter and then click **OK.**

Once again, Scott comments on how remarkably fast this process is compared to creating income statements manually. As with the balance sheet, he decides to create a comparison report—this time with the income statement.

Creating a Comparative Income Statement

QuickBooks has several features that allow you to create comparative reports as you did with the balance sheet. Scott suggests that you help him create a comparative income statement illustrating the performance of Century Kitchens in March and February. You guess that the process will be similar to how you prepared the comparative balance sheet. Scott also suggests changing the name and look of the statement as you've done previously.

To create a comparative income statement for March and February:

1   From the Report Center, click **Company & Financial**, and then double-click **Profit & Loss Standard** located under the title Profit & Loss (income statement).

2   Set the From date to **3/1/09** and the To date to **3/31/09**, and then click **Refresh**.

3   Click the **Modify Report. . .** button, and then check the **Previous Period, $ Change**, and **% Change** check boxes located under the caption Add subcolumns for (see Figure 3.5).

Figure 3.5

Creating a Previous Period for a Comparative Income Statement

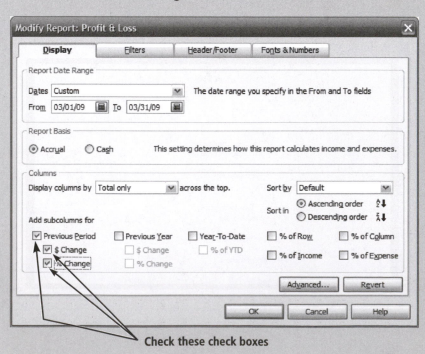

Check these check boxes

4 Click the **Header/Footer** tab, and then uncheck the **Date Prepared, Time Prepared**, and **Report Basis** check boxes.

5 Change the name of the statement from Profit & Loss to **Comparative Income Statements**, align the statement **Right**, put your name in the Footer, and then click **OK** to see the revised report. See Figure 3.6.

Later you will double-click this
amount to investigate its detail

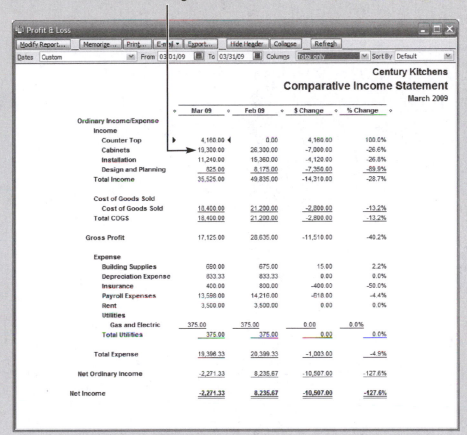

Figure 3.6

Comparative Income Statements for March and February 2009

6 Do not close this report, as it will be used in the next section.

Scott had been concerned about the company's performance in March and can now see how things differed between March and February. His most immediate concern is the drop-off in design and planning revenues, because he knows that will mean future reductions in revenues for cabinet and counter purchases and installations. Scott can see that his expenses are fairly consistent across periods, so his biggest concern is a decrease in revenues.

Using QuickZoom with the Income Statement

To investigate the decrease in revenues for March, Scott uses the QuickZoom feature of QuickBooks to examine the underlying source of various business events. He knows that he can "drill down" behind the income statement to view Transaction Detail By Account reports and further to an invoice. He explains that the invoice in this example is referred to as a *source document* and will prove helpful in his analysis.

To use QuickZoom with an income statement:

1 Place the QuickZoom cursor over the March Cabinets amount of $19,300.00 (as shown in Figure 3.6), and then double-click that amount to reveal a Transaction Detail By Account report; see Figure 3.7.

Figure 3.7

Transaction Detail By Account Report

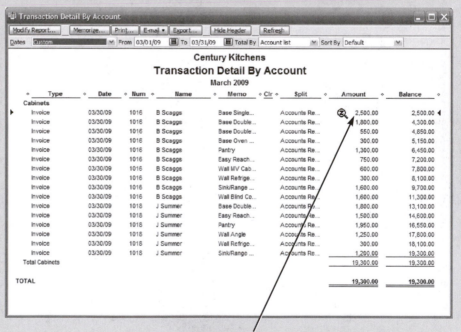

Double-click here to view detail

2 Double-click the **$2,500.00** as shown in Figure 3.7 to reveal the invoice used to bill this amount as shown in Figure 3.8.

3 Close your newly created Comparative Income Statements report, and memorize it in your Report Group.

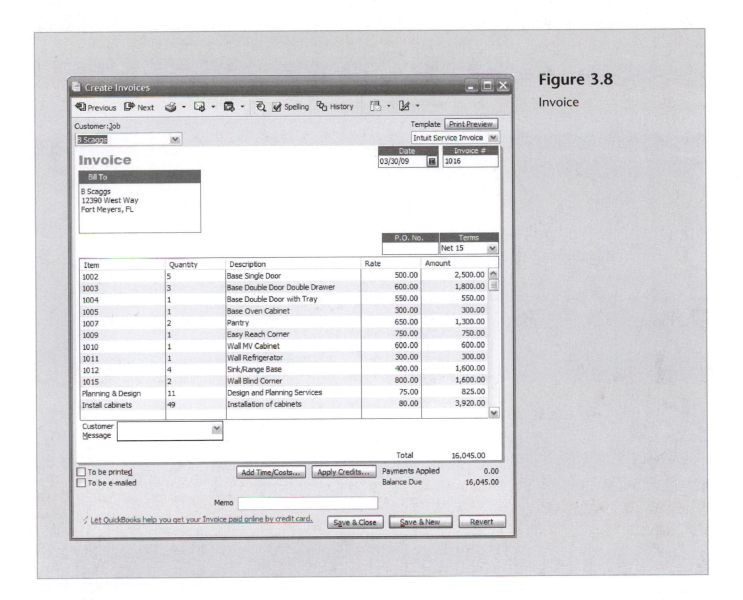

Figure 3.8

Invoice

You have now seen that the QuickZoom feature of QuickBooks is available with the income statement as well as with the balance sheet and that it provides background detail relating to revenues and expenses.

Modifying the Income Statement Report

The Income Statement report, like all other reports created in QuickBooks, can be modified using the report button bar. Scott knows from experience that when he works with income statements in the future he will definitely need to add columns, change report dates, use different number formats, modify headings, and so on. He therefore decides to explore additional ways of modifying an income statement. He decides first to create a first-quarter income statement and to add a percentage of net income column.

To add percentage of net income columns and to change the dates on an Income Statement report:

1   From the Report Center, click **Company & Financial**, and then double-click **Profit & Loss Standard** from the list of Profit & Loss Reports.

2   Click the **Modify Report** button on the report button bar, and then select the **Display** tab if it is not already selected.

3   Click the **% of Income** check box in the Columns section to report monthly amounts as a percent of total income—actually a percent of total revenue. See Figure 3.9.

Figure 3.9

The Modify Report Window

Change these dates

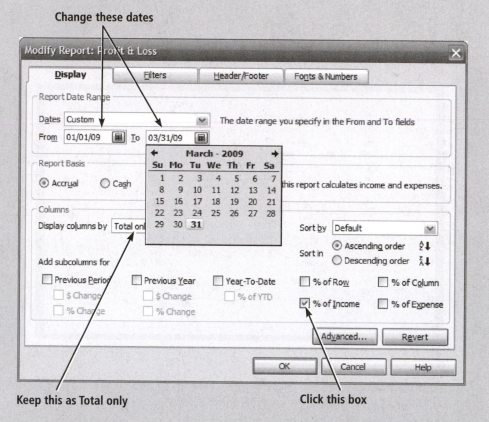

Keep this as Total only

Click this box

4   Click the **From** edit box, and change the date to **1/1/09.**

5   Click the **To** edit box, and change the date to **3/31/09** (see Figure 3.9). These two changes customize the report so it reports on the months of January through March only. (Alternatively, you can select the calendar icons and click the arrows to specific dates.)

6   Select the **Header/Footer** tab, and uncheck the **Date Prepared, Time Prepared**, and **Report Basis** check boxes.

7   Click **OK** to accept these changes. The revised report appears as Figure 3.10. Do not close this report window.

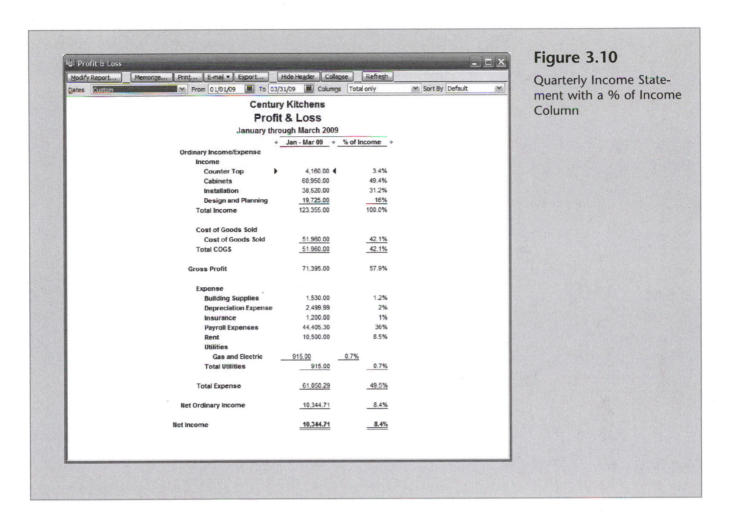

Figure 3.10

Quarterly Income Statement with a % of Income Column

Scott decides that he wants to report the numbers without cents and to collapse expenses.

To report the amounts without cents:

1 Click **Modify Report** on the report button bar, and then click the **Fonts & Numbers** tab.

2 Click the **Without Cents** check box under the Show All Numbers section of the Format Report window. A check mark appears in the box.

3 Click **OK** to accept these changes.

4 Click the **Collapse** button on the report button bar to view the revised quarterly Income Statement; see Figure 3.11.

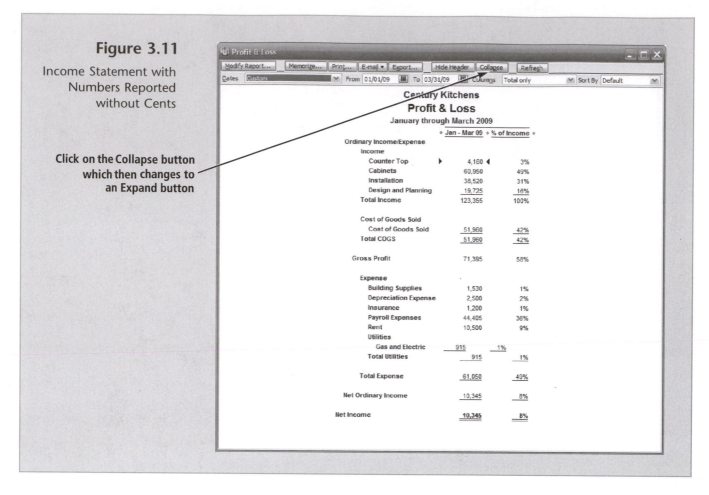

Figure 3.11

Income Statement with
Numbers Reported
without Cents

**Click on the Collapse button
which then changes to
an Expand button**

As Scott looks over this latest version of the income statement, he sees that he must correct the report title again. Also, he decides the title would look better if it appeared in the center of the report and if it included each separate month.

To modify the title and its layout:

1 Click **Modify Report** on the report button bar, and then click the **Header/Footer** tab.

2 Click inside the **Report Title** edit box, and change the name of the report from Profit & Loss to **Income Statement** as you have done before.

3 Change the title alignment by clicking the **Down Arrow** in the Page Layout section and changing the selection from Standard to **Centered**.

4 Before you accept these changes, look at the Subtitle edit box. Notice that QuickBooks had changed the subtitle of this report. QuickBooks does this automatically for you whenever you change the dates in the To and From edit boxes. (*Note:* Once again, you may want to type your name in the Extra Footer Line.)

5 Click **OK** to accept the changes. Change the Columns text box from Total Only to **Month**. The modified income statement appears as shown in Figure 3.12.

Change to Month

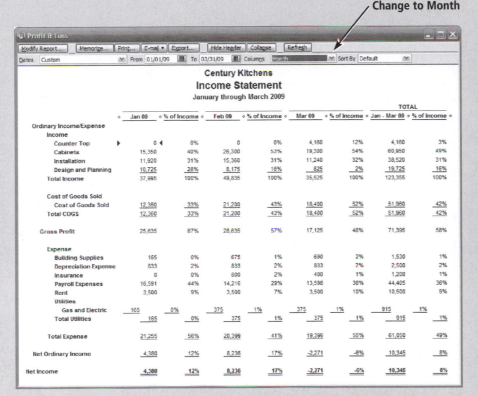

Figure 3.12

Modified Income Statement

6 Do not close this report window.

QuickBooks provides many other ways to modify a report—grouping and subtotaling data, sorting transactions, and specifying which columns appear in a report, to name just a few. Scott encourages you to explore these additional options when you generate reports in the future.

Printing the Income Statement

Scott would like to print this modified report so that he can show some Century Kitchens managers an example of the type of reports he can generate for them. He'd like this example to fit on one piece of 8½″ × 11″ paper—both to save paper and to make analysis of the report easier. He decides to use QuickBooks's preview option to see if the report will fit onto a single page.

To preview the modified income statement:

1 Click **Print** on the report button bar.

2 Click **Preview** in the Print Reports window. A miniature reproduction of the report appears. See Figure 3.13. (Do not resize the columns.) The heading "Page 1 of 2" may appear at the top of the window. This indicates how many pages the report contains and which page you are previewing.

Figure 3.13

The Print Preview Window

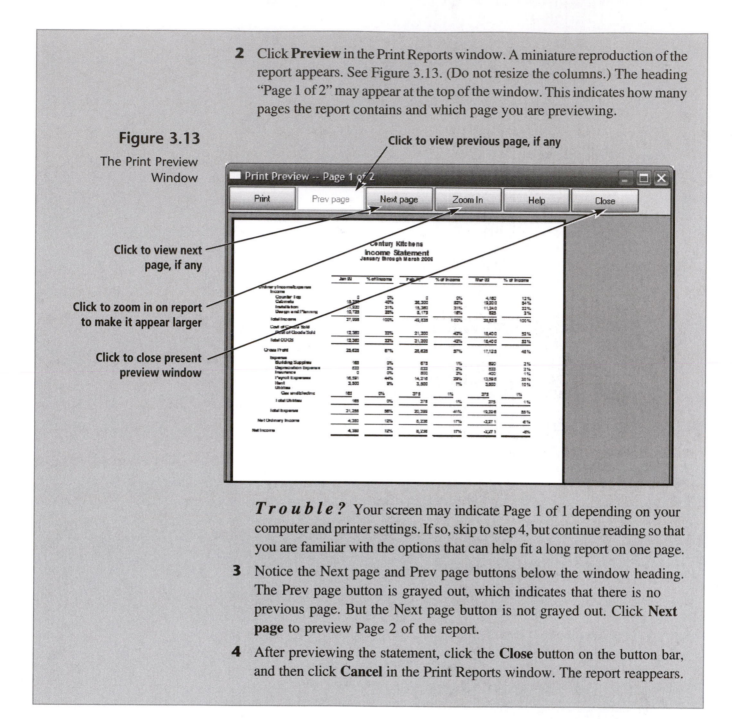

Click to view previous page, if any

Click to view next page, if any

Click to zoom in on report to make it appear larger

Click to close present preview window

Trouble? Your screen may indicate Page 1 of 1 depending on your computer and printer settings. If so, skip to step 4, but continue reading so that you are familiar with the options that can help fit a long report on one page.

3 Notice the Next page and Prev page buttons below the window heading. The Prev page button is grayed out, which indicates that there is no previous page. But the Next page button is not grayed out. Click **Next page** to preview Page 2 of the report.

4 After previewing the statement, click the **Close** button on the button bar, and then click **Cancel** in the Print Reports window. The report reappears.

Scott has seen that the report is not much more than one page; he might make it fit onto one page by reducing the size of the type font.

To reduce the font size of the type in a report:

1 Click **Modify Report** on the report button bar, and then click the **Fonts & Numbers** tab. See Figure 3.14.

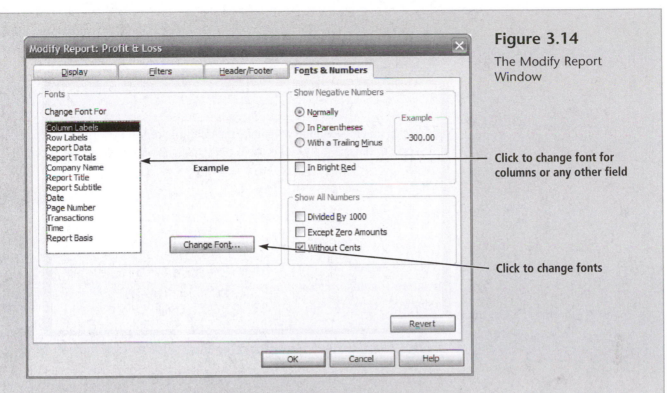

Figure 3.14

The Modify Report Window

2 Click the **Change Font** button located in the bottom center of the window. The Column Labels window appears (see Figure 3.15).

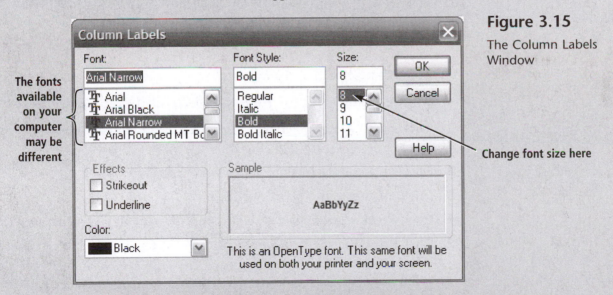

Figure 3.15

The Column Labels Window

3 Click the **Size** edit box. Delete 9 and type (or click on) **8** to reduce the font size by one. Then click the **Font** edit box, and choose **Arial Narrow**, if available, or choose another font that is small enough to accomplish your goal.

4 Click **OK** to accept this new size. A Changing Font window will appear asking if you want to make the change to all related fonts. Click **Yes.** Then click **OK** again. The revised report appears—now in size 8 font.

Scott hopes that this change will make the example report now fit on one page. To see if it worked, he again previews the report. If it fits on one page, he'll print it.

To preview the modified income statement again:

1 Click **Print** on the report button bar.

2 Click **Preview**. The Print Preview window appears. Notice that the heading for this window may still include the words "Page 1 of 2." The change of font size has reduced the report size but not enough that it will fit on one page.

3 Click **Close**, and then click **Cancel** in the Print Reports window.

Suddenly, Scott realizes there might be another way to fit the report on one page. He decides to change the orientation of the page from portrait, the default vertical orientation, to landscape, which is a horizontal orientation.

To change a document from portrait to landscape orientation:

1 Click **Print** on the report button bar to view the Print Reports window. See Figure 3.16.

2 Click the **Landscape** button in the Orientation box.

3 Click **Fit report to 1 page(s) wide.**

4 Click **Preview** once again. The report should now fit on one page.

5 Click **Print** from the Print Preview window. Your completed report should look like Figure 3.17.

Trouble? If your printer still prints this document on two pages, consult with your lab personnel. Different printers may generate different output.

6 Close all windows, and exit QuickBooks as you have done before. Do not memorize this report.

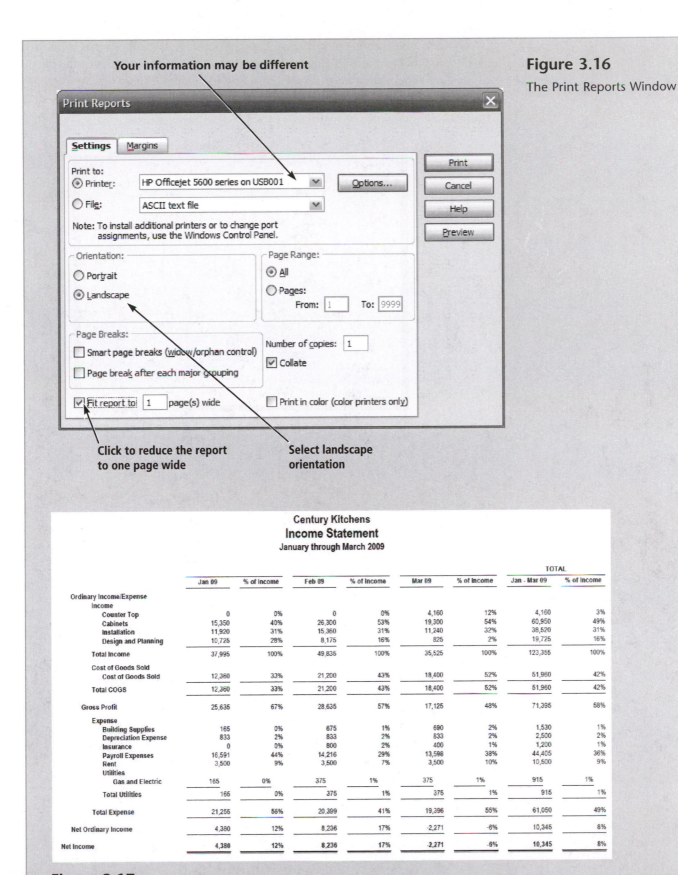

Figure 3.16

The Print Reports Window

Your information may be different

Click to reduce the report to one page wide

Select landscape orientation

Figure 3.17

Modified Income Statement on One Page

Now that you have completed Chapters 2 and 3, you see how easily QuickBooks creates the two financial reports most commonly used to communicate accounting information to external users—the balance sheet and the income statement. In Chapter 4, you will continue your brief overview of QuickBooks by creating a statement of cash flows.

Chapter 3 Questions

1 List at least three of the preset formats that QuickBooks provides for an income statement.

2 Identify the different periods of time that QuickBooks provides for an income statement.

3 Describe the steps necessary to create an income statement for a period other than one ending on the computer's current system date.

4 Describe the steps necessary to generate an income statement in QuickBooks.

5 Describe the steps necessary to reformat the columns of a comparative income statement.

6 Describe the steps necessary to modify an income statement so that it includes comparative information.

7 How does QuickZoom help you further investigate an income statement?

8 How could a manager use QuickZoom to access underlying information as reported in an income statement?

9 List five report modification features of QuickBooks that can be applied to an income statement.

10 How would you modify an income statement to include a column describing the percentage relationship between expenses and total revenues?

Chapter 3 Matching

Select the letter of the item below that best matches the definitions that follow. Use the text or QuickBooks Help to complete this assignment.

a. Date formats

b. Profit & Loss Standard report

c. % of Income

d. QuickZoom

e. Without Cents

f. Divided by 1000

g. Previous Period $ Change

_____ The end of the reporting period.

_____ When selected in the Modify Report window, this check box requires QuickBooks to report amounts in thousands.

_____ Adds a subcolumn to a Profit & Loss report that calculates the relative percentage change in each item from a previous period.

_____ The beginning of the reporting period.

_____ A financial statement reporting the revenues and expenses of a business for a specific accounting period.

_____ Adds a subcolumn to a Profit & Loss report that calculates the amount of change in each item from a previous period.

_____ A preference option that specifies whether years in date fields are shown as two digits or four digits.

h.   Previous Period %   _____ A feature in QuickBooks that allows you to view the transaction details
     Change   underlying amounts in a report.

i.   To date   _____ When selected in the Modify Report window, this check box requires
                                       QuickBooks to round amounts to the nearest whole dollar.

j.   From date   _____ When selected in the Modify Report window, this check box requires
                                       QuickBooks to add a column representing the percentage of each item
                                       compared to total revenues.

Chapter 3 Assignments

corporation

merchandising

1   *Preparing an Income Statement for Century Kitchens*

Scott has asked you to help him prepare a new income statement. Include
your name in the Extra Footer Line of all reports printed.

a.   First, he asks you to prepare and print a modified income statement that
     includes operating information for February 2009. He wants the income
     statement to include amounts (without cents) and columns reflecting the
     dollar change and percentage change between periods. (***Hint:*** Set the
     dates to reflect February only, and be sure the Previous Period box,
     $ Change, and % Change boxes are also checked in the Modify Report
     window.) He asks you to change the title to "Comparative Income
     Statements." Finally, he wants you to format the page layout to the
     left; collapsed; without a reference to the date prepared, time prepared,
     or report basis; and printed in portrait orientation. Memorize the report
     for use later.

b.   Next, Scott asks you to prepare and print a standard income statement for
     Century Kitchens for the month of January 2009 in a format different
     from what you used in Assignment 1a.

2   *Investigating the Century Kitchens Income Statement Using QuickZoom*

Scott would like more information on the $675.00 Building Supplies Expense
balance shown on a standard income statement created for the month of
February 2009. Investigate the $675.00 of Building Supplies expense.
Examine the check used to pay this expense.

a.   Which vendor provided the building supplies? *Home Depot*

b.   What check number was used to pay this expense? *#119*

3   *Modifying an Income Statement*

Modify the income statement created in Assignment 1 as follows, including
your name in the Extra Footer Line of all reports printed. Change the To/From

dates to include amounts from just March 2009. Change the columns so that they no longer reflect comparative information but do include year-to-date amounts and year-to-date percentages. (***Hint:*** Customize the report by checking the Year-to-Date and % of YTD boxes found in the Display section of the Modify Report window.) Print this customized income statement.

Chapter 3 Case Problem 1:
SIERRA MARINA

Meagan Casey, sole proprietor and owner of Sierra Marina (see Chapter 2 Case Problem 1), requires some additional financial reports.

Requirements:

Prepare, memorize, and print the following reports using Meagan's Sierra Marina QuickBooks file. (Use the file you restored in Chapter 2 or restore this file from the Data Files CD. Be sure to include your name in the Extra Footer Line of each report where possible.)

1 A standard Profit & Loss Report for the month of July 2007.

2 A standard Profit & Loss Report for the month of July 2007 without cents, formatted with a left layout, with the title "Income Statement," and with a % of Income column.

3 A report of those transactions recorded in July 2007 that affected the rental income—Personal Watercraft account. (***Hint:*** From your income statement already prepared, double-click the rental income—Personal Watercraft account.)

4 Modify the income statement that you created in Step 2 to be a comparative income statement for July and August 2007 with the title "Comparative Income Statement."

Chapter 3 Case Problem 2:
JENNINGS & ASSOCIATES

As you learned in Chapter 2, Kelly Jennings prepared a balance sheet to submit to her banker with her application for a business loan. When she delivered the balance sheet to the banker, he told her that he also needed information about her operations. In other words, her banker needed an income statement.

Kelly asks you to help her prepare and print three versions of the income statement, one of which she will include with her application. She gives you a QuickBooks file named Kelly Jennings.qbw. Include your name in the Extra Footer Line of all reports printed.

Requirements:

1 Prepare a standard Profit & Loss Report for the month of January 2008.

2 Prepare a standard Profit & Loss Report for the month of January 2008 without cents, formatted with a left alignment and with the title "Income Statement."

3 Modify the income statement you prepared for Step 2 by adding a % of Income column.

Preparing a Statement of Cash Flows Using QuickBooks

Case: Century Kitchens

One of the main financial statements used by businesses is the statement of cash flows. Your previous experience with this statement has not always been good, so the thought of a computer program preparing this one for you is quite enticing. You recall that this statement reports cash flow from operating, investing, and financing activities for a specific period.

Once again, as a part of your training with QuickBooks, Scott asks you to work with him while he prepares a statement of cash flows for the period January 1, 2009, through March 31, 2009.

Creating a Statement of Cash Flows

Unlike the balance sheet and the income statement, the statement of cash flows in QuickBooks is presented in only one format, although it can be modified after it is created. (Another report for cash flows, not addressed in this text, is called Forecast; it projects future cash flows based on the current period's cash flow.) Scott decides to create the statement of cash flows and modify it later.

Video Demonstration

DEMO 4A - Creating a statement of cash flows

To create a statement of cash flows:

1 Open Century Kitchens.qbw.

2 From the Report Center, click **Company & Financial**, and then click **Statement of Cash Flows**. *Remember*, this is not clicking the Reports menu item; it's clicking **Company & Financial** from the Report Center.

3 Change the From date to **1/1/09** and the To date to **3/31/09**, and then click **Refresh.**

4 Select the **Header/Footer tab**, and uncheck the Date Prepared and Time Prepared check boxes.

5 Scroll down this report and notice the three sections: operating activities, investing activities, and financing activities (see Figure 4.1). Observe that the net cash increase for the period is reported at the bottom of the statement. It is then added to the cash at the beginning of the period to yield cash at the end of the period.

Figure 4.1

Statement of Cash Flows for the Period January 1, 2009, through March 31, 2009

Make sure you've changed the From and To dates

Click here to modify the layout of the statement of cash flows

All text figures will exclude time, date, and accounting basis. Your screen will show these if you don't modify your report to exclude them.

Note current location of changes in accumulated depreciation

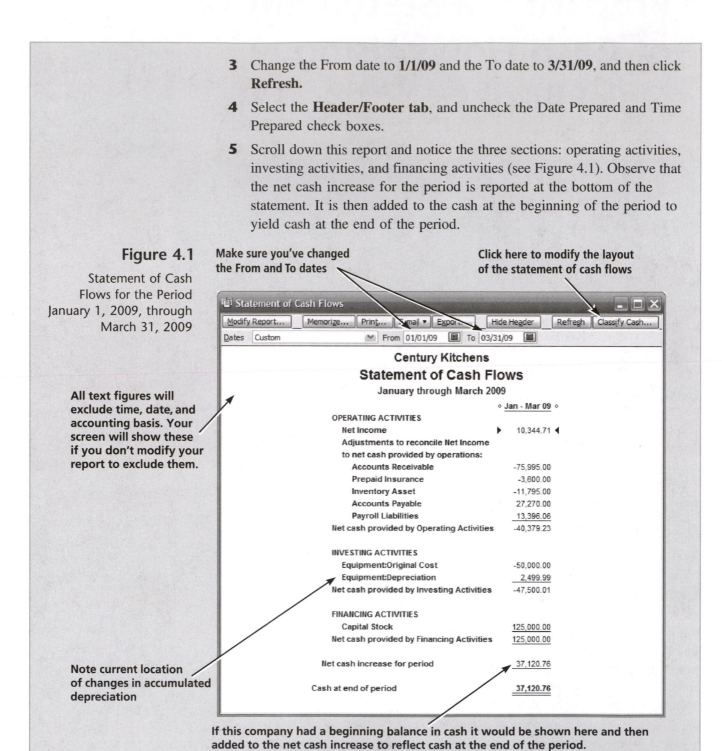

If this company had a beginning balance in cash it would be shown here and then added to the net cash increase to reflect cash at the end of the period.

In your examination of the Statement of Cash Flows, you notice in the operating activities section that several adjustments are made to reconcile net income to net cash provided by operations. Scott points out that one of the more common adjustments should be depreciation expense, since it reduces income but does not use cash. However, depreciation is not shown in this reconciliation. Instead, Scott finds that changes in accumulated depreciation (which, of course, usually result from depreciation expense) are shown in the investing activities section of the statement.

Scott says: "We need to modify this statement's layout to properly reflect changes in accumulated depreciation as adjustments to net income in the operating activities section, not as line items in the investing activities section." To do this, he uses the Classify Cash button on the Statement of Cash Flows window.

To modify the layout of the statement of cash flows:

1 Click **Classify Cash** to open the Preferences window with the Reports & Graphs icon selected and the Company Preferences tab selected, as shown in Figure 4.2.

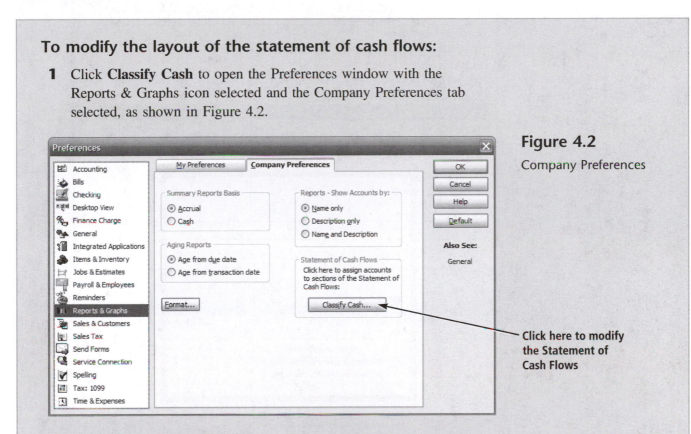

Figure 4.2

Company Preferences

Click here to modify the Statement of Cash Flows

2 Click **Classify Cash** in the Preferences window to view the Classify Cash window; see Figure 4.3.

3 Click in the Operating column next to **Equipment: Depreciation** to move the change in depreciation from an investing activity to an operating activity as shown in Figure 4.3.

Trouble? If you accidentally click in the wrong column, simply click the correct column for the item you accidentally reclassified.

4 Click **OK** in the Preferences window to close it. A "Report needs to be refreshed" window may appear, indicating that the changes you made require refreshing of the report. Click **Yes** to refresh the report. Note how the report has been adjusted to reflect changes in depreciation (depreciation expense) as an adjustment to operating activities and not an investing activity; See Figure 4.4.

Figure 4.3

Classify Cash Window for Modifying the Statement of Cash Flows Layout

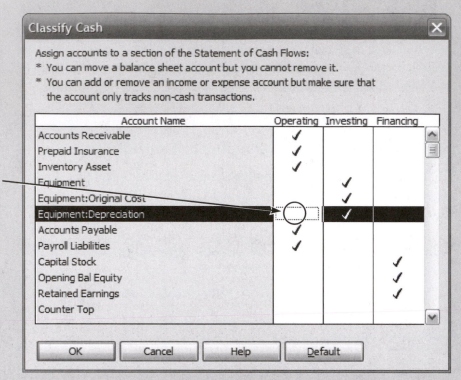

Click here to reclassify changes in accumulated depreciation to Operating Activities

Figure 4.4

Statement of Cash Flows after Changes in Types of Accounts

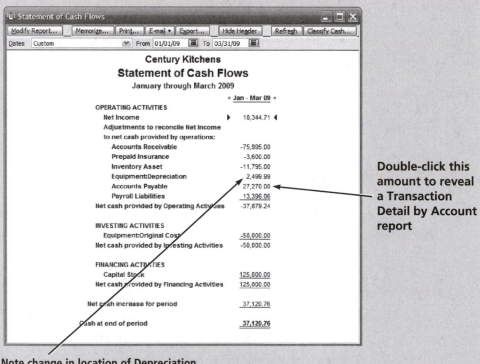

Double-click this amount to reveal a Transaction Detail by Account report

Note change in location of Depreciation

"How about modifying the Statement of Cash Flows to reflect comparative amounts like prior years? Isn't there a previous year comparative report available like we saw for the income statement?" you ask.

"Well, no." Scott explains. "Not only is there no present comparative report in QuickBooks, but there is no way to modify the report to show percentage changes or year-to-date amounts like we can do for the income statement. Maybe in the next version."

Using QuickZoom with the Statement of Cash Flows

You then ask about the QuickZoom feature you found so helpful in examining information on the income statement. Scott responds with a big smile. "Let's check it out!"

To use QuickZoom with the statement of cash flows:

1 Double-click the **27,270.00** amount in Figure 4.4 on the report reflecting changes in Accounts Payable to open a Transaction Detail by Account window as shown in Figure 4.5.

Double-click here to view the detail of this transaction

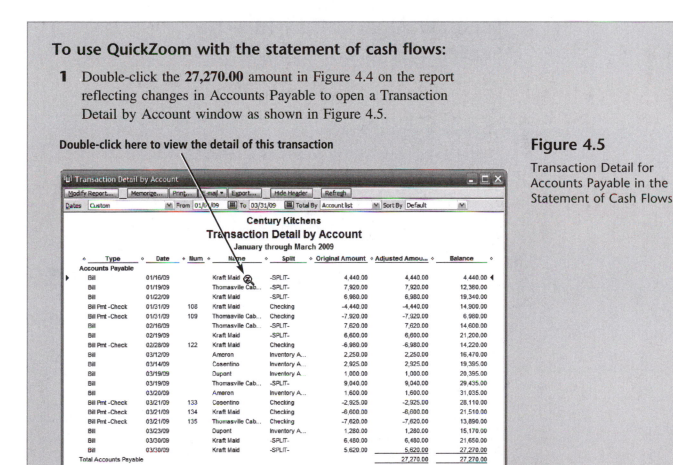

Figure 4.5

Transaction Detail for Accounts Payable in the Statement of Cash Flows

2 Double-click the **Kraft Maid** bill dated 1/16/09 as shown in Figure 4.5.

> **3** Close both the bill and the Transaction Detail by Account window. Do not memorize the Transaction Detail by Account window.
>
> **4** Do not close the revised Statement of Cash Flows.

You have now seen that the QuickZoom feature works for the balance sheet, income statement, and statement of cash flows. However, the QuickZoom feature in the statement of cash flows does not necessarily provide much help. In the case just described, the accounts payable amount in the statement of cash flows reflects the changes in accounts payable—here an increase, which needs to be added to net income in order to reconcile with cash provided by operating activities. It is therefore the change (in this case, an increase) that is being analyzed, not the underlying transactions.

Formatting and Printing the Statement of Cash Flows

Scott would like to print this statement of cash flows in a format without cents.

> **To modify and print the statement of cash flows:**
>
> **1** Click **Modify Report** on the report button bar, and then click the **Fonts & Numbers** tab.
>
> **2** Click in the **Without Cents** check box, and then click **OK** to close the window.
>
> **3** Click **Print** on the report button bar to reveal the Print Reports window.
>
> **4** Click **Print** in the Print Reports window to print the report.
>
> **5** Close all remaining windows. Memorize the revised Statement of Cash Flows report in your report group.

You've now seen how easily all three of the key financial statements—the balance sheet, income statement, and statement of cash flows—can be created, modified, and printed from within QuickBooks. In Chapter 5, you will complete your overview of QuickBooks by creating supporting reports for accounts receivable, inventory, and accounts payable.

Chapter 4 Questions

1 List the reports available for reporting cash flows.

2 Describe the steps necessary to create a statement of cash flows.

3 What additional steps are necessary to create a statement of cash flows for a period other than one ending on the computer's current system date?

4 Identify three different periods of time that QuickBooks provides for a statement of cash flows.

5 List the three sections of the statement of cash flows.

6 Describe the statement of cash flow operating section created by QuickBooks.

7 Describe the one adjustment necessary to reconcile net income to cash provided by operations that was not initially a part of the Century Kitchens statement of cash flows until you made some changes in the reports layout.

8 Describe the steps necessary to make changes in the statement of cash flows report layout in order to properly reflect the adjustments needed to reconcile net income with cash provided by operations.

9 Describe how the QuickZoom feature of QuickBooks does or does not provide the same help in the statement of cash flows as it does in the income statement.

10 Describe the steps necessary to format and print a statement of cash flows whose header differs from that of the software default of this statement.

Chapter 4 Matching

Select the letter of the item below that best matches the definitions that follow. Use the text or QuickBooks Help to complete this assignment.

a. Statement of cash flows   _____ The beginning of the reporting period.

b. Classify Cash   _____ When selected in the Modify Report window, this check box requires QuickBooks to round amounts to the nearest whole dollar.

c. Depreciation expense   _____ A feature in QuickBooks that allows you to view the transaction details underlying amounts in a report.

d. QuickZoom   _____ A financial report describing the change in cash during an accounting period.

e. Included in the operating activities section of the statement of cash flows

_____ The end of the reporting period.

f. Included in the investing activities section of the statement of cash flows

_____ Increases in long-term debt.

g. Included in the financing activities section of the statement of cash flows

_____ Button selected to correct QuickBooks's method of accounting for changes in accumulated depreciation.

h. From date

_____ Increases in equipment.

i. To date

_____ Net income.

j. Without Cents

_____ An adjustment to net income in the operating activities section of the statement of cash flows.

Chapter 4 Assignment

corporation   **merchandising**

1 *Preparing a Statement of Cash Flows for Century Kitchens*

Scott has asked you to prepare and print a customized statement of cash flows for the month of January 2009. He wants the statement to include amounts (without cents) with a left page layout. (*Hint:* Be sure accumulated depreciation is classified correctly.) Include your name in the Extra Footer Line of all reports printed.

Chapter 4 Case Problem 1:
SIERRA MARINA

sole proprietorship   **service**

Meagan Casey owns Sierra Marina and is proud of her business's success. After entering past transactions as described in Chapter 2 Case Problem 1, Meagan needs your help in preparing some basic financial reports related to Sierra Marina's cash flow.

Requirements:

Prepare, memorize, and print the following reports using Meagan's Sierra Marina QuickBooks file. (Use the file you restored in the previous chapter or restore this file from the Data Files CD, and be sure to include your name in the Extra Footer Line of each report where possible.)

1 A statement of cash flows for the month of July 2007 without cents and formatted with a left layout.

2 A report of those transactions recorded in July 2007 that affected the Accounts Receivable account. (*Hint:* From the statement of cash flows just created, double-click the **Accounts Receivable** account.)

Chapter 4 Case Problem 2:
JENNINGS & ASSOCIATES

Continuing your work from Chapter 3, Kelly has asked you to prepare two versions of the statement of cash flows, one of which she will include with her application. Open the Kelly Jennings.qbw file. Include your name in the Extra Footer Line of all reports printed.

corporation   service

Requirements:

1 Prepare a statement of cash flows for the period 1/1/08 to 1/31/08. (***Hint:*** Be sure accumulated depreciation accounts are properly classified.)

2 Prepare a statement of cash flows for the same period, 1/1/08 to 1/31/08, but without cents and with a right page layout.

Creating Supporting Reports to Help Make Business Decisions

Learning Objectives

In this chapter, you will:

- Create, print, and analyze an Accounts Receivable Aging report
- Create and print a Customer Account Balance Summary
- Create, print, and analyze an Inventory Valuation Summary
- Create, print, and analyze an Accounts Payable Aging report
- Create and print a Vendor Balance Summary

Case: **Century Kitchens**

You arrive at work, and two phones are ringing. As Scott hangs up from one call and is about to answer another, he quickly explains what's happening: he's thinking about expanding the business and needs to borrow from the bank, and they are requesting up-to-the-minute information. You quickly answer a phone and write down the banker's request for some information on inventory. As you hang up from the call, Scott asks you to come into his office. You compare notes—he has requests for information on accounts receivable and accounts payable. You show him your note requesting information on Century Kitchens' inventory.

Scott has shown you that QuickBooks can easily generate transaction reports, but you can see that the banker's requests require more detailed information. You remember from your accounting course that accountants frequently use what are called supporting schedules—reports that provide the underlying details of an account. You ask Scott if QuickBooks can help. He smiles and says, "You bet. QuickBooks calls these schedules 'reports,' but they are the same thing. Let's get to work."

Video Demonstration

DEMO 5A - Creating other useful reports

Creating and Printing an Accounts Receivable Aging Report

You know from your accounting course that accounts receivable are amounts due from customers for goods or services they have received but for which they have not yet paid. QuickBooks provides several preset accounts receivable reports that anticipate the information managers most often need.

The banker wants information on a particular customer's past due account balance, and she wants to know the total amount due from customers as of today.

Scott tells you that the best way to get information on past due accounts is to create a schedule that QuickBooks calls an "Accounts Receivable Aging report," but what you learned in your accounting course is usually called an "accounts receivable aging schedule." You remember that an aging schedule is a listing of how long each receivable has been uncollected.

To create an Accounts Receivable Aging report:

1   Open Century Kitchens.qbw.

2   From the Report Center, click **Customers & Receivables**, and then click **Summary** under the title A/R Aging.

3   Change the report date to **3/31/09**, and click **Refresh** to see the company A/R Aging Summary, as shown in Figure 5.1.

The number of days past the due date

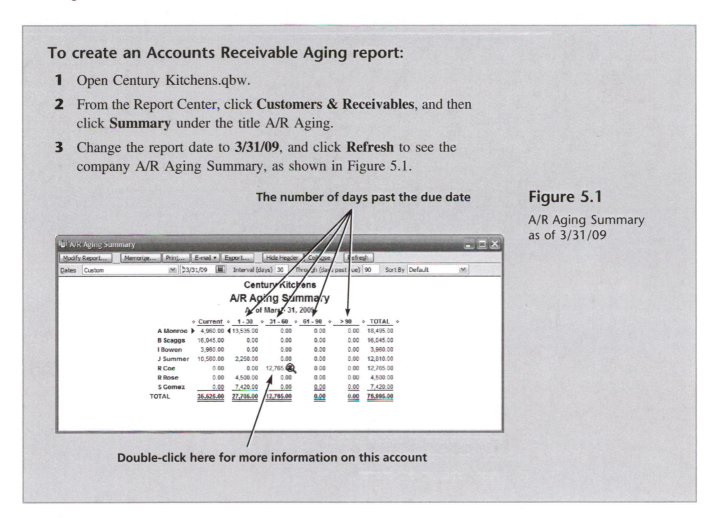

Double-click here for more information on this account

Figure 5.1

A/R Aging Summary as of 3/31/09

You can see that this report gives Scott an up-to-date listing of customers and their balances. It tells him how long each receivable has been uncollected so he can take appropriate action.

You ask Scott the name of the customer about whom the banker requested information. He says the customer's name is R Coe and that the banker wants to know the status of his account and his payment history. He says that, as you have done with other reports, you can use QuickZoom to gather this information.

To investigate a particular receivable on an Accounts Receivable Aging report:

1   Double-click the **$12,765.00** balance owed by R Coe.

2 An A/R Aging QuickZoom report appears; see Figure 5.2. This report indicates that invoice 1005, dated 1/31/09, was due 2/15/09 and is presently 44 days late.

Figure 5.2

A/R Aging QuickZoom Report

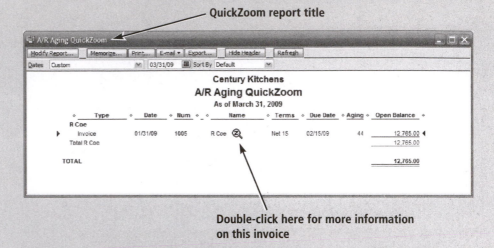

QuickZoom report title

Double-click here for more information on this invoice

3 Double-click this invoice to investigate further. Invoice 1005 appears (see Figure 5.3). Invoice 1005 describes the items purchased and installation fees charged.

Figure 5.3

Invoice 1005

Click here to display payment history

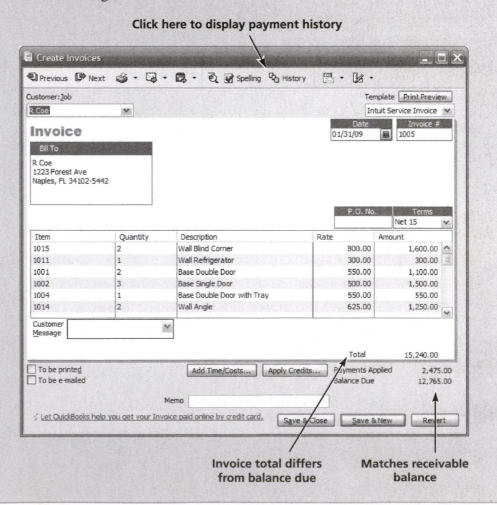

Invoice total differs from balance due

Matches receivable balance

4 Click the **Down Arrow** in the invoice's scroll box to view more of the invoice. Notice that the balance due—$12,765.00—matches the receivable balance you are investigating. But notice also that invoice 1005 totals $15,240.00. How can that be?

5 Click the **History** button on the top of the window to help you investigate this difference. The transaction history of this invoice appears; see Figure 5.4. Notice that a payment of $2,475.00 was applied to this invoice on 3/31/09. Let's investigate further.

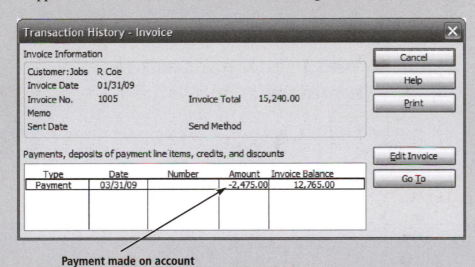

Figure 5.4

Invoice 1005 Transaction History

Payment made on account

6 Be sure that the $2,475.00 payment is highlighted. Then click **Go To** to examine the payment in more detail. The Receive Payments window appears (see Figure 5.5). Observe that a $3,000.00 check was received

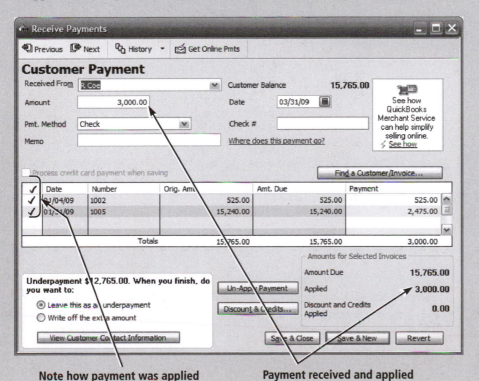

Figure 5.5

Receive Payments Window for R Coe

Note how payment was applied   **Payment received and applied**

from R Coe on 3/31/09. Of this payment, $525.00 was applied to pay off invoice 1002. The balance of the $3,000.00—$2,475.00—was applied to invoice 1005. This explains why the balance due and the invoice amount were different.

7 Close all open windows without memorizing any reports.

Scott has copied down the information the banker requested—R Coe is 44 days past due on invoice 1005, he owes $12,765.00 on that invoice, and invoice 1002 was paid off on 3/31/09. He is now ready to fulfill the banker's other request.

Creating and Printing a Customer Balance Summary

Scott says that the banker's request for the total amount due from customers as of today is easy to fulfill because QuickBooks has a built-in feature that prepares a customer balance summary. He can provide the banker this information with only a few clicks of the mouse.

To create a Customer Balance Summary:

1 From the Report Center, click **Customers & Receivables** and then click **Summary** located under the Customer Balance title; see Figure 5.6.

Figure 5.6

Customer Balance Summary for March 31, 2009

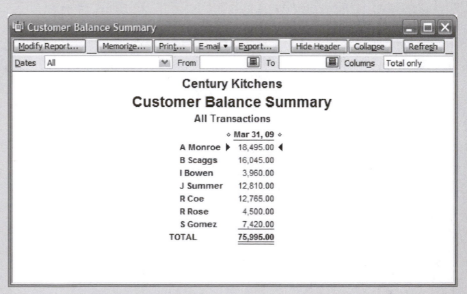

2 Notice that this is exactly the information the banker has requested—a list of the total amounts each customer owes Century Kitchens as of March 31, 2009. When you have finished viewing this report, close this window.

Scott prints this report for the banker and asks you to fax it. He's ready to handle the second request.

Creating and Printing an Inventory Valuation Summary Report

Scott asks you about the request you took over the phone. You show him your notes; you spoke to Kim Hui, one of the company's investors. He stopped by the other day and noticed a lot of cabinet inventory in the shop and wondered why we had so much.

Scott explains that in his business he never places a purchase order to a cabinet or counter top manufacturer unless it's been signed off by a customer. "We hold the inventory until we can schedule it for installation. Once installed, we then bill the customer and the inventory becomes cost of goods sold."

He suggests that you use QuickBooks to show, via an Inventory Valuation Summary report, just exactly what inventory you have and to which customer it will be billed.

To create an Inventory Valuation Summary:

1 From the Report Center, click **Inventory**, and then click **Summary** located under the Inventory Valuation title. Set the report date to **3/31/09.** The Inventory Valuation Summary appears; see Figure 5.7. Resize the columns as necessary to view this report.

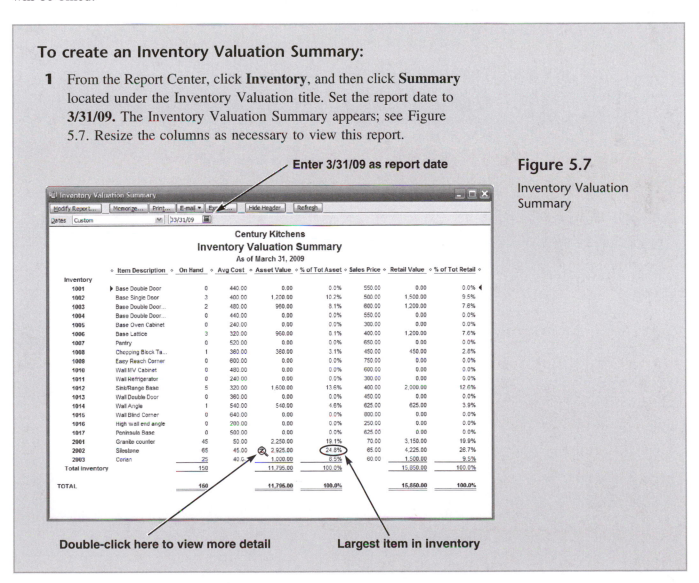

Figure 5.7

Inventory Valuation Summary

2 Scroll around this report to familiarize yourself with its contents. It describes the inventory on hand as of 3/31/09.

Scott decides to investigate the largest dollar value cost item in inventory to see to which customer it belongs.

To view the underlying documentation of the Inventory Valuation Summary:

1 Double-click on item **#2002 Silestone**, representing 24.8% of the cost of inventory on hand. An Inventory Valuation Detail appears. By default, this report shows activity for just 3/31/09. But Scott wants to know the *total* inventory on hand and to see activity for the quarter. To find this information, you need to change the From date to 1/1/09.

2 Type **1/1/09** in the box, and then click **Refresh.** A new report appears; see Figure 5.8.

Note that this report shows a beginning inventory of 0 and purchases of 65.

Figure 5.8

Inventory Valuation Detail from January 1 through March 31, 2009

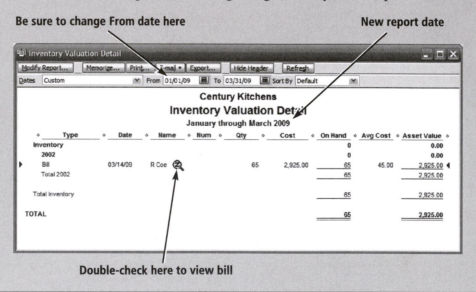

You ask Scott if QuickZoom lets you view the actual invoices. "Sure does," he says. "Let's look at one."

To view an actual bill:

1 Double-click anywhere in the row containing information on the bill for this item. The bill appears as shown in Figure 5.9 on the following page. Adjust your window size or scroll as necessary to view the entire invoice.

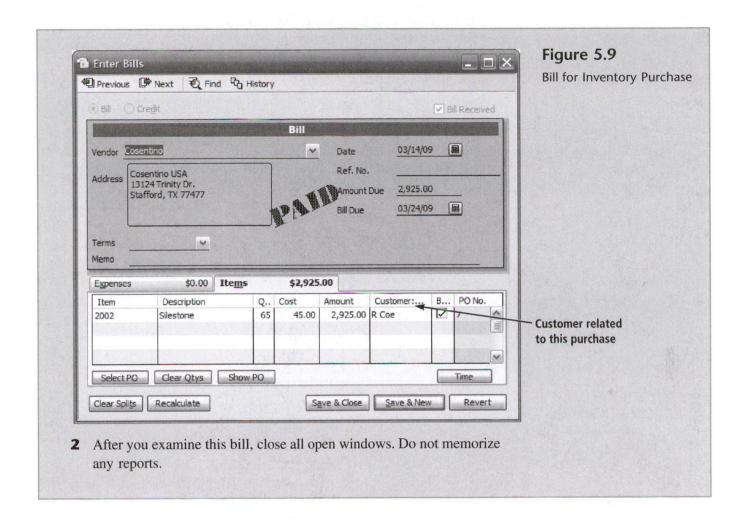

Figure 5.9

Bill for Inventory Purchase

2 After you examine this bill, close all open windows. Do not memorize any reports.

Scott retrieves the Inventory Valuation Summary and prints it for Kim. He notes that this item was purchased for customer R Coe, who has a fairly large past due account. Scott makes a note to contact Mr. Coe and find out what is going on, and he asks you to mail this report to Kim when you have a chance. He's now ready to fulfill the last request.

Creating, Printing, and Analyzing an Accounts Payable Aging Report

The last request to which you and Scott need to respond is from Juan Gomez, who handles all inventory purchase orders, pays bills, and monitors accounts payable. He wants two reports so he can plan next month's cash flow.

You quickly ask if QuickBooks handles accounts payable aging the same way it handles accounts receivable aging. Scott smiles. "You catch on fast," he says. "Let's start with an Accounts Payable Aging report. It provides the detail Juan needs. Then we'll print him a Vendor Balance Summary."

To create an Accounts Payable Aging report:

1 From the Report Center, click **Vendors & Payables**, and then click **Summary** under the title A/P Aging. Change the report date to **3/31/09**. The A/P Aging Summary report appears; see Figure 5.10.

Figure 5.10

Accounts Payable Aging Summary

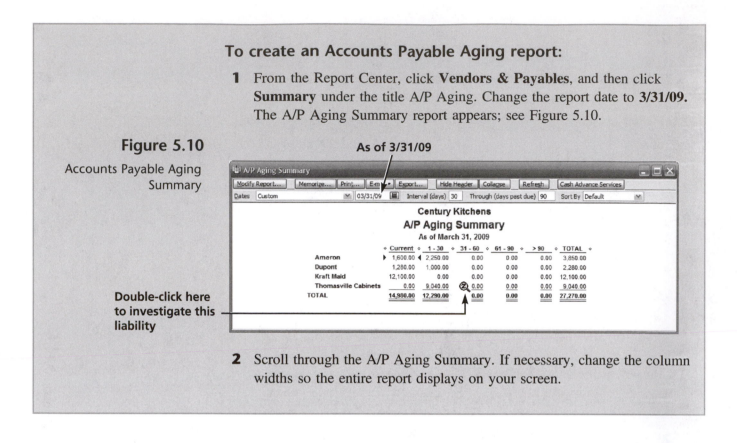

As of 3/31/09

Double-click here to investigate this liability

2 Scroll through the A/P Aging Summary. If necessary, change the column widths so the entire report displays on your screen.

After Scott prints this report for Juan, you look it over. You notice a large outstanding balance 1–30 days past due to Thomasville Cabinets, and you suggest using QuickZoom to investigate it further. Scott and you both decide to investigate this liability to whom Century Kitchens owes $9,040.00.

To analyze the Thomasville Cabinets liability:

1 Double-click the Thomasville Cabinets liability balance of **9,040.00**. An A/P Aging report appears; see Figure 5.11.

Figure 5.11

A/P Aging QuickZoom Report for Thomasville Cabinets

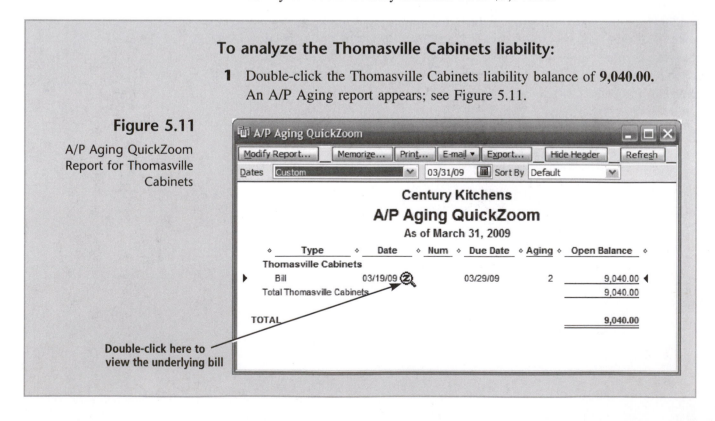

Double-click here to view the underlying bill

2 Double-click anywhere in the entry for the bill dated **3/19/09.** The
details of this bill appear (see Figure 5.12). Notice that this bill documents cabinet costs incurred in the B Scaggs kitchen remodeling job.

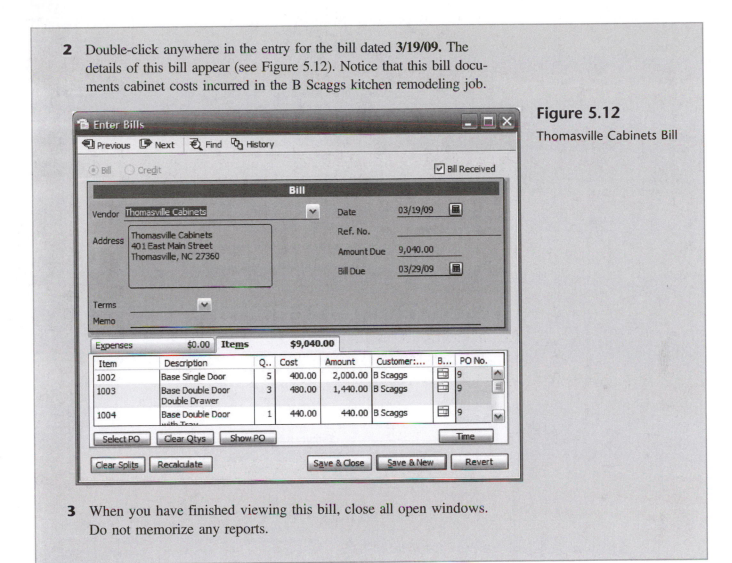

Figure 5.12

Thomasville Cabinets Bill

3 When you have finished viewing this bill, close all open windows.
Do not memorize any reports.

Creating and Printing a Vendor Balance Summary

The final supporting report for Juan is a Vendor Balance Summary. This report is
also a preset report available from the QuickBooks Reports menu. It will summarize for Juan all of the unpaid balances due to vendors and will be valuable
information for his cash planning.

To create and print a Vendor Balance Summary:

1 From the Report Center, click **Vendors & Payables**, and then
Vendor Balance Summary. Change the report To date to **3/31/09**
and the From date to **1/1/09.** The Vendor Balance Summary
appears; see Figure 5.13. Notice that the vendors are listed
alphabetically.

Figure 5.13

Vendor Balance Summary as of 3/31/09

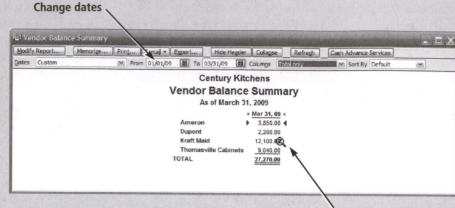

Change dates

Double-click here to look at the detail supporting the liability

2 To investigate, Scott suggests you look further into the Kraft Maid balance. Double-click the **$12,100.00** balance to reveal the Vendor Balance Detail report shown in Figure 5.14.

Figure 5.14

Vendor Balance Detail Report

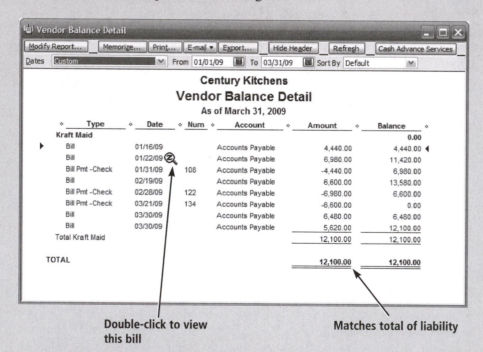

Double-click to view this bill

Matches total of liability

3 Double-click the **1/22/09** bill for $6,980.00 to reveal the paid bill as shown in Figure 5.15.

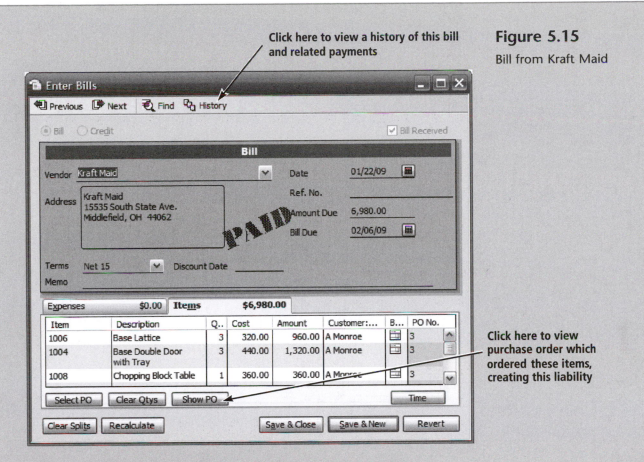

Figure 5.15

Bill from Kraft Maid

4   Click the **Show PO** button to view the purchase order Century Kitchens generated to order these cabinets; see Figure 5.16.

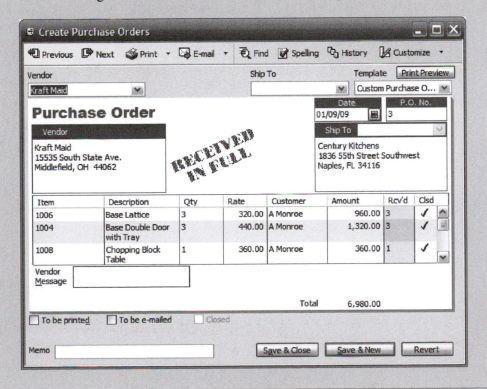

Figure 5.16

Purchase Order 3 to Kraft Maid

5 Close the purchase order, and then click the **History** button to reveal the bill's history; see Figure 5.17.

Figure 5.17

Transaction History of Kraft Maid Bill

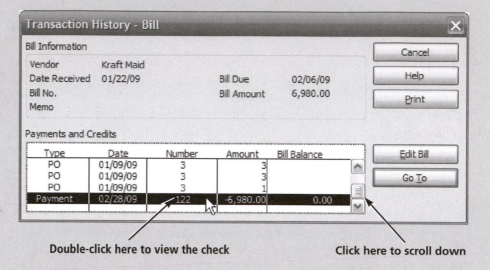

Double-click here to view the check   Click here to scroll down

6 Scroll down the history listing, and then double-click the payment reference to view the related check used to pay this bill. See Figure 5.18, Bill Payment (Check No. 122).

Figure 5.18

Bill Payment (Check No. 122)

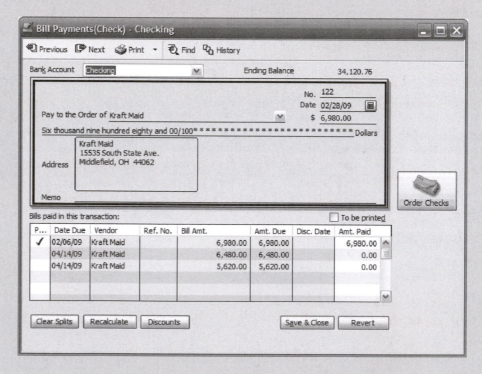

7 When you finish viewing this report, close all windows and do not memorize any reports.

Scott prints the Vendor Balance Summary for Juan, and looks at you. "Yes, I'll deliver this one too," you volunteer good-naturedly.

End Note

As you gather the reports and set out to deliver them, you are struck by how easily and quickly Scott has been able to respond to the managers' requests. Within a short time, QuickBooks has generated accurate, up-to-the-minute financial information to help Scott and his staff make important business decisions. The many preset reports—summaries, details, and supporting documentation—anticipate the information that owners often need to make sound business decisions.

Chapter 5 Questions

1 Which menu in QuickBooks provides you access to supporting reports?

2 What information does an Accounts Receivable Aging report provide?

3 What types of transactions might appear in a QuickZoom report created from an Accounts Receivable Aging report? Give two examples.

4 How might the payment history of an account receivable help you analyze the Accounts Receivable Aging report?

5 What information does an Inventory Valuation Summary provide?

6 What types of transactions might appear in a QuickZoom report created from an Inventory Summary? Give two examples.

7 What information does an Accounts Payable Aging report provide?

8 What types of transactions might appear in a QuickZoom report created from an Accounts Payable Aging report?

9 What options can you choose from the Print Reports dialog box to help you print a report?

10 How can you create a supporting report for a date other than the system date? Describe a situation for which you would want to do this.

Chapter 5 Matching

Select the letter of the item below that best matches the definitions that follow. Use the text or QuickBooks Help to complete this assignment.

a. Accounts Receivable Aging report

b. Vendor Balance Detail report

c. Inventory Valuation Detail report

d. Customer Balance Summary report

e. Inventory Valuation Summary report

_____ A report that describes how much the company owes to a vendor and is organized by date due.

_____ A feature in QuickBooks that allows you to view the transaction details that underlie amounts in a report.

_____ A document used to bill a customer for goods or services.

_____ A report that describes how much is owed to a company by customers and is organized by date due.

_____ A document used to remit amounts to vendors for bills received.

f. Accounts Payable   _____ A report that describes inventory on hand as of a particular date.
    Aging report

g. Invoice   _____ A report that describes inventory transactions for a particular inventory
                              item over a specified period of time.

h. Vendor Balance Sum-   _____ A report that describes bills received/payments made from/to a particular
    mary report   vendor over a specified period of time.

i. Bill payment check   _____ A report that describes how much each customer owes a company as of a
                              particular date.

j. QuickZoom   _____ A report that describes how much each vendor is owed as of a particular
                              date.

Chapter 5 Assignments

1 *Creating Supporting Reports for Century Kitchens*

Remember to include your name in the Extra Footer Line of all reports printed.
Scott wants you to help him provide supporting reports. Create the reports
Scott has requested, and write down the answers to the following questions:

corporation   merchandising

  a. Create and print a Customer Balance Summary as of 1/31/09. Other than
      the $15,765.00 receivable from R Coe, what is the amount of the largest
      customer receivable and what is the customer's name? What invoice
      supports that receivable? What was purchased on that invoice?

  b. Create and print an Accounts Receivable Aging Summary report as of
      1/31/09. List all past due invoices. When is each due? What is the nature
      of each invoice?

  c. Create and print an Accounts Payable Aging Summary report as of
      2/28/09. What is the largest vendor liability? What bill makes up this
      liability? What is the nature of this bill? When was it due?

  d. Create and print an Inventory Valuation Summary as of 1/31/09. What is
      the item with the largest asset cost? What was its cost and retail value?

2 *Creating More Supporting Reports for Century Kitchens*

Scott wants you to help him provide more supporting reports. Create the
reports he has requested, and write down the answers to the following
questions:

  a. Create and print a Customer Balance Summary as of 2/28/09 and ex-
      amine the QuickZoom reports for A Monroe. What invoice created this
      receivable? For what was A Monroe invoiced on 2/15/09? What are the
      terms of this invoice?

b. Create and print an Accounts Receivable Aging Summary report as of 2/28/09 and examine the QuickZoom reports for J Summer. What invoice is represented by this receivable? For what was J Summer invoiced? What are the terms of this invoice?

c. Create and print an Accounts Payable Aging Summary report as of 1/31/09 and examine the QuickZoom reports for Kraft Maid. What bill is represented by this payable? What was Century Kitchens billed for? What are the terms of this invoice?

d. Create and print an Inventory Valuation Summary as of 2/28/09. Describe the nature of items on hand as of this date.

Chapter 5 Case Problem 1:
SIERRA MARINA

sole proprietorship   service

Meagan Casey, the sole proprietor and owner of Sierra Marina, would now like you to help her prepare some basic financial reports related to the company's accounts receivable and payable.

Requirements:

Prepare, memorize, and print the following reports using Meagan's Sierra Marina QuickBooks file. (Use the file you restored in the previous chapter or restore this file from the Data Files CD. Be sure to include your name in the Extra Footer Line of each report where possible.)

1 A/R Aging Summary as of August 31, 2007.

2 A/P Aging Summary as of August 31, 2007.

Chapter 5 Case Problem 2:
JENNINGS & ASSOCIATES

corporation   service

Kelly Jennings created financial reports and submitted them to her banker to secure a loan. Today Kelly received a phone call from her banker, who told her that the balance sheet she submitted requires further explanation. He'd like to see some documentation to support her company's balances of receivables, inventory, and payables.

Requirements:

Kelly asks you to prepare and print three supporting reports using her QuickBooks file, Kelly Jenning.qbw.

1 Prepare an Accounts Receivable Aging Summary report for January 31, 2008. Print this report. Write a brief paragraph in which you explain the status of the two largest balances—that is, how old they are, what was sold, and so on.

2   Prepare an Accounts Payable Aging Summary report for January 31, 2008. Print this report. Write a brief paragraph in which you explain, as before, the status of the two largest balances.

3   Prepare an Inventory Valuation Summary for January 31, 2008. Print this summary. Drill down from this report and then write a brief paragraph in which you describe the most recent purchase of film. Be sure to include the date, vendor, amount, and cost per unit.

Creating a QuickBooks File to Record and Analyze Business Events

part 2

In this part, you will:

- **Set Up Your Business's Accounting System**
- **Enter Cash-Oriented Business Activities**
- **Enter Additional Business Activities**
- **Enter Adjusting Entries**
- **Perform Budgeting Activities**
- **Generate Reports of Business Activities**

Part 2 is designed to teach you how to use QuickBooks in conjunction with the accounting methods and concepts learned in your introductory accounting course. This part is divided into six chapters, each with its own set of questions, assignments, and case problems. You'll follow the adventures of Donna and Karen at Wild Water Sports, who have hired you to help them set up their business in QuickBooks, capture various business transactions, make adjusting entries, set up and use budgets, and generate key business reports. You'll use QuickBooks EasyStep Interview to establish accounts, customers, vendors, items, and employees and then record business transactions using key source documents such as sales receipts, invoices, bills, deposit forms, and checks. You will learn how to create journal entries in QuickBooks to accrue revenues and expenses, adjust deferred assets and liabilities, and record depreciation of long-lived assets. Finally, you'll learn how QuickBooks's budgeting and reporting process can help Wild Water Sports plan and control their business activities.

Setting Up Your Business's Accounting System

Case: Wild Water Sports, Inc.

Donna Chandler and her best friend Karen Wilson have been water sports enthusiasts since they were 6 years old. They would spend a good portion of each summer vacation wakeboarding and skiing the lakes and reservoirs of Central Florida. After high school, both went their separate ways. Donna went off to a four-year college and then a career in real estate, while Karen attended a local community college and began a career in small business accounting.

They became reacquainted at their 10-year high school reunion, reminiscing about their fun-filled weekends and summers with boats and boys. They pondered how they could mix their careers and their fun and love of boating into a business. Both vowed to keep in touch. Later that year, Donna called with a plan. She had run into a business investor, Ernesto Martinez, who had opened a retail boat dealership in Orlando, Florida, but didn't have the time to mind the details. Donna figured she could handle the marketing and sales if Karen could handle the day-to-day business operations. Wild Water Sports was born.

The company has some existing cash, receivables, inventory, equipment, and liabilities. The plan is for Karen and Donna to make an investment by purchasing common stock in the existing company. As a result, each will have a one-third interest in the corporation with the remaining third belonging to Ernesto.

Karen knew she would need some help with the daily accounting records, and she chose QuickBooks to replace the manual accounting system currently in place. She contacted an employment agency to find a part-time accountant. You answered her call as a student who could use some spending money and had completed a basic accounting course, and you were hired the same day.

Your job will be to work with Karen to establish and maintain accounting records for Wild Water Sports using QuickBooks. The company will open its doors for business under new ownership in January but needs to set up accounts, items, customers, vendors, and employees before it gets started. The company rents its showroom and service bays from a former auto dealership. It plans to sell top-of-the-line ski-boats from Malibu, Tige, and MB Sports. It also plans to service boats by providing engine repair, engine service, and boat cleaning.

You agree to meet with Karen the next day to get started.

Creating a New Company File Using the EasyStep Interview

easy step

When you return to Karen's office, she's already purchased a new computer, the QuickBooks software, Microsoft's Office suite, and supplies. The software is loaded and ready to go. Karen explains that you have two choices to begin setting up the company. QuickBooks has a built-in EasyStep Interview that can guide you through the company setup process, or you can skip the interview and set up the company yourself. Given this is your first time setting up a company in QuickBooks, you opt for the interview. The EasyStep Interview process provides a step-by-step guided series of questions that you can answer to help you choose various QuickBooks features. The alternative process requires you to enter basic company information, establish a set of accounts, provide sales tax information, and determine a file name.

"Starting with the interview is probably a good idea," Karen says. "Besides, no matter which method you start with, you can always change the decisions you make during setup later."

Video Demonstration

DEMO 6A - Starting a new company

To create a new company file:

1   Start QuickBooks. Close any previously created company if one appears.

2   Click **New Company** from the File menu. The EasyStep window appears.

3   Click the **Start Interview** button.

4   Type the information provided in Figure 6.1.

5   Click **Next.**

6   Scroll down the listing of industries, and select **Retail Shop or Online Commerce** as shown in Figure 6.2.

7   Click **Next.**

8   Select the **Corporation** option button and then click **Next.**

9   Select **January** in the My fiscal years starts in text box and then click **Next.**

10   Do not enter a password, and then click **Next** two times.

Figure 6.1

Starting the EasyStep Interview

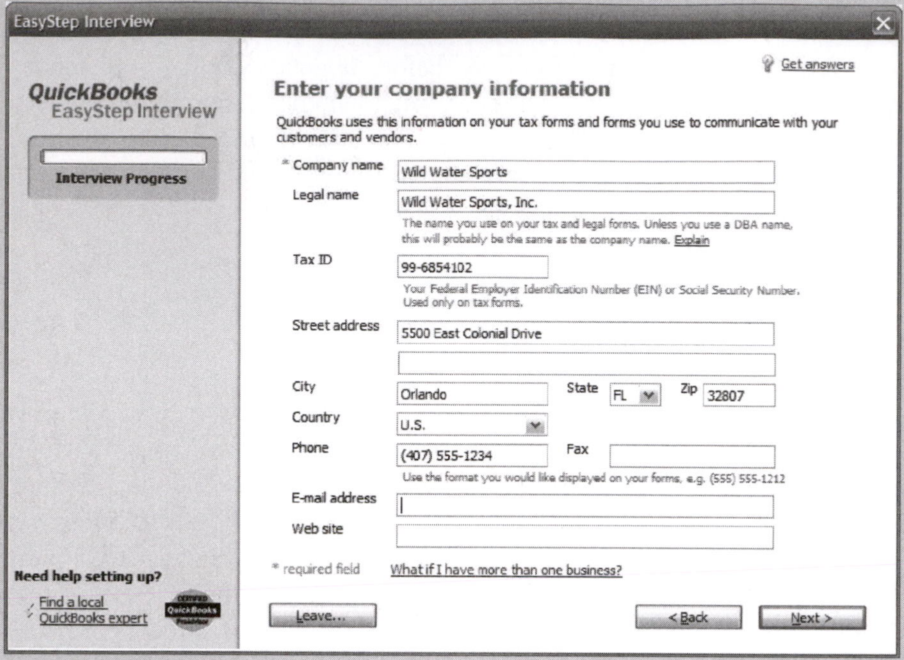

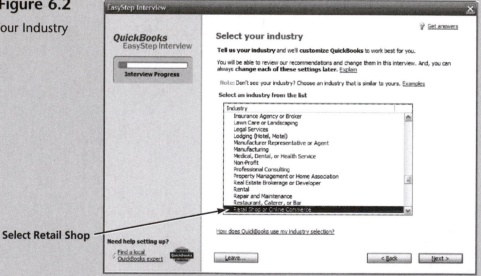

Figure 6.2

Selecting Your Industry

Select Retail Shop

11 Accept the default file name "Wild Water Sports" and then click the **Drop-down Arrow** in the Save in text box to specify where you want your data file saved. Note that in this example the file was saved in a folder called QuickBooks, as shown in Figure 6.3. Click **Save.**

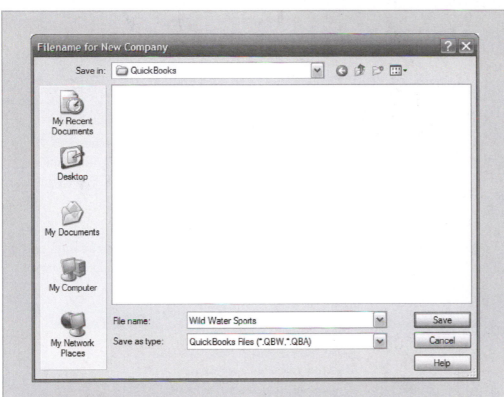

Figure 6.3

Saving Your Data File

12 Click **Next**, select **Both services and products** since Wild Water Sports will be selling and servicing boats, and then click **Next** to move to the next window. If a "Customizing QuickBook for your business" window appears, close it and continue.

13 Select **Record each sale individually** and then click **Next**.

14 Select **I don't sell online and am not interested in doing so** and then click **Next**.

15 Select **Yes** when asked if you charge sales tax and then click **Next**.

16 Select **No** when asked if you want to create estimates and then click **Next**.

17 Select **Yes** when asked if you want to use sales receipts and then click **Next**.

18 Select **No** when asked if you want to use billing statements and then click **Next**.

19 Select **Yes** when asked if you want to use invoices and then click **Next**.

20 Select **No** when asked if you want to use progress invoicing and then click **Next**.

21 Select **Yes** when asked if you want to keep track of bills and then click **Next**.

22 Select **I don't currently print checks and I don't plan to** when asked if you want to print checks and then click **Next**.

23 Select **Yes** when asked if you want to track inventory and then click **Next.**

24 Select **I accept credit cards and debit cards** when asked and then click **Next.**

25 Select **Yes** when asked if you want to track time and then click **Next.**

26 Select **Yes** when asked if you have employees, check **We have W-2 employees**, and then click **Next.** If a "Using accounts in Quickbooks window" appears, close it and continue. Click **No** when asked if you want to track multiple currencies and then click **Next.**

27 Click **Next** to set up your chart of accounts.

28 Select **Use today's date or the first day of the quarter or month**, and then click the calendar icon to select **1/1/2009** as the start date as shown in Figure 6.4. Click **Next** to continue.

Figure 6.4

Choosing Your Start Date

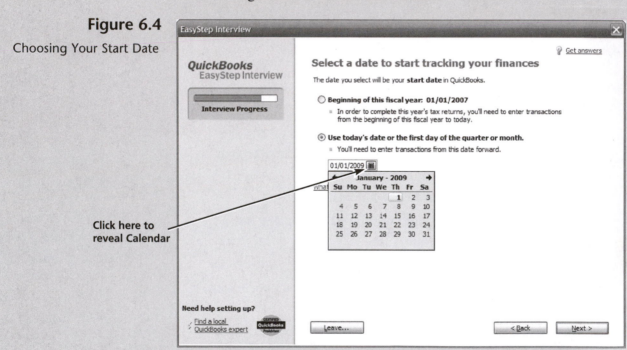

29 Click **Yes** to add an existing bank account and then click **Next.**

30 Type **Bank of Florida** as your bank account name, select **Before** to answer the question about when your account was opened, and then click **Next.**

31 Type **12/31/08** as the statement ending date and **25,000.00** as the ending balance as shown in Figure 6.5.

32 Click **Next** and then select **No** when asked if you want to add another bank account, and then click **Next.**

33 Click **Next** to continue and accept the given income and expense accounts.

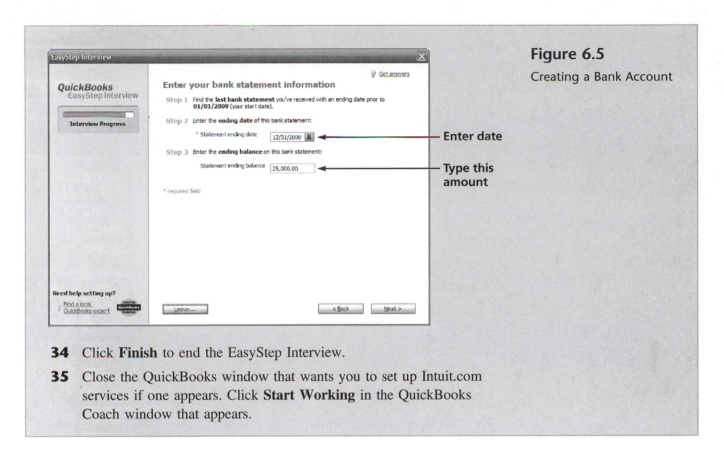

Figure 6.5

Creating a Bank Account

34 Click **Finish** to end the EasyStep Interview.

35 Close the QuickBooks window that wants you to set up Intuit.com services if one appears. Click **Start Working** in the QuickBooks Coach window that appears.

"That wasn't too bad," you comment. "QuickBooks seems pretty thorough in getting you started."

"That they are," Karen replies. "But we still have a long way to go before we can start entering transactions for January. We need to set up preferences, customers, vendors, employees, et cetera."

Set Up Company Preferences

"In QuickBooks," Karen explains, "preferences provide a way for turning certain features on or off, changing the look of the QuickBooks desktop, and customizing how QuickBooks performs."

Video Demonstration

DEMO 6B - Setting preferences

To set up preferences:

1 Close any Alert windows that may have popped up.

2 Click the **Edit** menu, and then click **Preferences**.

3 Scroll to the top of the preferences list and click **Accounting**.

4 Click the **Company Preferences** tab, and then check **Require accounts** if it is not already checked. Also make sure the **Use account numbers** check box is unchecked. Uncheck the two **Date Warnings** check boxes.

5 Click **Checking** from the preferences list, and click **Yes** if asked whether you want to save your changes.

6 Click the **My Preferences** tab, and then check all the boxes specifying default accounts to be used for different processes. Select **Bank of Florida** as the default account as shown in Figure 6.6.

Figure 6.6

Checking Account Preferences

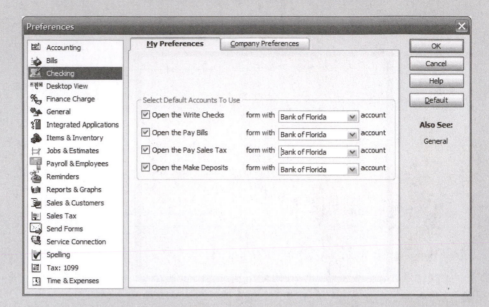

7 Click **Desktop View** from the preferences list, and click **Yes** when asked if you want to save your changes.

8 Select the **Multiple Windows** option, and make sure the **Show Home page** check box is checked. Also, uncheck the **Show Coach window and features** and the **Show Live Community** check boxes.

9 Click **General** from the preferences list, and click **Yes** if asked whether you want to save your changes.

10 Check all the items shown in Figure 6.7.

Figure 6.7

General Preferences

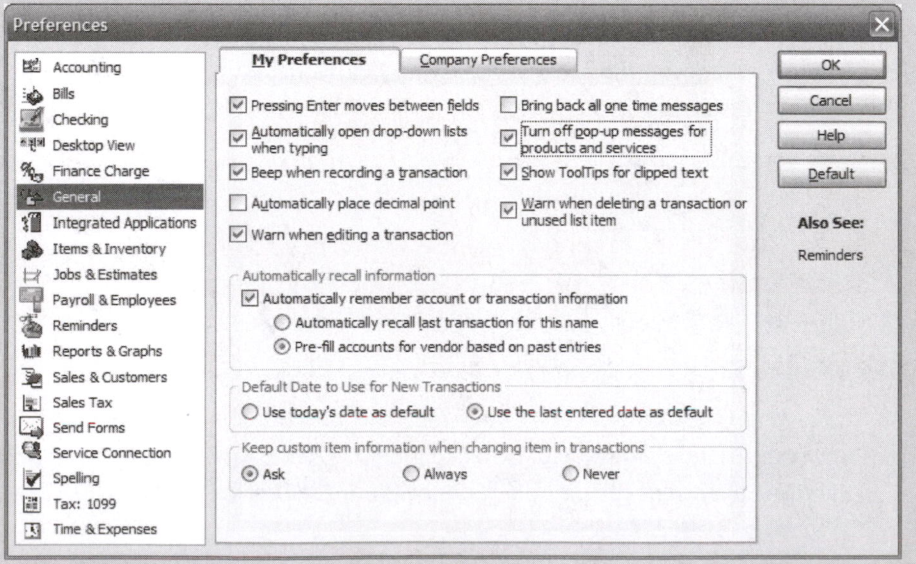

11 Click the **Company Preferences** tab, and uncheck the **Always show years as 4 digits** box.

12 Click **Reminders** from the preferences list, and click **Yes** when asked if you want to save your changes.

13 Click **OK** if you see a warning message.

14 Click the **Company Preferences** tab, and choose the **Don't Remind Me** option button for all the reminders as shown in Figure 6.8.

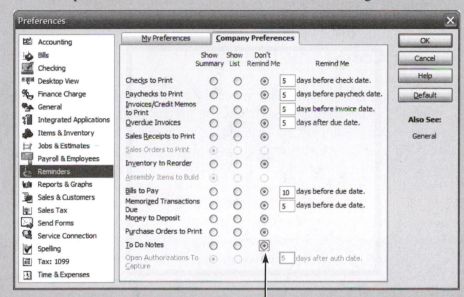

Figure 6.8

Reminders

Make sure all of these Don't Remind Me option buttons are selected

15 Click **Reports & Graphs** from the preferences list, and click **Yes** when asked if you want to save your changes.

16 Click the **My Preferences** tab, and choose the option to **Refresh automatically.**

17 Click **OK** to close the Preferences window and click **Yes** if asked to save changes.

18 Right-click the Icon Bar and then select Customize the Icon Bar.

19 Click **Online Banking** from the list of Icon Bar Content and then click the **Delete** button.

20 Follow the same procedure to delete the Company Snapshot, Doc Center, App Center, Cards & eChecks, Add Payroll, Services, (space), and Live Community icons.

21 Click **OK** to close the Customize the Icon Bar window.

"Why did we choose not to use account numbers?" you ask. "Why just use account names?"

Karen explains that some small businesses use account numbers to help manage their accounting systems. Certain account sequences are followed. For example, assets are commonly assigned numbers beginning with a 1, liabilities with a 2, equities with a 3, revenues with a 4, and expenses with a 5. QuickBooks will assign all assets a 1000–1999 account number depending on the asset type. Liabilities will be assigned a 2000–2999 number, and so forth. There is no requirement in QuickBooks for account numbers, but Karen has decided not to use them because she believes account names are more descriptive than account numbers.

You've accomplished quite a bit by telling QuickBooks that you collect sales tax and use the payroll features, accounts, accrual-based reports, etc. In addition, you've set certain "look and feel" features of QuickBooks to facilitate your navigation. Now it's time to specifically address income and expense accounts and items.

Set Up Company Items

Video Demonstration

DEMO 6C - Setting up new inventory and service items

Karen explains that it's now time to set up items. In QuickBooks, an *item* is anything that your company buys, sells, or resells in the course of business, such as products, shipping and handling charges, discounts, and sales tax (if applicable). You can think of an item as something that shows up as a line on an invoice or other sales form.

Items help you fill out the line item area of a sales or purchase form quickly. When you choose an item from your Item List, QuickBooks fills in a description of the line item and calculates its amount for you. QuickBooks provides 11 different types of items. Some—such as the service item or the inventory part item—help you record the services and products your business sells. Others—such as the subtotal item or discount item—are used to perform calculations on the amounts in a sale.

She suggests that you now set up some new service items and inventory part items. For Wild Water Sports, service items will be such things as changing engine oil and filter, engine tune-ups, and 20-hour service checks. Inventory part items will include boats and parts for repairs.

To set up items, Karen and Donna had to agree on prices for common service items, hourly service rates for nonstandard repairs, and pricing for products to be sold. They also had to set up item names and descriptions. One item they both notice is used for consignment sales, which they don't plan on doing, so they both agree to remove that item from the list. They must also edit the sales tax item to specify a tax rate and vendor.

"QuickBooks has a feature that allows us to enter multiple items at one time, which is a great time saver," says Karen. "I'll show you how it works."

To set up multiple items:

1 Click **Home** on the Icon Bar and then click **Items & Services** from the Company section of the home page. This opens the Item List window. Karen has decided you will set up specific service items and specific inventory items for Wild Water Sports.

2 Select the **Consignment Item** from the Item List.

3 Click the **Item** button in the lower left corner of the Item List window, and then select **Delete Item.**

4 Click **OK** to confirm.

5 Click the **Item** button again, and then select **Add/Edit Multiple Items.**

6 Select **Service Items** from the List drop-down list.

7 Click the **Customize Columns** button.

8 Click **Subitem of** from the Chosen Columns list.

9 Click the **Remove** button.

10 Now click **Sales Description** from the Available Columns list.

11 Click the **Add** button.

12 Click **OK** to close the Customize Columns window and then click in between each column, hold the left mouse button down, and then drag either left or right to re-size them to fit the information presented.

13 Type **20-Hour Service** in the space below the Item Name column then press [**Tab**].

14 Type **175** as the Sales Price then press [**Tab**].

15 Type **Service** as the Income Account then press [**Tab**].

16 Click **Setup** in the Account Not Found window.

17 Select **Income** in the Account Type drop-down list and then click **Save & Close**.

18 Select **Tax** as the Sales Tax Code and then press [**Tab**].

19 Type **Labor charge for 20 hour service check** in the Sales Description column and then press [**Tab**].

20 Type **Engine Service** as a new item in the Item Name column below 20-Hour Service and then press [**Tab**].

21 Type **125** in the Sales Price column and then press [**Tab**].

22 Select **Service** in the Income column and then press [**Tab**].

23 Select **Tax** in the Sales Tax Code column and then press [**Tab**].

24 Type **Labor charge for changing engine oil and filter** in the Sales Description column and then press [**Tab**]. Your screen should look like Figure 6.9.

Figure 6.9

Adding Multiple List
Entries

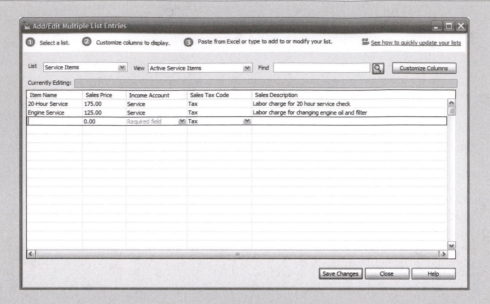

25 Click below the Engine Service item you just added in the Add/Edit Multiple List Entries window. Using the same process just illustrated add the following items:

Item Name	Sales Price	Income Account	Sales Tax Code	Sales Description
Engine Tune-Up	$250.00	Service	Tax	Labor charge for engine tune-up
Diagnostic Service	$ 85.00	Service	Tax	Labor charge for diagnostic service

26 Once you've entered all the service items above click **Save Changes.** Now, it is time to enter new inventory parts.

27 Reopen the Item List if you closed it and then click **Add/Edit Multiple Items** from the Item drop-down list. Select **Inventory Parts** from the List drop-down list.

28 Click the **Customize Columns** button.

29 Click **Subitem of** from the Chosen Columns list.

30 Click the **Remove** button. In addition remove Total Value, Preferred Vendor, and Manufacturer's Part Number columns.

31 Now click **Purchase Description** from the Available Columns list.

32 Click the Add button.

33 Click the **Purchase Description** column title and then click the **Move Up** button multiple times until the Purchase Description column title appears below Item Name column title. In addition add the As Of Date column to the end of the list.

34 Click **OK** to close the Customize Columns window and then click in between each column, hold the left mouse button down and then drag either left or right... to re-size them to fit the information presented.

35 Type **MS LXi** as the Item Name and then press [**Tab**].

36 Type **Malibu Sunsetter LXi** as the Purchase Description and then press [**Tab**].

37 Type **48000** in the Cost column and then press [**Tab**]. (*Note:* All merchandise is marked up 25% of cost; thus, all merchandise cost is 80% of the sales price.)

38 Type **60000** as the Sales Price and then press [**Tab**].

39 Type **Cost of Goods Sold** as the COGS Account and then press [**Tab**].

40 Select **Merchandise Sales** as the Income Account and then press [**Tab**].

41 Select **Inventory Asset** as the Asset Account and then press [**Tab**].

42 Type **0** as the Reorder Point, and then type **1** as the On Hand quantity indicating that, as of the beginning of the year, the firm had a quantity of one unit on hand for sale and then press [**Tab**].

43 Select **Tax** as the Sales Tax Code and then press [**Tab**].

44 Type **12/31/08** as the As Of Date. Your screen should look like Figure 6.10.

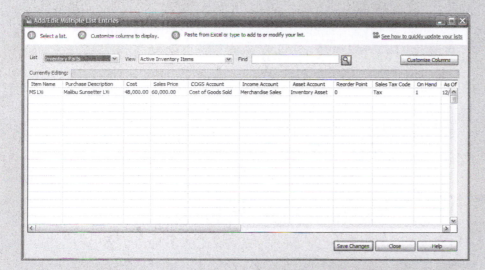

Figure 6.10

Adding a New Inventory Item

45 Press [**Tab**] to set up another inventory part item. Click **Add** whenever the Check Spelling on Form window appears as long as you've correctly typed the part name. If a warning window about dates appears, you can either ignore it or change preferences as instructed.

46 Continue this process for the remaining inventory part items listed next. Be sure to specify 12/31/08 in the As of text box for all items added, Tax as the Tax Code, Cost of Goods Sold as the COGS Account, 0 as the Reorder Point, and Merchandise Sales as the Income Account.

Item Name	Description	Cost	Sales Price	On Hand
MS LX	Malibu Sportster LX	$41,600	$52,000	1
MS LSV	Malibu Sunscape LSV	$52,000	$65,000	2
MV	Malibu Vride	$38,400	$48,000	2
MW VLX	Malibu WakeSetter VLX	$45,600	$57,000	1
MW XTI	Malibu WakeSetter XTI	$56,000	$70,000	1

47 Click **Save Changes** after you've entered all five additional inventory items. Click **Close** to close the Add/Edit Multiple List Entries window.

"Don't you agree that entering multiple items at a time is much more efficient than entering them one at a time?" says Karen.

"I do," you respond. "But we didn't enter a sales description. We only entered a purchase description. Won't that cause problems later?"

"Yes, that's a good point." Karen answers. "I'll show you how to edit the items using the same multiple entry format."

To edit multiple items:

1 Open the Item List window again by clicking **Items & Services** from the Company section of the home page.

2 Click the **Item** button and then select **Add/Edit Multiple Items.**

3 Select **Inventory Parts** from the List drop-down text box.

4 Click the **Customize Columns** button.

5 Click **Sales Description** from the list of Available Columns.

6 Click the **Add** button to move Sales Description to the list of Chosen Columns.

7 With Sales Description selected click the **Move Up** button 10 times to move it just below the Item Name column.

8 Click **OK** to close the Customize Column window.

9 Click and drag the mouse to select the text **Malibu Sunscape LSV** from the purchase description of item MS LSV then **right-click** and click **Copy.**

10 Click in the sales description text box for item MS LSV then **right-click** and click **Paste.**

11 Continue this process to copy the purchase description you had previous entered to the sales description column. Upon completion of this process your window should now look like Figure 6.11.

Figure 6.11

Updated Inventory Parts List

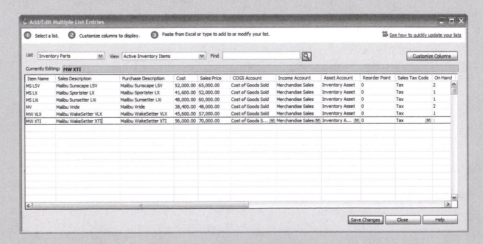

12 Click **Save Changes** and then click **Close.**

Karen explains that you have one more item to enter and then need to print a list of items.

1 From the Item List, double-click the **State Tax** item.

2 Type **6.5%** as the Tax Rate.

3 Type **Florida Department of Revenue** as the Tax Agency and then click **OK.**

4 Click the **Set Up** button.

5 Type **1379 Blountstown Hwy, Tallahassee, FL 32804-2716** in the Name and Address box just below the vendor name.

6 Click **OK** twice to accept the modifications for this new vendor and sales tax item.

7 Prepare this window for printing by clicking the **Reports** button at the bottom of the window and then selecting **Item Listing.**

8 Click the **Modify Report** button.

9 Click the **Display** tab, and then uncheck **Sales Tax Code, Quantity on Purchase Order, Reorder Point**, and **Preferred Vendor.**

10 Click the **Header/Footer** tab, and then uncheck **Subtitle, Date Prepared**, and **Time Prepared.**

11 Click **OK.**

12 Click the **Print** button on the top of the Reports window, choose **Landscape** orientation, and then click **Print.** Your printout should look like Figure 6.12.

13 Close both the Item Listing report and the Item List window. Click **Yes** to memorize the Item Listing report as modified and then click **OK** to memorize the report in no specific report group.

Wild Water Sports
Item Listing

Item	Description	Type	Cost	Price	Quantity On Hand
20-Hour Service	Labor charge for 20 hour service check	Service	0.00	175.00	
Dianostic Service	Labor charge for diagnostic service	Service	0.00	85.00	
Engine Service	Labor charge for changing engine oil and filter	Service	0.00	125.00	
Engine Tune-Up	Labor charge for engine tune-up	Service	0.00	250.00	
MS LSV	Malibu Sunscape LSV	Inventory Part	52,000.00	65,000.00	2
MS LX	Malibu Sportster LX	Inventory Part	41,600.00	52,000.00	1
MS LXi	Malibu Sunsetter LXi	Inventory Part	48,000.00	60,000.00	1
MV	Malibu Vride	Inventory Part	38,400.00	48,000.00	2
MW VLX	Malibu WakeSetter VLX	Inventory Part	45,600.00	57,000.00	1
MW XTI	Malibu WakeSetter XTI	Inventory Part	56,000.00	70,000.00	1
Non-inventory Item	Non-inventory part item description	Non-inventory Part	0.00	0.00	
Local Tax	Local Sales Tax	Sales Tax Item	0.00	0%	
Out of State	Out-of-state sale, exempt from sales tax	Sales Tax Item	0.00	0%	
State Tax	State Sales Tax	Sales Tax Item	0.00	6.5%	

Figure 6.12

Item Listing

"We are well on our way to getting this company set up," Karen explains.

"Should we save our work?" you ask.

"Funny you should mention that," Karen responds. "QuickBooks automatically saves every event you record. In fact, QuickBooks doesn't even have a Save or Save As feature like most other software."

"Shouldn't we at least make a copy of the file in case something happens to this one?" you inquire.

"Good point," Karen says. "Once we're set up we can use the QuickBooks backup procedure to save a copy."

Karen explains that it's now time to enter our existing customers and vendors into QuickBooks and to establish beginning balances.

Set Up Customers, Vendors, and Accounts

job costing

Video Demonstration

DEMO 6D - Setting up new customers and vendors

Donna has met with Ernesto and has determined he did have some outstanding balances from a few customers and also owed some vendors for purchases made in the previous months. He has an existing bank account and a MasterCard credit card account for the business. He also owned some equipment and a related note payable.

Karen has also decided to use QuickBooks's job tracking feature to follow service-related efforts for customers. The firm plans to market its service program to existing customers and will need to track costs for each job as well as bill customers based on hours worked and materials used for each job.

Karen has gathered the information she needs and is ready for you to input it into the system.

To set up existing customers:

1 Click **Customers** from the Customer section of the home page. This opens the Customer Center window.

2 Click **New Customer & Job**, and then click **Add Multiple Customer: Jobs** from the shortcut menu.

3 Click the **Customize Columns** button.

4 Remove all columns from the Chosen Columns list except Name and Company Name.

5 Add columns Customer Balance and Opening Balance as of Date so that you now have four items listed in the Chosen Columns section of the Customize Columns window and then click **OK**.

6 Type **Orlando Water Sports** in the Name and Company Name columns.

7 Type **48300** in the Customer Balance column.

8 Type **12/31/08** in the Opening Balance as of Date column.

9 Your window should look like Figure 6.13.

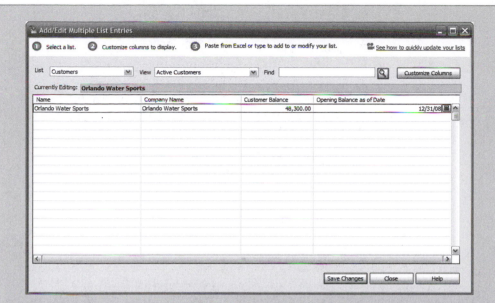

Figure 6.13

Adding a New Customer

10 Continue this process for the remaining customers listed below. Once again, be sure to type the date 12/31/08 in the Opening Balance as of Date for all customers.

Name/Company Name	Customer Balance
Buena Vista Water Sports	$33,000
Walking on Water	$15,000

11 Click **Save Changes** in the Add/Edit Multiple List Entries window. Click **OK** to acknowledge that 3 customer records have been saved and then click **Close**. Your Customer Center should now look like Figure 6.14.

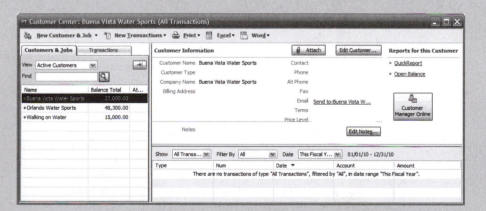

Figure 6.14

Completed Customer Center

12 Click **Report Center.** Click the **Standard** tab and then click **Customers & Receivables**, scroll down the page, and then select Customer Balance Summary in the Customer Balance section as shown in Figure 6.15.

Figure 6.15

Reports Center

Click here first

Click here next

Click here to display report

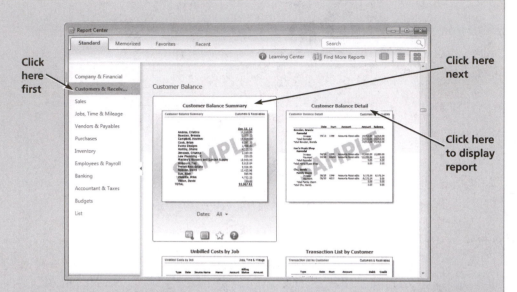

13 Click the **Display Report** icon shown below the Customer Balance Summary report. Type **12/31/08** as the From and To dates.

14 Click the **Modify Report** button.

15 Click the **Header/Footer** tab and then uncheck **Subtitle**, **Date Prepared**, and **Time Prepared.**

16 Click **OK** to close the Modify Report window.

17 Click the **Print** button on the top of the Reports window.

18 Choose the printer you want to print to, choose **Portrait** orientation, and click **Print.** Your printout should look like Figure 6.16.

Figure 6.16

Customer Balance Summary

Wild Water Sports
Customer Balance Summary

	Dec 31, 08
Buena Vista Water Sports	33,000.00
Orlando Water Sports	48,300.00
Walking on Water	15,000.00
TOTAL	**96,300.00**

19 Close the Customer Balance Summary window.

20 Memorize this report like you did before.

21 To print a customer contact list, scroll down the list of reports shown in the Customers & Receivables section of the Report Center, click **Customer Contact List**, then click the **Display Report** icon.

22 Remove the Subtitle, Date Prepared, and Time Prepared fields as you've done previously.

23 Click the **Display** tab and remove the Bill to, and Fax columns and then click **OK.**

24 Click the **Print** button on the top of the Reports window.

25 Choose the printer you want to print to, choose **Portrait** orientation, and then click **Print.** Your printout should look like Figure 6.17.

Wild Water Sports
Customer Contact List

Customer	Contact	Phone	Balance Total
Buena Vista Water Sports			33,000.00
Orlando Water Sports			48,300.00
Walking on Water			15,000.00

Figure 6.17

Customer Contact List

26 Close the Customer Contact List window and memorize the report. The close the Report Center and Customer Center.

"That will be fine for now, and as we add new customers, we'll follow the same process," Karen explains. "As you can see, we have several options for printing a list of customers. The Customer Balance Summary prints only the names of customers with outstanding balances at the dates we specified. The Customer Contact List prints all customers with the addresses and phone numbers we provided. Now let's set up Malibu Boats as our only current vendor."

To set up an existing vendor:

1 Click **Vendors** from the Vendor section of the home page. This opens the Vendor Center window.

2 Click **New Vendor** and then select **New Vendor** from the drop-down list. Click **OK** to close the New Feature window.

3 Type **Malibu Boats** in the Vendor Name text box and Company Name text box.

4 Type **76000** in the Opening Balance text box.

5 Type **12/31/08** in the As of text box. Your screen should look like Figure 6.18.

Figure 6.18

New Vendor

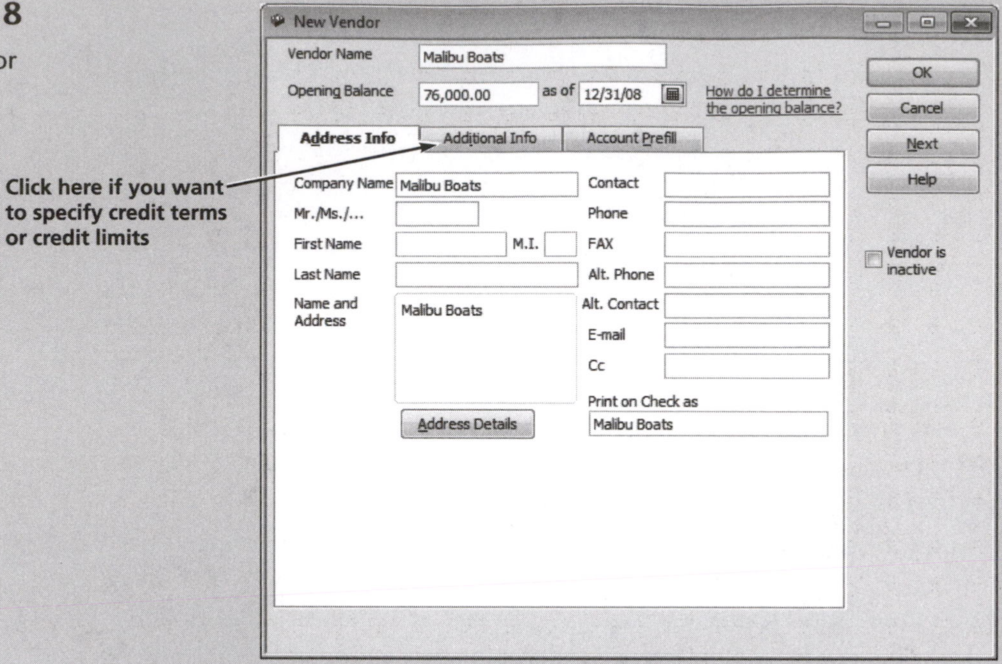

Click here if you want
to specify credit terms
or credit limits

6 Click the **Additional Info** tab and note that, if credit terms or credit limits were provided, you would enter them here. Click **OK** to finish adding existing vendors.

7 Open the Report Center, click **Vendors & Payables**, and then double-click **Vendor Balance Summary.**

8 Type **1/1/09** as the From and To dates.

9 Click the **Modify Report** button.

10 Click the **Header/Footer** tab, and then uncheck **Subtitle**, **Date Prepared**, and **Time Prepared.**

11 Click **OK** to close the Modify Report window.

12 Click the **Print** button on the top of the Reports window.

13 Choose the printer you want to print to, choose **Portrait** orientation, and then click **Print.** Your printout should look like Figure 6.19.

Figure 6.19

Vendor Balance
Summary

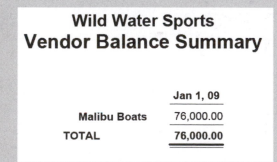

14 Memorize and then close the Vendor Balance Summary window.

15 To print a vendor contact list, double-click **Vendor Contact List** from the Reports Center.

16 Click **Modify Report** and then click **Display.** Remove Account No., Contact, Phone, and Fax columns. Remove Subtitle, Date Prepared, and Time Prepared fields as you've done before.

17 Click **OK** and then click the **Print** button on the top of the Reports window.

18 Choose the printer you want to print to, choose **Landscape** orientation, and then click **Print.** Your printout should look like Figure 6.20.

Wild Water Sports
Vendor Contact List

Vendor	Address	Balance Total
Florida Department of Revenue	Florida Department of Revenue 1379 Blountstown Hwy Tallahassee, FL 32804-2716	0.00
Malibu Boats	Malibu Boats	76,000.00

Figure 6.20

Vendor Contact List

19 Close the Vendor Contact List window and memorize this report.

20 Close the Report Center and Vendor Center windows.

Karen explains that, although Malibu Boats is the only vendor she needs to add at this time, later she'll be adding more vendors "on the fly" as she enters transactions for January. Now she suggests you complete the setup process by adding some new accounts to establish the company's credit card and long-term liability as well as its fixed asset balances as of 12/31/08.

To create and modify accounts:

1 Click **Chart of Accounts** from the Company section of the home page.

2 Click the **Account** button, and select **New.**

3 Select **Credit Card** from the list and then click **Continue.**

4 Type **MasterCard** in the Account Name text box.

5 Click the **Enter Opening Balance** button.

6 Type **1000** in the Statement Ending Balance text box.

7 Type **12/31/08** in the Statement Ending Date text box and then click **OK.** Your screen should look like Figure 6.21.

Figure 6.21

Establishing a Credit
Card Account

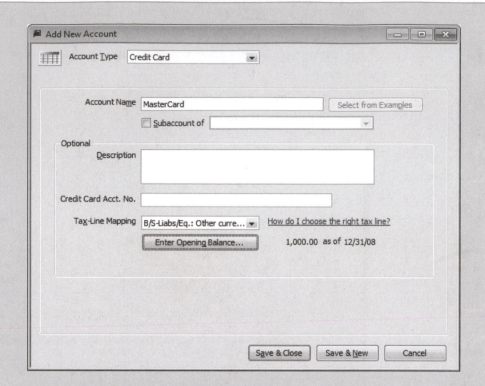

8   Click **Save & New** to enter another account.

9   Select **Long-Term Liability** from the Type drop-down list.

10 Type **Loan Payable** in the Account Name text box.

11 Click the **Enter Opening Balance** button.

12 Type **383800** in the Opening Balance text box and **12/31/08** in the As of text box and then click **OK.**

13 Click **Save & Close.**

14 Select **Furniture and Equipment** from the Chart of Accounts, click the **Account** button, and then click **Edit Account.**

15 Click the **Enter Opening Balance** button, type **75000** in the Opening Balance text box and **12/31/08** in the As of text box, and then click **OK.**

16 Click **Save & Close.**

17 Select **Accumulated Depreciation** from the Chart of Accounts, click the **Account** button, and then click **Edit Account.**

18 Click the **Enter Opening Balance** button, type **–7500** in the Opening Balance text box and **12/31/08** in the As of text box, and then click **OK.**

Trouble? Be sure to enter this amount as a negative number. If you don't, your trial balance will be out of balance. Accumulated depreciation is a contra-asset account that has a normal credit balance.

19 Click **Save & Close.**

20 Close the Chart of Accounts window.

You are curious whether, after entering all of these opening balances, the accounts are in balance. Karen explains that QuickBooks establishes an Opening Balance Equity account that is used to balance all the assets and liabilities established via this opening balances effort *except* for Accounts Receivable and Accounts Payable. The beginning accounts receivable balances were assigned to an account called Uncategorized Income on 12/31/08, and all beginning accounts payable balances were assigned to an account called Uncategorized Expenses as of the same date.

"But aren't we mostly concerned with balances beginning 1/1/09?" you question.

Karen points out that QuickBooks will automatically close these accounts to Retained Earnings as of 1/1/09. She does suggest, however, that you recategorize the retained earnings balance as of 1/1/09 to be part of the Opening Balance Equity account. She also suggests that it might make sense to transfer the resulting balance in the Opening Balance Equity account to the Common Stock account, because that is the basis the company will use for Karen and Donna's new investment in the company.

She enlightens you by explaining the arrangement that she and Donna have with Ernesto. The three agreed that the Opening Balance Equity (assets minus liabilities) was $100,000. Donna and Karen will each be purchasing stock in the company on January 1 for $100,000, thus giving the company a value of $300,000. Each stockholder—Ernesto, Donna, and Karen—will have a one-third interest in the company.

"Are we sure that our opening balance effort yielded an Opening Balance Equity of $100,000?" you ask.

"We'll check while we make the adjustments for the opening equity we just spoke of," Karen responds. "First let's look at a trial balance as of 1/1/09, which will give us the account balances as of that date."

To view opening balances and recategorize the opening balance equity and uncategorized account balances:

1 Open the Report Center, select **Accountant & Taxes**, and then double-click **Trial Balance.**

2 Change the To and From dates to **1/1/09** to view the trial balance shown in Figure 6.22.

Wild Water Sports
Trial Balance
As of January 1, 2009

	Jan 1, 09	
	Debit	Credit
Bank of Florida	25,000.00	
Accounts Receivable	96,300.00	
Inventory Asset	372,000.00	
Accumulated Depreciation		7,500.00
Furniture and Equipment	75,000.00	
Accounts Payable		76,000.00
MasterCard		1,000.00
Loans Payable		383,800.00
Opening Balance Equity		79,700.00
Retained Earnings		20,300.00
TOTAL	568,300.00	568,300.00

Figure 6.22

Trial Balance

3 Close the Trial Balance window and then close the Reports Center window. (No need to memorize this report since you didn't make any changes to the standard trial balance report.)

4 Select **Chart of Accounts** from the Company section of the home page.

5 Double-click the **Opening Bal Equity** account to use the register.

6 If necessary, scroll down the account until an empty row can be seen.

7 Type **1/1/09** in the date column in the first open row available.

8 Type **20300** in the increase column of that same row.

9 Select **Retained Earnings** from the Account drop-down list.

10 Click **Record.**

11 Click **OK** if asked whether you really want to make an adjustment to this account.

12 Type **1/1/09** in the date column in the next open row available if it is not already there.

13 Type **100000** in the decrease column of that same row.

14 Select **Capital Stock** from the Account drop-down list.

15 Click **Record.** Your screen should now look like Figure 6.23.

Figure 6.23

Opening Balance Equity Account Register

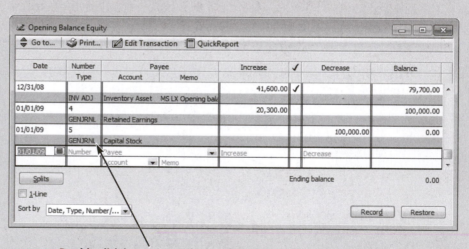

Double-click here to reveal journal entry

16 Double-click **GENJRNL** under the number 5 to reveal the general journal entry that was created when you adjusted the Opening Balance Equity account as shown in Figure 6.24. Close the Assigning Numbers to Journal Entries window.

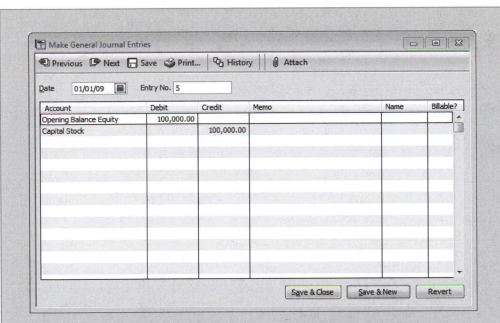

Figure 6.24

General Journal Entry

17 Close the **Opening Bal Equity** and the **Make General Journal Entries** windows.

18 The Opening Balance Equity and Retained Earnings accounts should now be zero, and the Capital Stock account should be $100,000. Your Chart of Accounts should now look like Figure 6.25.

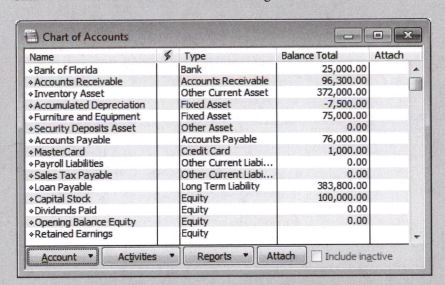

Figure 6.25

Chart of Accounts after Adjustments

"Much better," you proclaim.

Karen suggests you print this Chart of Accounts for later reference.

To print the Chart of Accounts:

1 Prepare this window for printing by clicking the **Reports** button at the bottom of the window and then selecting **Account Listing.**

2 Click the **Modify Report** button.

3 Click the **Header/Footer** tab, and then uncheck **Subtitle, Date Prepared,** and **Time Prepared.**

4 Click the **Display** tab, and then uncheck **Tax Line** and **Description** to remove those columns from your report.

5 Click **OK.**

6 Click the **Print** button on the top of the Reports window, choose **Portrait** orientation, and then click **Print.** Alternatively, you can access this list by clicking the **Reports** menu, then **List,** and then **Account Listing.**

7 Close both the Account Listing report and the Chart of Accounts window. Be sure to memorize the Accounting Listing report.

Karen points out the opening equity balance in the accounts listing is, in fact, the $100,000 they expected. Her stock purchase and Donna's stock purchase will occur in the first few days of January. All that's left in the company creation process is setting up payroll and adding employees.

Set Up Payroll and Employees

Video Demonstration

DEMO 6E - Setting up payroll for manual payroll calculations

"Now it's time to establish information about our employees in QuickBooks," Karen says. "QuickBooks has some very nice payroll features that will help us track employee information, prepare payroll tax reports, and account for our employee cost."

"Will it calculate payroll withholding for federal and state taxes?" you ask.

"It will if we purchase a payroll tax table service from Intuit," Karen answers, "but we decided not to do that."

First, we must set up QuickBooks so that it knows we want to compute payroll manually. As you will see, this is not a straightforward proposition. QuickBooks makes you do some fairly strange things to begin a manual payroll, and none is intuitive or easy to discover. To get started, we will use the Help menu.

To set up payroll:

1 First, note that the home page lists only two icons (Enter Time and Learn about Payroll Options) in the Employee section. Now press the F1 key to start QuickBooks Help.

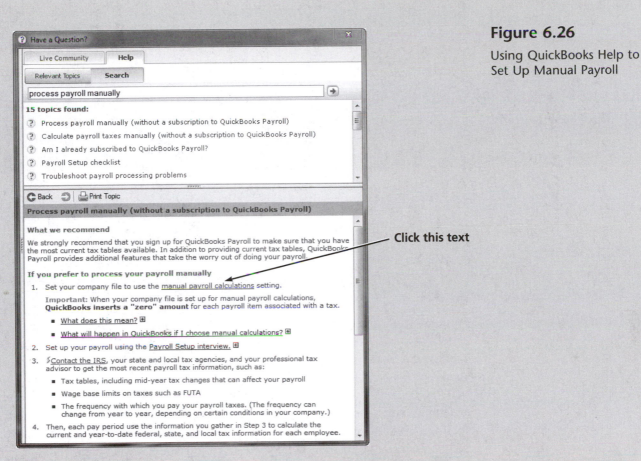

Figure 6.26

Using QuickBooks Help to Set Up Manual Payroll

2 Click the **Search** tab and then type **process payroll manually** in the text box, then press the **Enter** key.

3 Click the text **Process payroll manually (without a subscription to QuickBooks Payroll).** Your screen should look like Figure 6.26.

4 Click the text **manual payroll calculations.**

5 Click the text **Set my company file to use manual calculations.**

6 Click **OK** and then close the Have a Question? window. Notice that the home page now contains new icons that will allow you to process payroll as shown in Figure 6.27 below.

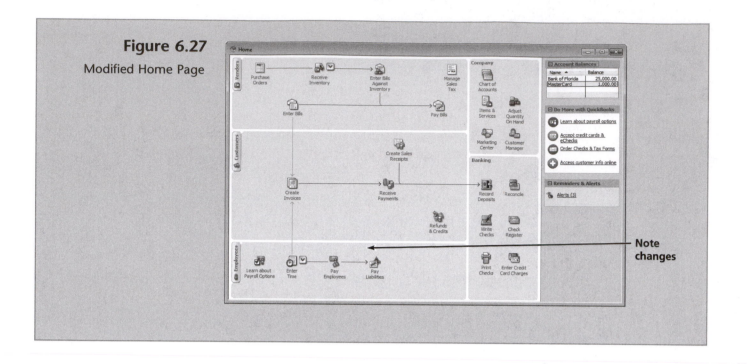

Figure 6.27

Modified Home Page

Note changes

Now it's time to enter payroll details for January. Karen explains that, during the month of January, she and Donna will work full time as salaried employees. Ryder and Pat, sales staff and service technicians, will work occasional days until the end of the month when the business is more established. For the first few weeks, most of their work will be setting up the business, passing out marketing flyers, and trying to sell boats. Later in the month, they will begin servicing some boats.

For each employee you'll need to add personal, address and contact, and tax information. In doing so, Karen points out, you'll also be setting up payroll tax items such as salary and hourly as well as identifying how often your employees are paid (monthly in this case). You'll also be identifying each employee's salary or hourly rate, taxes to be withheld, state worked, filing status, tax rates (e.g., unemployment), and tax payees (e.g., Florida Department of Revenue) to whom state taxes are paid. Karen then explains that the best way to get started is to use QuickBooks Payroll Setup.

Video Demonstration

DEMO 6F - Setting up payroll after setting manual payroll calculations

To set up payroll:

1 Click **Payroll Setup** from the Employees menu.

2 Click the **Continue** button after reading each window.

3 Make sure that only the **Salary** and **Hourly wage and overtime** check boxes are checked in the Add New window and then click **Finish**.

4 Click **Continue** to accept the Compensation list provided.

5 Click **Continue** again, check the **My company does not provide insurance benefits** check box, and then click **Finish**.

6 Proceed in the same manner through the payroll setup process, as the company does not provide retirement benefits and paid time off or have any special additions and deductions.

7 Click **Continue** when you get to the Set up your employees section.

8 Enter the information for Donna Chandler as shown in Figure 6.28.

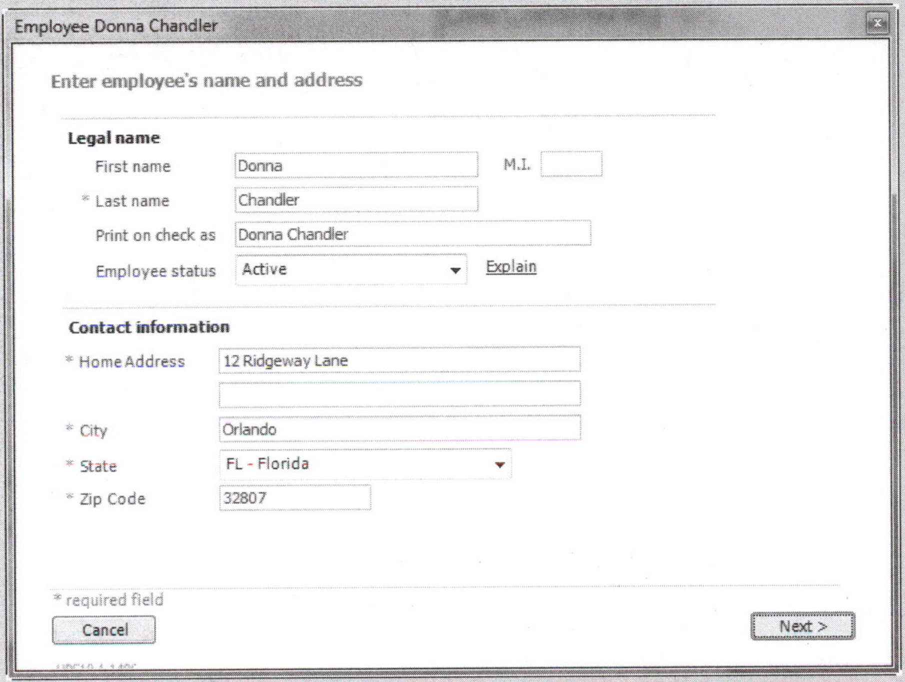

Figure 6.28

Personal Information for Donna Chandler

9 Click **Next** and then enter the hiring information for Donna Chandler as shown in Figure 6.29.

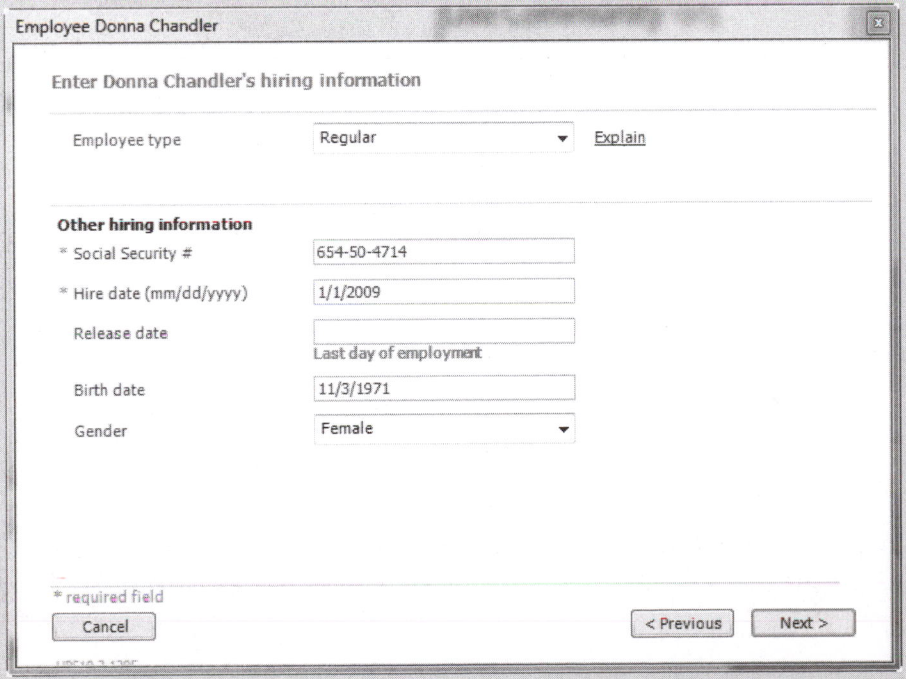

Figure 6.29

Hiring Information for Donna Chandler

10 Click **Next** and then enter the compensation information for Donna Chandler as shown in Figure 6.30.

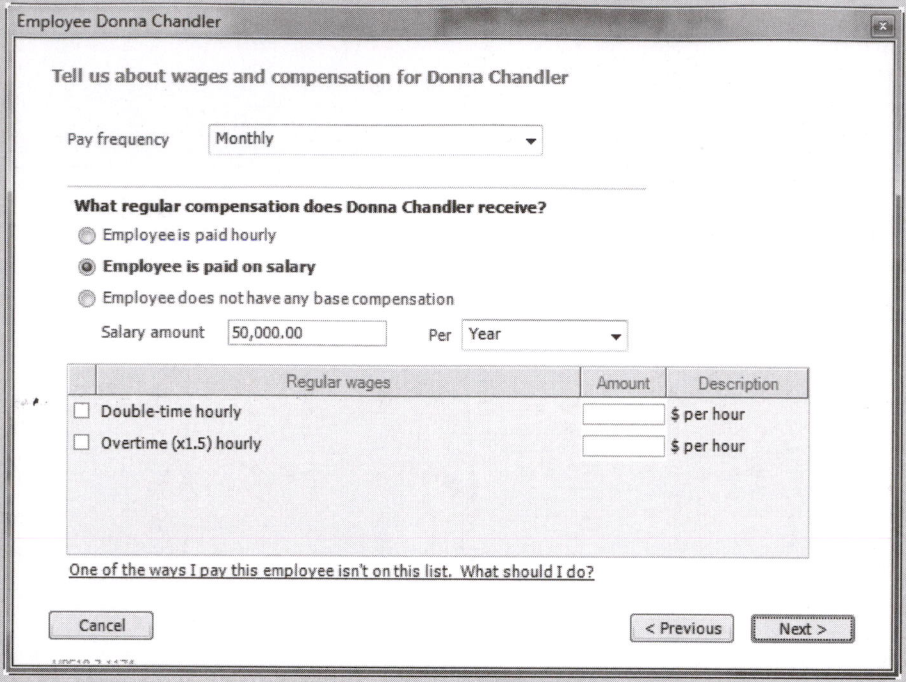

Figure 6.30

Compensation Information for Donna Chandler

Employee Donna Chandler

Tell us about wages and compensation for Donna Chandler

Pay frequency   Monthly

What regular compensation does Donna Chandler receive?
- Employee is paid hourly
- **Employee is paid on salary**
- Employee does not have any base compensation

Salary amount 50,000.00   Per Year

Regular wages	Amount	Description
☐ Double-time hourly		$ per hour
☐ Overtime (x1.5) hourly		$ per hour

One of the ways I pay this employee isn't on this list. What should I do?

Cancel   < Previous   Next >

11 Click **Next** two times and then enter the subject to tax information for Donna Chandler as shown in Figure 6.31.

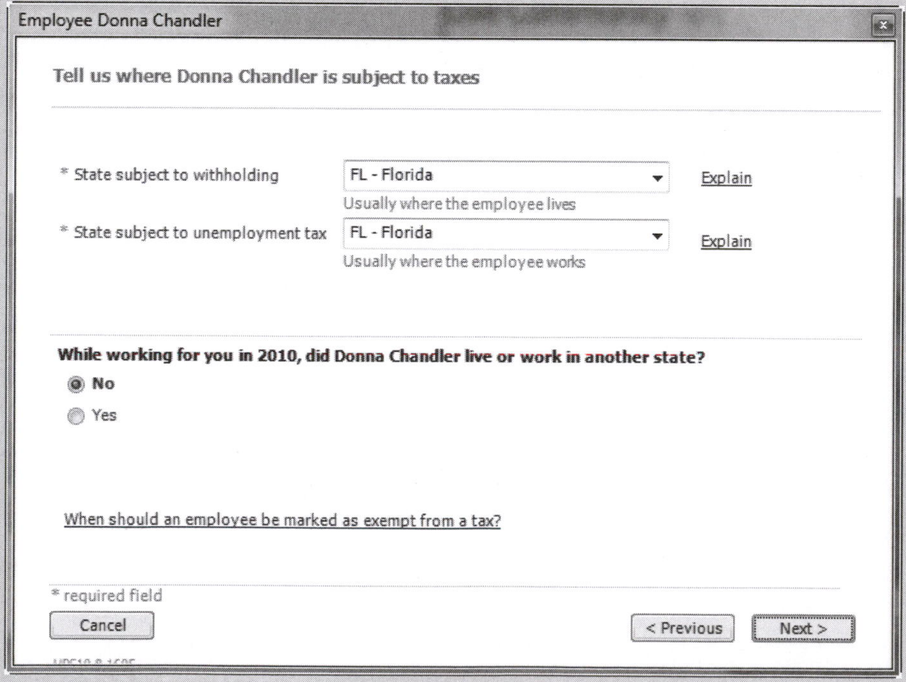

Figure 6.31

Subject to Tax Information for Donna Chandler

Employee Donna Chandler

Tell us where Donna Chandler is subject to taxes

* State subject to withholding   FL - Florida   Explain
Usually where the employee lives

* State subject to unemployment tax   FL - Florida   Explain
Usually where the employee works

While working for you in 2010, did Donna Chandler live or work in another state?
- **No**
- Yes

When should an employee be marked as exempt from a tax?

* required field
Cancel   < Previous   Next >

12 Click **Next** and then enter the federal tax information for Donna Chandler as shown in Figure 6.32.

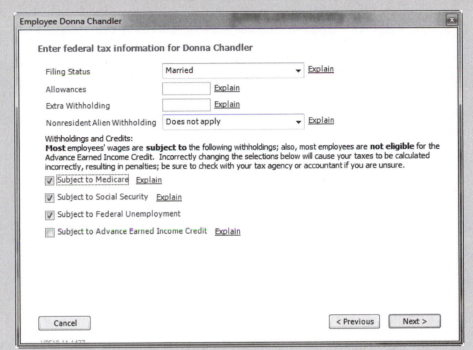

Figure 6.32

Federal Tax Information for Donna Chandler

13 Click **Next** and then enter the state tax information for Donna Chandler as shown in Figure 6.33.

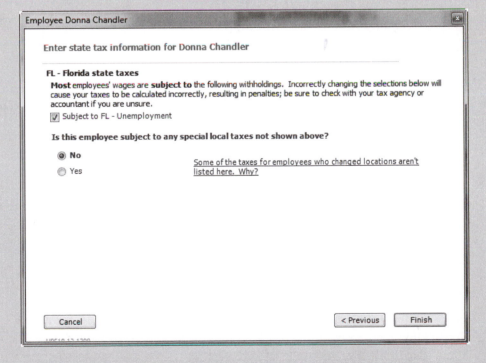

Figure 6.33

State Tax Information for Donna Chandler

14 Click **Finish** to finish adding Donna to the payroll system. Click **Continue** to carry on the payroll setup process.

15 Click **Continue** two more times to accept the tax items set up for you.

16   Type **2.7%** as the FL – Unemployment Company Rate and then click **Finish.**

17   Click **Continue** and then set the Payee to the default information provided and the Deposit Frequency to Quarterly for all tax payments. Click **Next.**

18   Type **6854102** as the FL Dept of Revenue UT Acct No and then click **Finish.**

19   Click **Continue** twice and then click **2009** if you are asked when you will start processing payroll in QuickBooks. If asked, select No to a question about your company issued paychecks this year.

20   Click **Continue** and then click **Go to the Payroll Center** to finish the payroll setup process.

You note that Donna Chandler is now set up as an employee for the company and that payroll is ready to go, but you still have more employees to enter. Karen suggests that you add one employee for now, perhaps Ryder Zacovic, an hourly employee. You respond that you are up to the task.

To add Ryder as an employee:

1   Click **New Employee.** A New Employee window appears.

2   Be certain that the Personal Info. tab is selected. Then, fill in the form with the following information:

Name: Mr. Ryder Zacovic

Social Security number: 556-74-6585

Gender: Male

Date of Birth: 2/19/85

3   Click the **Address and Contact** tab and then type **1554 Rose Avenue Apt. #4, Orlando, FL 32804** in the Home Address section.

4   Select **Payroll and Compensation Info** from the Change tabs drop-down text box.

5   Select **Hourly** as the Item Name.

6   Type **15** as the Hourly/Annual Rate.

7   Select **Monthly** as the Pay Frequency.

8   Click the **Taxes** button and enter the following information: Ryder is single and subject to Medicare, Social Security, and Federal Unemployment Tax.

9   Click the **State** tab and identify Ryder as working in Florida (FL) and subject to Florida (FL) withholding.

10 Click **OK** two times to finish entering Ryder as a new employee.

11 Click **Leave As Is** when asked if you want to set up other payroll information.

12 Click the **Reports** menu, click **List**, and then click **Employee Contact List.**

13 Click the **Modify Report** button.

14 Click the **Header/Footer** tab, and then uncheck **Date Prepared** and **Time Prepared.**

15 Click the **Display** tab, and then uncheck **Phone** from the list of columns.

16 Click **OK** to close the Modify Report window.

17 If necessary, resize the remaining columns of the report to fit it on to one page.

18 Click the **Print** button on the top of the Reports window.

19 Choose the printer you want to print to, choose **Portrait** orientation, and then click **Print.** Your printout should look like Figure 6.34.

20 Close the Employee Contact List window memorizing this report.

21 Close the Employee Center window.

Wild Water Sports
Employee Contact List

Employee	SS No.	Address	Gender
Donna Chandler	654-50-4714	12 Ridgeway Lane Orlando, FL 32807	Female
Ryder Zacovic	556-74-6585	1554 Rose Avenue Apt. #4 Orlando, FL 32804	Male

Figure 6.34

Employee Contact List

You have now finished setting up new company files, establishing company preferences, and setting up company items, customers, vendors, accounts, and employees.

Your final task is to backup your data file for safekeeping.

Backing Up Your Company File

"It is very important to keep a backup of your company file just in case your computer hard drive crashes or your data file gets corrupted or destroyed," Karen explains. She goes on to explain that some business users save their files to USB drives.

"USB drives are ideal," you point out. Karen suggests that the two of you backup and restore a file for practice.

To backup and restore a file to an external disk using QuickBooks Backup procedures:

1 Open the Wild Water Sports file if you closed it after the last lesson.

2 Click **Save Copy or Backup** from the File menu.

3 Choose the **Backup Copy** option and then click **Next.**

4 Choose the **Local backup** option and then click **Next.**

5 Choose a location to which you would like to backup your file. In Figure 6.35, we chose to backup the file to an external drive defined as Drive K in a folder we called My QuickBooks Backups. Uncheck the default check boxes checked to eliminate the date and time of the backup to the file name. Click **Browse** to locate the drive and location where you would like to backup your file.

Figure 6.35

Backing Up to an External Drive

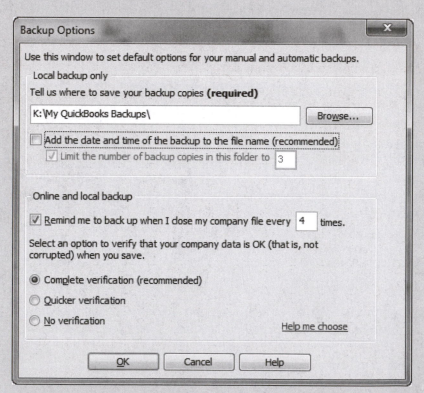

6 Click **OK**, click **Next**, and then click **Save** to begin the backup process.

7 Click **OK** again when QuickBooks informs you that your file has been backed up successfully.

8 To restore that same file from the external drive to your hard drive, choose **Open or Restore Company** from the QuickBooks File menu.

9 Choose the **Restore a backup copy** option and then click **Next.**

10 Choose the **Local backup** option and then click **Next.**

11 Identify the location of your backup file and then click **Open.**

12 Click **Next** to identify where the company file will be stored.

13 Once you've identified the location where the company file will be stored, click **Save.** Figure 6.36 shows an example where a backup file is being restored to a folder on a computer's hard drive.

14 Click **OK** when QuickBooks informs you that your file has been restored successfully.

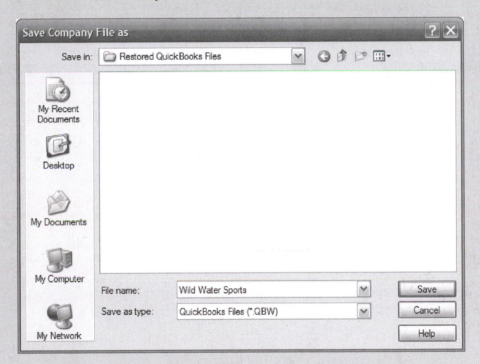

Figure 6.36

Restoring a QuickBooks File

End Note

Karen thanks you for your patience in helping to create a QuickBooks file for Wild Water Sports. You've created a new company and have also set up company preferences, company items, customers, vendors, accounts, and employees. Next, you'll begin recording business transactions.

Business Events Summary

Business Event	Process Steps	Page
New Company		
Create new company	Use EasyStep Interview	97
Set up company preferences	Select Edit menu, then Preferences	101
Customers		
Create customer	New Customer & Job from Customer Center	109
Print customer list	Customer Contact List from Reports Center	111
Vendors		
Create vendor	New Vendor from Vendor Center	112
Print vendor list	Vendor Contact List from Reports Center	113
Items		
Create service/inventory items	Select Items & Services	107
Set up sales taxes	Sales tax from Item List	107
Print item list	Select Reports, Item Listing	107
Employees		
Activate manual payroll	Use F1 to access help	119
Set up payroll	Payroll Setup from Employees menu	121
Create employee	New Employee from Employee Center	125
Print employee list	Employee Contact List from Reports Center	125
Accounts		
Create account	Chart of Accounts from Home page	114
Set up beginning balances	Enter Opening Balance in Account	114
Print account list	Reports menu: List: Account Listing	118
Other		
Trial balance	Accountant & Taxes in Reports Center	116
Recategorize opening balances	Use Opening Bal Equity account	116
Backup company file	Save Copy or Backup from File menu	126

Chapter 6 Questions

1 Describe the EasyStep Interview process to create a new QuickBooks company file.

2 What is the purpose of setting preferences in QuickBooks?

3 Do all businesses use account numbers?

4 Give examples of service items and inventory part items used by Wild Water Sports.

5 Why did Wild Water Sports choose to use QuickBooks's job tracking feature?

6 Explain the process of establishing new accounts for fixed assets that will be depreciated like equipment. Why is accumulated depreciation set up with a negative beginning balance?

7 What happens when you first establish beginning balances for Accounts Receivable and Accounts Payable?

8 Describe the process for telling QuickBooks you want to manage payroll manually.

9 When creating a new employee during the payroll setup process, what information is provided in the Payroll and Compensation Info tab?

10 Why is it important to backup your QuickBooks file?

Chapter 6 Matching

Select the letter of the item below that best matches the definitions that follow. Use the text or QuickBooks Help to complete this assignment.

a. EasyStep Interview   _____ Anyone who pays you.

b. Items   _____ Anyone you pay except employees.

c. Service items   _____ Anything that your company buys, sells, or resells in the course of business.

d. Inventory part items   _____ This QuickBooks setup process walks you through the setup procedure and helps you tailor QuickBooks to suit your business.

e. Customer   _____ Items representing services you sell.

f. Vendor   _____ Items representing products you sell.

g. Opening balance   _____ In traditional accounting, a document that adds up all the debits and credits so that mistakes can be traced if debits don't equal credits.

h. Job	_____ Property used in a productive capacity that will benefit your business for longer than one year.
i. Fixed asset	_____ An optional way to keep track of larger orders, such as those placed by different departments within the same organization.
j. Trial balance	_____ The amount of money in, or the value of, an account as of the start date of your records in QuickBooks.

Chapter 6 Exercises

Chapter 6 Exercise 1
CREATE A NEW COMPANY

Having just completed your second year of college studying business and accounting, you are looking for summer employment when you run across an ad from a Jessica Gil, a local CPA, who is in need of part-time help. After an hour-long interview you get the job and are anxious to apply your newfound knowledge in accounting to help a business gain success. Jessica has just taken on a new client, Boston Catering, a catering firm located in Cambridge, Massachusetts that provides catering services to businesses in the Cambridge and Boston area. So far they have been manually keeping their accounting records but wish to convert to QuickBooks starting July 1, the beginning of their fiscal year. Jessica would like you to spearhead this effort by creating a QuickBooks file containing their existing customers, vendors, and employees and then entering their business events in July.

The company's federal tax ID is 99-2158715 and state tax ID is 4513-41. They are located at 305 Hampshire Street, Cambridge, MA 02139 with a phone number 617-555-2806. The company is organized as a corporation and sells both services and products. They do not sell products online, do charge sales tax of 5% on all items which is paid to the Massachusetts Department of Revenue, but do not create estimates and do not use sales receipts because all products and services are invoiced. Statements and progress invoices are not used but they do wish to use QuickBooks to manage the bills they owe. They do not print checks but do keep track of inventory (change standard inventory account to food inventory) and do accept credit cards. Customers of this catering business are billed a fixed fee, but the company wants to keep track of hourly employees hours so they have chosen to track time in QuickBooks. They will need a chart of accounts and will starting using QuickBooks 7/1/2010.

The company's existing bank account is with Bank of America in Cambridge. The 6/30/2010 statement reveals an ending balance of $8,345. You decide to use the following income and expense accounts:

Account Name	Type
Bar Sales	Income
Catering Sales	Income
Bar Purchases	Cost of Goods Sold
Food Purchases	Cost of Goods Sold
Restaurant Supplies	Cost of Goods Sold
Advertising and Promotion	Expense
Bank Service Charges	Expense
Depreciation Expense	Expense
Insurance Expense	Expense
Payroll Expenses	Expense
Professional Fees	Expense
Rent Expense	Expense
Telephone Expenses	Expense
Uniforms	Expense
Utilities	Expense

Any additional accounts already present in your file are to remain as is except for the Inventory Asset account which should be changed to Food Inventory. You decide to not sign up for an account at intuit.com and to set up preferences exactly as you did in Chapter 6. Create a new company using QuickBooks's EasyStep Interview. Use Boston Catering Ch 6 Ex 1 as the Company Name. The company is in the general service based industry. Each sale is recorded individually, using the US dollar. They have W-2 employees. Hint: be sure to set up your sales tax item information now for use in later exercises.

Print an Account Listing report after removing the description and tax lines and then create a backup file with the name Boston Catering Ch 6 Ex 1 (Backup).

Chapter 6 Exercise 2
ADD CUSTOMERS

You must have completed Exercise 1 in this chapter to complete this exercise.

Restore the backup file you created in Exercise 1. Change the company name to Boston Catering Ch 6 Ex 2. Add the following customers to your file.

	MA General Hospital	Fidelity Investments	John Hancock
Address	55 Fruit St.	1 Devonshire St.	601 Congress St.
City	Boston	Boston	Boston
State	MA	MA	MA
Zip	02114	02109	02210
Phone	617-555-2000	617-555-1000	617-555-3000
Beginning Balance	$7,000	$8,000	$9,000
Terms	Net 30	Net 30	Net 30
Sales Tax Item	Sales Tax 5%	Sales Tax 5%	Sales Tax 5%

Print a Customer Balance Summary report as of 6/30/10.

Chapter 6 Exercise 3
ADD VENDORS

You must have completed Exercise 1 in this chapter to complete this exercise.

Restore the backup file you created in Exercise 1. Change the company name to Boston Catering Ch 6 Ex 3. Add the following vendors to your file.

	Sanford Winery	Fiddlehead Cellars	US Food Service
Address	5010 Santa Rosa Rd.	1597 East Chestnut Ave.	One Technology Dr.
City	Lompoc	Lompoc	Peabody
State	CA	CA	MA
Zip	93436	93436	01960
Phone	805-555-5900	805-555-0204	978-555-5100
Beginning Balance	$2,000	$3,000	$4,000
Terms	Net 30	Net 30	Net 30

Print a Vendor Balance Summary report as of 6/30/10.

Chapter 6 Exercise 4
ADD ITEMS

You must have completed Exercise 1 in this chapter to complete this exercise.

Restore the backup file you created in Exercise 1. Change the company name to Boston Catering Ch 6 Ex 4. Add the following items to your file.

#	Type	Description	Vendor	Cost	Price /Unit	Income Account	Quantity
A100	Service	Appetizers Heavy	-	-	$18	Catering Sales	-
A200	Service	Appetizers Light	-	-	$12	Catering Sales	-
S100	Service	Spring Supper	-	-	$35	Catering Sales	-
S200	Service	Summer Supper	-	-	$40	Catering Sales	-
S300	Service	Fall Supper	-	-	$65	Catering Sales	-
S400	Service	Winter Supper	-	-	$50	Catering Sales	-
D100	Service	Desserts	-	-	$6	Catering Sales	-
P100	Service	Pastries	-	-	$5	Catering Sales	-
W100	Inventory Part	Sanford Chardonnay	Sanford Winery*	$45	$60	Bar Sales	25
W200	Inventory Part	Fiddlehead Pinot Noir	Fiddlehead Cellars*	$50	$65	Bar Sales	30

*You will need to add these vendors to complete this assignment.

Print an Item Listing report.

Chapter 6 Exercise 5
ADD EMPLOYEES

You must have completed Exercise 1 in this chapter to complete this exercise.

Restore the backup file you created in Exercise 1. Change the company name to Boston Catering Ch 6 Ex 5. You will need to create two new payroll items: Salary and Hourly, which both track to a Payroll Expense account. Payroll is paid monthly at the end of the month. All employees are subject to Medicare, Social Security, and Federal Unemployment federal taxes and state unemployment taxes which are paid quarterly. The company's state tax ID is 4513-41. All state taxes are paid to the Massachusetts Department of Revenue quarterly. The company's state unemployment tax rate is 3%. The company is also subject to a workforce training fund tax of .01%. (Note: use this information even if the QuickBooks software warns you about account numbers and payees.) Make sure you set up your company file to use manual calculations and then add the following employees:

	Nathan Chambers	Kyle Hain	Amy Casey
Address	One Leighton St.	101 Canal St. #9	1449 Main St. #30
City	Cambridge	Boston	Waltham
State	MA	MA	MA
Zip	02141	02114	02451
Phone	617-555-9822	617-555-0905	617-555-1234
SS#	154-74-8745	541-84-7312	641-87-9825
Earnings	$50,000/year	$16/hour	$18/hour
Filing Status	Single	Single	Married
Type	Regular	Regular	Regular

Print an Employee Contact List report with phone number.

Chapter 6 Exercise 6
ADD ACCOUNTS AND SET OPENING BALANCES

You must have completed Exercise 1 in this chapter to complete this exercise.

Restore the backup file you created in Exercise 1. Change the company name to Boston Catering Ch 6 Ex 6. Add accounts and set opening balances so that your chart of accounts looks like the following as of 6/30/10 (Use information from the previous exercises for details of accounts receivable, inventory, and accounts payable.):

Description	Dr.	Cr.
Bank of America	8,345	
Accounts Receivable	24,000	
Prepaid Insurance	3,000	
Inventory Asset	2,625	
Furniture and Equipment	62,030	
Accumulated Depreciation		2,030
Accounts Payable		9,000
Note Payable		50,000
Opening Balance Equity		23,970
Retained Earnings		15,000
Total	100,000	100,000

Make journal entries as of 7/1/10 to adjust retained earnings to zero and capital stock to 38,970. Print the Account Listing report as of 7/1/10.

Chapter 6 Assignments

Chapter 6 Assignment 1

corporation   *merchandising*

ADDING MORE INFORMATION: WILD WATER SPORTS

Restore the file Wild Water Sports Ch 6A (Backup) found on the text CD or download it from the text Web site. Add a new income type account titled "Part Sales." Add a new other current asset account titled "Inventory Parts." Change the title of the existing Inventory Asset account to Inventory Boats. Change the title of the existing Merchant Sales account to Boat Sales.

Add the following service items:

Item Name	Sales Description	Sales Price	Tax Code	Income Account
Cleaning	Labor charge for cleaning boat	$75.00	Tax	Service
Painting & Body Repairs	Labor charge for painting and repairs	$80.00	Tax	Service

Add the following inventory parts:

Item Name & Description	Sales Price	Tax Code	Income Account	Asset Account	Cost	On Hand
Engine Oil	$ 5.00	Tax	Part Sales	Inventory Parts	$ 4.00	0
Oil Filter	$ 15.00	Tax	Part Sales	Inventory Parts	$ 12.00	0
Tune-Up Parts	$250.00	Tax	Part Sales	Inventory Parts	$200.00	0
Air Filter	$ 35.00	Tax	Part Sales	Inventory Parts	$ 28.00	0

Add the following customers:

Customer/Company	Balance Due
Freebirds	$0
Florida Sports Camp	$0

Add the following vendors:

Vendor/Company	Address	Phone	Balance Owed
MB Sports	280 Air Park Road, Atwater, CA 95301	209-357-4153	$0
Tige Boats	6803 US Hwy 83 N., Abilene, TX 79601	325-676-7777	$0

Add the following employees:

Employee Data	Karen Wilson	Pat Ng
Social Security number	654-85-7844	125-95-4123
Gender	Female	Male
Salary	$50,000 per year	n/a
Hourly Wage	n/a	$18 per hour
Filing Status	Single	Single
Taxes	Subject to Medicare, Social Security, FUTA, and all applicable state taxes	Subject to Medicare, Social Security, FUTA, and all applicable state taxes
Filing State	Florida	Florida
Pay Period	Monthly	Monthly

Print the following as of 1/1/09 (similar to what you did in the chapter):

a. Customer Balance Summary

b. Customer Contact List

c. Vendor Balance Summary

d. Vendor Contact List

e. Employee Contact list

f. Account Listing (Account, Type, and Balance Total only)

g. Item Listing (list only Item, Description, Type, Cost, Quantity On Hand, and Price)

h. Trial Balance

Chapter 6 Assignment 2
CREATING A NEW COMPANY: CENTRAL COAST CELLULAR

Van Morrison would like to use QuickBooks for his new company, Central Coast Cellular. You choose to use QuickBooks EasyStep Interview. The company's federal tax ID is 77-9418745. The company is located at 950 Higuera St., San Luis Obispo, CA 93401. The company's phone number is 805-555-9874, and its fiscal and tax year begins in January 2009. The company's main business is cellular phone sales and rentals (which will not be done online), but it also earns revenue by consulting with customers on alternative cellular phone plans. Choose Professional Consulting as the Industry for this company. The company is organized as a sole proprietorship selling both products and services. Sales tax at 8% is collected on all products and services and then paid to the State Board of Equalization. (**Hint:** Be sure to create a tax item.) No estimates are used, but sales receipts are used to record cash sales and invoices to record credit sales. Customer billing statements may be used to remind customers of monthly balances owed. Progress billing is not used, but Van wants to keep track of bills that he owes. All checks are handwritten, inventory needs to be tracked, and credit cards are accepted. Van does plan on keeping time records for his hourly W-2 employees. He will use accounts (but not account numbers) starting on 1/1/09, at which time he plans to establish a checking account with a local bank. In addition to the recommended income and expense accounts, Van would like to have a Product Sales (Type: Income) account.

Change the preferences in QuickBooks as follows: Set QuickBooks to move between fields after pressing the Enter key. Set dates to a two-digit year format. Enable reports and graphs to refresh automatically. Enable manual payroll features.

Set up the following customers:

- Tribune, 3825 S. Higuera St., San Luis Obispo, CA 93401, 805-781-7800, Terms: Net 30, Contact: Sara Miles, Subject to state sales taxes.

- City of San Luis Obispo, 990 Palm Street, San Luis Obispo, CA 93401, 805-781-7100, Terms: Net 30, Contact: Robert Preston, Subject to state sales taxes.

- Sterling Hotels Corporation, 4115 Broad Street, Suite B-1, San Luis Obispo, CA 93401, 805-546-9388, Terms: Net 30, Contact: Monica Flowers, Subject to state sales taxes.

Set up the following vendors:

- Verizon Communications, 1255 Corporate Drive, Irving, TX 75038, 972-507-5000, Terms: Net 30, Contact: Francisco Rojas.

- Nokia Mobile Phones, 23621 Park Sorrento Road, Suite 101, Calabasas, CA 91302, 818-676-6000, Terms: Net 30, Contact: Brandy Parker.

- Ericsson, Inc., 740 East Cambell Road, Richardson, TX 75081, 972-583-0000, Terms: Net 30, Contact: Monty Python.

- Employment Development Department (EDD).

Set up the following employees using the company's federal and state tax ID 779-4187-4 All employees are paid semi-monthly and subject to Social Security, FUTA, Medicare, CA state withholding, SUI (CA Unemployment Company Rate: 3%), SDI, and California's Employment Training Taxes payable to the Employment Development Department (EDD). The California wage plan code for all employees is U (Voluntary DI, State UI Plan). Payroll taxes are paid quarterly.

- Name: Mr. Jay Bruner, Address: 552 Olive St., San Luis Obispo, CA 93401, Phone: 805-555-7894, SSN 578-94-3154, Start date: 1/1/09, Salary: $36,000 per year, Filing status: Single.

- Name: Mr. Alex Rodriguez, Address: 1480 Monterey St., San Luis Obispo, CA 93401, Phone: 805-555-1579, SSN 487-98-1374, Start date: 1/1/09, Salary: $48,000 per year, Filing status: Married with two incomes.

- Name: Ms. Megan Paulson, Address: 400 Beach St., San Luis Obispo, CA 93401, Phone: 805-555-4489, SSN 547-31-5974, Start date: 1/1/09, Hourly: $12 per hour, Filing status: Married with one income.

Modify the existing chart of accounts to include an Accounts Receivable account and a checking account.

Set up the following items:

- Consulting Services: Type: Service, Rate: $95, Taxable, and using income account: Consulting Income.

- Inventory Part: Item name/description: Nokia 8290, Cost: $150, Preferred vendor: Nokia Mobile Phones, Sales price: $225, Taxable, and using income account: Product Sales.

- Inventory Part: Item name/description: Nokia 8890, Cost: $175, Preferred vendor: Nokia Mobile Phones, Sales price: $250, Taxable, and using income account: Product Sales.

- Inventory Part: Item name/description: Nokia 3285, Cost: $200, Preferred vendor: Nokia Mobile Phones, Sales price: $300, Taxable, and using income account: Product Sales.

- Inventory Part: Item name/description: Ericsson LX588, Cost: $50, Preferred vendor: Ericsson, Inc., Sales price: $85, Taxable, and using income account: Product Sales.

- Inventory Part: Item name/description: Ericsson T19LX, Cost: $75, Preferred vendor: Ericsson, Inc., Sales price: $100, Taxable, and using income account: Product Sales.

Print the following as of 1/1/09.

a. Customer Contact List (include only the columns for Customer, Bill to, Contact, and Phone; print in landscape orientation).

b. Vendor Contact List (include only the columns for Vendor, Address, Contact, and Phone; print in landscape orientation).

c. Employee Contact List (include only the columns for Employee, SSN, Phone, and Address; print in portrait orientation).

d. Account Listing (include only the columns for Account, Type, and Balance Total).

e. Item Listing (list only Item, Description, Type, Cost, Price, and Quantity On Hand).

Chapter 6 Assignment 3
CREATING A NEW COMPANY: SANTA BARBARA SAILING

easy step

service

corporation

Rob Dutton, an old friend from your high school days, has just purchased Santa Barbara Sailing Center and is getting ready to start business July 1, 2008. He purchased the corporation from its previous owner for $50,000 and assumed the company's existing long-term debt of $264,900. In return, he now owns 100% of the outstanding capital stock. The company owns several sailboats, which it charters and rents to the public and businesses in town. As of 6/30/08, these boats had an estimated value of $300,000. There is an existing company bank account at Coast Hills Federal Credit Union, and there are existing customer receivable balances and vendor accounts payable balances that are expected to be collected/paid in the near future. The only remaining asset owned by the company is some furniture and equipment valued at $2,450. Rob has asked you to help him set up QuickBooks to account for and report on his business activities for the bank's information.

Company Information

- Company name: Santa Barbara Sailing Center

- Legal name: Santa Barbara Sailing Center, Inc.

- Tax ID: 99-9851206

- Address: 133 Harbor Way, Santa Barbara, CA 93109

- Phone: (805) 962-2826

- Industry: Rental

- Company Organization: Corporation

- Fiscal Year Starts: July

- Services only, sales tax at 8%, without estimates, with sales receipts, and statements, some corporate customers are invoiced but no progress invoicing, keep track of bills you owe, no to print checks, accept credit and debit cards, keep track of time, they have W-2 employees, use 7/1/08 as the first day of the quarter (since they are a calendar year company starting business 7/1/08)

- Existing bank account name "Checking," account number 122541584 with a balance of $10,000 on 6/30/08

- Income and expense accounts: accept recommended accounts

Preferences

- Accounting: Use and require accounts but no account numbers. Turn off date warnings.

- Checking: Use the checking account as the default to write checks, pay bills, pay sales tax, and make deposits.

- Desktop View: Use multiple windows and open the home page when opening a company file.

- General: Check the **Pressing Enter moves between fields** check box in addition to the default settings. Uncheck the **Always show years as 4 digits** check box.

- Sales Tax: Add sales tax item; Type: Sales Tax Item; Sales Tax Name: Tax; Description: Sales Tax; Tax Rate: 8%; Tax Agency: State Board of Equalization. Then set Your most common sales tax item to Tax.

Item Information

- Type: Service, Item Name: CAT 28, Description: Catalina 28, Rate: $220 per day, Account: Rental Income

- Type: Service, Item Name: CAT 32, Description: Catalina 32, Rate: $275 per day, Account: Rental Income

- Type: Service, Item Name: CAT 42, Description: Catalina 42, Rate: $465 per day, Account: Rental Income

- Type: Service, Item Name: CAT 50, Description: Catalina 50, Rate: $560 per day, Account: Rental Income

Customer Information

- Customer Name: SBMED, Opening Balance as of 6/30/08: $1,485, Company Name: Santa Barbara Medical, Address: 470 South Patterson, Santa Barbara, CA 93111, Terms: Net 30, Credit limit: $25,000

- Customer Name: RAY, Opening Balance as of 6/30/08: $8,465, Company Name: Raytheon, Address: 7418 Hollister Ave., Goleta, CA 93117, Terms: Net 30, Credit limit: $20,000

Vendor Information

- Vendor Name: Catalina, Opening Balance as of 6/30/08: $7,500, Company Name: Catalina Yachts, Address: 21200 Victory Blvd., Woodland Hills, CA 91367, Terms: Net 30, Credit limit: $50,000

Other Account Information

- Furniture & Equipment (Fixed Asset) opening balance at 6/30/08: $2,450

- Boats (new Fixed Asset) opening balance at 6/30/08: $300,000

- Accumulated Depreciation (Fixed Asset) opening balance at 6/30/08: $0

- Loan Payable (Long-Term Liability) opening balance at 6/30/08: $264,900

Payroll and Employee Information

- Payroll is calculated manually. The company does not provide insurance benefits, retirement benefits, paid time off, or have any special additions and deductions. All employees are subject to CA withholding, CA unemployment, Medicare, Social Security, federal unemployment, CA employment training, and CA disability taxes. The California wage plan code for all employees is U (Voluntary DI, State UI Plan). Payroll taxes are paid quarterly.

- Employee Name: Rob Dutton, Social Security number: 239-0974-6, Gender: Male, Address: 1044 Padre St., Santa Barbara, CA 93105. Hire date 7/1/08. Payroll Item: Regular, which represents an annual salary of $65,000 recorded to the Payroll Expenses account and paid semi-monthly. Filing Status: Single.

- Employee Name: Jeanne Winestock, Social Security number: 222-32-0298, Gender: Female, Address: 4678 Berkeley Rd., Goleta, CA 93117. Hire date 7/1/08. Payroll Item: Staff Hourly, which represents a regular hourly salary of $18 per hour recorded to the Payroll Expense account and paid semi-monthly. Filing Status: Married, one income.

- CA Unemployment rate is 3.4%, CA Employment Training Tax is 0.1%, CA Disability Employee Rate is 1.1%. CA taxes are paid to the EDD quarterly (Acct. No. 203-8232-1). Federal taxes are paid to the U.S. Treasury quarterly.

Use the EasyStep Interview to create Santa Barbara Sailing Center's QuickBooks file. Reclassify Opening Balance Equity, Uncategorized Income, and Uncategorized Expense as Capital Stock. Print the following reports as of 7/1/08 without a Subtitle, Date Prepared, or Time Prepared reference. Place your name in the Extra Footer Line and print with a Landscape orientation. (Be sure to keep this QuickBooks file in a safe place, because it will be used as the starting file for this case in Chapter 7.)

a. Customer Contact List (Customer, Company, Balance Total, City, and State columns only)

b. Vendor Contact List (Vendor, Address, Company, and Balance Total columns only)

c. Employee Contact List (Employee, SS No., Address, and Gender columns only)

d. Item List (Item, Description, Type, Price, and Sales Tax Code columns only)

e. Trial Balance

Chapter 6 Cases

Chapter 6 Case 1:
FOREVER YOUNG

Sebastian Young played quarterback for the Los Angeles Raiders for the 12 years of his professional football career. As a team leader, Sebastian guided his team to three Super Bowl victories and earned the respect of his teammates, the coaching staff, the press, and fans across the country. Now retired, Sebastian is a guest commentator for a variety of sports talk shows on radio and television. He recently formed a sole proprietorship called Forever Young to promote himself as a motivational speaker to large corporations and organizations. He has hired Cory Walsh to promote and coordinate his appearances and Anne Sunshine to manage the office. Sebastian has contacted some vendors and customers and is about to embark on a new business adventure. He has asked you to set up an accounting system for the business and has given you the following information.

Company Information

* Company and legal name: Forever Young

* Tax ID: 94-9723900

* Address: 100 Westwood Blvd., Los Angeles, CA 90024

* Phone: 310-555-2324

* Industry: Professional Consulting

* Company Organization: Sole Proprietor

* Fiscal year starts: January 2008

* Services only, no sales tax, with estimates, with sales receipts, and statements, no progress invoicing, keep track of bills you owe, print checks,

accept credit and debit cards, keep track of time, has W-2 employees, use 1/1/08 as the first day of the quarter

- Existing bank account: Washington Mutual, bank account name: "Checking," account number: 390093912, opened 1/1/08

- Income and expense accounts: accept recommended accounts

Preferences

- Accounting: Use accounts but do not require account numbers.

- Checking: Use the checking account as the default to write checks, pay bills, pay sales tax, and make deposits.

- Desktop View: Use multiple windows and show home page when opening a company file.

- General: Check the **Pressing Enter moves between fields** check box in addition to the default settings. Uncheck the **Always show years as 4 digits** check box.

Item Information

- Type: Service, Number: 001, Description: Full-Day Seminar, Rate: $10,000, Consulting Income

- Type: Service, Number: 002, Description: Half-Day Seminar, Rate: $6,000, Consulting Income

- Type: Service, Number: 003, Description: One-Hour Presentation, Rate: $2,000, Consulting Income

Customer Information

- Customer Name: Levi, Company Name: Levi Strauss, Address: 100 Market St., San Francisco, CA 94099, Terms: Net 30, Credit limit: $25,000

- Customer Name: Boeing, Company Name: Boeing Aerospace, Address: 139 Boeing Park Dr., El Segundo, CA 90233, Terms: Net 30, Credit limit: $25,000

Vendor Information

- Vendor Name: Fleet, Company Name: Fleet Promotions, Address: 3099 Wilshire Blvd. #300, Los Angeles, CA 90024, Terms: Net 30, Credit limit: $50,000

- Vendor Name: Galas, Company Name: Galas & Associates, Address: 37321 Santa Monica Blvd. #100, Los Angeles, CA 90024, Terms: Net 30, Credit limit: $50,000

Account Information

- Checking account (already created)

- Accounts receivable (not yet created)

Payroll and Employee Information

- Payroll is calculated manually.

- Employee Name: Cory Walsh, Social Security number: 339-09-7466, Gender: Male, Address: 399 Sunset Blvd., Bel Air, CA 90033. Payroll item: Officer Salary, which represents a regular annual salary of $80,000 recorded to the Payroll Expenses account and paid semi-monthly. Filing Status: Single. Hire date 1/1/08.

- Employee Name: Anne Sunshine, Social Security number: 232-38-0098, Gender: Female, Address: 2983 Olympic Blvd., Los Angeles, CA 90032. Payroll item: Staff Hourly, which represents a regular hourly salary of $20 per hour recorded to the Payroll Expense account and paid semi-monthly. Filing Status: Single. Hire date 1/1/08.

- State: California, State tax, unemployment, and state disability vendor: Franchise Tax Board, ID number: 930808, Liability account: Payroll Liabilities, California Unemployment tax rate: 3.4%, California Disability tax rate: 1.1%, all employees are subject to the California Training Tax. The California wage plan code for all employees is U (Voluntary DI, State UI Plan). Payroll taxes are paid quarterly.

Requirements:

Use the EasyStep Interview to create Forever Young's QuickBooks file and then print the following reports as of 1/1/08 without a Subtitle, Date Prepared, or Time Prepared reference. Place your name in the Extra Footer Line and print with a Landscape orientation. (Be sure to keep this QuickBooks file in a safe place; it will be used as a starting file for this case in Chapter 7.)

1   Customer Contact List

2   Vendor Contact List

3   Employee Contact List

4   Item List

Chapter 6 Case 2:
OCEAN VIEW FLOWERS

corporation   merchandising

Ocean View Flowers is in the wholesale distribution and sales industry and is located at 100 Ocean Ave. in Lompoc, CA, 93436. Ocean View started business as a corporation on January 1, 2008, and owner Scott Cruz would like you to use QuickBooks to keep track of its business transactions. Ocean View is a calendar year corporation (for both fiscal and tax purposes) and will need to use the inventory, purchase order, and manual payroll features of QuickBooks. The company established a bank account, titled Union Checking, at the beginning of the year. In addition, the company filed for federal (91-3492370) and state (234-3289-4) tax ID numbers. All employees are paid semi-monthly but do not earn sick or vacation pay. All of their customers are product resellers and thus no state sales tax is collected. They don't use estimates or progress invoicing, but do use sales receipts, invoices, and statements. They keep track of the bills they owe but don't print checks. They accept checks and credit cards as payment from customers but don't keep detailed records of the time employees work. All state payroll taxes are paid to the Employment Development Department. The state unemployment tax (SUTA) rate is 3.4%, and the state disability tax rate is 1.1%. The company's expected customers, items, and vendors are tabulated as follows.

Customer	Address	Terms	Contact
Valley Florists	101 Main St., Los Angeles, CA 90113	2/10 net 30	Sam Davies
FTD	2033 Lakewood Dr., Chicago, IL 60601	Net 30	Beverly Rose
California Beauties	239 Hyde Street, San Francisco, CA 95114	2/10 net 30	Farrah Faucet
Eastern Scents	938 42nd Street, New York, NY 10054	2/10 net 30	Nick Giovanni
Latin Ladies	209 Zona Rosa, Mexico City, Mexico	2/10 net 30	Juan Valdez

Item Type	Item Name/Description	Cost	Sales Price	Income Account
Inventory part	Almond Puff	$12.00	$24.00	Sales
Inventory part	Calistoga Sun	$ 8.00	$16.00	Sales
Inventory part	Caribbean Pink Sands	$13.00	$26.00	Sales

Vendor	Address	Terms	Contact
Hawaiian Farms	2893 1st Street, Honolulu, HI 05412	Net 30	Mahalo Baise
Brophy Bros. Farms	90 East Hwy 246, Santa Barbara, CA 93101	Net 30	Tim Beach
Princess Flowers	92 West Way, Medford, OR 39282	Net 30	Bonnie Sobieski
Keenan's Pride	10 East Betteravia, Santa Maria, CA 93454	2/10 net 30	Kelly Keenan
Vordale Farms	62383 Lido Isle, Newport, CA 90247	Net 30	Deana Vordale

Ocean View Flowers employees (all of whom are considered regular-type employees) were hired on 1/4/08 and are subject to federal and state taxes and withholdings, state unemployment, state disability, and state employee training taxes. Two wage items are used: Hourly and Salary. The California wage plan code for all employees is U (Voluntary DI, State UI Plan). Payroll taxes are paid quarterly. A list of employees is shown below.

Employee	Address	Social Security #	Compensation	Filing Status
Margie Cruz	2322 Courtney, Buellton, CA 93246	654-85-1254	$12/hour	Single
Kelly Gusland	203 B St., Lompoc, CA 93436	567-78-1334	$15/hour	Single
Stan Comstock	383 Lemon St., Lompoc, CA 93436	126-85-7843	$50,000/year	Married with one income
Marie McAninch	1299 College Ave., Santa Maria, CA 93454	668-41-9578	$60,000/year	Married with two incomes
Edward Thomas	1234 St. Andrews Way, Lompoc, CA 93436	556-98-4125	$70,000/year	Single

Requirements:

Create a new company file for Ocean View Flowers using the EasyStep Interview. Then add the customers, vendors, employees, accounts, items, and other information as just described. (Be sure to keep this QuickBooks file in a safe place; it will be used as a starting file for this case in Chapter 7.) Print the following as of 1/1/08:

1   Customer Contact List (Customer, Bill to, and Contact fields only)

2   Vendor Contact List (Vendor, Address, and Contact fields only)

3   Employee Contact List (Employee, SS No., and Address fields only)

4   Item List (Item, Description, Type, Cost, and Price fields only)

Chapter 6 Case 3:
ALOHA PROPERTIES

corporation   service

Aloha Properties is located at 4-356 Kuhio Highway, Suite A-1, Kapaa Kauai, HI 96746. Its phone number is 808-823-8375, and the corporation specializes in Hawaii Vacation Rentals. Its federal tax ID number is 72-6914707, and it plans to start using QuickBooks as its accounting program on January 1, 2008. It has been in business for two years using a manual accounting system. Aloha hopes that you can help it migrate to QuickBooks. It is a property rental firm, files Form 1120 each year, and collects a 4% general excise tax (Tax name: HI Sales Tax, Description: Sales Tax) on all rental income, which must be paid to the State of Hawaii Department of Taxation located at P.O. Box 1425, Honolulu, HI 96806-1425. It has chosen to use sales receipts for its cash sales and invoices and statements for its credit sales. The firm would like to use QuickBooks to keep track of bills it owes but will continue to handwrite checks. It accepts credit and debit cards.

Aloha plans to use QuickBooks's service invoice format but not use progress invoicing. It also plans to use QuickBooks's payroll features but to continue calculating payroll manually, because it currently has only two W-2 employees. The firm doesn't prepare estimates and does not track employee time or segments. It does, however, plan to enter bills as received and then enter payments later. Reports are to be accrual based, and Aloha plans to use the income and expense accounts created in QuickBooks for a property management company. It will be providing services only, no products. Most of its revenue comes from renting properties located on the island of Kauai to individual and corporate accounts. The company's policy is to collect a 50% deposit upon reservation and the balance upon arrival. Some customers (those that have prior credit approval) are invoiced upon arrival with the remaining payment due within 30 days. Deposits are recorded as payments on account, even though revenue is not recorded until customers arrive. Other customers (those without prior credit approval) must pay upon arrival, at which time a sales receipt is generated and the remaining payment is collected. Service items are used, but no inventory is maintained. Existing service items, customers, vendors, and employee information are provided below. *Note:* Deposits for rentals not yet provided are shown as negative numbers.

Service Item Name	Description	Income a/c	Rate
Moana Unit #1	Moana Unit #1	Rental Income	$ 2,000
Moana Unit #2	Moana Unit #2	Rental Income	$ 2,500
Moana Unit #3	Moana Unit #3	Rental Income	$ 4,000
Moana Unit #4	Moana Unit #4	Rental Income	$12,000
Villa Kailani Unit #1	Villa Kailani Unit #1	Rental Income	$ 3,000
Villa Kailani Unit #2	Villa Kailani Unit #2	Rental Income	$ 4,500
Villa Kailani Unit #3	Villa Kailani Unit #3	Rental Income	$ 4,200
Villa Kailani Unit #4	Villa Kailani Unit #4	Rental Income	$ 6,000

Customer Name	Balance Due (Deposits) at 12/31/07
Boeing	$10,000
General Motors	$75,000
Brice Montoya	–$ 3,000
Sara Rice	–$ 6,000
Apple Computer	$25,000

Vendor Name	Balance Owed
Reilly Custodial	$4,500
Blue Sky Pools	$1,800

Employee Data	Fran Aki	Daniele Castillo
Social Security #	128-85-7413	984-74-1235
Hire date	1/1/06	1/1/06
Salary	$75,000 per year	n/a
Hourly wage	n/a	$20 per hour
Filing status	Married with one income	Single
Taxes	Subject to Medicare, Social Security, FUTA, and all applicable state taxes	Subject to Medicare, Social Security, FUTA, and all applicable state taxes
Filing state	Hawaii	Hawaii

The company owns two properties: Moana located in Princeville and Villa Kailani located in Poipu. As of 12/31/07, it owed $3,875,000 (a 25-year mortgage classified as a long-term liability called Notes Payable) on the two properties for which it originally paid $2,000,000 and $3,000,000 (respectively) several years ago. Of this amount, $500,000 was identified as land, $250,000 as furniture and equipment, and $4,250,000 as buildings. Use Buildings as the fixed asset account name for the buildings. Accumulated depreciation for all fixed assets as of 12/31/07 was $1,200,000.

The company has one checking account, which had a balance of $15,000 on 12/31/07 with the Bank of Hawaii (account name: checking). Its Hawaii withholding, unemployment, and disability identification number is 8432518452. Its unemployment rate is 1.9%, and the disability rate is 0.01%. Only two payroll items are used: Salary and Hourly. Federal taxes are paid to the U.S. Treasury, and state taxes are paid to the State of Hawaii Department of Taxation quarterly. All employees are paid monthly.

You've been asked to reclassify the balance in the Opening Balance Equity account as Capital Stock ($10,000) and Retained Earnings ($70,000). You've also been asked to use account names, not numbers, for all accounts.

Use the information provided here to create a new QuickBooks file for Aloha. (*Hint:* Read the entire case before you begin, establish the new company file accepting the default name provided, and modify preferences as you did earlier in the chapter. Enter all beginning asset, liability, and equity account balances as of 12/31/07. Use journal entry adjustments to close the Opening Balance Equity account so that there is $10,000 in the Capital Stock account and $24,700 in the Retained Earnings account. Change account names and delete accounts not used so they match up with the following trial balance.) After adjustments, the trial balance at 1/1/08 should look like Figure 6.37.

Figure 6.37

Aloha Properties Trial Balance as of January 1, 2008

Aloha Properties
Trial Balance
As of January 1, 2008

	Jan 1, 08	
	Debit	Credit
Checking	15,000.00	
Accounts Receivable	101,000.00	
Accumulated Depreciation		1,200,000.00
Buildings	4,250,000.00	
Furniture and Equipment	250,000.00	
Land	500,000.00	
Accounts Payable		6,300.00
Notes Payable		3,875,000.00
Capital Stock		10,000.00
Opening Bal Equity	0.00	
Retained Earnings		24,700.00
TOTAL	5,116,000.00	5,116,000.00

Requirements:

Once you've entered all the beginning information, print the following reports as of 1/1/08. (Be sure to keep this QuickBooks file in a safe place; it will be used as a starting file for this case in Chapter 7.)

1   Customer Balance Summary

2   Vendor Balance Summary

3   Employee Contact List (Employee and SS No. only)

4   Account Listing (Account, Type, and Balance Total only)

5   Item Listing (List only Item, Description, Type, and Price)

6   Trial Balance

Cash-Oriented Business Activities

Learning Objectives

In this chapter, you will:

- Record cash-oriented business transactions classified as financing activities, such as owner contributions
- Record cash-oriented business transactions classified as investing activities, such as equipment purchases
- Record cash-oriented business transactions classified as operating activities, such as inventory purchases, sales, and payroll
- Evaluate a firm's performance and financial position

Case: **Wild Water Sports, Inc.**

You and Karen completed the initial setup of the QuickBooks program at the beginning of January and are ready to begin recording business transactions for the month. The new company has completed its first month of business, and Ernesto is pleased with the new business relationship he established with Karen and Donna. However, no one knows the extent of their profitability or financial position because none of the accounting events has yet been recorded into QuickBooks. You had to start the spring semester, and Karen has been busy just keeping the business going.

"I'm brand new to QuickBooks," you explain. "I know a little about financial accounting and I'm taking a managerial class right now, but I haven't had a course in QuickBooks or any other computerized accounting program for that matter."

"No problem," Karen says, trying to reassure you. "QuickBooks is very easy for first-time users to learn, and you'll be pleased with how much it will help the company understand its performance and financial position."

The two of you agree to meet today to review the business transactions that took place in January. Karen agrees to explain the nature of each transaction and how it should be recorded in QuickBooks. She suggests that the best way to accomplish this is to view each transaction in terms of the three fundamental business activities: financing, investing, and operating.

"I remember studying those concepts in my first accounting course," you comment. "If I remember correctly, financing activities are initiated when money or other resources are obtained from short-term nontrade creditors, long-term creditors, and/or owners. Financing activities are completed when amounts owed are repaid to or otherwise settled with these same creditors and/or owners. Investing activities are initiated when the money obtained from financing activities is applied to nonoperating uses, such as buying investment securities and/or productive assets like equipment, buildings, land, or furniture and fixtures. Investing activities are completed when the investment securities and/or productive assets are sold. Finally, operating activities occur when the money obtained from financing activities and the productive assets obtained from investing activities are applied to either purchase or produce goods and services for sale. These operating activities are substantially completed when goods are delivered or when services are performed."

"Wow, they taught you well!" Karen exclaims. "Let's begin with a few cash-oriented financing activities."

Video Demonstration

DEMO 7A - Receive cash from stock sales and borrowings

Recording Cash-Oriented Financing Activities

You begin with two financing activities. The first occurred on January 2 when the company received $200,000 from Karen and Donna ($100,000 each) as their purchase of stock in the company.

To record the deposit received from Karen and Donna:

1 Start the QuickBooks program.

2 Restore the Wild Water Sports Ch 7 (Backup) file from your Data Files CD or download it from the Internet. See "Data Files CD" in Chapter 1 if you need more information.

3 The newly restored Wild Water Sports Ch 7.qbw file should now be open.

4 Click the **Record Deposits** icon from the Banking section of the home page. The Make Deposits window appears. Note that QuickBooks has automatically inserted today's date.

5 Enter the information for Karen and Donna's stock purchase as shown in Figure 7.1. Be sure to enter the correct date.

6 Click **Save & New** to record the deposit. Do not close the Make Deposits window.

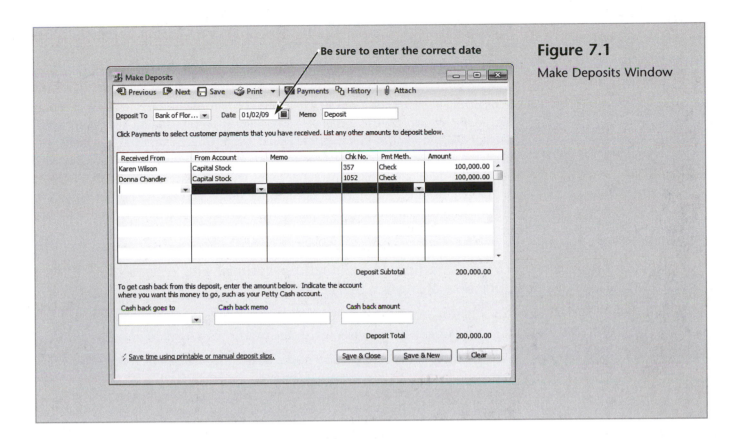

Be sure to enter the correct date

Figure 7.1

Make Deposits Window

The second deposit was made on January 5 when the company borrowed $250,000 from their bank (Bank of Florida) at 5%, payable in five years.

To record the long-term loan from the Bank of Florida:

1 Select account **Bank of Florida** as the Deposit To account.

2 Type **1/5/09** as the deposit date.

3 Type **Bank of Florida** in the received from text box and then press **[Tab]**.

4 Click **Quick Add** in the Name Not Found window.

5 Click **Other** in the Select Name Type window and then click **OK**.

6 Select account **Loans Payable** as the From account.

7 Type **250000** as the amount and then click **Save & Close**.

You have now recorded two different cash-oriented financing activities: the sale of stock to investors and the borrowing of funds on a long-term basis. Now it's time to look at recording cash-oriented investing activities.

Recording Cash-Oriented Investing Activities

After making the deposits from investors and creditors, the company decided to temporarily invest those funds in a money market account with its bank. By transferring those funds from its checking account to a money market account, the company expected to generate some interest revenue until the funds were needed. To accomplish this transfer, Karen wrote Check No. 1001 on January 8 from the company's checking account with Bank of Florida and deposited the check into their new money market account with ETrade.

"Do we have a general ledger account for this?" you ask.

"No, but we can create one while we record this transaction," Karen answers.

To create a new general ledger account and record the purchase of money market funds:

1 Click the **Write Checks** icon from the Banking section of the home page. The Write Checks window appears.

2 Uncheck the **To be printed** check box if it is checked.

3 Type **1001** as the check number.

4 Type **1/8/09** as the date.

5 Type **ETrade** in the Pay to the Order of section of the check, and then press **[Tab]**.

6 Click **Quick Add** in the Name Not Found window.

7 Select **Other** in the Select Name Type window and then click **OK.**

8 Type **300000** as the check amount, and then press **[Tab]** five times or until the cursor is in the account section of the check.

Trouble? Near the bottom of the Write Checks window are two tabs—one labeled Expenses and one labeled Items. The Expenses tab is somewhat misleading because you can type or select any account to appear here, including assets. On the other hand, you use the Items tab to enter inventory acquisitions only. The main difference between them is that the Items tab has a column for quantities purchased and the Expenses tab has a column for an account.

9 In the Expenses tab, select **<Add New>** from the drop-down arrow list of accounts. (*Note:* You may have to scroll up the list to the top to find <Add New>.) An Add New Account: Choose Account Type window should appear.

10 Select **Bank** as the Account Type, and then click **Continue.**

11 Type **Short-Term Investments** as the Account Name. Your screen should look like Figure 7.2.

12 Click **Save & Close** to record this new general ledger account. Your Write Checks window should look like Figure 7.3.

13 Click **Save & New** to record this transaction. Do not close this window.

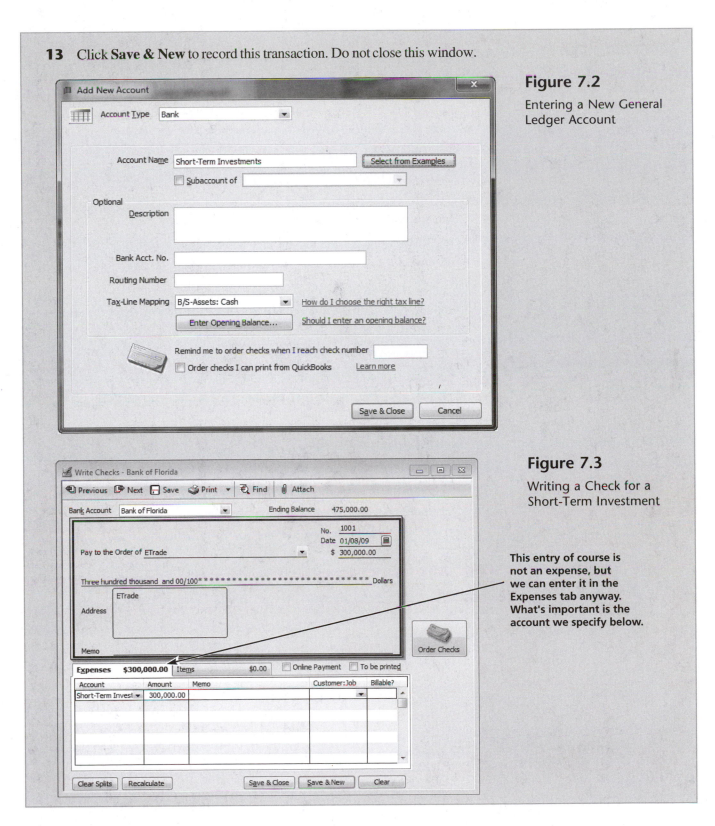

Figure 7.2

Entering a New General Ledger Account

Figure 7.3

Writing a Check for a Short-Term Investment

This entry of course is not an expense, but we can enter it in the Expenses tab anyway. What's important is the account we specify below.

Wild Water also had other cash-oriented investment activity in January. On January 9, it purchased new office furniture for the sales, marketing, and service staff from the local Staples store and new equipment for the service bays from AJ Marine Equipment.

To record the purchase of furniture and equipment:

1 Type **1002** as the check number (if it is not already there).

Trouble? If you previously closed the Write Checks window, open it again by clicking the Write Checks icon on the home page.

2 Type **1/9/09** as the date of purchase in the Write Checks window.

3 Type **Staples** in the Pay to the Order of section of the check, and then press **[Tab].**

4 Click **Quick Add** in the Name Not Found window.

5 Select **Vendor** in the Select Name Type window and then click **OK.**

6 Type **70000** as the check amount, and then press **[Tab]** five times or until the cursor is in the account section of the check.

7 In the Expenses tab, select **Furniture and Equipment** from the drop-down arrow list of accounts.

8 Click **Save & New** to enter another purchase.

9 Type **1003** as the check number.

10 Type **1/12/09** as the date of purchase in the Write Checks window.

11 Type **AJ Marine Equipment** in the Pay to the Order of section of the check, and then press **[Tab].**

12 Click **Quick Add** in the Name Not Found window.

13 Select **Vendor** in the Select Name Type window and then click **OK.**

14 Type **100000** as the check amount, and then press **[Tab]** five times or until the cursor is in the account section of the check.

Figure 7.4

Writing a Check to Purchase Equipment

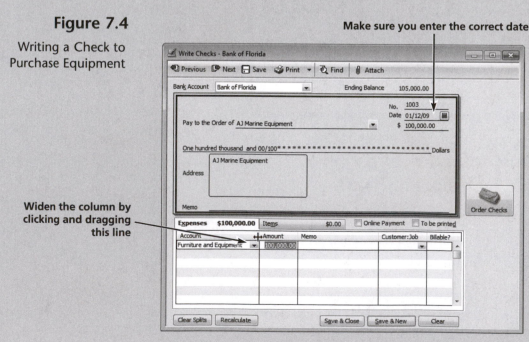

> **15** In the Expenses tab, select **Furniture and Equipment** from the drop-down arrow list of accounts and then press **[Tab]** twice. Your check should look like Figure 7.4.
>
> **16** Click **Save & Close** to complete this process.

"When is depreciation recorded on fixed assets?" you ask.

"Not until the end of the accounting period, before we create financial statements," Karen responds. "But we have lots to do before that."

Recording Cash-Oriented Operating Activities

Video Demonstration

DEMO 7C - Order, receive, and pay for inventory

Karen explains that Wild Water uses purchase orders to help manage its business activities. She remarks that purchase orders do not usually have an impact on financial statements, but they do play an important role as a control feature in QuickBooks. So she plans on using them.

"For example," she says, "we ordered two custom boats for two customers in January using purchase orders 4001 and 4002. Let me show you how purchase orders are used in QuickBooks."

"Are all purchase orders related to customers?" you ask.

"Not necessarily," Karen responds. "Sometimes we order for inventory to have in our showroom, but in these two we were ordering boats for specific customers."

The first boat was an existing inventory item (Malibu WakeSetter XTI sold for $70,000) and was ordered for an existing customer from an existing vendor. The second boat was for a new item (Tige 22v sold for $78,750) and was ordered from an existing vendor but for a new customer. In both transactions, the customer was required to pay a 25% deposit upon order ($17,500.00 and $19,687.50, respectively).

"How do you account for the amounts received?" you ask.

"We treat them just like payments received from customers, but since there is no invoice to allocate them to, we just leave them as credit balances in customers' accounts," Karen answers. "Accounting would normally require you to treat these as unearned revenue and record them as liabilities; however, we make adjustments for credit balances in accounts only if, prior to preparing financial statements, we still have remaining credits in customer accounts."

Karen decides first to show you the purchase orders generated to place the order with the vendors and then how to account for the two deposits on sales.

> **To create a purchase order:**
>
> **1** Click the **Purchase Orders** icon from the Vendors section of the home page to open the Create Purchase Orders window.
>
> **2** Select **Malibu Boats** from the Vendor drop-down list.

3 Type **1/12/09** as the date.

4 Type **4001** as the purchase order number.

5 Select **MW XTI** as the item, type **1** as the Qty (quantity), and select **Florida Sports Camp** as the customer for which we are ordering the boat. Your purchase order should now look like Figure 7.5.

Figure 7.5

Purchase Order No. 4001

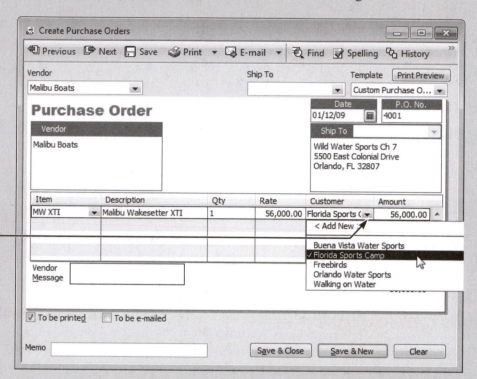

Be sure to specify the customer name here so that later you will properly bill them for this boat

6 Click **Save & New.** Note that QuickBooks may identify a word it doesn't know and, before processing this purchase order, a Check Spelling on Form window may appear to verify the spelling of Wakesetter. Click **Add** to add Wakesetter and then click **Add** again to add XTI to the dictionary.

7 Select **Tige Boats** from the Vendor drop-down list in the new purchase order form.

8 Type **1/12/09** as the date (if it's not already there).

9 Type **4002** as the purchase order number (if it's not already there).

10 Select **Add New** from the drop-down Item list to display the New Item window.

11 Select **Inventory Part** from the drop-down Type list.

12 Type **T 22v** as the Item Name/Number and **Tige 22v** as the Description for both purchase and sales transactions.

13 Type **63000** as the Cost.

14 Leave Cost of Goods Sold as the COGS Account.

15 Select **Tige Boats** as the Preferred Vendor.

16 Type **78750** as the Sales Price.

17 Leave Tax as the Tax Code.

18 Select **Boat Sales** as the Income Account.

19 Leave Inventory Boats as the Asset Account. The New Item window should look like Figure 7.6.

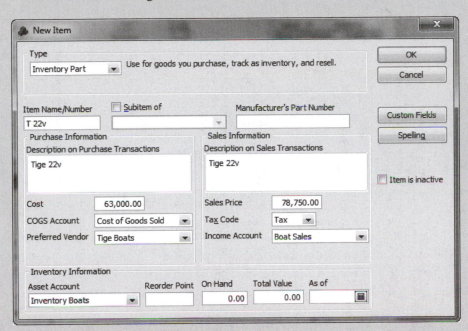

Figure 7.6

Creating a New Item from a Purchase Order

20 Click **OK** to accept this new item and add Tige to the dictionary if necessary.

21 Type **1** as the Qty.

22 Select **Add New** from the drop-down Customer list to display the New Customer window.

23 Type **Performance Rentals** as the Customer Name and Company Name.

24 Type **15 Hwy 22, Orlando, FL 32807** as the customer's address.

25 Click **Copy >>** to copy the Bill To address to the Ship To address section. Click **OK** to accept. Your New Customer window should look like Figure 7.7.

26 Click **OK** to add this new customer.

27 Click **Save & Close** to add this new purchase order.

Figure 7.7

Adding a New Customer

New Customer

Customer Name [Performance Rentals]

Opening Balance [   ] as of [   ] 📅 How do I determine the opening balance?

OK

Cancel

Help

Address Info | Additional Info | Payment Info | Job Info

Company Name [Performance Rentals]   Contact [   ]
Mr./Ms./... [   ]   Phone [   ]
First Name [   ] M.I. [   ]   FAX [   ]
Last Name [   ]   Alt. Phone [   ]
Alt. Contact [   ]
E-mail [   ]
Cc [   ]

☐ Customer is inactive

Addresses

Bill To   Ship To [Ship To 1   ▼]

Performance Rentals   Performance Rentals
15 Hwy 22   [Copy >>]   15 Hwy 22
Orlando, FL 32807   Orlando, FL 32807

[Edit]   [Add New] [Edit] [Delete]
                                 ☑ Default shipping address

Customer Manager Online

Click here to copy information from Bill To across to the Ship To box

---

Karen has shown you how to create purchase orders and now would like to show you how to account for the customers' deposits. Remember, in both cases customers remitted cash to Wild Water, but a sale could not be recorded because the products had not been delivered and thus the earnings process was not complete.

Video Demonstration

DEMO 7D - Receive and deposit cash

To record the receipt of deposits on future sales:

1 Click the **Receive Payments** icon located in the Customers section of the home page. Check the **Do not display** check box and then click **No** in the QuickBooks information window.

2 Select **Florida Sports Camp** as the customer from which the first deposit was received.

3 Type **17500** as the amount received.

4 Type the date **1/12/09.**

5 Select **Check** as the payment method.

6 Type **8755** as the check number. Your Receive Payments window should look like Figure 7.8.

7 Click **Save & New** to record another deposit.

8 Click **OK** to save the credit on the customer's account and not print a credit memo.

9 Select **Performance Rentals** as the customer from which the second deposit was received.

10 Type **19687.50** as the amount received.

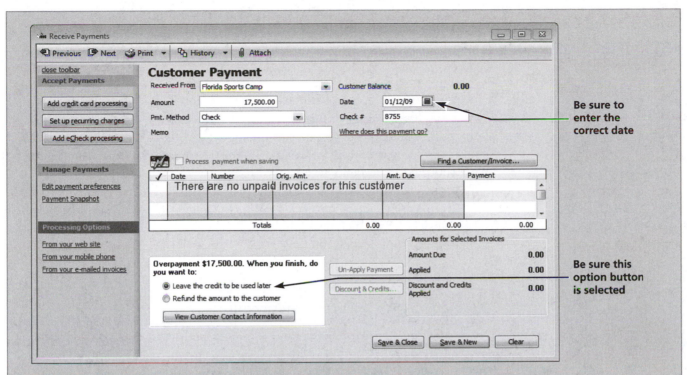

Be sure to enter the correct date

Be sure this option button is selected

Figure 7.8

Receive Payments Window

11 Type the date **1/12/09.**

12 Select **MasterCard** as the payment method.

13 Type **2158-6412-9842-9855** as the credit card number and **04/10** as the expiration date. Your Receive Payments window should look like Figure 7.9.

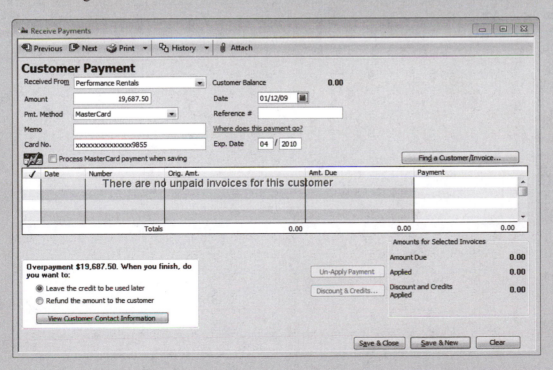

Figure 7.9

Processing a Credit Card Received as a Deposit

14 Click **Save & Close** to exit, and then click **OK** once again to leave this credit balance for the customer.

"Typically, we collect cash from sales on account, such as sales made to customers where we gave them credit terms like net 30," Karen comments. "If you recall when we set up our accounting system on January 1, 2009, we had some customers who owed us money from previous sales. The balances owed were reflected in accounts receivable."

"Do you record those cash collections like we just recorded deposits?" you ask.

"Yes, plus we had some cash sales during January that I'll show you as well," Karen answers. "We had one cash boat sale and one cash boat service during the month, both from new customers."

To record cash collected on account:

1 Click the **Receive Payments** icon located in the Customers section of the home page.

2 Select **Buena Vista Water Sports** from the Received From drop-down list.

3 Type **30000** as the amount received.

4 Type **1/15/09** as the date received.

5 Select **Check** as the payment method and type **65454** as the check number. Your screen should look like Figure 7.10.

Figure 7.10

Receipt of Payments from Customer on Account

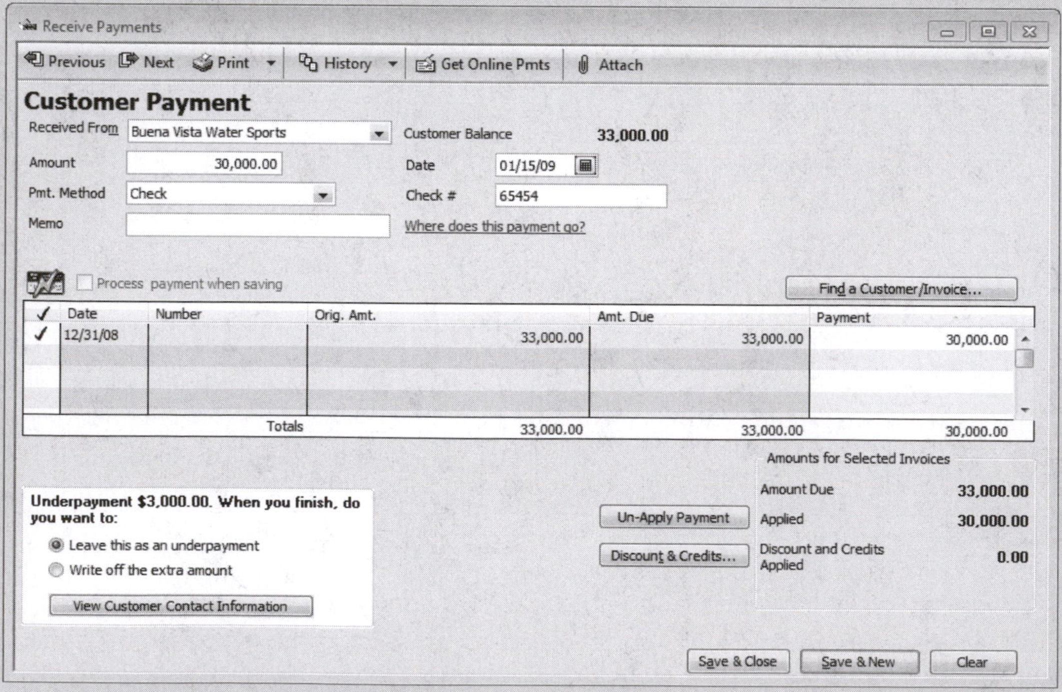

6 Click **Save & Close** to complete this transaction.

To record cash sales:

1 Click the **Create Sales Receipts** icon located in the Customers section of the home page.

2 Select **Add New** from the Customer:Job drop-down list.

3 Type **Seth Backman** as both the Customer Name and Company Name.

4 Type this customer's Bill To and Ship To address as **140 Fir Ave., Miami, FL 33109.**

5 Click **OK** to accept this new customer.

6 Type **1/16/09** as the date of sale and **6001** as the Sale No.

7 Type **161** as the check number and select **Check** as the payment method.

8 Select **MS LX** from the drop-down list of items.

9 Type **1** as the Qty.

10 Select **State Tax** from the Tax drop-down list if it is not already there.

11 Make sure the To be printed check box is unchecked. Your screen should look like Figure 7.11.

Video Demonstration

DEMO 7E - Sell inventory and apply deposits

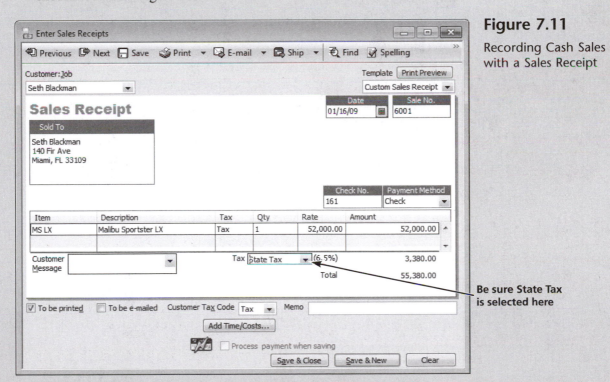

Figure 7.11

Recording Cash Sales with a Sales Receipt

Be sure State Tax is selected here

12 Click **Save & New** to record another sales receipt. Click **Yes** if asked to have the new tax item appear next time.

13 Select **Add New** from the Customer:Job drop-down list.

14 Type **Alisa Hay** as both the Customer Name and Company Name.

15 Type this customer's Bill To and Ship To address as **2999 Dover Blvd., Daytona Beach, FL 32114.**

16 Click **OK** to accept this new customer.

17 Type **1/26/09** as the date of sale and **6002** as the Sale No.

18 Select **Cash** as the payment method.

19 Select **Engine Service** from the drop-down list of items.

20 Type **1** as the Qty.

21 Select **Engine oil** from the drop-down list of items.

22 Click **OK** in the warning window which appears. (Since you're recording these transactions after the events have already occurred, your timing may be off from the actual acquisition of inventory items like engine oil and the date you record the receipt of those items.)

23 Type **5** as the Qty.

24 Select **Oil filter** from the drop-down list of items.

25 Click **OK** in the warning window which appears.

26 Type **1** as the Qty.

27 Select **State Tax** from the Tax drop-down list.

28 Make sure the To be printed check box is unchecked. Your screen should look like Figure 7.12.

Figure 7.12

Recording More Cash Sales with a Sales Receipt

Click and drag here to increase width of column to view all of the items

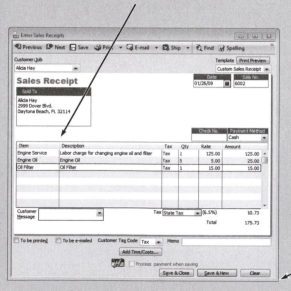

Click and drag here to increase the size of the receipt to view more lines

29 Click **Save & Close.** Click **Yes** to accept tax change.

"Have all of these cash receipt transactions been recorded in our checking account?" you ask.

"No, one of the preferences we specified in the company setup was that all cash receipts like payments on account, advance payments, et cetera, are to be recorded into an Undeposited Funds account since bank deposits are often made at a different time than cash is actually received," Karen answers. "We've made those deposits now, so let me show you how we record them in QuickBooks."

To record cash deposits made to banks:

1 Click the **Record Deposits** icon located in the Banking section of the home page. The Payments to Deposit window should appear as shown in Figure 7.13.

Place two check marks here next to the two 01/12/09 dates

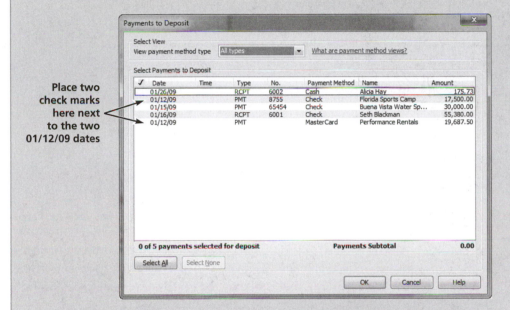

Figure 7.13

Payments to Deposit

2 Click next to the two **1/12/09** dates to place a check next to each, and then click **OK.**

3 Type **1/13/09** as the date of deposit. Your window should look like Figure 7.14. Note the default Deposit To account should be the account Bank of Florida. Note also that the From Account is the Undeposited Funds account, which is where the payments were recorded when first received and accounted for.

4 Click **Save & New.**

5 Click next to the **1/15/09** and **1/16/09** dates to place a check next to each and then click **OK.**

6 Type **1/16/09** as the date of deposit.

7 Click **Save & New.**

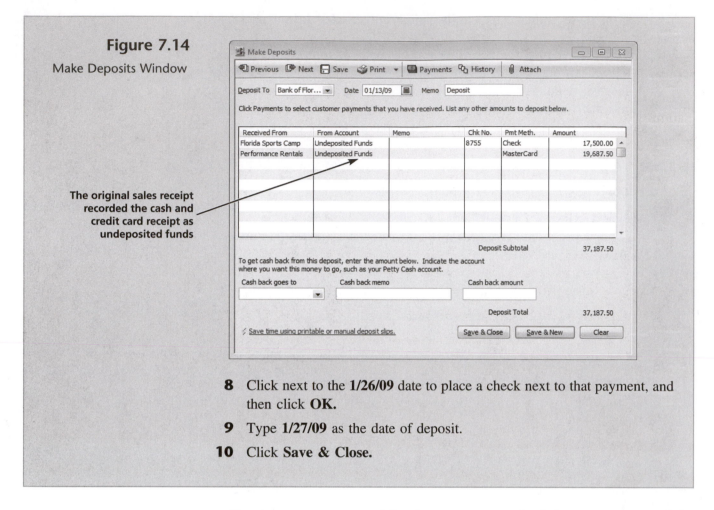

Figure 7.14

Make Deposits Window

The original sales receipt recorded the cash and credit card receipt as undeposited funds

8   Click next to the **1/26/09** date to place a check next to that payment, and then click **OK.**

9   Type **1/27/09** as the date of deposit.

10 Click **Save & Close.**

You have now accounted for the payments received from customers and the bank deposits that reflect amounts deposited to the checking account. Karen explains that the next item on your list is to record the inventory received from purchase order 1001 and the related payment to the vendor.

"When inventory received is related to a purchase order, it's important to do more than just record the check which paid for the inventory," Karen points out. "We also have to close out the purchase order and properly record the receipt of inventory. In this case, we received the two boats ordered under purchase orders 1001 and 1002. Both of these were cash-only purchases in that the vendor did not extend us credit and thus payment was due on receipt. Thus, we'll use the Write Checks process to record these transactions."

Video Demonstration

DEMO 7C - Order, receive, and pay for inventory

To record the receipt and payment of inventory:

1   Click the **Write Checks** icon located in the Banking section of the home page.

2   Select **Malibu Boats** from the Pay to the order of drop-down list. An Open PO's Exist window should appear as shown in Figure 7.15.

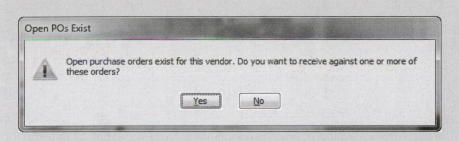

Figure 7.15

Open Purchase Order
Warning

3 Click **Yes.** An Open Purchase Orders window should appear as shown in Figure 7.16.

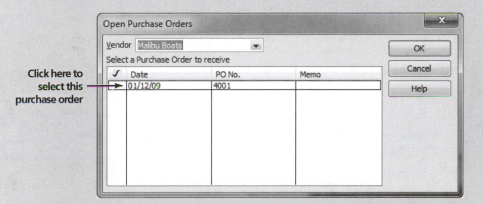

Figure 7.16

Open Purchase Orders for
Malibu Boats

4 Click next to the **1/12/09** date to place a check mark on the purchase order 4001 line and then click **OK.** If a Warning window appears then click **OK** and ignore the warning since, although we owe funds to Malibu Boats from a previous purchase, we are not accounting for that payment at this point.

5 Type **1004** as the check number if it is not already present.

6 Type **1/29/09** as the check date. Your window should look like Figure 7.17.

7 Note that, because this transaction was treated as the payment for and receipt of inventory, the transaction is recorded using the Items tab, and the item being received is that item ordered under purchase order 4001 for $56,000. Click **Save & New** to continue.

8 Select **Tige Boats** from the Pay to the order of drop-down list. An Open PO's Exist window should appear.

9 Click **Yes.** An Open Purchase Orders window should appear.

10 Click next to the **1/12/09** date to place a check mark on the purchase order 4002 line and then click **OK.**

11 Type **1005** as the check number if it is not already present.

12 Type **1/30/09** as the check date.

13 Click **Save & Close.**

Figure 7.17

Payment for Inventory Received

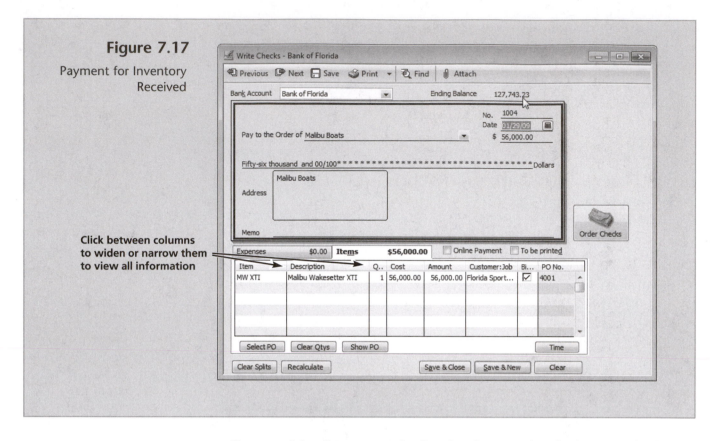

Click between columns to widen or narrow them to view all information

Karen explains that, as a result of paying these vendors for boats received under purchase orders, cash has decreased and inventory has increased. Both customers for whom these boats were ordered were contacted, and they picked up their boats on January 30.

"I'll show you how we record the sales of these boats via the invoice process," Karen says. "Remember that both of these customers remitted their deposits when we placed the order, and thus we only need to collect the remaining 75% balance owed."

"How do we account for the deposits already received?" you ask.

"Recall that, when we received these deposits earlier in January, we credited each of these customers' accounts receivable balances," she answers. "Because of that, we need to use the invoicing process to record the sales first, apply the existing credits, and then separately record the receipt of the balance due on the sale. Let me first show you how to record these two invoices."

Video Demonstration

DEMO 7E - Sell inventory and apply deposits

To record the sales of inventory, application of advanced deposits received, and receipt of payment for the balance due:

1 Click the **Create Invoices** icon located in the Customers section of the home page.

2 Select **Florida Sports Camp** from the Customer:Job drop-down list. A Billable Time/Costs window should appear indicating that this customer has billable costs.

3 Check the **Save this as a preference** check box as shown in Figure 7.18 and then click **OK.**

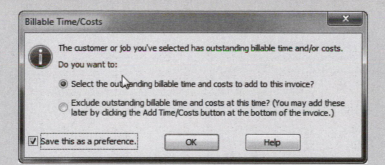

Figure 7.18

Billable Time/Costs

4 Click the **Items** tab to reveal the information shown in Figure 7.19. Note that this window identifies that an item has been received for Florida Sports Camp and is available for billing. Click next to the **1/29/09** date in the ✓column to place a check mark there, indicating you would like to bill the customer for this item.

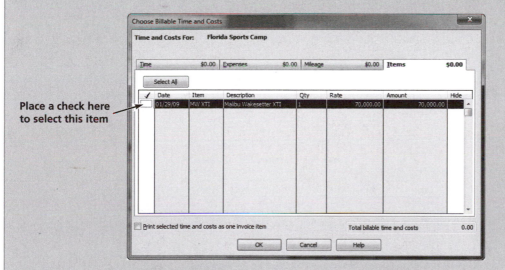

Figure 7.19

Choosing Billable Costs

5 Click **OK.**

6 Type **1/30/09** as the invoice date and **10001** as the Invoice #.

7 Complete the invoice by adding a Bill To address, Ship To address, and Tax item as shown in Figure 7.20.

8 Click the **Apply Credits** button.

9 Click **Yes** two times to accept the changes you made to the invoice and customer. An Apply Credits window should appear like that shown in Figure 7.21.

10 Note that the credit balance shown is the deposit we recorded earlier this month and that it is prechecked for application. Click **Done** to apply this credit to the balance owed on the invoice.

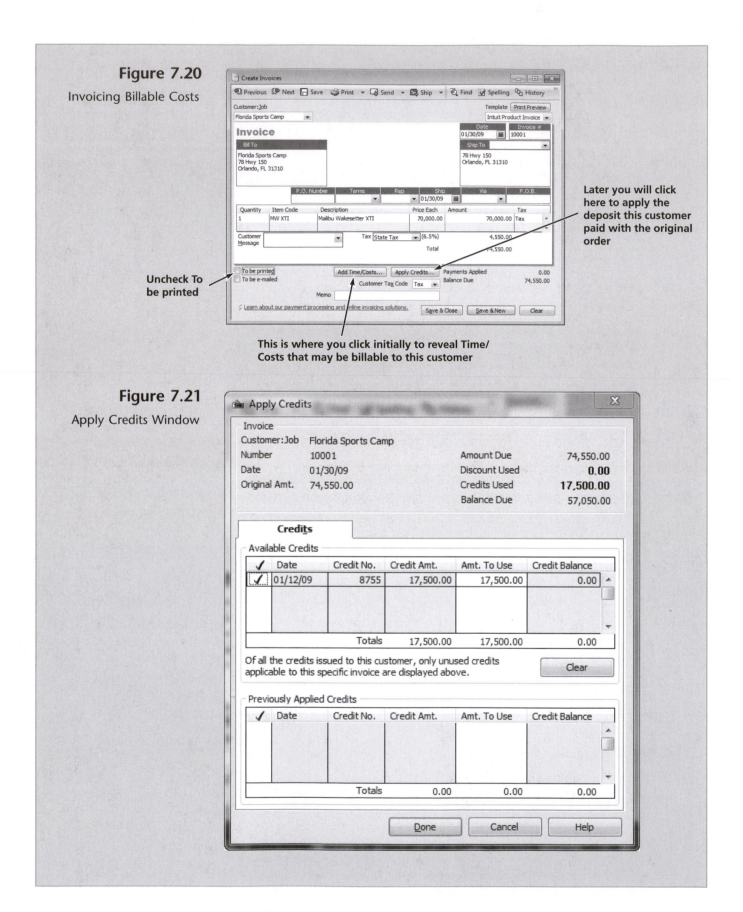

Figure 7.20

Invoicing Billable Costs

Figure 7.21

Apply Credits Window

11 Click **Save & New** to record this invoice.

12 Select **Performance Rentals** from the Customer:Job drop-down list and then click the **Items** tab.

13 Check the ✓**column** next to the 1/30/09 date.

14 Click **OK.**

15 Click **Apply Credits**, click **Yes** to save your changes, and then click **Done.**

16 Change the Tax to State Tax**.**

17 Click **Save & Close**, and then click **Yes** to save the changed tax item.

Now that the invoices are recorded, it follows that sales and accounts receivable have been increased, cost of goods sold has been increased, and inventory has been decreased. Wild Water can now record the receipt of full payment from the customers and record the related deposit to their bank account. Florida Sports Camp remitted $57,050 as the balance due on their purchase, while Performance Rentals remitted $64,181.25.

To record the payment and deposit of funds from boat sales:

1 Click the **Receive Payments** icon located in the Customers section of the home page.

2 Select **Florida Sports Camp** from the Received From drop-down list.

3 Type **57050** as the amount received. (Note that this is the amount shown as due from them.)

4 Type **1/30/09** as the date received.

5 Type Check No. **4532.** Your Receive Payments window should look like Figure 7.22.

6 Click **Save & New.**

7 Select **Performance Rentals** from the Received From drop-down list.

8 Type **64181.25** as the amount received. (Note that this is the amount shown as due from them.)

9 Type **1/30/09** as the date received.

10 Type Check No. **10885.**

11 Click **Save & Close.**

12 Click **Record Deposits** from the Banking section of the home page.

Figure 7.22

Recording Balance of
Payment Due from
Customer

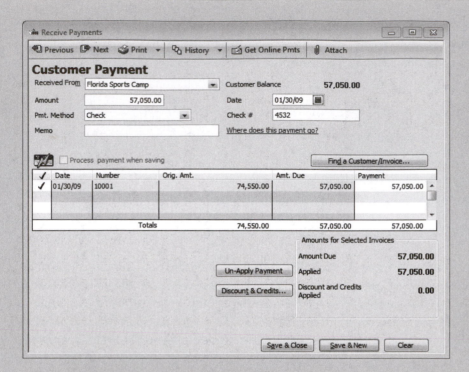

13 Click next to both cash receipts dated **1/30/09** to include them in this deposit, and then click **OK.**

14 Click **Save & Close** to record this deposit.

"Next," Karen comments, "I'd like to show you how Wild Water will pay for monthly expenses and bills. Currently, most of our vendors want us to pay on receipt of their bills, so we've been recording expenses only when we pay the bills. In a couple of months, we will be in a position to ask for credit terms from most of our vendors. In the meantime, we write checks at the end of the month to pay for expenses."

Video Demonstration

DEMO 7F - Pay expenses

One of their payments was for insurance for the year, which will be treated as prepaid insurance and adjusted prior to preparing financial statements. A second payment represents inventory parts received earlier in the month (oil, air filters, and oil filters used in servicing boats). Still another represents an amount due to Malibu Boats, which was established as a liability when the company was first set up. This payment requires the use of QuickBooks's bill payment process. The balance of their payments this month relate to expenses already incurred.

"Let's first look at how we pay for expenses and inventory parts," Karen suggests.

To record checks written for expenses and inventory parts:

1 Click the **Write Checks** icon in the Banking section of the home page.

2 Type **1006** as the check number if it is not already there.

3 Type **1/31/09** as the check date.

4 Type **Manchester Insurance** in the Pay to the Order of section of the check and then press **[Tab]**.

5 Click **SetUp** in the Name Not Found window.

6 Select **Vendor** from the Select Name Type window, and then click **OK**.

7 Type **Manchester Insurance** in the Company Name text box.

8 Type the vendor's address as **234 Wilshire Blvd., Los Angeles, CA 91335.**

9 Click **OK** in the New Vendor window.

10 Type **22000** as the check amount and then press **[Tab]** five times.

11 Select **Add New** from the Account drop-down list.

12 Select the **Other Account Types** option and then select **Other Current Asset** from the drop-down list in the Add New Account window.

13 Click **Continue.**

14 Type **Prepaid Insurance** in the Account section, and then click **Save & Close.**

15 Press **[Tab]** twice. Your window should look like Figure 7.23.

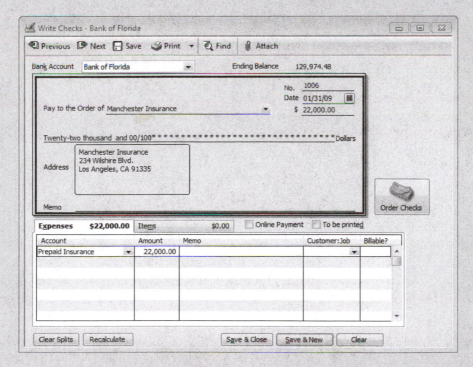

Figure 7.23

Payment for Prepaid Insurance

16 Click **Save & New.**

17 Type **1007** as the check number if it is not already there.

18 Type **1/31/09** as the check date if it is not already there.

19 Type **Chevron/Mobil** in the Pay to the Order of section of the check, and then press **[Tab]**.

20 Click **SetUp** in the Name Not Found window.

21 Select **Vendor** from the Select Name Type window, and then click **OK**.

22 Type **Chevron/Mobil** in the Company Name text box.

23 Type the vendor's address as **2389 Peachtree Blvd., Atlanta, GA 30311.**

24 Click **OK** in the New Vendor window.

25 Type **1600** as the check amount and then press **[Tab]**.

26 Click the **Items** tab to make it active.

27 Select **Air filter** from the Item drop-down list.

28 Type **25** as the Qty.

29 Click in the next line below the air filter you just added.

30 Select **Engine Oil** from the Item drop-down list.

31 Type **150** as the Qty.

32 Click in the next line below the engine oil you just added.

33 Select **Oil Filter** from the Item drop-down list.

34 Type **25** as the Qty and then press **[Tab]**. Your screen should look like Figure 7.24.

Figure 7.24

Payment for Inventory Parts

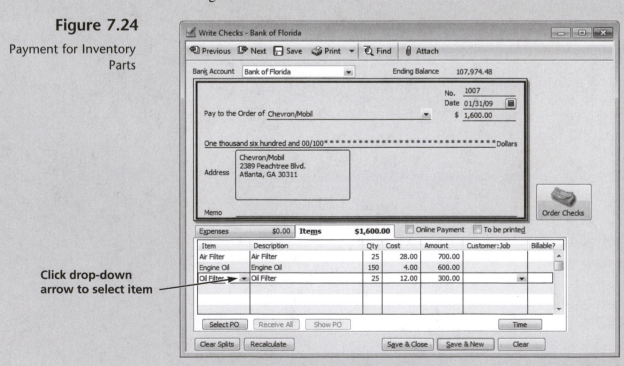

Click drop-down arrow to select item

35 Click **Save & New.**

36 Type **1008** as the check number if it is not already there.

37 Type **1/31/09** as the check date if it is not already there.

38 Type **Central Florida Gas & Electric** in the Pay to the Order of section of the check and then press **[Tab].**

39 Click **Quick Add** in the Name Not Found window.

40 Select **Vendor** from the Select Name Type window, and then click **OK.**

41 Type **890** as the amount.

42 Click the **Expenses** tab to make it active.

43 Select **Utilities** from the Account drop-down list and press **[Tab]** twice. Your window should look like Figure 7.25.

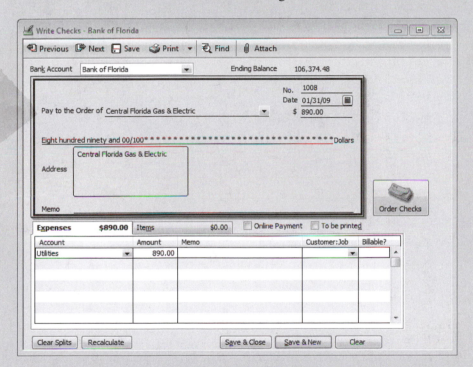

Figure 7.25
Payment of Utilities

44 Click **Save & New.**

45 Type **1009** as the check number if it is not already there.

46 Type **1/31/09** as the check date if it is not already there.

47 Type **Verizon** in the Pay to the Order of section of the check, and then press **[Tab].**

48 Click **Quick Add** in the Name Not Found window.

49 Select Vendor from the Select Name Type window, and then click **OK.**

50 Type **1700** as the amount.

---

51 Click the **Expenses** tab to make it active.

52 Select **Telephone Expense** from the Account drop-down list.

53 Click **Save & Close.**

"Let's now look at how we pay for bills already established in accounts payable," Karen suggests.

To record checks written to pay bills:

1 Click the **Pay Bills** icon in the Vendor section of the home page. The Pay Bills window should appear as shown in Figure 7.26.

Figure 7.26

Payment of Bills

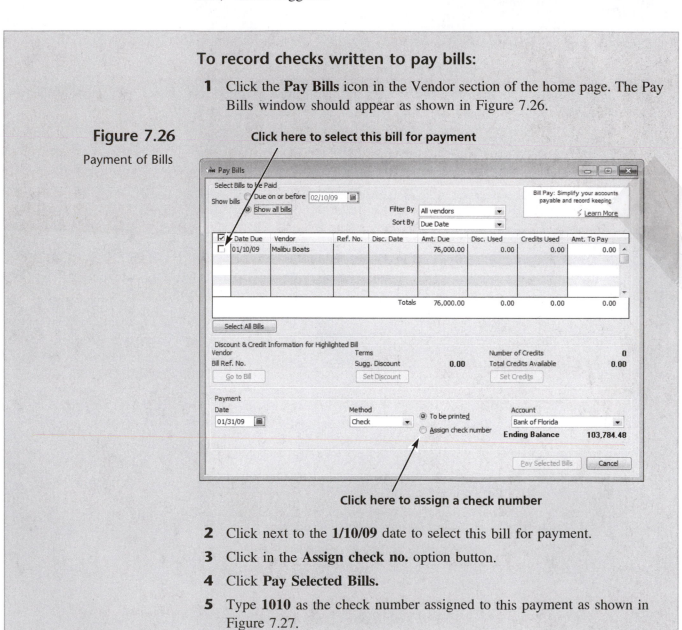

Click here to select this bill for payment

Click here to assign a check number

2 Click next to the **1/10/09** date to select this bill for payment.

3 Click in the **Assign check no.** option button.

4 Click **Pay Selected Bills.**

5 Type **1010** as the check number assigned to this payment as shown in Figure 7.27.

6 Click **OK** and then click **Done.**

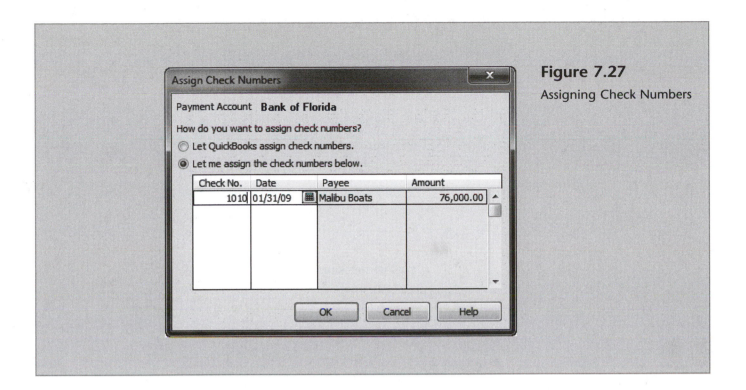

Figure 7.27
Assigning Check Numbers

Now it's time to calculate payroll. Karen explains that entering information about payroll is a little tricky because Wild Water has decided not to use QuickBooks's payroll service. To participate at any level would have required a monthly or annual fee and, since Wild Water has so few employees, the company has decided to compute payroll manually.

Video Demonstration

⏵

DEMO 7G - Recording payroll timesheets

"Is that why we previously set up Wild Water to calculate payroll manually?" you ask.

"Exactly," Karen answers. "That was a part of the QuickBooks setup process. Now we are going to enter payroll information for the month of January."

"Wouldn't it be faster to use the payroll service?" you ask.

"Well, yes," she responds, "but, as you'll see, entering payroll withholding and tax information manually isn't that difficult."

"QuickBooks has a nice time sheet capability, which is how we'll track Ryder's and Pat's time," Karen explains. "It also has a job cost tracking feature so that, when either Ryder or Pat works on a specific boat, their time can be automatically charged to a customer and a specific job for that customer. Time sheets are typically used when a company is trying to keep track of hours worked on specific jobs, but they are not required. Many companies who don't track job costs will only enter the hours for each employee right before processing the payroll. However, in this company's situation, time sheets are very helpful. Before we can enter the employees' time, we must make sure that a customer/job entry is set up. Later, we'll do this during the month as each job is started, but for now we'll enter them after the fact. Two jobs were started in the last couple of days of January, one for Florida Sports Camp and one for Freebirds. Let me show you how to create those jobs entries, both of which are for customers we've already created in QuickBooks."

To create new jobs for existing customers:

1 Click the **Customers** button in the Customers section of the home page to open the Customer Center.

2 Select **Florida Sports Camp** from the list of customers and jobs.

3 Click the **New Customer & Job** button and then select **Add Job** from the menu options provided as shown in Figure 7.28.

Figure 7.28

Creating a New Job

Click Add Job →

Select this customer first before clicking Add Job

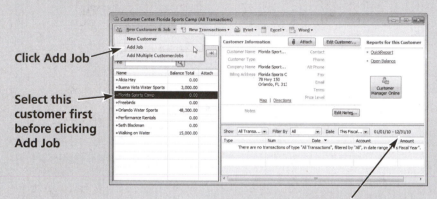

Depending on your current system date this information may be different

4 Type **50001** as the Job Name, and then click **OK.**

5 Select **Freebirds** from the list of customers and jobs.

6 Click the **New Customer & Job** button, and then select **Add Job** from the menu options provided.

7 Type **50002** as the Job Name, and then click **OK.**

8 The Customer Center should now reflect the two new jobs added and should look like Figure 7.29.

Figure 7.29

Customer Center Window

Note the two new jobs added ←

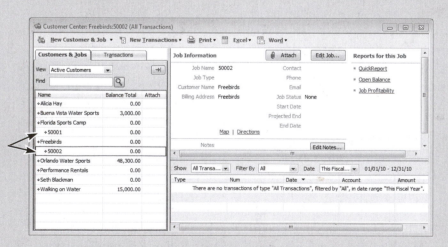

9 Close the Customer Center window.

With the two new jobs added, Karen explains that you can now enter the hours worked into QuickBooks's time sheets, which are organized by week.

To complete weekly time sheets for January:

1 Click the **Enter Time** icon from the Employees section of the home page.

2 Select **Use Weekly Time Sheet** from the menu options provided.

3 Click the **Calendar** icon and then click either the right or left arrow to navigate to the month of January 2009 as shown in Figure 7.30.

Your dates here will be different as this corresponds to the week that includes your current system date

Figure 7.30

Setting Time Sheet Date

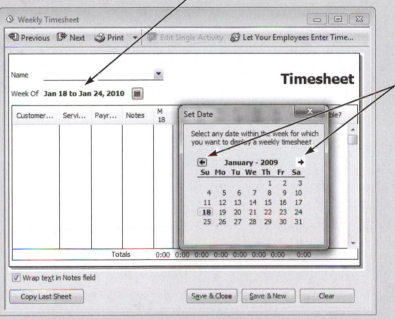

Click either arrow to navigate to January 2009

4 Click on the 5 in the January calendar.

5 Select **Ryder Zacovic** from the drop-down name list presented in the weekly time sheet. Click **Yes** to set up this employee to use time data.

6 Choose **Hourly** from the Payroll Item drop-down list.

7 Type **6** and **4** as the hours worked on M 1/5/09 and Tu 1/6/09, respectively.

8 Click on the **Billable** column (the far right column), which will uncheck the billable check box and so indicate that this line is not billable. Your screen should look like Figure 7.31.

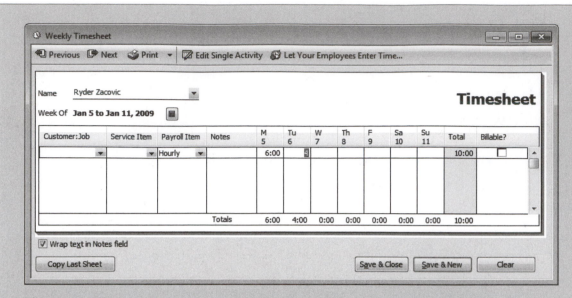

Figure 7.31

Time Sheet for Ryder Zacovic for the Week Beginning 1/5/09

9   Click the **Next** button. (*Note:* This creates a new time sheet for the next week for the current employee.)

10 Choose **Hourly** from the Payroll Item drop-down list.

11 Type **8**, **6**, and **4** as the hours worked on M 1/12/09, W 1/14/09, and F 1/16/09.

12 Click on the **Billable** column (the far right column) to indicate that this line is not billable.

13 Click the **Next** button.

14 Use the same process to record hourly nonbillable hours for Ryder Zacovic of 8 hours each day on 1/19/09, 1/21/09, and 1/23/09. Then click **Next.**

15 Select **50002** as the Customer:Job from the drop-down list in the first column's first row.

16 Select **20 Hour Service** as the Service Item.

17 Select **Hourly** as the Payroll Item.

18 Type **3** in the F 30 column to record 3 hours worked on Friday 1/30/09.

19 Leave the Billable column checked.

20 Select **50002** as the Customer:Job from the drop-down list in the first column's second row.

21 Select **Painting & Body Repairs** as the Service Item.

22 Select **Hourly** as the Payroll Item.

23 Type **4** in the F 30 column to record 4 hours worked on Friday 1/30/09.

24 Leave the Billable column checked.

25 Select **Hourly** as the Payroll Item in the third row.

26 Type **1** in the F 30 column to record 1 hour worked on Friday 1/30/09.

27 Click in the **Billable** column to uncheck the box. Your screen should look like Figure 7.32.

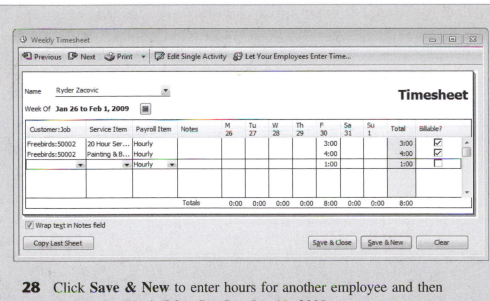

Figure 7.32

Time Sheet for Ryder Zacovic for the Week of Jan 26 to Feb 1, 2009

28 Click **Save & New** to enter hours for another employee and then change the Week Of to Jan 5 to Jan 11, 2009.

29 Select **Pat Ng** from the Name drop-down list.

30 Click **Yes** to set up this employee to use time data.

31 Use the process you have learned to enter the following time data on time sheets for Pat Ng (all times use the Hourly Payroll Item).

Date	Hours	Customer:Job	Service Item	Billable ?
1/5/09	6	n/a	n/a	No
1/6/09	4	n/a	n/a	No
1/12/09	2	n/a	n/a	No
1/14/09	4	n/a	n/a	No
1/16/09	6	n/a	n/a	No
1/19/09	8	n/a	n/a	No
1/21/09	8	n/a	n/a	No
1/23/09	8	n/a	n/a	No
1/29/09	6	50001	Engine Tune-Up	Yes
1/29/09	1	50001	Cleaning	Yes
1/29/09	1	n/a	n/a	No

32 When you've entered all the hours for Ryder and Pat, click **Save & Close** to close the Weekly Time sheet window.

"That takes care of January's hourly time sheets, but now we have to process payroll for those time sheets and for our two salaried employees," Karen remarks.

To process payroll for January:

1 Click **Pay Employees** from the Employees section of the home page.

2 Click **No** if the QuickBooks Payroll Service window appears.

3 Type **1/31/09** in the Pay Period Ends text box and then press **[Tab].**

4 Click **Yes** to refresh the data for time-card employees.

5 Type **1/31/09** in the Check Date text box and then press **[Tab].**

6 Select **Bank of Florida** in the Bank Account text box.

7 Resize the columns if need be to view all columns, and then click **Check All.** Your window should look like Figure 7.33.

Figure 7.33

Selecting Employees to Pay

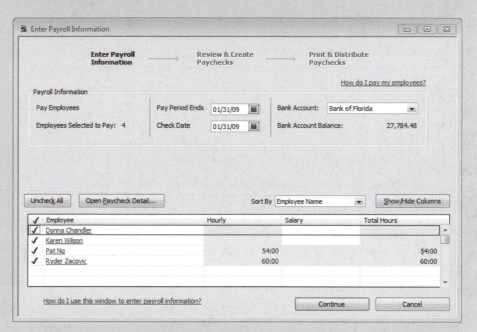

8 Click the **Continue** button in the lower right-hand corner of your window.

Trouble? If the window doesn't show all of the information you were expecting, just double-click the title bar of that window so that it enlarges to the maximum size of your screen.

9 Verify the number of hours for both hourly employees to make sure you have accounted for all hours specified in the schedule provided. In this case, the Review and Create Paychecks window indicates 54 hours for Pat Ng and 60 hours for Ryder Zacovic.

10 Click the text **Donna Chandler** in the Employee column. Enter information for Donna Chandler's paycheck from Figure 7.34. Be sure to put employee amounts as negative numbers and company amounts as positive numbers.

11 Verify the net check amount on your screen with the net check amount in Figure 7.34, and then click **Save & Next.**

If a company doesn't use time sheets, you would place hours worked (for hourly employees) here

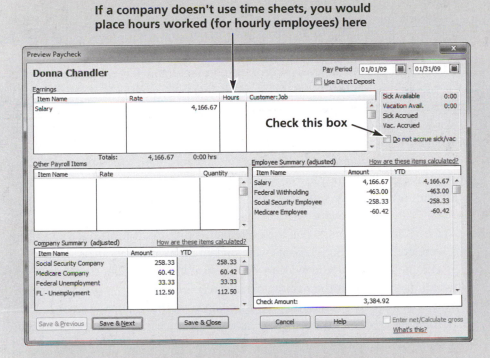

Figure 7.34

Payroll Information for Donna Chandler

12 Continue the payroll process based on the following payroll information. Click **Save & Next** after entering each of the following employees' payroll information:

Item	Karen	Pat	Ryder
Earnings	4,166.67	972.00	900.00
Federal Withholding	–710.00	–133.16	–123.30
Social Security Employee	–258.33	–60.26	–55.80
Medicare Employee	–60.42	–14.09	–13.05
Social Security Company	258.33	60.26	55.80
Medicare Company	60.42	14.09	13.05
Federal Unemployment	33.33	7.78	7.20
FL Unemployment company	112.50	26.24	24.30
Check Amount	3,137.92	764.49	707.85

13 Click **Save & Close** after entering the last paycheck.

14 Select the **Assign check numbers to handwritten checks** option button located in the Paycheck Options section of the Review and Create Paychecks window.

15 Type **1011** as the First Check Number.

16 Click the **Create Paychecks** button located in the lower right-hand corner of the window.

17 Click **Close** without printing paychecks.

"How did you determine the withholding amounts and the other tax items?" you ask.

"Withholding amounts came from the payroll tax withholding tables I downloaded from the Internal Revenue Service Web site at http://www.irs.gov," says Karen. "The others were provided by our local CPA, as follows: Social Security is 6.2% of earnings, Medicare is 1.45% of earnings, and federal unemployment is 0.8% of earnings up to $7,000, while state unemployment is 2.7% of earnings up to $7,000." (See Appendix 1: Payroll Accounting.)

Karen further explains that, since the hourly employees' time was recorded on time sheets, she did not need to enter hours on each employee's paycheck. However, if her company didn't use time sheets then we would enter hours worked by hourly employees in each Preview Paycheck window.

"What about the two customer jobs we charged for Ryder's and Pat's time?" you ask. "Don't we have to bill the customers for the time charged?"

"Yes," Karen answers. "You are quite perceptive. As it turns out, both of these jobs were completed and the boats were picked up by the customers. Had they not been completed, we would wait to bill them until they were complete. Let me show you the process for generating a sales receipt based on time recorded via the payroll system. This should look familiar, since we have already invoiced customers for boats purchased on their behalf. In those cases, when we generated an invoice to a particular customer who had unbilled costs, QuickBooks reminded us of that fact and hence we billed the customer."

"How do we know when to create an invoice and when to create a sales receipt?" you ask.

"Good question," Karen answers. "Invoices are used in two cases. If we've received advance payments (deposits) from a customer, we must create an invoice in order to apply his or her credit balance in accounts receivable. Invoices are also used whenever we bill a customer and don't receive cash payment at the same time. Thus, sales receipts are always used when we want to bill a customer for time or costs incurred or product sales, and we collect full payment at the same time."

Video Demonstration

DEMO 7H - Billing customers

To bill customers for time recorded via the payroll system:

1 Click the **Create Sales Receipts** icon in the Customers section of the home page.

2 Click job **50001**, located under the customer name Florida Sports Camp.

3 Click the **Time** tab, and then click **Select All** to place a check next to the time charged by Pat Ng to this job. Your screen should look like Figure 7.35.

4 Click **OK.**

Click the Time tab to view time charged to this customer

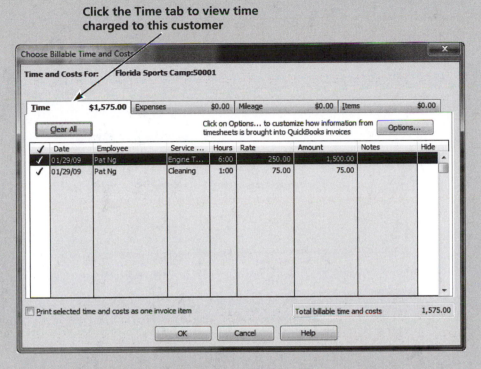

Figure 7.35

Billable Time and Costs

5 Type **1/31/09** as the sales receipt date.

6 Type **6003** as the sale number.

7 Click **Save & New.**

8 Click job **50002** located under the customer name Freebirds.

9 Click the **Time** tab, and then click **Select All** to place a check next to the time charged by Ryder Zacovic to this job.

10 Click **OK.**

11 Type **1/31/09** as the sales receipt date.

12 Type **6004** as the sale number.

13 Type **1000 Boomer St., Tallahassee, FL 32303** in the Sold To section of the sales receipt under the Freebirds name. Select State Tax as the Tax item. Your screen should look like Figure 7.36.

14 Click **Save & Close.**

15 Click **Yes** in the Name Information Changed window to preserve your changes.

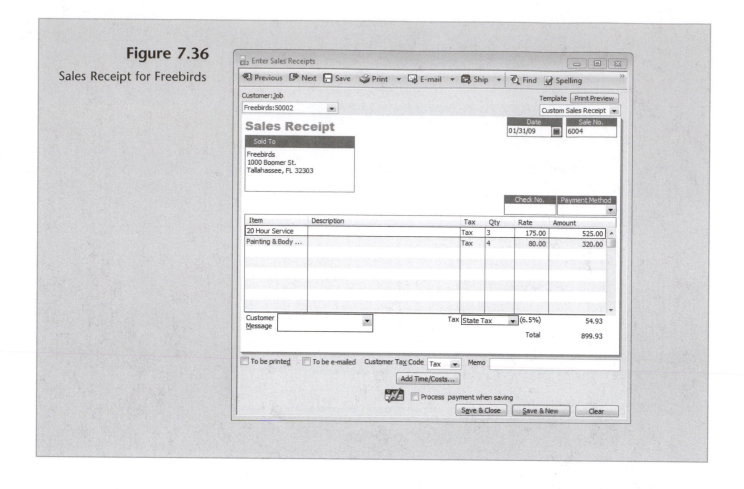

Figure 7.36

Sales Receipt for Freebirds

"Did we deposit funds collected from those two transactions?" you ask.

"No," Karen answers. "We didn't deposit them until the next month. Thus, they will stay in the Undeposited Funds account until we do."

You've now recorded many operating activities including cash sales, purchase orders, writing checks, and processing payroll, and you'd like to know how the business did for the month.

Evaluate a Firm's Performance and Financial Position

The best way to evaluate a firm's performance and financial position at this point is to generate an income statement and a balance sheet as of January 31, 2009. Karen suggests that you apply what you learned from past experience with QuickBooks to create and print a standard income statement and a standard balance sheet for January.

To prepare a standard income statement and a balance sheet for January:

1 Click the **Report Center** icon from the icon toolbar and then click the **Standard** tab.

2 Double-click the **Profit & Loss Standard** view under the Profit & Loss section.

3 Change the From date to **1/1/09.**

4 Change the To date to **1/31/09**, and then click **Refresh.** Remove the Subtitle, Date Prepared, Time Prepared and Report Basis fields from the header as you have done before.

5 Click the **Print** button from the toolbar and then click **Print** in the Print Reports window. Your report should look like Figure 7.37.

Figure 7.37

Income Statement for January 2009

Wild Water Sports Ch 7
Profit & Loss

	Jan 09
Ordinary Income/Expense	
Income	
Boat Sales	200,750.00
Part Sales	40.00
Service	2,545.00
Total Income	203,335.00
Cost of Goods Sold	
Cost of Goods Sold	160,632.00
Total COGS	160,632.00
Gross Profit	42,703.00
Expense	
Payroll Expenses	11,343.22
Telephone Expense	1,700.00
Utilities	890.00
Total Expense	13,933.22
Net Ordinary Income	28,769.78
Net Income	28,769.78

6 Close the Profit & Loss report window and then minimize the Report Center.

7 Click **Chart of Accounts** from the home page, click and move the Accumulated Depreciation account below Furniture and Equipment, and then close the Chart of Accounts window.

8 Expand the Report Center and then double-click the **Balance Sheet Standard** view from the Balance Sheet & Net Worth section.

9 Change the As of date to **1/31/09**, and then click **Refresh.** Remove the Subtitle, Date Prepared, Time Prepared, and Report Basis fields from the header as you have done before.

10 Click the **Print** button from the toolbar and then click **Print** in the Print Reports window. Your report should look like Figure 7.38.

Figure 7.38

Balance Sheet

Wild Water Sports Ch 7
Balance Sheet

	Jan 31, 09
ASSETS	
Current Assets	
Checking/Savings	
Bank of Florida	19,789.30
Short-Term Investments	300,000.00
Total Checking/Savings	319,789.30
Accounts Receivable	
Accounts Receivable	66,300.00
Total Accounts Receivable	66,300.00
Other Current Assets	
Inventory Boats	330,400.00
Inventory Parts	1,568.00
Prepaid Insurance	22,000.00
Undeposited Funds	2,577.31
Total Other Current Assets	356,545.31
Total Current Assets	742,634.61
Fixed Assets	
Furniture and Equipment	245,000.00
Accumulated Depreciation	-7,500.00
Total Fixed Assets	237,500.00
TOTAL ASSETS	**980,134.61**
LIABILITIES & EQUITY	
Liabilities	
Current Liabilities	
Credit Cards	
MasterCard	1,000.00
Total Credit Cards	1,000.00
Other Current Liabilities	
Payroll Liabilities	3,348.04
Sales Tax Payable	13,216.79
Total Other Current Liabilities	16,564.83
Total Current Liabilities	17,564.83
Long Term Liabilities	
Loans Payable	633,800.00
Total Long Term Liabilities	633,800.00
Total Liabilities	651,364.83
Equity	
Capital Stock	300,000.00
Net Income	28,769.78
Total Equity	328,769.78
TOTAL LIABILITIES & EQUITY	**980,134.61**

11 Close the Balance Sheet report window.

"Is there a way for us to see what transactions made up these balances?" you ask.

"Yes," Karen responds. "We'll print a Transaction List by Date report, which will show us every transaction recorded in chronological order. It will include the type of transaction, the date it was recorded, a number reference (check number, invoice number, etc.), the name of the entity (vendor name, customer name, employee name, etc.), the balance sheet account affected (checking, accounts receivable, undeposited funds, etc.), other accounts affected (inventory, revenue, expenses, etc.), and the amount. Let me show you how to create this report."

To prepare a Transaction List by Date report for January:

1 Click the **Accountant and Taxes** section in the Report Center.

2 Double-click the **Transaction List by Date** view from the Account Activity section of Accountant and Taxes.

3 Type **1/1/09** in the From text box.

4 Type **1/31/09** in the To text box.

5 Click the **Refresh** button. Your window should look like Figure 7.39.

Wild Water Sports Ch 7
Transaction List by Date
January 2009

Type	Date	Num	Name	Memo	Account	Clr	Split	Amount
Jan 09								
General Journal	1/1/09	4			Opening Balance E...		Retained Earni...	-20,300.00
General Journal	1/1/09	5			Opening Balance E...		Capital Stock	100,000.00
Deposit	1/2/09			Deposit	Bank of Florida		-SPLIT-	200,000.00
Deposit	1/5/09			Deposit	Bank of Florida		Loans Payable	250,000.00
Check	1/8/09	1001	ETrade		Bank of Florida		Short-Term In...	-300,000.00
Check	1/9/09	1002	Staples		Bank of Florida		Furniture and ...	-70,000.00
Check	1/12/09	1003	AJ Marine Equipment		Bank of Florida		Furniture and ...	-100,000.00
Payment	1/12/09	8755	Florida Sports Camp		Undeposited Funds	X	Accounts Rec...	17,500.00
Payment	1/12/09		Performance Rentals		Undeposited Funds	X	Accounts Rec...	19,687.50
Deposit	1/13/09			Deposit	Bank of Florida		-SPLIT-	37,187.50
Payment	1/15/09	65454	Buena Vista Water ...		Undeposited Funds	X	Accounts Rec...	30,000.00
Sales Receipt	1/16/09	6001	Seth Blackman		Undeposited Funds	X	-SPLIT-	55,380.00
Deposit	1/16/09			Deposit	Bank of Florida		-SPLIT-	85,380.00
Sales Receipt	1/26/09	6002	Alisa Hay		Undeposited Funds	X	-SPLIT-	175.73
Deposit	1/27/09			Deposit	Bank of Florida		Undeposited F...	175.73
Check	1/29/09	1004	Malibu Boats		Bank of Florida		Inventory Boats	-56,000.00
Check	1/30/09	1005	Tige Boats		Bank of Florida		Inventory Boats	-63,000.00
Invoice	1/30/09	10001	Florida Sports Camp		Accounts Receivable		-SPLIT-	74,550.00
Invoice	1/30/09	10002	Performance Rentals		Accounts Receivable		-SPLIT-	83,868.75
Payment	1/30/09	4532	Florida Sports Camp		Undeposited Funds	X	Accounts Rec...	57,050.00
Payment	1/30/09	10885	Performance Rentals		Undeposited Funds	X	Accounts Rec...	64,181.25
Deposit	1/30/09			Deposit	Bank of Florida		-SPLIT-	121,231.25
Check	1/31/09	1006	Manchester Insuran...		Bank of Florida		Prepaid Insura...	-22,000.00
Check	1/31/09	1007	Chevron/Mobil		Bank of Florida		-SPLIT-	-1,600.00
Check	1/31/09	1008	Central Florida Gas ...		Bank of Florida		Utilities	-890.00
Check	1/31/09	1009	Verizon		Bank of Florida		Telephone Ex...	-1,700.00
Bill Pmt -Check	1/31/09	1010	Malibu Boats	Opening bala...	Bank of Florida		Accounts Pay...	-76,000.00
Paycheck	1/31/09	1011	Donna Chandler		Bank of Florida		-SPLIT-	-3,384.92
Paycheck	1/31/09	1012	Karen Wilson		Bank of Florida		-SPLIT-	-3,137.92
Paycheck	1/31/09	1013	Pat Ng		Bank of Florida		-SPLIT-	-764.49
Paycheck	1/31/09	1014	Ryder Zacovic		Bank of Florida		-SPLIT-	-707.85
Sales Receipt	1/31/09	6003	Florida Sports Cam...		Undeposited Funds		-SPLIT-	1,677.38
Sales Receipt	1/31/09	6004	Freebirds:50002		Undeposited Funds		-SPLIT-	899.93
Jan 09								

Figure 7.39

Transaction List by Date for January 2009

Trouble? On occasion, you might accidentally enter the wrong date for a transaction (e.g., accepting the default date, which might be before January 2009 or after January 2009). If you're pretty sure you entered a transaction but don't see it on your transactions list, it is likely that dates are your problem. To verify this, try entering 1/1/06 as the From date and 12/31/10 as the To date. If your missing transaction appears, double-click it to correct the date and you'll be good to go!

6 Close the Report and Report Center windows.

"Not bad for our first month," Karen comments. "But we need to pay off some of the debt acquired with the company acquisition. Plus, we can't forget that some costs such as interest and depreciation expenses have not been accrued or paid, so this information is not complete."

End Note

The two of you decide to quit for the day because you've accomplished quite a lot. You've recorded the firm's financing, investing, and operating activities for the month of January, which included processing purchase orders, receiving inventory, paying for inventory and other bills, recognizing cash sales, and writing checks, including some for payroll. Next up are February transactions and a few noncash activities.

Business Events Summary

Business Event	Process Steps	Page
Financing Activities:		
Receive cash from the sale of stock	Record deposits from Banking section	150
Receive cash from borrowings	Record deposits from Banking section	151
Investing Activities:		
Invest funds	Write checks from Banking section	152
Purchase furniture and equipment	Write checks from Banking section	154
Operating Activities:		
Order inventory	Purchase order from Vendor section	155
Receive cash as a deposit on future sales	Receive payments from Customer section	158
Receive cash on account	Receive payments from Customer section	160
Receive cash from a cash sales	Create sales receipts from Customer section	161
Deposit cash	Record deposits from Banking section	163
Receive and pay for inventory	Write checks from Banking section	164
Sell inventory and apply deposit	Create invoices from Customer section	166
Pay expenses	Write checks from Banking section	170
Pay for inventory parts	Write checks from Banking section	172
Pay bills	Pay bills from Vendor section	174
Create new jobs	Add job from Customer section	176
Enter employee hours	Enter time from the Employees section	177
Process payroll and pay employees	Pay employees from the Employees section	179
Bill customers for billable hours	Create sales receipts from Customers section	182
Evaluate a firm's financial performance	Report center from the icon toolbar	185

Chapter 7 Questions

1 Compare and contrast operating, investing, and financing activities.

2 Describe some of the financing activities you recorded for Wild Water in January.

3 Describe some of the investing activities you recorded for Wild Water in January.

4 Describe some of the operating activities you recorded for Wild Water in January.

5 How are purchase orders closed out?

6 Explain the difference between the Expenses tab and the Items tab in the Write Checks window.

7 How should you account for advanced deposits received on customer orders?

8 Why are cash receipts initially recorded as undeposited funds?

9 Are time sheets required for QuickBooks to process payroll?

10 How does a business know when to create an invoice and when to create a sales receipt?

Chapter 7 Matching

Select the letter of the item below that best matches the definitions that follow. Use the text or QuickBooks Help to complete this assignment.

a. Operating activity

_____ A source document used to track cash sales, calculate sales tax, and totals.

b. Investing activity

_____ This document shows the time spent by one person doing any number of activities for any number of jobs within a seven-day period.

c. Financing activity

_____ A source document that has no effect on financial statements but helps in managing a company's ordering process.

d. Time sheet

_____ Cash received by a company for which a sale cannot be recorded because the product has not been delivered.

e. Customer deposits

_____ An account used to record cash receipts not yet deposited to the bank.

f. Accounts receivable

_____ A source document that includes details about a sale to a customer who owes you money.

g. Undeposited Funds
    account
    _____ An activity where cash or other resources are obtained from or paid to nontrade creditors, long-term creditors, and/or owners.

h. Sales receipt
    _____ An activity where cash or other resources are applied to nonoperating uses such as making long-term productive investments in equipment, buildings, land, equipment, etc.

i. Sales invoice
    _____ An activity where cash or other resources are used to purchase or produce goods and services for sale.

j. Purchase order
    _____ Money that is owed to a business for sales that have already been made but for which payment has not yet been received.

Chapter 7 Exercises

Chapter 7 Exercise 1
CASH-ORIENTED FINANCING ACTIVITIES

Restore the file Boston Catering Ch 7 (Backup) found on the text CD or download it from the text Web site. Add the following transactions and then print a standard balance sheet as of 7/31/10.

a. On 7/6/10 the company sold 1,000 shares of common stock to a new private investor (Broad Investments) for $50,000. Funds were deposited directly into the company's checking account on the same date on their check 23413.

b. On 7/8/10 the company borrowed $25,000 from Bank of America at 8% due in 4 years. Bank of America's check 823908 was deposited directly into the company's checking account on the same date after the company signed the long-term note payable.

Chapter 7 Exercise 2
CASH-ORIENTED INVESTING ACTIVITIES

Restore the file Boston Catering Ch 7 (Backup) found on the text CD or download it from the text Web site. Do not use the file created in Exercise 1 above. Add the following transactions and then print a standard balance sheet as of 7/31/10.

a. On 7/13/10 the company purchased new equipment for $3,000 using check 1501 from Outlet Tool Supply, a vendor.

b. On 7/15/10 the company invested $5,000 on a short-term basis with an investment firm named North Eastern Investments using check 1502.

Chapter 7 Exercise 3

CASH-ORIENTED OPERATING ACTIVITIES – SALES

Restore the file Boston Catering Ch 7 (Backup) found on the text CD or download it from the text Web site. Do not use the file created in Exercise 1 or 2 above. Add the following transactions and then print a standard balance sheet as of 7/31/10 and a standard income statement for the month ended 7/31/10.

a. On 7/14/10 the company received check 25141 from MA General Hospital in the amount of $7,000 as payment on account. Amount was deposited to the bank the same day.

b. On 7/16/10 the company recorded sales receipt 930 for a new customer MIT, terms due on receipt, sales tax applicable, for 50 item A100 and 50 item A200, delivered. On the same date they received check 523420 from MIT in the amount of $1,575 as payment in full. Amount was deposited to the bank the same day. Hint: you can modify QuickBooks preferences to show the Create Sales Receipts icon on the home page to access a new sales receipt or you can select Enter Sales Receipts from the Customer menu.

Chapter 7 Exercise 4

CASH-ORIENTED OPERATING ACTIVITIES – PURCHASES

Restore the file Boston Catering Ch 7 (Backup) found on the text CD or download it from the text Web site. Do not use the file created in the exercises above. Add the following transactions and then print a standard balance sheet as of 7/31/10 and an item listing report showing just the item, description, type, cost, price, quantity on hand, and quantity on purchase order.

a. On 7/5/10 the company ordered 24 bottles of item W100 from the Sanford Winery on purchase order 101.

b. On 7/7/10 the company ordered 48 bottles of a new item W201 (Fiddlehead Syrah, Cost $25, Sales Price $40) on purchase order 102.

c. On 7/28/10 the company ordered 12 bottles of a new item W300 (Foley Pinot Noir, Cost $50, Sales Price $70) from a new vendor Foley Estates (6121 Hwy. 246, Lompoc, CA 93436) on purchase order 103 with terms net 15.

d. On 7/22/10 the company received the 24 bottles of item W100 from Sanford Winery which had been ordered using purchase order 101 along with a bill due in 30 days.

e. On 7/29/10 the company received the 48 bottles of item W201 from Fiddlehead Winery which had been ordered using purchase order 102 along with a bill due in 30 days.

Chapter 7 Exercise 5

CASH-ORIENTED OPERATING ACTIVITIES – EXPENSES

Restore the file Boston Catering Ch 7 (Backup) found on the text CD or download it from the text Web site. Do not use the file created in the exercises above. Add the following transactions and then print a standard balance sheet as of 7/31/10 and a standard income statement for the month ended 7/31/10.

a. On 7/15/10 the company paid rent to New England Property Management (a new vendor) on check 1503 for $3,000.

b. On 7/29/10 the company paid a bill due Sanford Winery for $2,000 on check 1504.

c. During the month of July, Kyle Hain worked 8 hours a day from the 19th through the 23rd, all of which was unbilled time. He also worked 6 hours of billable time on Saturday July 24th during the John Hancock summer supper catered event. Use a new service item (X100, Wait Staff, Rate $25, Account: Catering Sales, Tax Code: Non taxable). Amy Casey also worked 8 hours a day from the 19th through the 23rd, all of which was unbilled time. She also worked 8 hours of billable time on Saturday, July 24th during the John Hancock summer supper catered event. Payroll checks are issued starting with check #1505. Paycheck information is shown below:

Pay/Tax/Withholding	Chambers	Hain	Casey
Hours	n/a	46	48
Rate	$ 50,000	$ 16.00	$ 18.00
Gross pay	4,166.67	736.00	864.00
Federal withholding	570.83	100.83	118.37
Social Security employee	258.33	45.63	53.57
Medicare employee	60.42	10.67	12.53
MA withholding	283.99	23.26	32.99
MA Training Fund	0.42	0.07	0.09
Social Security employer	258.33	45.63	53.57
Medicare company	60.42	10.67	12.53
Federal unemployment	33.33	5.89	6.91
MA unemployment	125.00	22.08	25.92
Check amount	2,993.10	555.61	646.54

d. On 7/31/10 the company recorded sales receipt 931 for John Hancock, terms due on receipt, sales tax applicable, for 175 item S200 and 30 W200 delivered, and 14 hours of wait staff time. On the same date, they received check 12311 from the customer in the amount of $9,747.50 as payment in full. Amount was deposited to the bank the same day.

e. On 7/31/10 the company paid $2,000 to the US Food Service for food purchased and consumed for the various events in July using check 1508. (Note: this transaction is in addition to the existing liability to US Food Service.)

f. Change all wine items COGS Account from costs of goods sold to bar purchases.

Chapter 7 Assignments

Chapter 7 Assignment 1

ADDING MORE INFORMATION: WILD WATER SPORTS

Restore the file Wild Water Sports Ch 7A (Backup) found on the text CD or download it from the text Web site, and then add the following transactions.

Event #	Date	Business Event
1	2/2/09	Wrote Check No. 1015 for $1,000 to Delco (new vendor) as payment for the purchase of five sets of tune-up parts.
2	2/2/09	Accepted a new job (50003) to tune up a boat owned by Orlando Water Sports.
3	2/2/09	Paid $24,000 to Coe Marketing (new vendor) for new advertising campaign, which will last one year, with Check No. 1016. (**Hint:** You'll need to create a new other current asset account type titled Prepaid Advertising.)
4	2/2/09	Deposited funds received 1/31 in the amount of $2,577.31 into the Bank of Florida account.
5	2/2/09	Created Purchase Order No. 4003 to MB Sports to order an MB B52 V23 (a new item) on behalf of our customer, Performance Rentals. Cost: $60,000; Sales Price: $75,000.
6	2/2/09	Collected $18,750 as an advance payment from Performance Rentals (their Check No. 2003), which was equal to the 25% down payment required on all boat orders. (**Hint:** Use the Receive Payments function to record receipt of this payment, and do not apply this payment to any existing balances owed.)
7	2/2/09	Pat Ng worked four hours on Job No. 50003, tuning up a boat owned by Orlando Water Sports. (**Hint:** Record on a time sheet now!)
8	2/3/09	Deposited $100,000 from a new investor, Sam Ski, in exchange for common stock representing a 25% interest in the company. Payment received was in the form of his Check No. 987.
9	2/3/09	Recorded Sales Receipt No. 6005 from Orlando Water Sports under Job No. 50003, based on work performed by Pat Ng and one set of tune-up parts. $1,331.25 was collected via Check No. 9774.

Event #	Date	Business Event
10	2/5/09	Deposited the advance payment received from Performance Rentals and the check received from Orlando Water Sports.
11	2/5/09	Received Check No. 390 for $3,000 as payment on account from Buena Vista Water Sports.
12	2/5/09	Deposited a $50,000 check, No. 188774, from CitiBank (new vendor) as the proceeds from a three-year 6% loan negotiated by Sam Ski. The company plans to use these funds in the future to pay down some older, more expensive debt.
13	2/6/09	Wrote Check No. 1017 in the amount of $75,000 to ETrade as a short-term investment.
14	2/6/09	Deposited a $3,000 check received on 2/5.
15	2/6/09	Created Purchase Order No. 4004 to Malibu Boats to order a MS LSV and a MV on behalf of a new customer, Fantasy Sports, located at 345 Sunset Rd., Orlando, FL 31312.
16	2/6/09	Collected $28,250 as an advance payment from Fantasy Sports (its Check No. 1005), which was equal to the 25% down payment required on all boat orders.
17	2/9/09	Received Check No. 1988 for $43,000 as payment on account from Orlando Water Sports.
18	2/9/09	Sold a MW VLX from inventory to Walking on Water for $57,000 plus tax of $3,705, and recorded the sale with Sales Receipt No. 6006. Received the customer's Check No. 232 as payment in full. Updated the customer's address as 874 Nightingale Dr., Kissimmee, FL 34743.
19	2/9/09	Accepted a new job (50004) to paint a boat owned by Alisa Hay.
20	2/9/09	Made a deposit of $131,955 from checks received on 2/6 and 2/9.
21	2/9/09	Ryder Zacovic worked five hours on Job No. 50004, painting a boat owned by Alisa Hay.
22	2/10/09	Recorded Sales Receipt No. 6007 from Alisa Hay under Job No. 50004, based on work performed by Ryder Zacovic. Check No. 741 collected for $426.
23	2/10/09	Deposited $426 from Sales Receipt No. 6007.
24	2/16/09	Wrote Check No. 1018 to Sunset Auto (vendor) for $45,000 to purchase a truck for the business. (Use Furniture and Equipment account.)
25	2/19/09	Wrote Check No. 1019 to MB Sports for $60,000 as payment for Purchase Order No. 4003 because the MB B52 V23 ordered on behalf of Performance Rentals was received.
26	2/20/09	Created Invoice No. 10003 to Performance Rentals for sale of MB B52 V23 received under Purchase Order No. 4003 on 2/19. Applied the deposit received upon order.
27	2/20/09	Record receipt of payment from Performance Rentals of $61,125 with their Check No. 23098 on Invoice No. 10003.
28	2/23/09	Deposited Performance Rentals check received 2/20.
29	2/26/09	Wrote Check No. 1020 to Bank of Florida to pay MasterCard liability of $1,000. (**Hint:** Record this payment to the MasterCard liability account.)
30	2/26/09	Wrote Check No. 1021 to Central Florida Gas & Electric for $930 for utilities expense.
31	2/26/09	Wrote Check No. 1022 to Verizon for $1,820 for telephone expense.

Event #	Date	Business Event
32	2/26/09	Wrote Check No. 1023 to Brian Ski (new vendor) for $2,700 for advertising and promotion expense.
33	2/26/09	Wrote Check No. 1024 to Staples for $4,500 for office supplies expense.
34	2/27/09	Record time sheet information provided in Table 7.1. **Note:** Some of these hours are in connection with jobs for which time had already been recorded and should already be on your time sheet. Those hours are designated in the table with an *. All other hours not designated by an * are for nonbillable activities.
35	2/27/09	Process payroll per the information provided in Table 7.2, starting with Check No. 1025.

Table 7.1

Time Sheet Information

Date	Ryder Zacovic	Date	Pat Ng
2/2/09	8 hrs.	2/2/09	4 hrs.*
2/5/09	5 hrs.	2/5/09	8 hrs.
2/6/09	5 hrs.	2/6/09	8 hrs.
2/9/09	5 hrs.*	2/9/09	8 hrs.
2/11/09	8 hrs.	2/11/09	8 hrs.
2/13/09	8 hrs.	2/13/09	8 hrs.
2/23/09	8 hrs.	2/23/09	8 hrs.
2/24/09	8 hrs.	2/24/09	8 hrs.
2/25/09	8 hrs.	2/25/09	8 hrs.
Total	63 hrs.		68 hrs.

Table 7.2

Payroll Information for Wild Water Sports

Item	Donna	Karen	Pat	Ryder
Earnings	4,166.67	4,166.67	1,224.00	945.00
Federal Withholding	−463.00	−710.00	−167.69	−129.47
Social Security Employee	−258.33	−258.33	−75.89	−58.59
Medicare Employee	−60.42	−60.42	−17.75	−13.70
Social Security Company	258.33	258.33	75.89	58.59
Medicare Company	60.42	60.42	17.75	13.70
Federal Unemployment	33.33	33.33	9.79	7.56
State Unemployment	112.50	112.50	33.05	25.52
Check Amount	3,384.92	3,137.92	962.67	743.24

Print the following as of 2/28/09.

    a.   Customer Balance Summary

    b.   Vendor Balance Summary

    c.   Account Listing (Account, Type, and Balance Total only)

    d.   Item Listing (list only Item, Description, Type, Cost, Quantity On Hand, and Price.)

    e.   Balance Sheet Standard

f.   Profit & Loss Standard

g.   Transaction List by Date

Chapter 7 Assignment 2
ADDING MORE INFORMATION: CENTRAL COAST CELLULAR

sole proprietorship

merchandising

Restore the file Central Coast Cellular Ch 7 (Backup) found on the text CD or download it from the text Web site, and then add the following transactions. **Hint:** You may want to disable the warning about transaction dates being greater than 90 days from the current system date; this is done in the Accounting Preferences section.

Event #	Date	Business Event
1	1/3/09	Mr. Van Morrison deposited $200,000 of his personal funds into the company checking account. (Remember, this is a sole proprietorship.) Use the Opening Balance Equity account to record this transaction.
2	1/3/09	Signed a lease with Central Coast Leasing (2830 McMillan Ave. #7, San Luis Obispo, CA 93401, 805-544-2875) to rent retail space at $3,000 a month for five years. Payment is due on the 13th of the month.
3	1/6/09	The company temporarily invested $75,000 by writing Check No. 3001 to Schwab Investments (a new vendor located at 1194 Pacific St., San Luis Obispo, CA 93401, 805-788-0502). (**Hint:** You will need to create an other bank type account named Short-Term Investments.)
4	1/7/09	The company borrowed and then deposited $125,000 from Wells Fargo Bank (a new vendor located at 665 Marsh St., San Luis Obispo, CA 93401, 805-541-0143), due in five years with annual interest of 8% and payments made monthly. (**Hint:** You will need to create a long-term liability account named Loan Payable.)
5	1/8/09	The company purchased furniture & equipment by writing Check No. 3002 for $20,000 to Russco (a new vendor located at 3046 S. Higuera St. #A, San Luis Obispo, CA 93401, 805-547-8440).
6	1/9/09	The company ordered inventory from the following vendors:

Purchase Order #	Vendor	Product	Quantity
101	Ericsson, Inc.	Ericsson LX588	40
		Ericsson T19LX	60
102	Nokia Mobile Phones	Nokia 3285	25
		Nokia 8290	50
		Nokia 8890	15

Event #	Date	Business Event
7	1/10/09	The company purchased supplies from Russco for $3,000 using Check No. 3003. These supplies are expected to last over the next year. (**Hint:** You will need to create a new other current asset type account named Supplies.)

Event #	Date	Business Event
8	1/13/09	The company wrote Check No. 3004 to Central Coast Leasing for $6,000 ($3,000 for January's rent and $3,000 as a security deposit). (**Hint:** You will need to create a new other asset type account named Security Deposit.)
9	1/14/09	The company received and deposited an advance payment of $10,000 from the City of San Luis Obispo (a customer) as part of a consulting contract to begin in February.
10	1/15/09	The company received a shipment of phones from Ericsson, Inc., on Purchase Order No. 101. Items were received and a bill was recorded that is due in 30 days.
11	1/16/09	The company created Sales Receipt No. 501 to record 50 hours of consulting services and the sale of 25 Ericsson LX588 phones to Sterling Hotels Corporation. A check was received and deposited for $7,425.
12	1/17/09	The company paid semi-monthly payroll starting with Check No. 3005 for the period January 1 to January 15, 2009. Megan Paulson worked 80 hours during the period. Payroll tax information is shown in Table 7.3.

Table 7.3

Payroll Information for Central Coast Cellular

Item	Alex	Jay	Megan
Earnings	2,000.00	1,500.00	960.00
Federal Withholding	−300.00	−225.00	−144.00
Social Security Employee	−124.00	−93.00	−59.52
Medicare Employee	−29.00	−21.75	−13.92
CA Withholding	−100.00	−75.00	−48.00
CA Disability Employee	−10.00	−7.50	−4.80
CA Employee Training Tax	2.00	1.50	0.96
Social Security Company	124.00	93.00	59.52
Medicare Company	29.00	21.75	13.92
Federal Unemployment	6.40	4.80	3.07
CA Unemployment	24.00	18.00	11.52
Check Amount	1,437.00	1,077.75	689.76

Print the following as of 1/17/09.

a. Profit & Loss Standard

b. Balance Sheet Standard

c. Transaction List by Date

Chapter 7 Assignment 3
ADDING MORE INFORMATION: SANTA BARBARA SAILING

corporation   service

Restore the file Santa Barbara Sailing Ch 7 (Backup) found on the text CD or download it from the text Web site, and then add the following transactions.

Event #	Date	Business Event
1	7/2/08	Rob Dutton contributed an additional $100,000 to the company in exchange for capital stock; this amount was then immediately deposited into the company's checking account.
2	7/4/08	Rented the CAT 50 to Raytheon (RAY) for seven days using Sales Receipt No. 10001 and collected Check No. 983 for $4,233.60. Amounts are deposited later.
3	7/4/08	Rented the CAT 42 to a new customer, Deckers (Deckers Outdoor Corporation located at 495-A South Fairview Ave., Goleta, CA 93117, Terms: Due on receipt), for seven days using Sales Receipt No. 10002 and collected $3,515.40. Amounts are deposited later.
4	7/7/08	Purchased a new J-24 sailboat (to rent to customers) for $42,000 with Check No. 101 from a new vendor (J-Boats, P.O. Box 90, Newport, RI 02840. Phone: 401-846-8410. Terms: Due on receipt).
5	7/7/08	Created a new service item J-24, to be rented out at a rate of $160 per day.
6	7/8/08	Deposited checks (two different deposits) from Raytheon and Deckers received on 7/4/08.
7	7/9/08	Paid existing bill from Catalina of $7,500 using Check No. 102.
8	7/9/08	Hired a new hourly employee, Nathan Snyder (SS# 390-09-2877, single male, earning $8 per hour and subject to all normal California and federal taxes).
9	7/10/08	Received full payment on account from Raytheon of $8,465 (their Check No. 39892).
10	7/11/08	Received advance payment of $1,000 (Check No. 974565) from a new customer, Montecito Bank (Montecito Bank and Trust, P.O. Box 2460, Santa Barbara, CA 93120. Phone: 805-963-7511. Terms: Due on receipt).
11	7/11/08	Deposited checks from Raytheon and Montecito Bank, a single deposit totaling $9,465.
12	7/14/08	Wrote Check No. 103 for $24,000 to Levy Property Management (new vendor) for rent of harbor facilities and docks for one year. (Classify all of this payment as Prepaid Rent, a new other current asset account that will be adjusted monthly.)
13	7/14/08	Rented the CAT 50 to Montecito Bank for 14 days using invoice 7001. Applied the advance deposit received 7/11/08 to this invoice and collected the balance owed of $7,467.20 via Check No. 974637.
14	7/14/08	Rented the CAT 42 to Santa Barbara Medical (SBMED) for 14 days using Sales Receipt No. 10003 and received a MasterCard payment for $7,030.80.
15	7/15/08	Rented the J-24 and CAT 28 to Deckers for 14 days using Sales Receipt No. 10004 and received a Visa payment for $5,745.60.
16	7/16/08	Paid employees for the period 7/1/08–7/15/08. Nathan and Jeanne worked 20 and 38 hours, respectively, during that period. Payroll tax information is shown in Table 7.4.

Item	Rob	Jeanne	Nathan
Table 7.4			
	Earnings	2,708.33	684.00	160.00

Table 7.4

Payroll and Earnings Information for Santa Barbara Sailing

Item	Rob	Jeanne	Nathan
Earnings	2,708.33	684.00	160.00
Federal Withholding	−514.58	−129.96	−30.40
Social Security Employee	−167.92	−42.41	−9.92
Medicare Employee	−39.27	−9.92	−2.32
CA Income tax	−216.67	−54.72	−12.80
CA Disability	−16.25	−4.10	−0.96
Check Amount	1,753.64	442.89	103.60
CA Employee Training Tax	2.71	0.68	0.16
Social Security Employer	167.92	42.41	9.92
Medicare Employer	39.27	9.92	2.32
Federal Unemployment	21.67	5.47	1.28
CA Unemployment	92.08	23.26	5.44

Print the following as of 7/16/08.

a. Profit & Loss Standard

b. Balance Sheet Standard

c. Statement of Cash Flows

d. Transaction List by Date

Chapter 7 Cases

Chapter 7 Case 1:
FOREVER YOUNG

sole proprietorship   *service*

In Chapter 6, you created a new QuickBooks file for Forever Young. Make a copy of that file, and use that copy to enter the following transactions.

Event #	Date	Business Event
1	1/2/08	Sebastian deposited $20,000 into his new company's checking account as his initial investment.
2	1/3/08	Paid Galas $6,000 in legal fees for setting up contracts with future customers (classify as Professional Fees Expense) using Check No. 1.
3	1/3/08	Signed a contract with Panasonic (new customer with terms due on receipt) to speak at its sales convention (half-day seminar) on 1/5/08. Collected a 50% deposit of $3,000 and immediately deposited this Check No. 9873 into the checking account.
4	1/4/08	Paid Office Depot (a new vendor) $4,000 for furniture using Check No. 2.
5	1/4/08	Paid Classic Leasing (a new vendor) $8,000 rent on office space using Check No. 3. (Half of payment represents January rent and half represents a security deposit.) (**Hint:** Create a new other asset account, named Security Deposit Asset.)
6	1/5/08	Spoke at the Panasonic sales convention, received remaining amount owed, provided invoice 501 to customer (billing them for services rendered), and applied previous credit.

Event #	Date	Business Event
7	1/7/08	Received and deposited Panasonic Check No. 9898 for $3,000 into checking account as final payment for services rendered.
8	1/9/08	Signed a contract with Gateway (new customer with terms due on receipt) to speak at its sales convention (full-day seminar) on 1/12/08. Collected a 50% deposit of $5,000 and immediately deposited this Check No. 15487 into the checking account.
9	1/10/08	Purchased supplies (new other current asset type of account) from Office Depot for $1,500 using Check No. 4; the supplies will be used over the next six months.
10	1/11/08	Signed a contract with Adobe (new customer with terms due on receipt) to speak at its officers' retreat (full-day seminar) on 1/19/08. Collected a 50% deposit of $5,000 and immediately deposited this Check No. 698747 into the checking account.
11	1/12/08	Spoke at the Gateway sales convention, received remaining amount owed, provided invoice 502 to customer (billing them for services rendered), and applied previous credit.
12	1/14/08	Received and deposited Gateway Check No. 15623 for $5,000 into checking account as final payment for services rendered.
13	1/15/08	Paid semi-monthly payroll starting with Check No. 5 for the period 1/1/08 to 1/15/08. Anne worked 23 hours during this period. Payroll tax information is shown in Table 7.5.

Item	Cory	Anne	
Earnings	3,333.33	460.00	**Table 7.5**
Federal Withholding	−633.33	−87.40	Payroll and Earnings
Social Security Employee	−206.67	−28.52	Information for Forever
Medicare Employee	−48.33	−6.67	Young
CA Income tax	−266.67	−36.80	
CA Disability	−20.00	−2.76	
Check Amount	2,158.33	297.85	
CA Employee Training Tax	3.33	0.46	
Social Security Employer	206.67	28.52	
Medicare Employer	48.33	6.67	
Federal Unemployment	26.67	3.68	
CA Unemployment	113.33	15.64	

Requirements:

Print the following as of 1/15/08.

1 Profit & Loss Standard

2 Balance Sheet Standard

3 Statement of Cash Flows

4 Transaction List by Date

Chapter 7 Case 2:
OCEAN VIEW FLOWERS

In Chapter 6, you created a new QuickBooks file for Ocean View Flowers, a wholesale flower distributor. Make a copy of that file and use that copy to enter the following transactions.

Event #	Date	Business Event
1	1/4/08	The company sold capital stock to investor Scott Cruz for $100,000 cash. The company deposited the check into the Union checking account.
2	1/4/08	The company borrowed $50,000 from Santa Barbara Bank & Trust. The long-term note payable (new account) is due in three years with interest due annually at 10%. The company deposited the check into the Union checking account.
3	1/4/08	The company temporarily invested $25,000 in a certificate of deposit, due in three months, that will earn 7% per annum. Check No. 101, drawn on the Union checking account, was made payable to Prudent Investments, 100 Main Street, San Francisco, CA 95154. (**Hint:** Create a new other current asset type account called Short-Term Investments to record this transaction.)
4	1/11/08	The company purchased office equipment from Stateside Office Supplies (324 G St., Lompoc, CA 93436) for $20,000 with Check No. 102.
5	1/12/08	The company purchased a used tractor from Gateway (100 Cowabunga Blvd., Sioux City, IA 23442) for $15,000 with Check No. 103.
6	1/14/08	The company created Purchase Order No. 5001 to order the following items from Brophy Bros. Farms, which specializes in daylilies.

Item	Quantity Ordered
Almond Puff	1,000
Calistoga Sun	2,000
Caribbean Pink Sands	500

Event #	Date	Business Event
7	1/15/08	The company paid payroll. All employees worked the entire period. Kelly Gusland worked 60 hours and Margie Cruz worked 75 hours. Checks were written using the Union Bank account starting with Check No. 104. (Do not print these checks.) Payroll taxes and withholding for employees during the period 1/1/08 through 1/15/08 are shown in Table 7.6.
8	1/18/08	The company received its order in full from Brophy Bros. Farms and paid the bill with Union Bank Check No. 109 in the amount of $34,500.
9	1/21/08	The company paid Stateside Office Supplies for supplies expected to last over the next six months using Union Bank Check No. 110 for $1,500. (**Hint:** Create a new other current asset account called Supplies.)

Item	Edward	Kelly	Margie	Marie	Stan
Earnings	2,916.67	900.00	900.00	2,500.00	2,083.33
Federal Withholding	−667.00	−118.00	−118.00	−402.00	−286.00
Social Security Employee	−180.83	−55.80	−55.80	−155.00	−129.17
Medicare Employee	−42.29	−13.05	−13.05	−36.25	−30.21
CA Withholding	−192.30	−19.32	−9.32	−153.55	−61.86
CA Disability employee	−14.58	−4.50	−4.50	−12.50	−10.42
Check Amount	1,819.67	689.33	699.33	1,740.70	1,565.67
CA Employee Training Tax	2.92	0.90	0.90	2.50	2.08
Social Security Company	180.83	55.80	55.80	155.00	129.17
Medicare Company	42.29	13.05	13.05	36.25	30.21
Federal Unemployment	23.33	7.20	7.20	20.00	16.67
CA Unemployment	1.46	0.45	0.45	1.25	1.04

Table 7.6

Earnings Information 1/1/08 through 1/15/08

Event #	Date	Business Event
10	1/22/08	The company recorded its first cash sale to Valley Florists, selling 100 Almond Puffs, 100 Calistoga Suns, and 100 Caribbean Pink Sands (Sales Receipt No. 701). The $6,600 sale was deposited directly to Union Bank.
11	1/25/08	The company recorded its second cash sale (Sales Receipt No. 702) to Eastern Scents, selling 600 Almond Puffs and 300 Caribbean Pink Sands. The $22,200 sale was deposited directly to Union Bank.
12	1/28/08	The company received a check as an advance payment on account from FTD in the amount of $5,000, which was deposited directly to the Union Bank account.
13	1/29/08	The company wrote the following three checks:

Check #	Payee	Amount	Category
111	Hawaiian Farms	$3,000	Rent Expense
112	Edison Inc.	$ 500	Utilities
113	GTE	$ 400	Telephone Expense

Event #	Date	Business Event
14	1/29/08	The company paid payroll for the period ended 1/31/08. All employees worked the entire period. Kelly Gusland worked 65 hours and Margie Cruz worked 70 hours. Checks were written using the Union Bank account starting with Check No. 114. (Do not print these checks.) Payroll taxes and withholding for employees during the period 1/16/08 through 1/31/08 are shown in Table 7.7.

Requirements:

Record business transactions in chronological order (remember, dates are in the month of January 2008). After recording the transactions, create and print the

Table 7.7	Item	Edward	Kelly	Margie	Marie	Stan
Earnings Information 1/16/08 through 1/31/08	Earnings	2,916.67	975.00	840.00	2,500.00	2,083.33
	Federal Withholding	−667.00	−130.00	−109.00	−402.00	−286.00
	Social Security Employee	−180.84	−60.45	−52.08	−155.00	−129.16
	Medicare Employee	−42.29	−14.14	−12.18	−36.25	−30.21
	CA Withholding	−192.30	−23.63	−8.12	−153.55	−61.86
	CA Disability employee	−14.59	−4.88	−4.20	−12.50	−10.41
	Check Amount	1,819.65	741.90	654.42	1,740.70	1,565.69
	CA Employee Training Tax	2.91	0.98	0.84	2.50	2.09
	Social Security Company	180.84	60.45	52.08	155.00	129.16
	Medicare Company	42.29	14.14	12.18	36.25	30.21
	Federal Unemployment	23.34	7.80	6.72	20.00	16.66
	CA Unemployment	1.46	0.49	0.42	1.25	1.04

following for January 2008. (Be sure to keep this QuickBooks file in a safe place, since it will be used as a starting file for this case in Chapter 8.)

1 Balance Sheet Standard

2 Profit & Loss Standard

3 Statement of Cash Flows

4 Transaction List by Date

Chapter 7 Case 3:
ALOHA PROPERTIES

corporation   *service*

In Chapter 6, you created a new QuickBooks file for Aloha Properties. Make a copy of that file, and use that copy to enter the following transactions.

Event #	Date	Business Event
1	1/3/08	Adventure Travel purchased capital stock from Aloha in exchange for $50,000 cash, which was deposited to the company's checking account.
2	1/4/08	Received payment on account from General Motors in the amount of $75,000 (their Check No. 6874).
3	1/4/08	Deposited the check from General Motors into the checking account.
4	1/7/08	Wrote Check No. 984 for $40,000 to World Investments (a new other name) as a short-term investment. (**Hint:** Create a new other current asset account called Short-Term Investments.)
5	1/8/08	Wrote Check No. 985 for $24,000 to GEICO Insurance (a new vendor) as payment for a one-year insurance policy with coverage provided from January 1, 2008, through December 31, 2008; recorded this transaction as Prepaid Insurance (a new account).

Event #	Date	Business Event
6	1/9/08	Received a $24,000 deposit from a new customer, Pixar Studios.
7	1/9/08	Deposited the check received from Pixar into the checking account.
8	1/11/08	Recorded Sales Receipt No. 5115 for rent of Villa Kailani Unit #1 for one week. Collected MasterCard payment in full of $3,120 from a new customer, Coast Union Bank.
9	1/11/08	Recorded Invoice No. 7508 for rental of Moana Unit #4 for one week to Sara Rice. Applied her previously received advance payment of $6,000 to this invoice, noted terms due on receipt, and recorded receipt of balance owed of $6,480 via Check No. 654.
10	1/11/08	Recorded Sales Receipt No. 5116 for rent of Villa Kailani Unit #2 for one week. Collected MasterCard payment in full of $4,680 from a new customer, Berkshire Hathaway.
11	1/14/08	Deposited checks and MasterCard payments of $14,280 to checking account.
12	1/14/08	Wrote Check No. 986 for $23,000 to Furniture King (a new vendor) as payment for new furniture.
13	1/15/08	Wrote Check No. 987 as payment on account to Reilly Custodial. (**Hint:** Use Pay Bills.)
14	1/18/08	Recorded Sales Receipt No. 5117 for rent of Moana Unit #3 and Villa Kailani Unit #3 for one week each. Collected American Express payment in full of $8,528 from a new customer, Bridgette Hacker.
15	1/18/08	Recorded Sales Receipt No. 5118 for rent of Moana Unit #4 for one week. Collected Check No. 909 as payment in full of $12,480 from a new customer, Lockheed Martin.
16	1/18/08	Recorded Invoice No. 7509 for rental of Villa Kailani Units #1 and #2 for one week to Boeing (Terms: net 30); net invoice $7,800.
17	1/21/08	Deposited $21,008 of undeposited funds to checking account.
18	1/23/08	Paid Reilly Custodial $3,000 via Check No. 988 for Cleaning (a new expense account).
19	1/24/08	Collected a $5,125 check from a new customer, ExxonMobil.
20	1/25/08	Recorded Invoice No. 7510 for rental of Villa Kailani Unit #4 for one week to Brice Montoya. Applied his advance payment to this invoice, noted terms due on receipt, and recorded receipt of balance owed of $3,240 via Check No. 1874.
21	1/28/08	Deposited $8,365 of undeposited funds to Bank of Hawaii.
22	1/30/08	Wrote Check No. 989 for $12,000 to Pacific Electric (a new vendor) for Utilities.
23	1/30/08	Wrote Check No. 990 for $3,700 to AT&T (a new vendor) for Telephone Expenses.
24	1/30/08	Wrote Check No. 991 for $15,000 to Sunset Media (a new vendor) for Advertising and Promotion.
25	1/31/08	Process payroll per the information provided in Table 7.8, starting with Check No. 992.

Requirements:

Record business transactions in chronological order (remember, dates are in the month of January 2008). After recording the transactions, create and print the

Item	Fran	Daniele
Hours	n/a	150
Rate		$ 20.00
Earnings	6,250.00	3,000.00
Federal Withholding	−856.25	−411.00
Social Security Employee	−387.50	−186.00
Medicare Employee	−90.63	−43.50
HI Withholding	−442.33	−195.33
HI Disability	−1.25	−0.60
HI E&T	0.63	0.30
Social Security Employer	387.50	186.00
Medicare Company	90.63	43.50
Federal Unemployment	50.00	24.00
HI Unemployment	187.50	90.00
Check Amount	4,472.04	2,163.57

Table 7.8

Earnings Information for Aloha Properties

following for January 2008. (Be sure to keep this QuickBooks file in a safe place; it will be used as a starting file for this case in Chapter 8.)

1 Balance Sheet Standard (Be sure to show the Accumulated Depreciation account as the last fixed asset account.)

2 Profit & Loss Standard

3 Statement of Cash Flows

4 Transaction List by Date

service

sole proprietorship

easy step

job costing

Comprehensive Problems

Comprehensive Problem 1: SARAH DUNCAN, CPA

Use the following information to create a new company in QuickBooks using the EasyStep Interview. Then create and print the reports as requested below.

Sarah Duncan, CPA, is starting her new sole proprietorship at One Constellation Road, Vandenberg Village, CA 93436. She'll start effective 9/1/09 and use a calendar year for fiscal and tax purposes. She'll be using QuickBooks's manual payroll calculations feature to account for herself and her one employee, and her federal tax ID number, EIN, and California EDD number is 574-8541-2. Both employees were hired 9/1/09, payroll taxes are paid quarterly, and no wage code is necessary as they file manually. (Be sure to set payroll to monthly manual calculations and perform payroll setup before entering transactions below.) Sarah lives at 259 St. Andrews Way, Vandenberg Village, CA 93436. Her Social Security number is 574-85-4125. She's married (one income) and earns $72,000 per year. Bob Humphrey, her other employee, lives at 453 Sirius, Vandenberg Village, CA 93436. His Social Security number is 632-78-1245. He's single and earns $20 per hour. Sarah's California unemployment tax rate is 3.4%, the disability rate is 1.1%, and she pays all state taxes to the Employment Development Department. Her business, of course, is in the Accounting industry as a Certified Public Accountant. She does not collect sales tax for her services, nor does she use sales receipts because she invoices her clients for services provided and gives them 15-day credit terms. She does accept credit card payments and tracks time spent on each client's services for billing purposes. She will have two payroll items: salary and hourly wage. She will perform audit, tax, and accounting services for $150, $150, and $100 per hour, respectively. (**Hint:** Create service items for each of these and assign the appropriate income accounts and descriptions to each.) Modify the Consulting Income account to be Auditing Services Income. Employees are paid monthly but file weekly time sheets on Friday of each week. Clients are also invoiced on Fridays of each week after time sheets have been processed. Add the following transactions. (**Note:** Be sure to enter these transactions in the proper date period.)

Chronological List of Business Events

Event #	Date	Business Event
1	9/1/09	Opened a business checking account at Union Bank with a $50,000 deposit as her investment in the business (Bank account name: Checking).
2	9/1/09	Borrowed $15,000 from Union Bank to purchase a copier. Term was three years with monthly payments of $463.16 beginning 10/1/09.
3	9/1/09	Purchased a $15,000 copier from Xerox Corporation using Check No. 1001.
4	9/1/09	Signed an engagement letter to perform tax services for Valley Medical Group, a new client located at 234 Third St., Lompoc, CA 93436. Terms: net 15. Created a new job: 2009 Tax Services for Valley Medical.
5	9/4/09	Purchased furniture and fixtures from Sam Snead, a prior tenant in her rented office space, for $4,000 using Check No. 1002 from Union Bank.
6	9/4/09	Sarah worked four hours each day on 9/2, 9/3, and 9/4 on the Valley Medical job and four hours more on each of those days that were not billable. Bob worked six hours each day on 9/3 and 9/4 on the Valley Medical job and two more hours on each of those days that were not billable.
7	9/4/09	Created Invoice No. 5001 to Valley Medical based on time costs incurred (Terms: net 15). When you choose the hours worked for the week to be billed, be sure to click the Option button and then select the option "Combine activities with the same service items."
8	9/4/09	Wrote Check No. 1003 for $15,000 to Dean Witter for a short-term investment, another current asset.
9	9/7/09	Wrote Check No. 1004 to Wiser Realty as payment for the first and last months' rent and security deposit for $9,000 (one-third for rent, one-third for last month's rent recorded as prepaid rent, and one-third for the security deposit). (**Note:** Both the prepaid rent and security deposit are considered other assets.)

Event #	Date	Business Event
10	9/8/09	Signed an engagement letter to perform audit services for Pactuco, a new client located at 345 Central Ave., Lompoc, CA 93436. Created a new job: 2009 Audit Services for Pactuco.
11	9/9/09	Signed an engagement letter to perform compilation services for Celite Corporation, a new client located at 20 Central Ave., Lompoc, CA 93436. Created a new job: Second Quarter Accounting Services for Celite.
12	9/9/09	Received a payment in the amount of $5,000 from Celite Corporation as an advance on services to be rendered. Be sure to record this as a receipt from the job and not just the customer. Sarah anticipates completing services for this client by the end of the month. She then deposited the check into the Union checking account.
13	9/11/09	Sarah worked five hours each day on 9/7, 9/8, and 9/9 on the Valley Medical job, and three more hours on each of those days that were not billable. She also worked eight hours on 9/10 on the Pactuco job as well as eight hours on 9/11 on the Celite job. Bob worked three hours each day on 9/7, 9/8, and 9/9 on the Valley Medical job and four more hours on each of those days that were not billable. He also worked eight hours on 9/10 on the Pactuco job and eight hours on 9/11 on the Celite job.
14	9/11/09	Created Invoice Nos. 5002, 5003, and 5004 to Valley Medical, Pactuco, and Celite based on time costs incurred (Terms: net 15). Applied credits available for Celite.
15	9/14/09	Signed an engagement letter to perform compilation services for Lompoc Hospital, a new client located at 233 D St., Lompoc, CA 93436. Created a new job: Second Quarter Accounting Services for Lompoc Hospital.
16	9/16/09	Received check for $7,200 from Valley Medical as payment on account.
17	9/17/09	Deposited Valley Medical's check into the Union savings account.
18	9/18/09	Sarah worked four hours each day from 9/14 to 9/18 on the Pactuco job as well as two hours on 9/14 and 9/15 on the Celite job. She also worked five hours each on 9/17 and 9/18 on the Lompoc Hospital job. Bob worked eight hours on 9/14 on the Valley Medical job, eight hours on 9/15 on the Pactuco job, and eight hours each day on 9/16 and 9/17 on the Celite job. On 9/18, he attended eight hours of training at a local university.
19	9/18/09	Created Invoice Nos. 5005, 5006, 5007, and 5008 to Valley Medical, Pactuco, Celite, and Lompoc Hospital based on time costs incurred (Terms: net 15). Applied credits available for Celite.
20	9/25/09	Sarah worked six hours each day from 9/21 through 9/24 on the Pactuco audit and two hours each of those days as nonbillable hours. Bob worked six hours each day from 9/21 through 9/25 on the Lompoc Hospital job.
21	9/25/09	Created Invoice Nos. 5009 and 50010 to Pactuco and Lompoc Hospital based on time costs incurred (Terms: net 15).
22	9/29/09	Wrote Check No. 1005 to Pacific Gas & Electric for $400 in utilities expenses.

Event #	Date	Business Event
23	9/29/09	Wrote Check No. 1006 to Mark Jackson Insurance for $8,000 in professional liability insurance for the year 9/1/09 through 8/31/10. (Record to prepaid insurance!)
24	9/29/09	Wrote Check No. 1007 to Allan Hancock College for $300 in continuing education fees for Bob's training.
25	9/29/09	Received a bill from Verizon Wireless in the amount of $525 for telephone expenses for September. Terms are net 30.
26	9/29/09	Received a bill from Staples in the amount of $1,500 for supplies (a current asset). Terms are net 30.
27	9/30/09	Used Check Nos. 1008 and 1009 to pay herself her $6,000 monthly salary and her assistant Bob Humphrey for 123 hours of work at $20 per hour, as shown in Table 7.9.

Item	Sarah	Bob
Hours	n/a	123
Annual Salary/Hourly Rate	$ 72,000.00	$ 20.00
Earnings	6,000.00	2,460.00
Federal Withholding	−770.50	−305.05
Social Security Employee	−372.00	−152.52
Medicare Employee	−87.00	−35.67
CA Withholding	−231.40	−77.98
CA Disability	−4.80	−1.97
CA Employee Training Tax	6.00	2.46
Social Security Employer	372.00	152.52
Medicare Company	87.00	35.67
Federal Unemployment	48.00	19.68
CA Unemployment	204.00	83.64
Check Amount	4,534.30	1,886.81

Table 7.9

Earnings Information for Sarah Duncan, CPA

Requirements:

Create a QuickBooks file for Sarah Duncan, CPA, using the EasyStep Interview. Add vendors, inventory items, customers, and employees first. Record business transactions in chronological order (remember, dates are in the month of September 2009). After recording the transactions, create and print the following for September 2009.

a. Customer Contact List (Customer, Bill to, and Balance Total only)

b. Vendor Contact List (Vendor, Address, and Balance Total only)

c. Employee Contact List (Employee, SS No., and Address only)

d. Profit & Loss Standard

e. Standard Balance Sheet

f. Statement of Cash Flows

g. Transaction List by Date (Type, Date, Number, Name, Account, and Amount Fields)

easy step   *merchandising*

corporation

Comprehensive Problem 2: PACIFIC BREW

Pacific Brew was incorporated January 1, 2009, upon the issuance of 50,000 shares of $1 par value capital stock for $50,000. The business is located at 500 West Ocean, Arcata, California, 95521, and Michael Patrick oversees this whole-sale distribution and sales operation. The company will have a calendar fiscal year, has a federal employer ID number of 77-1357465 and a state ID number of 387-1724-0, and plans to use QuickBooks's inventory, purchase orders, and payroll features. Payroll taxes are paid quarterly, and no wage code is necessary as they file manually. Listed below are the items the company intends to carry in its inventory, the suppliers it purchases from, and the customers (whose billing and shipping addresses are the same) it has lined up. No sales tax is collected because all of its customers are resellers.

In addition to distributing beer, Pacific Brew provides consulting services to customers on bar operations, menu plans, and beverage selection. These services are billed to customers at the rate of $85 per hour and are recorded in an income account called Consulting.

Pacific has two other employees, as shown below. The company's unemployment rate is 3%, its employee training tax rate is 0.1%, its disability tax rate is 1.1%, and it uses only two payroll items for wages: salary and hourly wage. All payroll taxes are paid quarterly. There is no need to track time for these employees because there are no jobs per se. Federal withholding, unemployment, Social Security, and Medicare are paid to the U.S. Treasury, while California withholding, unemployment, employee disability, and employee training tax are paid to the EDD. Payroll is paid semi-monthly and is handled manually. The company does not provide insurance or retirement benefits. Employees do not receive paid time off.

Vendors

	Mad River	Lost Coast	JD Salinger	Humboldt
Address	195 Taylor Way	123 West Third St.	101 Market St.	865 10th St.
City	Blue Lake	Eureka	San Francisco	Arcata
State	CA	CA	CA	CA
Zip	95525	95501	94102	95521

Items

#	Description	Cost	Price	Income Account
100	Consulting	—	$85.00	Consulting
302	Mad River Pale Ale	$5.00	$6.00	Sales
303	Mad River Stout	$6.00	$7.00	Sales
304	Mad River Amber Ale	$4.00	$5.00	Sales
305	Mad River Porter	$5.50	$6.50	Sales
402	Lost Coast Pale Ale	$5.25	$6.25	Sales
403	Lost Coast Stout	$6.25	$7.25	Sales
404	Lost Coast Amber Ale	$4.25	$5.25	Sales
502	Humboldt Pale Ale	$5.50	$6.50	Sales
506	Humboldt IPA	$6.50	$7.50	Sales
507	Humboldt Red Nectar	$7.00	$8.00	Sales

Customers

	Avalon Bistro	Hole in the Wall	Ocean Grove
Address	1080 3rd St.	590 G St.	570 Ewing St.
City	Arcata	Arcata	Trinidad
State	CA	CA	CA
Zip	95521	95521	95570

	River House	Michael's Brew House	Bon Jovi's
Address	222 Weller St.	2198 Union St.	4257 Petaluma Hill
City	Petaluma	San Francisco	Santa Rosa
State	CA	CA	CA
Zip	95404	94123	95404

Employees

	Michael Patrick	Shawn Lopez	Emilio Duarte
Address	333 Spring Rd.	234 University Dr.	23 Palm Dr. #23
City	Arcata	Arcata	Arcata
State	CA	CA	CA
Zip	95521	95521	95521
Hire Date	1/1/09	1/1/09	1/1/09
SS#	655-85-1253	702-54-8746	012-58-4654
Earnings	$50,000/year (salary)	$12/hour (wage)	$11/hour (wage)
Filing Status	Married (one income)	Single	Single

Chronological List of Business Events

Event #	Date	Business Event
1	1/2/09	Sold 50,000 shares of $1 par value common stock for $50,000 cash to various shareholders. Deposited these funds into a newly created Wells Fargo checking account (Name: Checking).
2	1/5/09	Using Purchase Order No. 1001, ordered 500 each of Items 302, 303, 304, and 305 for immediate delivery from Mad River (Terms: due on receipt). (**Hint:** Use QuickBooks Help to customize the purchase order so that the terms of the sale are specified on both the screen and print versions of the purchase order. Always save the terms for the vendor.)
3	1/5/09	Using Purchase Order No. 1002, ordered 400 each of Items 502, 506, and 507 for immediate delivery from Humboldt (Terms: due on receipt).
4	1/5/09	Using Purchase Order No. 1003, ordered 300 each of Items 402, 403, and 404 for immediate delivery from Lost Coast (Terms: 30 days).
5	1/5/09	Rented a warehouse from JD Salinger, landlord, for $2,500 per month by paying first month's rent and a security deposit with Wells Fargo Check No. 101 for $5,000. (**Hint:** Add a new other asset type account called Security Deposit.)
6	1/6/09	Purchased shelving, desks, and office equipment from JD Salinger for $8,000 via Wells Fargo Check No. 102.

Event #	Date	Business Event
7	1/7/09	Invested $30,000 in a short-term investment with Schwab Investments using Wells Fargo Check No. 103.
8	1/8/09	Borrowed $40,000 from Wells Fargo Bank as a long-term note due in three years. The money was deposited into the company's Wells Fargo account.
9	1/9/09	Purchased warehouse equipment for $10,200 from West Coast Supply using Wells Fargo Check No. 104.
10	1/12/09	Received and paid for items on Purchase Order No. 1001 to Mad River via Check No. 105 for $10,250.
11	1/12/09	Provided 50 hours of consulting services (Sales Receipt No. 5001) to Michael's Brew House. Payment of $4,250 in the form of a check was deposited into Wells Fargo Bank that same day.
12	1/12/09	Paid for items (Purchase Order No. 1002) received from Humboldt using Check No. 106 for $7,600.
13	1/13/09	Recorded Sales Receipt No. 5002 to Bon Jovi's for 25 units of Item 305, 30 units of Item 506, and 50 units of Item 507. Payment of $787.50 (in the form of a check) was deposited into Wells Fargo Bank that same day.
14	1/13/09	Provided 60 hours of consulting services (Sales Receipt No. 5003) to River House. Payment of $5,100 in the form of a check was deposited into Wells Fargo Bank that same day.
15	1/14/09	Recorded Sales Receipt No. 5004 to Ocean Grove for 30 units of Item 304, 40 units of Item 302, and 50 units of Item 502. Payment of $715 in the form of a check was deposited into Wells Fargo Bank that same day.
16	1/16/09	Paid employees. Duarte worked 80 hours and Lopez worked 75 hours during the period. Assign check numbers to handwritten checks starting with Check No. 107. See tax information in Table 7.10.
17	1/16/09	Recorded Sales Receipt No. 5005 to Avalon Bistro for 40 units of Item 302, 50 units of Item 507, and 35 units of Item 506. Payment of $902.50 in the form of a check was deposited into Wells Fargo Bank that same day.
18	1/16/09	Recorded Sales Receipt No. 5006 to Michael's Brew House for 100 each of Items 302, 305, and 506. Payment of $2,000 in the form of a check was deposited into Wells Fargo Bank that same day.

Requirements:

Create a QuickBooks file for Pacific Brew. Add vendors, inventory items, customers, and employees first. Record business transactions in chronological order (remember, dates are in the month of January 2009). After recording the transactions, create and print the following for January 2009. (Be sure to keep this QuickBooks file in a safe place, since it will be used as a starting file for this case in Chapter 11.)

    a.   Customer Contact List (Customer, Bill to, and Balance Total only)

    b.   Vendor Contact List (Vendor, Address, and Balance Total only)

Item	Emilio	Shawn	Michael	
Earnings	880.00	900.00	2,083.33	**Table 7.10**
Federal Withholding	−120.56	−123.30	−285.42	Earnings Information for Pacific Brew
Social Security Employee	−54.56	−55.80	−129.17	
Medicare Employee	−12.76	−13.05	−30.21	
CA Withholding	−48.40	−49.50	−114.58	
CA Disability	−4.40	−4.50	−10.42	
CA Employee Training Tax	0.88	0.90	2.08	
Social Security Company	54.56	55.80	129.17	
Medicare Company	12.76	13.05	30.21	
Federal Unemployment	7.04	7.20	16.67	
CA Unemployment Company	26.40	27.00	62.50	
Check Amount	639.32	653.85	1,513.53	

c. Employee Contact List (Employee, SS No., and Address only)

d. Item Listing (Item, Description, Type, Cost, Price, and Quantity On Hand only)

e. Balance Sheet Standard

f. Profit & Loss Standard

g. Statement of Cash Flows

h. Transaction List by Date

Comprehensive Problem 3: SUNSET SPAS

easy step

merchandising

corporation

service

A family friend of your parents, Nancy Mandela, called and said she heard you were studying accounting and might be able to help her set up QuickBooks for a business she just purchased called Sunset Spas. She acquired the existing checking account, accounts receivable, inventory, fixed assets, and accounts payable as of 12/31/07. She would like to use QuickBooks starting January 1, 2008, and needs you to help set up and record the first two weeks of business transactions. You agree and are anxious to get started.

The company's checking account at Bank of America (Name: Checking) had a reconciled balance on 12/31/07 of $23,558.75. Furniture and equipment were valued at $55,000.00, inventory at $23,000.00, accounts receivable at $33,941.25, accounts payable at $35,500.00, and capital stock at $100,000.00. Bryan Christopher oversees this retail operation, which is located at 300 West Street, Del Mar, California, 92014. The company will have a calendar fiscal year, a federal employer ID number of 77-9851247, and a California EDD number of 012-3435-8. It plans to use QuickBooks's inventory, purchase orders, and payroll features. The tables that follow list the suppliers Sunset purchases from, the items it intends to carry in inventory, and the customers it has lined up. The customers' billing and shipping addresses are the same. The company collects 7.75% sales tax on all spa sales and remits amounts collected to the State Board of Equalization quarterly. No sales tax is collected on installation or consulting services. The company records each sale individually.

In addition to selling spas, Sunset Spas also provides installation and consulting services to customers. These services are billed to customers at the rate of $75 and $80 per hour, respectively, and are recorded in an income account called Service Sales. Spa sales are recorded in an income account titled Merchandise Sales. All customers currently have credit terms of "due on receipt."

Sunset also employs two other people, as shown in the following tables. It does not provide insurance, retirement benefits, or paid time off. All employees were hired effective 1/1/08. All taxes are paid quarterly. The company's unemployment insurance rate is 3.4%. It uses only two payroll items for wages: salary and hourly wage. Federal withholding, unemployment, Social Security, and Medicare are paid to the U.S. Treasury, while California withholding, unemployment, employee disability, and employee training tax are paid to the EDD. Payroll is paid semi-monthly. The company would like to use time tracking in Quick Books, but it plans to calculate payroll manually. Payroll taxes are paid quarterly, and no wage code is necessary as they file manually.

Vendors

	Sundance Spas	Cal Spas
Address	14525 Monte Vista Ave.	1462 East Ninth Street
City	Chino	Pomona
State	CA	CA
Zip	91710	91766
Phone	(909) 614-0679	(909) 623-8781
Beginning Balance	$18,000	$17,500
Terms	Due on receipt	Due on receipt

Inventory Service/Items

#	Description	Vendor	Cost	Price	Income Account	Beginning Balance
100	Installation	—	—	$75	Service Sales	—
101	Consulting	—	—	$85	Service Sales	—
201	Maxus	Sundance	$5,000	$7,000	Merchandise Sales	1
202	Optima	Sundance	$6,000	$8,000	Merchandise Sales	1
203	Cameo	Sundance	$7,000	$9,000	Merchandise Sales	0
301	Galaxy	Cal Spas	$4,500	$6,500	Merchandise Sales	1
302	Ultimate	Cal Spas	$5,500	$7,500	Merchandise Sales	0
303	Aqua	Cal Spas	$7,500	$9,500	Merchandise Sales	1

Customers

	J's Landscaping	Marriott Hotels	Pam's Designs
Address	12 Bones Way	97444 Miramar	5144 Union
City	San Diego	San Diego	San Diego
State	CA	CA	CA
Zip	92354	92145	92129
Phone	(858) 555-1348	(858) 555-7407	(707) 555-5748
Beginning Balance	$8,081.25	$18,317.50	$7,542.50
Terms	Due on receipt	Due on receipt	Due on receipt

Employees

	Bryan Christopher	**Loriel Sanchez**	**Sharon Lee**
Address	12 Mesa Way	2342 Court	323 Ridgefield Pl.
City	Del Mar	Del Mar	Del Mar
State	CA	CA	CA
Zip	92014	92014	92014
Phone	(858) 555-1264	(858) 555-3365	(858) 555-9874
SS#	556-95-4789	475-54-8746	125-58-8452
Earnings	$60,000/year (salary)	$13/hour (wage)	$12/hour (wage)
Filing Status	Married (one income)	Married (one income)	Single
Type	Regular	Regular	Regular

Chronological List of Business Events

Event #	Date	Business Event
1	1/4/08	Borrowed $200,000 from Hacienda Bank as a long-term note due in three years. The money was deposited into the company's bank account and a "Notes Payable" long-term liability type account was recorded.
2	1/4/08	Using Purchase Order No. 5001, ordered 10 each of Items 201, 202, and 203 for immediate delivery (Terms: due on receipt) from Sundance. (**Note:** Use QuickBooks Help to customize the purchase order so that the terms of the sale are specified on both the screen and print versions of the purchase order.) (**Hint:** Type **customize a purchase order** in the ask text box.)
3	1/4/08	Using Purchase Order No. 5002, ordered five each of Items 301, 302, and 303 for immediate delivery from Cal Spas (Terms: due on receipt).
4	1/4/08	Rented a retail store front from K Realty, landlord, for $3,000 per month by paying first and last month's rent with Check No. 101 for $6,000. This is a long-term lease for five years.
5	1/7/08	Time sheets were completed for the week ended 1/5/08. Sharon Lee worked eight hours of nonbillable time each day Wednesday (1/2/08) through Friday (1/4/08) and three hours on Saturday (1/5/08). Loriel Sanchez worked seven hours on 1/2/08, seven hours on 1/3/08, and six hours on 1/4/08, all of which was nonbillable time.
6	1/7/08	Received payment on account from Marriott of $18,317.50 and deposited their check immediately.
7	1/8/08	Purchased shelving, desks, and office equipment from Office Max for $8,000 using Check No. 102.
8	1/9/08	Invested $30,000 in a short-term investment (an "Other Current Asset" type of account) with Poole Investments via Check No. 103.
9	1/10/08	Purchased several computer systems and printers from Coast Computer Supply with Check No. 104 for $8,900.
10	1/11/08	Paid for items (Purchase Order No. 5001) received from Sundance using Check No. 105.
11	1/11/08	Created a new job (JL401) for J's Landscaping to consult on various clients.

Event #	Date	Business Event
12	1/11/08	Time sheets were completed for the week ended 1/11/08. Sharon Lee and Loriel Sanchez both worked eight hours of nonbillable time each day Monday (1/7/08) through Thursday (1/10/08). Sharon and Loriel worked five hours each on Job JL401 on Friday (1/11/08) and three hours each of nonbillable time.
13	1/11/08	Invoiced J's Landscaping for consulting (Job JL401) using invoice 6001. Payment was received and deposited that same day.
14	1/14/08	Paid for items (Purchase Order No. 5002) received from Cal Spas using Check No. 106.
15	1/14/08	Created a new job (PD402) for Pam's Design to install 3 Item 301, 1 Item 202, and 1 Item 303 spas in various locations.
16	1/15/08	Sharon Lee spent eight hours on 1/14/08 and eight hours on 1/15/08 installing spas on Job PD402. (Record on time sheet.)
17	1/15/08	Created a new job (JL403) for J's Landscaping to install 3 Item 201 and 2 Item 203 spas in various locations.
18	1/15/08	Created a new job (MH404) for Marriott to consult on future spa designs.
19	1/16/08	Loriel Sanchez spent seven hours on 1/15/08 and eight hours on 1/16/08 installing spas on Job JL403. (Record on time sheet.)
20	1/16/08	Bryan Christopher spent 10 hours on 1/15/08 consulting with Marriott on Job MH404. (Record on time sheet, but keep in mind that Bryan is paid a salary and not for hours worked.)
21	1/16/08	Invoiced Pam's Design for Job PD402 for both installation and spas sold (Invoice No. 6002). A check was received in payment but was not immediately deposited.
22	1/16/08	Invoiced J's Landscaping for Job JL403 for both installation and spas sold (Invoice No. 6003). A check was received in payment but was not immediately deposited.
23	1/16/08	Paid employees for work performed through 1/16/08. Sanchez worked 75 hours and Lee worked 83 hours during the period. Checks are to be handwritten starting with Check No. 107. See tax information in Table 7.11.
24	1/16/08	Received a check from Marriott Hotels for future consulting services of $5,000, which was deposited into the checking account that same day.
25	1/16/08	Deposited remaining balances in Undeposited Funds to checking account.
26	1/16/08	Paid a portion of bill owed to Sundance Spas for $5,000 with Check No. 110. (Be sure to use the Pay Bills feature; refer to QuickBooks Help if necessary.)

Requirements:

Create a QuickBooks file for Sunset Spas. Add vendors, inventory items, customers, and employees first. All quantities and balances on hand as of 12/31/07, including the Checking account and Furniture and Equipment account, should be recorded. Then record a journal entry to transfer the uncategorized income and expenses and opening balance equity as of 12/31/07 to capital stock. (**Hint:** The resulting capital stock balance should be $100,000.00.) Record business transactions in chronological order. (Remember, dates are in the month of January 2008.) After recording the transactions, create and print the following for January 2008.

Item	Bryan	Loriel	Sharon
Hours	n/a	75	83
Rate	$60,000.00	$ 13.00	$ 12.00
Earnings	2,500.00	975.00	996.00
Federal Withholding	–342.50	–133.58	–136.45
Social Security Employee	–155.00	–60.45	–61.75
Medicare Employee	–36.25	–14.14	–14.44
CA Withholding	–137.50	–53.63	–54.78
CA Disability	–12.50	–4.88	–4.98
CA Employee Training Tax	2.50	0.98	1.00
Social Security Employer	155.00	60.45	61.75
Medicare Company	36.25	14.14	14.44
Federal Unemployment	20.00	7.80	7.97
CA Unemployment	6.25	2.44	2.49
Check Amount	1,816.25	708.32	723.60

Table 7.11

Earnings Information for Sunset Spas, Inc.

(Be sure to keep this QuickBooks file in a safe place; it will be used as a starting file for this case in Chapter 11.)

a. Customer Contact List (Customer, Bill to, Phone, and Balance Total only)

b. Customer Balance Summary

c. Vendor Contact List (Vendor, Address, Phone, and Balance Total only)

d. Vendor Balance Summary

e. Employee Contact List (Employee, SS No., Phone, and Address only)

f. Item Listing (Item, Description, Type, Cost, Price, and Quantity On Hand only)

g. Trial Balance as of 1/1/08

h. Standard Balance Sheet as of 1/16/08

i. Profit & Loss Standard for 1/1/08 to 1/16/08

j. Statement of Cash Flows for 1/1/08 to 1/16/08

k. Transaction List by Date for 1/1/08 to 1/16/08

8

Additional Business Activities

Learning Objectives

In this chapter, you will:

- Record additional business transactions classified as financing activities, such as repayment of loans
- Record additional business transactions classified as investing activities, such as selling short-term investments for a gain or loss
- Record additional business transactions classified as operating activities, such as purchasing and selling inventory on account
- Record business transactions classified as noncash investing and financing activities, such as the purchase of equipment with long-term debt

Case: **Wild Water Sports, Inc.**

You and Karen have completed entering business events that took place during the months of January and February and are ready to begin recording transactions for March. Karen explains that, so far, the transactions entered have involved cash-related financing activities such as owner contributions; cash-related investing activities such as equipment purchases; and cash-related operating activities such as creating purchase orders, receipt of customer payments, cash sales, making deposits, receiving inventory, payment of purchases, invoicing time and costs, payment of expenses, accounting for employees' time, and payment of payroll.

In March and April, the company had similar business events to record in addition to some new ones. During these months, the company entered into some additional cash-related financing activities such as the payment of loans, additional cash-related investing activities such as the sale of short-term investments, and additional cash-related operating activities such as the purchase and sale of inventory on account and the related payment and receipt of those transactions. Further, the company entered into some noncash investing and financing activities when it purchased some equipment with long-term debt.

Karen suggests that you work through these transactions for March, paying particular attention to those you haven't encountered yet.

Recording Additional Financing Activities

You recall that as of December 31, 2008, the company had a long-term liability of $383,800. Then, in January, the company borrowed an additional $250,000 from the Bank of Florida, which was due in five years and carried a 5% interest cost.

"When do we make payments on those loans?" you ask.

"Our agreement on the $250,000 loan with the Bank of Florida called for monthly payments of $4,717.81 beginning February 4th," Karen answers. "I was so busy with QuickBooks and the business that I completely forgot! I wrote two checks yesterday to cover our first two payments, and the bank has been kind enough to waive the late payment fee."

The company also borrowed an additional $50,000 from Citibank on February 5th. Payments on that loan are due annually. The loan payable of $383,800 has payments due July 1 of every year.

Video Demonstration

DEMO 8A - Record payment of a loan

To record the checks written to make payment on the Bank of Florida loan:

1 Restore the Wild Water Sports Ch 8 (Backup) file from your Data Files CD or download it from the Internet. See "Data Files CD" in Chapter 1 if you need more information.

2 Click the **Write Checks** icon from the Banking section of the home page. The Write Checks window appears with your current system date and with Check No. 1029 ready for entry. The bank provided the loan amortization schedule shown in Figure 8.1.

Month	Payment	Interest	Principal	Balance
				250,000.00
1	4,717.81	1,041.67	3,676.14	246,323.86
2	4,717.81	1,026.35	3,691.46	242,632.40
3	4,717.81	1,010.97	3,706.84	238,925.56
4	4,717.81	995.52	3,722.29	235,203.27
5	4,717.81	980.01	3,737.79	231,465.48
6	4,717.81	964.44	3,753.37	227,712.11
7	4,717.81	948.80	3,769.01	223,943.10
8	4,717.81	933.10	3,784.71	220,158.39
9	4,717.81	917.33	3,800.48	216,357.91
10	4,717.81	901.49	3,816.32	212,541.59
11	4,717.81	885.59	3,832.22	208,709.37
12	4,717.81	869.62	3,848.19	204,861.19

Figure 8.1

Loan Amortization Schedule

3 Enter the information for the check as shown in Figure 8.2. Be sure to enter the correct date.

Figure 8.2

Recording Payment on a Bank Loan

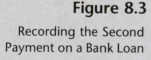

Enter correct date

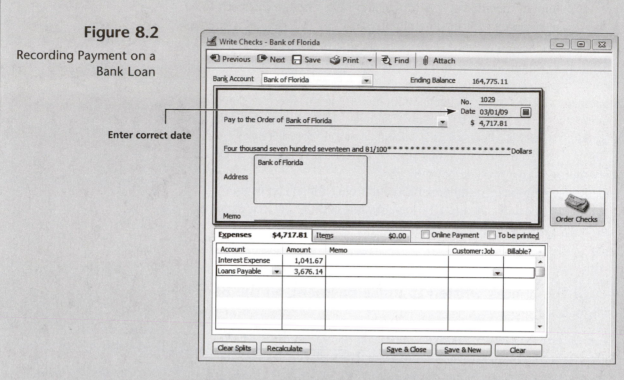

4 Click **Save & New** to record the check.

5 Using the amortization schedule, enter information for Check No. 1030, on the same date, to record the second payment using interest expense and principal information provided. Your screen should look like Figure 8.3.

Figure 8.3

Recording the Second Payment on a Bank Loan

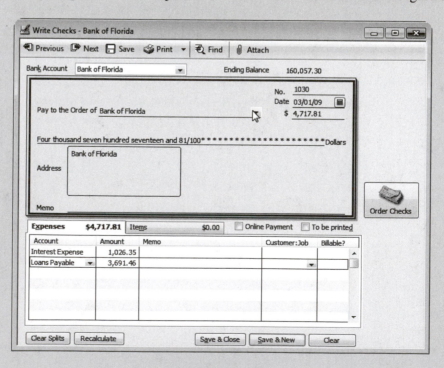

6 Click **Save & Close** to record the check.

With the addition of a new owner and the related funds received from their investment, the company decided to pay down the older, higher-interest (10%) debt with the Bank of Orlando. It made a payment of $387,690.58, which represented the interest at 10% for 37 days ($3,890.58) plus the principal balance due of $383,800. Before the company made this payment, it decided to electronically transfer $300,000 from its Short-Term Investments account with ETrade to its Bank of Florida checking account. Electronic transfers require no check and are recorded by using the account register. Karen suggests you try recording this transfer and loan payment that was made on 3/6 with Check No. 1031.

To record the electronic transfer of funds and record payment on a loan:

1 Click the **Chart of Accounts** icon in the Company section of the home page.

2 Double-click account **Short-Term Investments** to open the Short-Term Investments account register.

3 Type **3/6/09** in the Date section of the account register and leave the number field blank.

4 Type **Bank of Florida** in the Payee section of the account register.

5 Type **300000** in the Payment section of the account register.

6 Select **Bank of Florida** in the Account section of the account register.

7 Click **Record** to record this transaction. Your screen should look like Figure 8.4.

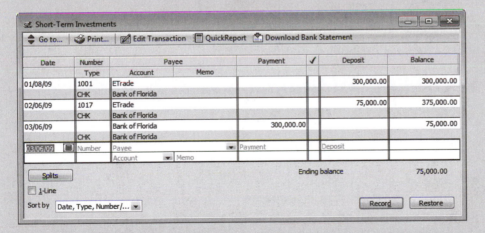

Figure 8.4

Transfer of Funds from ETrade to Bank of Florida

8 Close the Short-Term Investments window.

9 Close the Chart of Accounts window.

10 Click the **Write Checks** icon from the Banking section of the home page. The Write Checks window appears with your current system date and with Check No. 1031 ready for entry.

11 Enter the information for the check as shown in Figure 8.5. Be sure to enter the correct date and add a new name (type: Other) as required.

Figure 8.5

Recording a Check to Pay Off a Loan Payable

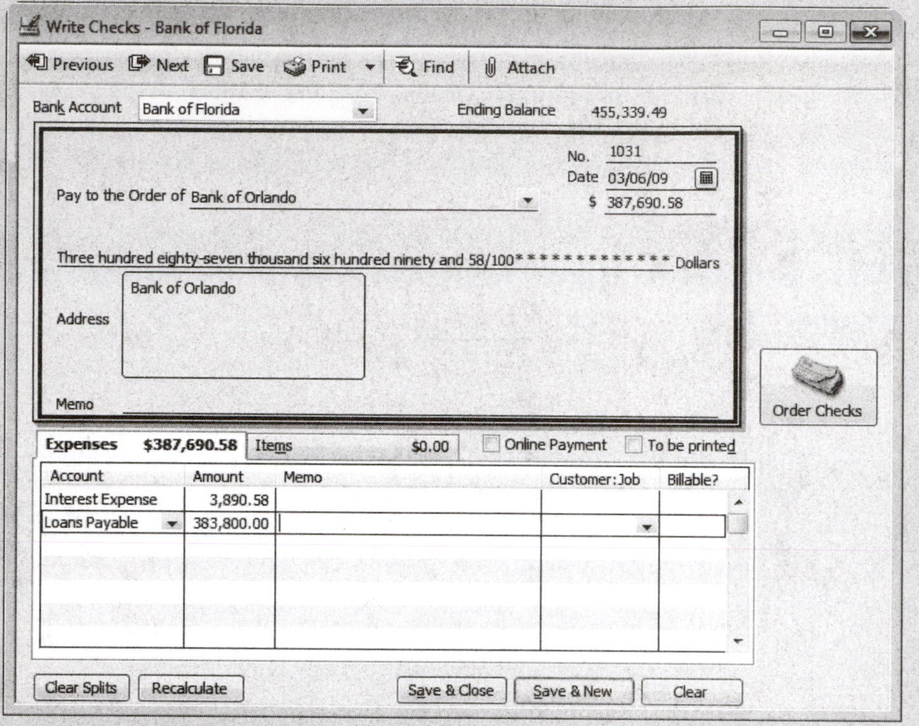

12 Click **Save & Close** to finish this transaction.

You have now recorded payments of long-term debt. Now it's time to look at some additional investing activities.

Recording Additional Investing Activities

You may recall from your accounting courses that investing activities generally result in the acquisition of noncurrent assets from buying or selling investment securities or productive equipment. Wild Water Sports engaged in several investing activities that you and Karen need to record in March. The company made some additional short-term investments, and it sold previously purchased investment securities for a profit.

In February, Wild Water Sports made an investment with ETrade for $75,000. On March 7, it sold that investment for a profit of $3,000. All funds were retained with ETrade. In addition, it used $35,000 of those money market funds to purchase stock in Apple Computer, again as a short-term investment.

To record short-term investment activity:

1 Click the **Chart of Accounts** icon in the Company section of the home page.

2 Double-click account **Short-Term Investments** to open the Short-Term Investments account register.

3 Type **3/9/09** in the Date section of the account register and leave the number field blank.

4 Type **ETrade** in the Payee section of the account register.

5 Type **3000** in the Deposit section of the account register.

6 Click **Add New** in the Account section of the account register. Create a new other income type of account with the name Other Income in the Account section of the account register.

7 Click **Record** to record this transaction. Your screen should look like Figure 8.6.

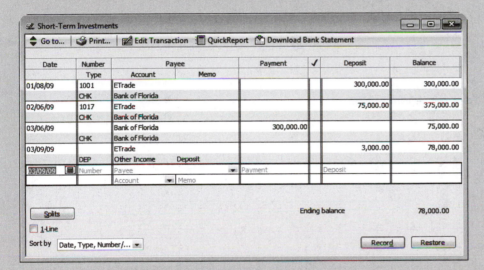

Figure 8.6

Recording Profit on a Short-Term Investment

8 Close the Short-Term Investments window.

9 Close the Chart of Accounts window.

"Why didn't we record the Apple Computer stock purchase in our records?" you ask.

"Well, remember that the funds used to purchase this stock were already in our Short-Term Investments account," Karen answers. "Thus, this is just a reallocation of our short-term investment from a money market category to a stock category. We, as shareholders, consider both the money market funds and the stock investment to be short-term investments; thus, we don't differentiate them in the accounting records."

Recording Additional Operating Activities

Donna has been working hard to establish credit with the company's suppliers. Recently, she's convinced both Malibu, MB Sports, and Tige to give Wild Water 15-day credit terms. Several purchase orders have been created to acquire more inventory for the company's showroom and to purchase inventory ordered by some new customers.

"Now that we have some credit with our suppliers, we'll be able to offer credit to some of our better customers," Donna points out. She suggests that you input the purchase orders created in March and the related bills received from suppliers.

To record purchase orders for the month of March:

1 Click the **Purchase Orders** icon from the Vendors section of the home page. Use QuickBooks Help to add a "terms" field to the customized purchase order form.

2 Enter purchase order information from Figure 8.7. Be sure to provide address information for Malibu, which isn't currently a part of our information for this vendor.

Figure 8.7

Purchase Order No. 4005

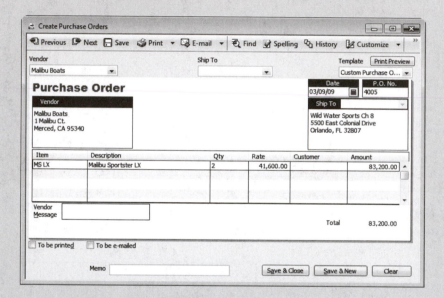

3 Click **Save & New.**

4 Click **Yes** to save the updated address for Malibu Boats.

5 Create Purchase Order No. **4006** to Tige Boats on 3/12/09 ordering 1 T 22v and 1 T 24v (a new item with a description Tige 24v, cost of $70,000 and a sales price of $87,500 using the same cost of goods sold and income accounts as all other boats).

6 Create Purchase Order No. **4007** to MB Sports on 3/16/09 ordering 1 MB 220V (a new item with a cost of $52,000 and a sales price of $65,000 using the same cost of goods sold and income accounts as all other boats) for a new customer (Spirit Adventures, 500 Butterfly Lake Rd., Fort Lauderdale, FL 33308.). Be sure to place this customer's name in the Customer text box as shown in Figure 8.8.

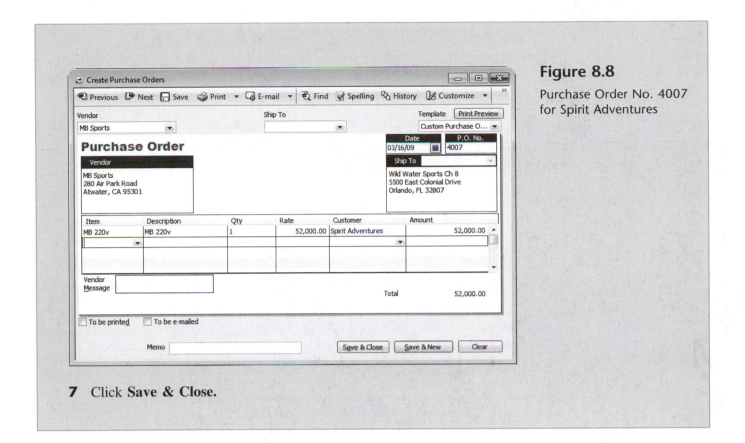

Figure 8.8

Purchase Order No. 4007 for Spirit Adventures

7 Click **Save & Close.**

Some of the boats ordered via the purchase orders entered above were received in the month of March. Because these were all ordered on account, QuickBooks requires that you record the receipt of inventory at the same time you record the receipt of the bill invoicing the company for payment. In addition, boats ordered with Purchase Order No. 4004 issued in February were received in March.

To record receipt of inventory and bill:

1 Click the **Receive Inventory** icon from the Vendors section of the company's home page.

2 Select **Receive Inventory with Bill.**

3 Select **Malibu Boats** from the Vendor list.

4 Click **Yes** when asked if you want to receive against one or more of the open purchase orders for this vendor.

5 Select Purchase Order No. **4004** as shown in Figure 8.9.

Video Demonstration

DEMO 8B - Record receipt of inventory and bill

Figure 8.9

Selecting Purchase
Orders When Receiving
Inventory

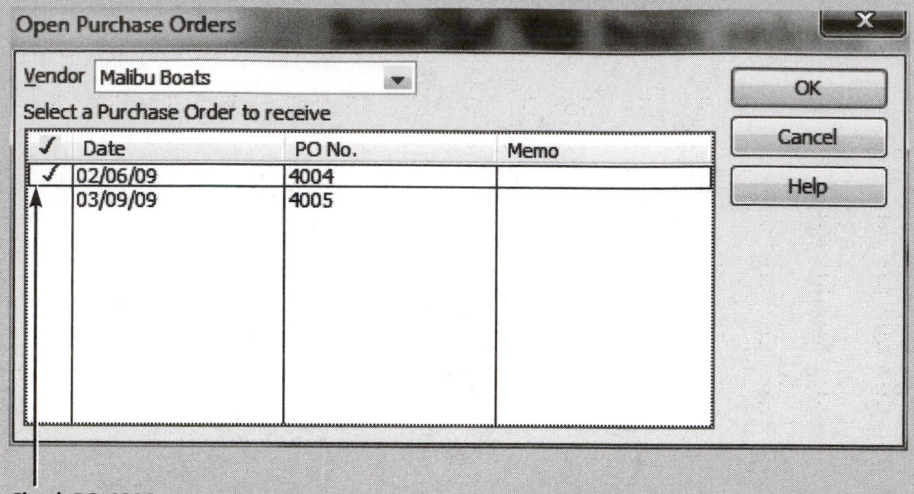

Check PO 4004

6   Click **OK.**

7   Type **3/6/09** as the bill date, set the Terms to Net 15, and then press
    [Tab].

8   Your screen should look like Figure 8.10.

Figure 8.10

Malibu Bill

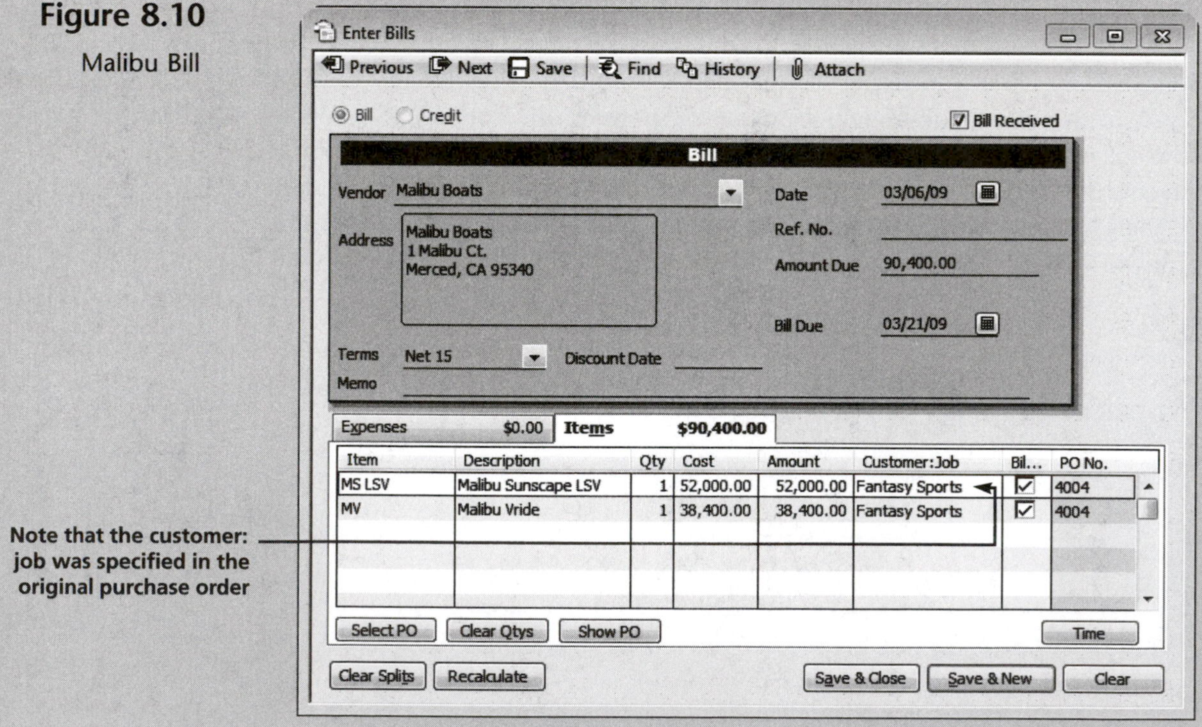

Note that the customer:
job was specified in the
original purchase order

9   Note the Bill Due date of 3/21/09 (15 days from the date of receipt).
    Click **Save & New.** Click **Yes** to save the changed terms.

10   Select **Malibu Boats** from the Vendor list.

11 Click **Yes** when asked if you want to receive against one or more of the open purchase orders for this vendor.

12 Select Purchase Order No. **4005.**

13 Click **OK.**

14 Type **3/16/09** as the bill date, select Net 15 as the terms, and then press **[Tab].**

15 Note the Bill Due date of 3/31/09 (15 days from the date of receipt). Click **Save & New.** Click **Yes** to save the changed terms.

16 Select **Tige Boats** from the Vendor list.

17 Click **Yes** when asked if you want to receive against one or more of the open purchase orders for this vendor.

18 Select Purchase Order No. **4006.**

19 Click **OK.**

20 Type **3/30/09** as the bill date, set the terms to Net 15, and then press **[Tab].**

21 Note the Bill Due date of 4/14/09 (15 days from the date of receipt). Click **Save & Close.** Click **Yes** to save the changed terms.

Two service-related jobs (50005 and 50006) were started and completed in the month of March. Both were for customers who were invoiced and given 15-day credit terms. Karen explains that, for both of these cases, jobs need to be created, time needs to be recorded, and invoices need to be recorded. Invoices are the source documents usually used to record sales on account.

job costing

To record service-related activity on account:

1 Click the **Customers** button from the Customers section of the home page.

2 Double-click **Buena Vista Water Sports.**

3 Click the **Additional Info** tab.

4 Change the Terms to **Net 15,** and then click **OK** to close the window.

5 Click **New Customer & Job** (while Buena Vista Water Sports is still selected).

6 Click **Add Job** from the drop-down menu presented.

7 Type **50005** as the Job Name and then click **OK.**

8 Double-click **Performance Rentals.**

9 Click the **Additional Info** tab.

10 Change the Terms to **Net 15,** and then click **OK** to close the window.

11 Click **New Customer & Job** (while Performance Rentals is still selected).

job costing

12 Click **Add Job** from the drop-down menu presented.

13 Type **50006** as the Job Name and then click **OK.**

14 Close the **Customer Center** window.

15 Click **Enter Time** and then click **Use Weekly Timesheet** from the Employees section of the home page.

16 Select **Ryder Zacovic** as the employee name.

17 Select the week of March 16 to March 22, 2009.

18 Enter the information shown in Figure 8.11.

Figure 8.11

Time Sheet for Ryder Zacovic for Week of 3/16

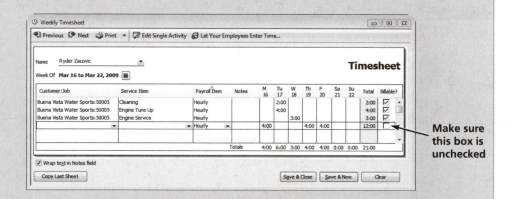

19 Click **Next.**

20 Enter the information shown in Figure 8.12.

Figure 8.12

Time Sheet for Ryder Zacovic for Week of 3/23

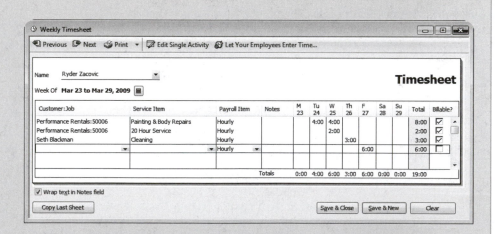

21 Click **Save & Close.**

22 Click Create **Invoices** from the Customers section of the home page.

23 Select **Buena Vista Water Sports 50005** from the Customer:Job list.

24 Click **Select All** to select all three employee charges.

25 Click the **Options** button, select **Combine activities with the same service items**, and then click **OK.**

26 Type **3/18/09** as the invoice date.

27 Type **10005** as the invoice number.

28 Add the tune-up parts, engine oil, air filter, and oil filter to the invoice as shown in Figure 8.13. Also add the address and tax information provided.

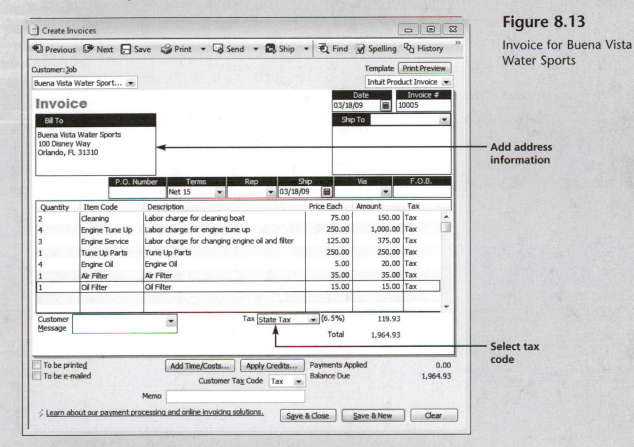

Figure 8.13

Invoice for Buena Vista Water Sports

29 Click **Save & New.**

30 Click **Yes** to save the new address and tax information for this customer.

31 Select **Performance Rentals 50006** from the Customer:Job list.

32 Click **Select All** and then click **OK.**

33 Type **3/26/09** as the invoice date.

34 Type **10006** as the invoice number. Your screen should look like Figure 8.14.

35 Click **Save & Close.**

Figure 8.14

Invoice to Performance Rentals

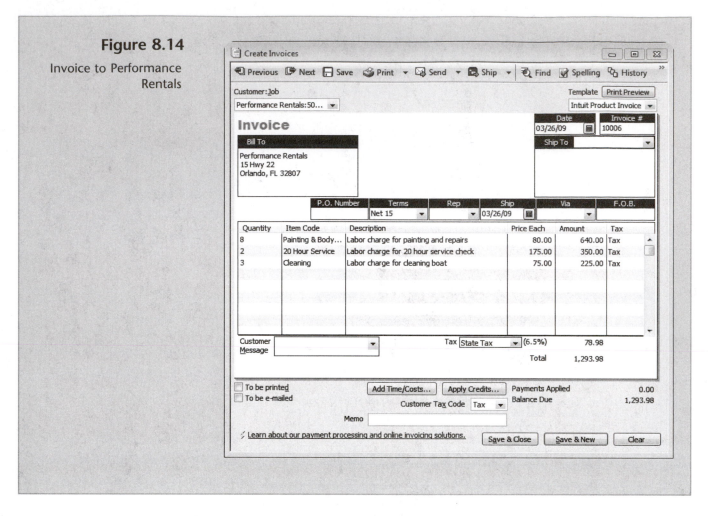

There was one cash boat purchase during the month to a new customer, Sonia Garcia. She purchased a Malibu Vride off the showroom floor on March 12 for $51,120 (including sales tax) using Check No. 8593.

To record a cash sale and deposit cash received:

1 Click **Create Sales Receipts** from the Customers section of the home page. (Click **No Thanks** if prompted to set up cash receipts.)

2 Type **Sonia Garcia** in the Customer:Job text edit box.

3 Click **Quick Add.**

4 Type **3/12/09** as the date of sale and **6008** as the sale number.

5 Type **8593** as the check number, and select **Check** as the Payment Method.

6 Select **MV** as the Item.

7 Type **1** as the Qty.

8 Make sure **State Tax** is shown as the Tax item click **Save & Close** to enter this sales receipt and then click **Yes** when asked to confirm changes.

9 Click **Record Deposits** from the Banking section of the home page.

10 Select the deposit shown and click **OK.**

11 Type **3/12/09** as the deposit date.

12 Click **Save & Close** to record the deposit.

Three invoices were generated in the month of March for boat sales. One, to Fantasy Sports (Invoice No. 10004), represented an order received during the month for which Fantasy had already paid a deposit. Upon Fantasy's request, Donna approved net 15 credit terms on the balance owed. Credit terms specify the discount, if any, and amount of time that customers have to pay an invoice. The other two invoices were for sales from the showroom floor: sales on account using Invoice No. 10007 and No. 10008, respectively. Sales on account are sales to customers who are not required to pay the invoice immediately.

To record invoices from the sale of boats on account:

1 Click **Create Invoices** from the Customers section of the home page.

2 Select **Fantasy Sports** from the Customer:Job list.

3 Click the **Items** tab.

4 Click the **Select All** button to select both boats received from Malibu, and then click **OK** to close the window.

5 Type **3/6/09** as the invoice date.

6 Type **10004** as the invoice number.

7 Click the **Apply Credits** button, and then click **Yes** to save this invoice.

8 Click **Done** to apply the credit of $28,250.

9 Select terms of **Net 15** from the Terms list, select **State Tax** from the Tax field, and type **3/6/09** as the ship date. The completed invoice should look like Figure 8.15.

10 Click **Save & New.**

11 Click **Yes** to save changes, and then click **Yes** again to save the changed terms and tax for this customer.

12 Select **Freebirds** from the Customer:Job list.

13 Type **3/23/09** as the invoice date.

14 Type **10007** as the invoice number.

15 Select terms of **Net 15** from the Terms list and type **3/23/09** as the ship date. Type the Bill To, Quantity, and Item Code information as found in Figure 8.16.

16 Click **Save & New.**

Video Demonstration

DEMO 8C - Record invoices and apply payments

Figure 8.15
Invoice to Fantasy Sports

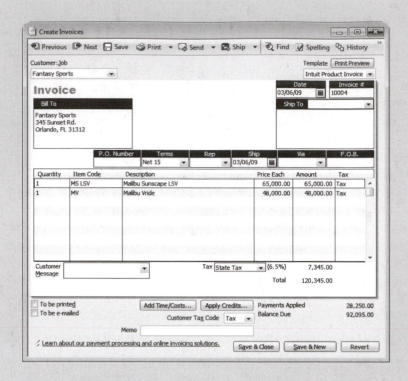

Figure 8.16
Invoice to Freebirds

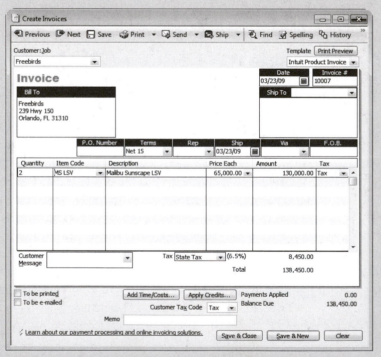

17 Click **Yes** to save the new billing address and terms.

18 Select **Florida Sports Camp** from the Customer:Job list.

19 Type **3/30/09** as the invoice date.

20 Type **10008** as the invoice number.

21   Select terms of **Net 15** from the Terms list, and type **3/30/09** as the ship date.

22   Enter Quantity **1**, Item Code **T 22v**, and Tax **State Tax.**

23   Click **Save & Close.**

24   Click **Yes** to save the new terms.

At the end of the month, Wild Water Sports received a check from Performance Rentals for $10,000 as a deposit toward the purchase of a boat on its showroom floor.

To record receipt of deposit from Performance Rentals:

1   Click **Receive Payments** from the Customers section of the home page.

2   Select **Performance Rentals** from the Received from drop-down list.

3   Type **10000** as the amount.

4   Type **3/31/09** as the date, **Check** as the Pmt. Method, and **15687** as the Check #.

5   Click the **Un-Apply Payment** button, since this is a deposit on another transaction and not a payment on Invoice No. 10006 as suggested.

6   Click **Save & Close.**

7   Click **OK** in the Payment Credit window.

8   Click **Record Deposits**, select the **3/31/09** check box, and click **OK** to record the deposit of this $10,000.

9   Click **Save & Close.**

"When do we get around to paying the bills and collecting cash from these invoices?" you ask.

"It's important to pay bills on a timely basis, since this will keep our suppliers happy and keep our good credit," Karen answers. "First off, we can view what bills are outstanding and when they are due and then choose which to pay and when."

To choose which bills to pay and to pay those bills:

1   Click **Pay Bills** from the Vendors section of the home page.

2   Click the option button to **Show all bills.**

3   Click next to the due date **3/21/09.**

4 Click the option button to **Assign check number.**

5 Type **3/20/09** as the payment date. Your screen should look like Figure 8.17.

Figure 8.17

Pay Bills Window

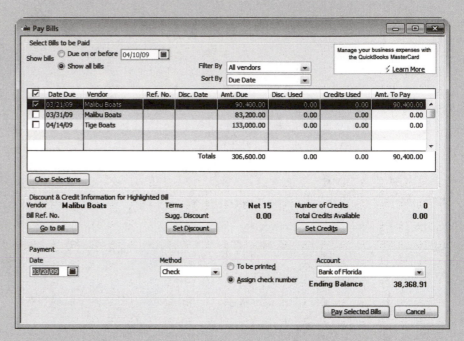

6 Click **Pay Selected Bills.**

7 Type **1032** as the check number in the Assign Check Numbers window, and then click **OK.**

8 Click **Done** in the Payment Summary window.

"We collected two payments from customers on account in March," Karen says. "Orlando Water Sports paid us $5,300 on 3/20, and Buena Vista paid us $1,964.93 on 3/27. Let's record those now."

To record cash collections on account and related deposit:

1 Click **Receive Payments** from the Customers section of the home page.

2 Select **Orlando Water Sports** as the customer received from.

3 Type **5300** as the Amount received.

4 Type **3/20/09** as the Date received.

5 Type **9152** as the check number of the check received as payment. Your screen should look like Figure 8.18.

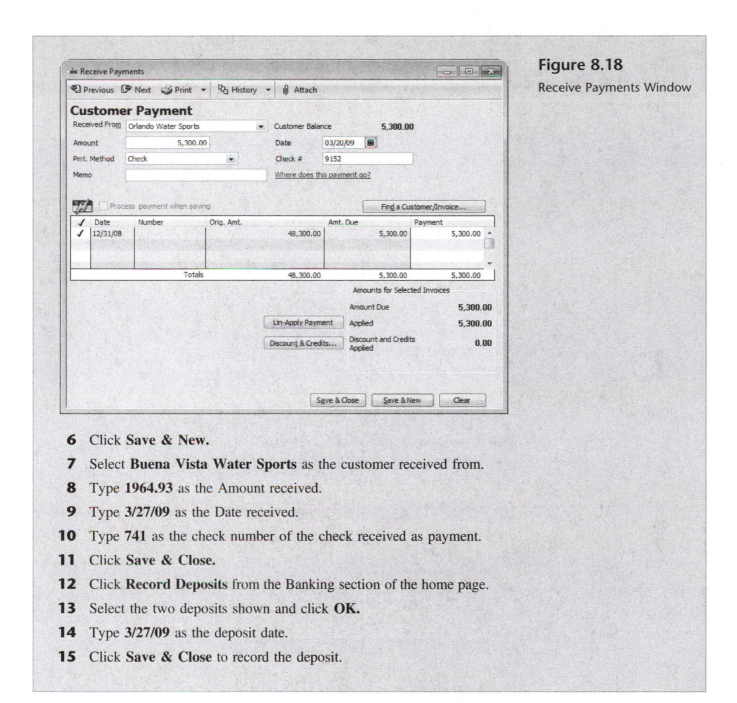

Figure 8.18

Receive Payments Window

6　Click **Save & New.**

7　Select **Buena Vista Water Sports** as the customer received from.

8　Type **1964.93** as the Amount received.

9　Type **3/27/09** as the Date received.

10　Type **741** as the check number of the check received as payment.

11　Click **Save & Close.**

12　Click **Record Deposits** from the Banking section of the home page.

13　Select the two deposits shown and click **OK.**

14　Type **3/27/09** as the deposit date.

15　Click **Save & Close** to record the deposit.

"In addition to paying bills from vendors for merchandise purchased, the company also has to pay its sales tax and payroll tax liabilities," Karen reminds you. "Sales tax liabilities are created when we sell merchandise and collect sales tax from a customer. Payroll tax liabilities are created when we withhold payroll tax from employees' paychecks and recognize our obligation to pay employer payroll taxes. Before we can do that and pay the rest of our end-of-month bills and payroll, we'll need to transfer some funds from our Short-Term Investments account at ETrade to our checking account."

Donna offers to make the electronic transfer of $40,000 from ETrade to Bank of Florida, and you agree to record the accounting effect of that transfer and prepare checks to pay the sales tax and payroll tax obligations.

Video Demonstration

DEMO 8E - Pay sales and payroll taxes

To transfer funds and pay sales tax and payroll tax obligations:

1 Click the **Chart of Accounts** icon in the Company section of the home page.

2 Double-click the **Short-Term Investments** account.

3 Type **3/30/09** as the date.

4 Type **Bank of Florida** as the payee.

5 Type **40000** as the payment.

6 Select **Bank of Florida** as the Account.

7 Click **Record** and then close the Short-Term Investments and the Chart of Accounts windows.

8 Click the **Manage Sales Tax** icon from the Vendors section of the home page.

9 Click **Pay Sales Tax** and then type **3/30/09** as the check date.

10 Type **2/28/09** as the Show sales tax due through date.

11 Press the **[Tab]** key to refresh the screen.

12 Type **1033** as the Starting Check No.

13 Click in the **Pay** column next to State Tax. Your screen should look like Figure 8.19.

Figure 8.19

Pay Sales Tax Window

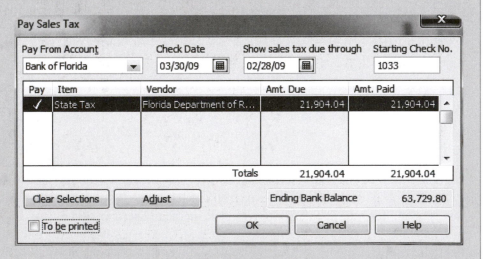

14 Click **OK** and then close the Manage Sales Tax window.

15 Click the **Pay Liabilities** icon from the Employees section of the home page.

16 Type **1/1/09** as the From date.

17 Type **2/28/09** as the Through date, and then click **OK.**

18 Uncheck the **To be printed** check box.

19 Select all of the Payroll Items.

20 Select the **Review liability check to enter expenses/penalties** option button.

21 Type **3/31/09** as the Check Date. Your screen should look like Figure 8.20.

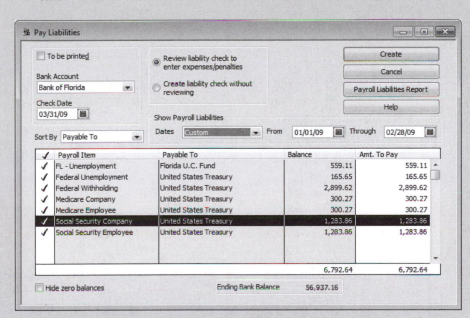

Figure 8.20

Pay Liabilities Window

22 Click **Create.**

23 A Liability Check—Bank of Florida window should appear as in Figure 8.21.

24 Click **Next** to view the United States Treasury check, which should look like Figure 8.22.

25 Close the check window.

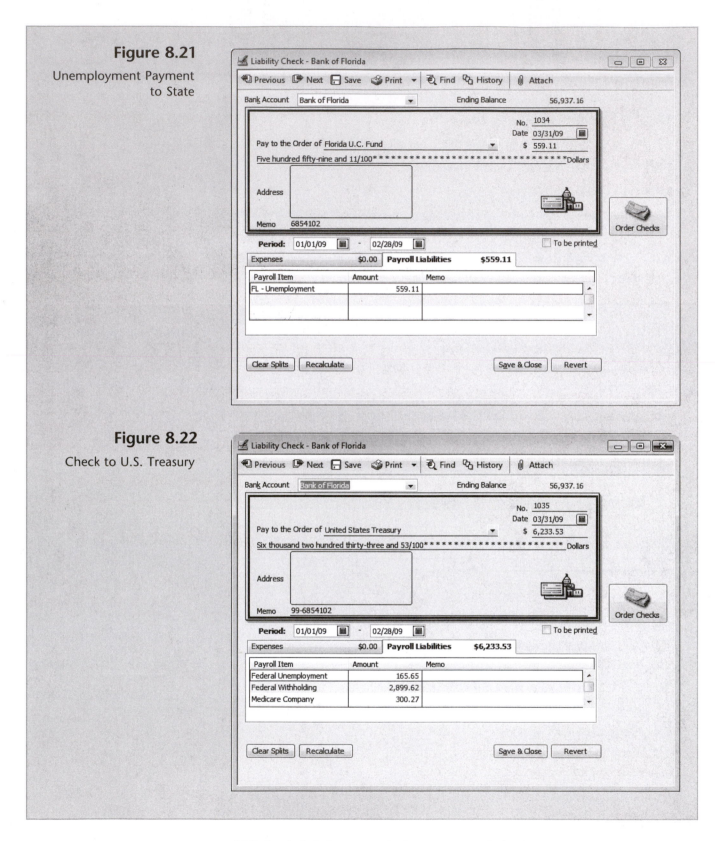

Figure 8.21

Unemployment Payment
to State

Figure 8.22

Check to U.S. Treasury

"All that is left for March is for us to record checks written for expenses and to record payroll," Karen states. "Our expenses are about the same each month, so you shouldn't see too much variation in what you did the last two months. We didn't have much in the way of service this month, so Pat didn't work and Ryder just worked the hours we recorded earlier."

To record end-of-month expenses:

1   Click the **Write Checks** icon in the Banking section of the home page.

2   Type **1036** as the check number if it is not already there.

3   Type **3/31/09** as the Check Date.

4   Select **Central Florida Gas & Electric** from the Pay to the Order of section of the check.

5   Type **1050** as the amount and then press **[Tab]**.

6   Note that **Utilities** should already be selected from the Account drop-down list. If it is not, select it now.

7   Click **Save & New.**

8   Type **1037** as the check number if it is not already there.

9   Type **3/31/09** as the Check Date if it is not already there.

10   Select **Verizon** in the Pay to the Order of section of the check.

11   Type **1500** as the amount and then press **[Tab]**.

12   Note that **Telephone Expense** should already be selected from the Account drop-down list. If it is not, select it now.

13   Click **Save & Close.**

Video Demonstration

DEMO 8D - Pay bills

To record end-of-month payroll:

1   Click the **Pay Employees** icon in the Employees section of the home page.

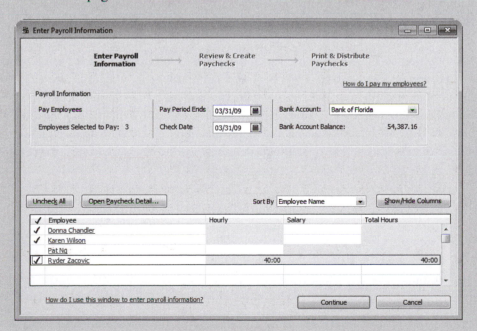

Figure 8.23

Select Employees to Pay

2 Type **3/31/09** as the Check Date and **3/31/09** as the Pay Period Ends date. Click **Yes** when asked if you want to update the hours worked from the new pay period. Then place a check next to Donna, Karen, and Ryder's names. Your screen should look like Figure 8.23.

3 Use the information below to create payroll for Donna, Karen, and Ryder. Click each employee's name to provide tax information. (*Note:* Pat Ng did not work any hours this month.)

4 Click **Continue.**

   Trouble? Depending on your monitor size, the Continue and Cancel buttons may not be visible. To view them, just maximize the window.

Item	Donna	Karen	Ryder
Earnings	4,166.67	4,166.67	600.00
Federal Withholding	−463.00	−710.00	−82.20
Social Security Employee	−258.33	−258.33	−37.20
Medicare Employee	−60.42	−60.42	−8.70
Social Security Company	258.33	258.33	37.20
Medicare Company	60.42	60.42	8.70
Federal Unemployment	33.33	33.33	4.80
FL Unemployment Company	112.50	112.50	16.20
Check Amount	3,384.92	3,137.92	471.90

5 Assign Check No. 1038 as the first check number for these paychecks. Then click **Create Paychecks.**

6 Click **Close.**

Recording Noncash Investing and Financing Activities

Although noncash investing and financing activities do not affect the cash position of a company, they do have an impact on a firm's financial position. One example of such an activity was Wild Water Sports's purchase of computer equipment in March, which was completely financed with long-term debt (a loan payable to Staples with no interest and no payment due until 10/1/09). Karen explains the nature of this transaction to you and demonstrates how it should be recorded.

To record the purchase of equipment with long-term debt:

1 Click the **Chart of Accounts** icon from the Company section of the home page.

2 Double-click the **Furniture and Equipment** account.

3 Type **3/31/09** as the Date.

4 Type **Staples** as the Payee.

5 Type **5000** as the amount in the Increase column.

6 Select **Loans Payable** as the Account.

7 Click **Record.** Your screen should look like Figure 8.24.

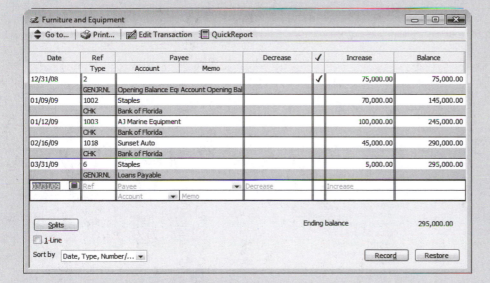

Figure 8.24

Entering an Equipment Purchase in Exchange for a Loan

8 Close the Furniture and Equipment window and the Chart of Accounts window.

Evaluate a Firm's Performance and Financial Position

Once again, the best way to evaluate a firm's performance and financial position at this point is to generate an income statement and balance sheet. Karen suggests that you do this for the entire three months ended March 31, 2009 (the first quarter of 2009) and then prepare a Transaction List by Date report like you did last month.

To prepare a comparative income statement, balance sheet, and transaction by date report for the first quarter of 2009:

1 Click the **Report Center** icon from the icon toolbar. Select the **Standard** Tab and then click the **Company & Financial** section.

2 Double-click the **Profit & Loss Standard** view under the Profit & Loss section.

3 Change the From date to **1/1/09.**

4 Change the To date to **3/31/09**, and then click **Refresh.**

5 Select **Month** from the Columns list.

6   Modify the report header to remove the date prepared, time prepared, and report basis fields.

7   Click the **Print** button from the toolbar, and then click **Print** in the Print Reports window. Your report should look like Figure 8.25.

Figure 8.25

Income Statement for the Three Months Ending March 31, 2009

Wild Water Sports Ch 8
Profit & Loss
January through March 2009

	Jan 09	Feb 09	Mar 09	TOTAL
Ordinary Income/Expense				
Income				
Boat Sales	200,750.00	132,000.00	369,750.00	702,500.00
Part Sales	40.00	250.00	320.00	610.00
Service	2,545.00	1,400.00	2,740.00	6,685.00
Total Income	203,335.00	133,650.00	372,810.00	709,795.00
Cost of Goods Sold				
Cost of Goods Sold	160,632.00	105,800.00	296,056.00	562,488.00
Total COGS	160,632.00	105,800.00	296,056.00	562,488.00
Gross Profit	42,703.00	27,850.00	76,754.00	147,307.00
Expense				
Advertising and Promotion	0.00	2,700.00	0.00	2,700.00
Interest Expense	0.00	0.00	5,958.60	5,958.60
Office Supplies	0.00	4,500.00	0.00	4,500.00
Payroll Expenses	11,343.22	11,673.35	9,929.40	32,945.97
Telephone Expense	1,700.00	1,820.00	1,500.00	5,020.00
Utilities	890.00	930.00	1,050.00	2,870.00
Total Expense	13,933.22	21,623.35	18,438.00	53,994.57
Net Ordinary Income	28,769.78	6,226.65	58,316.00	93,312.43
Other Income/Expense				
Other Income				
Other Income	0.00	0.00	3,000.00	3,000.00
Total Other Income	0.00	0.00	3,000.00	3,000.00
Net Other Income	0.00	0.00	3,000.00	3,000.00
Net Income	28,769.78	6,226.65	61,316.00	96,312.43

8   Close the **Profit & Loss** report window, but do not memorize this report.

9   Double-click the **Balance Sheet Standard** view under the Balance Sheet and Net Worth section.

10 Change the As of date to **3/31/09**, and then click **Refresh.**

11 Modify the report header to remove the date prepared, time prepared, and report basis fields.

12 Click the **Print** button from the toolbar and then click **Print** in the Print Reports window. The assets section of your report should look like Figure 8.26, and the liabilities and equity section of your report should look like Figure 8.27.

13 Close the Balance Sheet report window; do not memorize this report.

14 Click the **Accountant & Taxes** section and then double-click the **Transaction List by Date** view from the Account Activity section.

15 Type **3/1/09** in the From text box.

Figure 8.26

Assets Section of the Balance Sheet

Wild Water Sports Ch 8
Balance Sheet
As of March 31, 2009

	Mar 31, 09
ASSETS	
Current Assets	
Checking/Savings	
Bank of Florida	47,392.42
Short-Term Investments	38,000.00
Total Checking/Savings	85,392.42
Accounts Receivable	
Accounts Receivable	320,707.73
Total Accounts Receivable	320,707.73
Other Current Assets	
Prepaid Advertising	24,000.00
Inventory Boats	295,600.00
Inventory Parts	2,112.00
Prepaid Insurance	22,000.00
Total Other Current Assets	343,712.00
Total Current Assets	749,812.15
Fixed Assets	
Furniture and Equipment	295,000.00
Accumulated Depreciation	-7,500.00
Total Fixed Assets	287,500.00
TOTAL ASSETS	1,037,312.15

Figure 8.27

Liabilities and Equity Section of the Balance Sheet

LIABILITIES & EQUITY	
Liabilities	
Current Liabilities	
Accounts Payable	
Accounts Payable	216,200.00
Total Accounts Payable	216,200.00
Other Current Liabilities	
Payroll Liabilities	2,934.66
Sales Tax Payable	24,232.66
Total Other Current Liabilities	27,167.32
Total Current Liabilities	243,367.32
Long Term Liabilities	
Loans Payable	297,632.40
Total Long Term Liabilities	297,632.40
Total Liabilities	540,999.72
Equity	
Capital Stock	400,000.00
Net Income	96,312.43
Total Equity	496,312.43
TOTAL LIABILITIES & EQUITY	1,037,312.15

16   Type **3/31/09** in the To text box, and then click **Refresh**.

17   Click the **Print** button from the toolbar and then click **Print** in the
Print Reports window. Modify the report header to remove the date
prepared and time prepared fields. The report as shown in
Figure 8.28 should appear.

Wild Water Sports Ch 8
Transaction List by Date
March 2009

Type	Date	Num	Name	Memo	Account	Clr	Split	Amount
Mar 09								
Check	3/1/09	1029	Bank of Florida		Bank of Florida		-SPLIT-	-4,717.81
Check	3/1/09	1030	Bank of Florida		Bank of Florida		-SPLIT-	-4,717.81
Check	3/6/09		Bank of Florida		Short-Term Investm...		Bank of Florida	-300,000.00
Check	3/6/09	1031	Bank of Orlando		Bank of Florida		-SPLIT-	-387,690.58
Bill	3/6/09		Malibu Boats		Accounts Payable		-SPLIT-	-90,400.00
Invoice	3/6/09	10004	Fantasy Sports		Accounts Receivable		-SPLIT-	120,345.00
Deposit	3/9/09		ETrade	Deposit	Short-Term Investm...		Other Income	3,000.00
Sales Receipt	3/12/09	6008	Sonia Garcia		Undeposited Funds	X	-SPLIT-	51,120.00
Deposit	3/12/09			Deposit	Bank of Florida		Undeposited F...	51,120.00
Bill	3/16/09		Malibu Boats		Accounts Payable		Inventory Boats	-83,200.00
Invoice	3/18/09	10005	Buena Vista Water ...		Accounts Receivable		-SPLIT-	1,964.93
Bill Pmt -Check	3/20/09	1032	Malibu Boats		Bank of Florida		Accounts Pay...	-90,400.00
Payment	3/20/09	9152	Orlando Water Sports		Undeposited Funds	X	Accounts Rec...	5,300.00
Invoice	3/23/09	10007	Freebirds		Accounts Receivable		-SPLIT-	138,450.00
Invoice	3/26/09	10006	Performance Rental...		Accounts Receivable		-SPLIT-	1,293.98
Payment	3/27/09	741	Buena Vista Water ...		Undeposited Funds	X	Accounts Rec...	1,964.93
Deposit	3/27/09			Deposit	Bank of Florida		-SPLIT-	7,264.93
Bill	3/30/09		Tige Boats		Accounts Payable		-SPLIT-	-133,000.00
Invoice	3/30/09	10008	Florida Sports Camp		Accounts Receivable		-SPLIT-	83,868.75
Check	3/30/09		Bank of Florida		Short-Term Investm...		Bank of Florida	-40,000.00
Sales Tax Payment	3/30/09	1033	Florida Department ...		Bank of Florida		Sales Tax Pay...	-21,904.04
Payment	3/31/09		Performance Rentals		Undeposited Funds	X	Accounts Rec...	10,000.00
Deposit	3/31/09			Deposit	Bank of Florida		Undeposited F...	10,000.00
Liability Check	3/31/09	1034	Florida U.C. Fund	6854102	Bank of Florida		Payroll Liabiliti...	-559.11
Liability Check	3/31/09	1035	United States Treas...	99-6854102	Bank of Florida		-SPLIT-	-6,233.53
Check	3/31/09	1036	Central Florida Gas ...		Bank of Florida		Utilities	-1,050.00
Check	3/31/09	1037	Verizon		Bank of Florida		Telephone Ex...	-1,500.00
Paycheck	3/31/09	1038	Donna Chandler		Bank of Florida		-SPLIT-	-3,384.92
Paycheck	3/31/09	1039	Karen Wilson		Bank of Florida		-SPLIT-	-3,137.92
Paycheck	3/31/09	1040	Ryder Zacovic		Bank of Florida		-SPLIT-	-471.90
General Journal	3/31/09	6	Staples		Furniture and Equip...		Loans Payable	5,000.00
Mar 09								

Figure 8.28

Transaction List by Date for March 2009

18 Close all report windows.

"Not bad for our first three months," Karen comments. "But we still need to accrue some revenues and expenses, adjust some prepaid assets and unearned revenue, and record depreciation."

End Note

You've now helped Karen understand even more of QuickBooks's features, including how to record the repayment of loans, sale of investments, receipt of inventory items and related bills, credit sales, and receipt of payments on account.

Business Events Summary

Business Event	Process Steps	Page
Financing Activities:		
Pay loan	Write checks from Banking section	219
Transfer funds	Open account registers from chart of accounts	221
Investing Activities:		
Record short-term investment activity	Open account register from chart of accounts	222
Operating Activities:		
Order inventory; create purchase orders	Purchase orders from Vendors section	224
Receive inventory and enter bill	Receive inventory from Vendors section	225
Create new jobs	Add job from Customers section	227
Enter employee hours	Enter time from the Employees section	228
Invoice customers for billable hours	Create invoices from Customers section	228
Sell inventory for cash	Create sales receipts from Customers section	230
Invoice customers for sales on account	Create invoices from Customers section	231
Record deposits from customers	Receive payments from Customers section	233
Pay bills	Pay bills from Vendors section	233
Collect cash from customers	Receive payments from Customers section	234
Pay sales taxes	Manage sales tax from Company section	236
Pay payroll taxes	Pay liabilities from Employees section	237
Process payroll and pay employees	Pay employees from the Employees section	239
Other:		
Purchase assets with long-term debt	Open account register from chart of accounts	240
Evaluate a firm's financial performance		241

Chapter 8 Questions

1 Of the information contained in a loan amortization schedule, what part is recorded in QuickBooks?

2 How does a firm account for a transfer of funds from one bank to another bank in QuickBooks?

3 How do you update vendor records for changes in terms from the home page?

4 What payment terms are available in QuickBooks for vendors?

5 Consider this statement: "QuickBooks records revenue when an invoice is generated even though cash has not been received." Is this practice acceptable? Why or why not?

6 What icon is clicked in the Vendors section to record the receipt of inventory and the related bill?

7 What steps are necessary to record services performed on account for Wild Water Sports?

8 How does the QuickBooks software respond if a bill is entered with a vendor name that is not included on the vendor list?

9 What are the steps for paying sales tax?

10 What are noncash investing and financing activities, and how are they recorded in QuickBooks?

Chapter 8 Matching

Select the letter of the item below that best matches the definitions that follow. Use the text or QuickBooks Help to complete this assignment.

a. Loan amortization table

b. Electronic transfers

c. Credit terms for customers

d. Credit terms from suppliers

e. Purchases on account

_____ Sales to a customer for which the company allows some time for the invoice to be paid.

_____ Used on invoices to specify how previous payments made by customers should be applied to an invoice.

_____ A source document used to record sales on account.

_____ A schedule of the payments, including interest and principal, that are required to pay down a loan.

_____ Purchases from a supplier who allows the purchaser some time to pay the bill.

f. Sales on account   _____ Liabilities created when a company sells merchandise and collects sales taxes from a customer.

g. Sales invoices   _____ Specify the discount, if any, and amount of time that customers have to pay an invoice.

h. Apply credits   _____ Used to move amounts from one bank account to another.

i. Sales tax liabil-   _____ Liabilities created when payroll taxes are withheld from an employee's
    ities   paycheck.

j. Payroll tax   _____ Specify the discount, if any, and amount of time that companies have to pay a
    liabilities   bill.

Chapter 8 Exercises

Chapter 8 Exercise 1
FINANCING ACTIVITIES

Restore the file Boston Catering Ch 8 (Backup) found on the text CD or download it from the text Web site. Add the following transactions and then print a standard balance sheet as of 8/31/10.

  a. On 8/2/10 the company wrote check #1509 to CitiBank for $926.29 as an installment on notes payable ($416.67 of which was for interest expense)

  b. On 8/2/10 the company wrote check #1510 to Bank of America for $610.32 as an installment on notes payable ($166.67 of which was for interest expense).

  c. On 8/3/10 the company electronically transferred $20,000 from the Bank of America checking account to the short-term investments account.

Chapter 8 Exercise 2
INVESTING ACTIVITIES

Restore the file Boston Catering Ch 8 (Backup) found on the text CD or download it from the text Web site. Do *not* use the file created in Exercise 1 above. Add the following transactions and then print a standard balance sheet as of 8/31/10.

  a. On 8/6/10 the company purchased some additional equipment from a restaurant that closed the previous month. The equipment was valued at $10,000 for which the company signed a two-year 6% note payable to Evian Sprinter with no payment due until maturity.

  b. On 8/9/10 the company purchased furniture from Outlet Tool Supply for $1,000 using check 1511.

Chapter 8 Exercise 3

OPERATING ACTIVITIES – PURCHASES AND PAYMENTS FROM/TO VENDORS

Restore the file Boston Catering Ch 8 (Backup) found on the text CD or download it from the text Web site. Do *not* use the file created in the exercises above. Add the following transactions and then print a vendor contact list showing only the vendor, address, and balance totals columns.

    a. On 8/5/10 the company ordered 48 bottles of a new item W400 Vintage Brut from Domain Chandon, 1 California Drive, Yountville, CA 94599 terms net 30, on purchase order 104. This champagne cost $36 per bottle and sells for $48 per bottle.

    b. On 8/6/10 the company paid bills due Fiddlehead Cellars and US Food Service as of 7/30/10 assigning check numbers 1512 and 1513.

    c. On 8/26/10 the company received the 48 bottles of item W400 from Domain Chandon along with a bill due in 30 days.

Chapter 8 Exercise 4

OPERATING ACTIVITIES – EXPENSES & SALES

Restore the file Boston Catering Ch 8 (Backup) found on the text CD or download it from the text Web site. Do *not* use the file created in the exercises above. Add the following transactions and then print a standard balance sheet as of 8/31/10 and a standard income statement for the month ended 8/31/10.

    a. On 8/6/10 the company contracted with a new customer, Boston College, terms net 15, that is subject to sales tax. The company anticipates many future engagements with this customer and thus created a new job (Event 1).

    b. On 8/15/10 the company paid rent to New England Property Management (a new vendor) on check 1513 for $3,000.

    c. On 8/16/10 the company contracted with MIT. The company anticipates many future engagements with this customer and thus created a new job (Dean Bumble).

    d. On 8/21/10 the company paid all bills outstanding using checks 1514-1516.

    e. During the month of August Kyle Hain worked 10 hours and Amy Casey worked 9 hours on 8/15 during the Boston College Event 1 party as wait staff. Kyle worked 12 hours and Amy worked 10 hours on 8/29 during the MIT Dean Bumble party as wait staff. Otherwise they did not work. Payroll checks are issued on 8/31/10 starting with check #1517. Paycheck information is shown below (Note: no premium is paid for overtime.):

Pay/Tax/Withholding	Chambers	Hain	Casey
Hours	n/a	22	19
Rate	$ 50,000	$ 16.00	$ 18.00
Gross pay	4,166.67	352.00	342.00
Federal withholding	570.83	48.22	46.85
Social Security employee	258.33	21.82	21.20
Medicare employee	60.42	5.10	4.96
MA withholding	283.99	5.92	6.68
MA Training Fund	0.42	0.04	0.03
Social Security employer	258.33	21.82	21.20
Medicare company	60.42	5.10	4.96
Federal unemployment	33.33	2.82	2.74
MA unemployment	125.00	10.56	10.26
Check amount	2,993.10	270.94	262.31

f. On 8/15/10 the company catered the Boston College Event 1 party. On 8/16/10 the company invoiced Boston College using invoice number 1123. They used 30 bottles of W100 and served 150 heavy appetizers (A100).

g. On 8/29/10 the company catered the MIT Dean Bumble party. On 8/30/10 the company invoiced MIT using invoice number 1124. They used 45 bottles of W201 and served 200 light appetizers (A200).

h. On 8/31/10 the company received a bill from US Food Service for $800 in food purchases for the Boston College event. A bill for the MIT party food purchases was expected next month.

i. On 8/31/10 the company paid sales tax due as of 8/31/10 using check 1520.

j. On 8/31/10 the company paid payroll liabilities due as of 7/31/10 using check 1521 and 1522. (Hint: be sure to modify payroll items and set vendor for federal withholding to the IRS.)

Chapter 8 Assignments

Chapter 8 Assignment 1
ADDING MORE INFORMATION: WILD WATER SPORTS

corporation

merchandising

Restore the file Wild Water Sports Ch 8A (Backup) found on the text CD or download it from the text Web site, and then add the following transactions in chronological order.

Event #	Date	Business Event
1	4/2/09	Wrote Check No. 1041 for $4,717.81 as payment no. 3 on loan to Bank of Florida. See loan amortization schedule in Figure 8.1 for interest and principal breakdown.
2	4/3/09	Received $92,095 as payment on account from Fantasy Sports (their Check No. 234).
3	4/3/09	Deposited payment received from Fantasy Sports.

Event #	Date	Business Event
4	4/3/09	Paid Malibu Boats bill by writing Check No. 1042 for $83,200.
5	4/6/09	Created Purchase Order No. 4008 to Tige Boats for the purchase of one T 22v and one T 24v for showroom floor inventory.
6	4/6/09	Received items ordered and bill on Purchase Order No. 4007 from MB Sports.
7	4/9/09	Received $1,293.98 as payment on account from Performance Rentals (their Check No. 987).
8	4/9/09	Accepted a new job (50007) to service a boat owned by Seth Blackman.
9	4/10/09	Pat Ng worked two hours performing an engine service and three hours cleaning on job 50007.
10	4/10/09	Sold the investment in Apple Computer stock, originally purchased for $25,000, for a loss of $2,000.
11	4/10/09	Deposited payment received from Performance Rentals.
12	4/10/09	Created Invoice No. 10009 to Spirit Adventures to record the sale of an MB 220v (Terms: net 30), with a balance due of $69,225.00.
13	4/10/09	Created Invoice No. 10010 to Seth Blackman for service under job 50007 and five quarts of oil, one air filter, and one oil filter. Terms: net 15, with a balance due of $585.75.
14	4/13/09	Created Purchase Order No. 4009 to MB Sports for the purchase of one MB 220v and one MB B52 V23 for showroom floor inventory.
15	4/13/09	Received $83,868.75 as payment on account from Florida Sports Camp (their Check No. 8741).
16	4/13/09	Deposited payment received from Florida Sports Camp.
17	4/13/09	Transferred $20,000 from short-term investments to checking.
18	4/13/09	Paid Tige Boats bill by writing Check No. 1043 for $133,000.
19	4/16/09	Accepted a new job (50008) to paint a boat owned by Fantasy Sports.
20	4/16/09	Ryder Zacovic worked eight hours painting and repairing on job 50008.
21	4/17/09	Created Invoice No. 10011 to High Flying Fun (a new customer, subject to state sales tax) to record sale of one T 24v and one MW XTI (Terms: net 15).
22	4/17/09	Created Sales Receipt No. 6009 to Orlando Water Sports to record the sale of one MS LXi in exchange for their Check No. 10005.
23	4/17/09	Deposited payment received from Orlando Water Sports.
24	4/20/09	Created invoice 10012 to Fantasy Sports for service under job 50008.
25	4/23/09	Created Purchase Order No. 4010 to Malibu Boats for the purchase of one MS LX for Freebirds, one MS LSV for Buena Vista Water Sports, and one MV for showroom floor inventory.
26	4/24/09	Received items ordered and bill on Purchase Order No. 4009 from MB Sports.
27	4/24/09	Received items ordered and bill on Purchase Order No. 4008 from Tige Boats.
28	4/24/09	Created invoice 10013 to Half Moon Sports (a new customer, subject to sales tax) to record sale of one MB 220v (Terms: net 15).
29	4/27/09	Purchased a computer, printer, and other electronic equipment from Staples for $12,000—again completely financed with a no-interest loan and with no payment due until 11/1/10.
30	4/27/09	Paid payroll tax liabilities (accrued during March) of $2,934.66 using Check No. 1044 to the Florida U.C. Fund and Check No. 1045 to the United States Treasury.
31	4/27/09	Paid sales tax liability (accrued during March) of $24,232.66 to the Florida Dept. of Revenue using Check No. 1046.

Event #	Date	Business Event
32	4/27/09	Wrote Check No. 1047 to Central Florida Gas & Electric in the amount of $1,250 for utilities expense.
33	4/27/09	Wrote Check No. 1048 to Verizon in the amount of $1,800 for telephone expense.
34	4/27/09	Wrote Check No. 1049 to Brian Ski in the amount of $3,000 for advertising and promotion expense.
35	4/30/09	Pat Ng worked 8 hours per day on 4/1, 4/2, and 4/3. He worked 4 hours per day on 4/6, 4/7, 4/8, 4/9, 4/13, 4/14, 4/15, 4/16, 4/20, 4/21, 4/22, 4/23, and 4/24. All of these hours were unbillable. Pat also worked 5 (billable) hours on 4/10, which were already recorded, for a total of 81 hours during the month of April. Ryder Zacovic worked 8 hours per day on 4/1, 4/2, and 4/3. He worked 4 hours per day on 4/6, 4/7, 4/8, 4/9, 4/13, 4/14, 4/15, 4/17, 4/20, 4/21, 4/22, 4/23, and 4/24 as well as 8 hours on 4/27. All of these hours were unbillable. Ryder also worked 8 (billable) hours on 4/16, which were already recorded, for a total of 92 hours during the month of April.
36	4/30/09	Received $681.60 as payment on account from Fantasy Sports (their Check No. 1874).
37	4/30/09	Received $585.75 as payment on account from Seth Blackman (his Check No. 1547).
38	4/30/09	Received $13,000 as a deposit from Freebirds (their Check No. 2514) toward the purchase of a Malibu Sportster LX ordered 4/23. **Note:** Do not apply this amount to their existing balance.
39	4/30/09	Received $16,250 as a deposit from Buena Vista Water Sports (their Check No. 8742) toward the purchase of a Malibu Sunscape LSV ordered 4/23.
40	4/30/09	Deposited $30,517.35 worth of checks received 4/30 into checking account.
41	4/30/09	Process payroll per the information provided in Table 8.1, starting with Check No. 1050.

Item	Donna	Karen	Pat	Ryder	Table 8.1
Earnings	4,166.67	4,166.67	1,458.00	1,380.00	Earnings Information for Wild Water Sports
Federal Withholding	−463.00	−710.00	−199.75	−189.06	
Social Security Employee	−258.33	−258.33	−90.40	−85.56	
Medicare Employee	−60.42	−60.42	−21.14	−20.01	
Social Security Company	258.33	258.33	90.40	85.56	
Medicare Company	60.42	60.42	21.14	20.01	
Federal Unemployment	0	0	11.66	11.04	
State Unemployment	0	0	39.37	37.26	
Check Amount	3,384.92	3,137.92	1,146.71	1,085.37	

Print the following as of 4/30/09.

   a.   Customer Balance Summary

   b.   Vendor Balance Summary

   c.   Item Listing (list only Item, Description, Type, Price, Quantity On Hand, and Cost)

   d.   Balance Sheet Standard

e. Profit & Loss Standard by month for January through April

f. Transaction List by Date for the month of April

Chapter 8 Assignment 2
ADDING MORE INFORMATION: CENTRAL COAST CELLULAR

sole proprietorship

merchandising

Restore the file Central Coast Cellular Ch 8 (Backup) found on the text CD or download it from the text Web site, and then add the following transactions.

Event #	Date	Business Event
1	1/20/09	The company received a shipment of phones from Nokia on Purchase Order No. 102. Items were received and a bill recorded (due in 30 days).
2	1/21/09	The company invoiced the City of San Luis Obispo, using Invoice No. 10001 for 20 Nokia 8290 phones, 15 Nokia 8890 phones, 30 hours of consulting time, and 35 commissions earned. (You'll need to add a new service item called Commissions, with a description of Commissions earned on cell phone contracts ($50 per contract) and recorded to a new income account titled Commissions.) Applied available credits to this invoice.
3	1/22/09	The company purchased equipment in the amount of $95,000 cash from Kyle Equipment, Inc., using Check No. 3008.
4	1/23/09	The company paid the Ericsson bill of $6,500 with Check No. 3009.
5	1/31/09	The company paid semi-monthly payroll starting with Check No. 3010 for the period of January 16 to January 31, 2009. Megan Paulson worked 85 hours during the period. Payroll tax information is shown in Table 8.2.

Table 8.2				
Payroll Information for Central Coast Cellular	**Item**	**Alex**	**Jay**	**Megan**
	Earnings	2,000.00	1,500.00	1,020.00
	Federal Withholding	−300.00	−225.00	−153.00
	Social Security Employee	−124.00	−93.00	−63.24
	Medicare Employee	−29.00	−21.75	−14.79
	CA Withholding	−100.00	−75.00	−51.00
	CA Disability Employee	−10.00	−7.50	−5.10
	CA Employee Training Tax	2.00	1.50	1.02
	Social Security Company	124.00	93.00	63.24
	Medicare Company	29.00	21.75	14.79
	Federal Unemployment	6.40	4.80	3.26
	CA Unemployment	24.00	18.00	12.24
	Check Amount	1,437.00	1,077.75	732.87

Print the following:

a. Profit & Loss Standard report for the month of January 2009

b. Balance Sheet Standard as of January 31, 2009

c. Transaction List by Date for the period January 1 through January 31, 2009

Chapter 8 Assignment 3

ADDING MORE INFORMATION: SANTA BARBARA SAILING

corporation

service

Restore the file Santa Barbara Sailing Ch 8 (Backup) found on the text CD or download it from the text Web site, and then add the following transactions.

Event #	Date	Business Event
1	7/17/08	Deposited three checks, which had been collected earlier in the week, into the checking account for a total of $20,243.60.
2	7/17/08	Hired a new employee, Jack Sparrow, to serve as a charter boat captain. Jack is single and earns $25 per hour but is billed out to customers at $50 per hour (a new service item called Charter Boat Captain with a new income type account called Charter Income). His Social Security number is 999-23-8722, and his address is 1 Black Pearl Road, Montecito, CA 93109. He is paid semi-monthly like other employees, but all of his hours are billable to customers. Maximum billing is eight hours per day.
3	7/18/08	Borrowed an additional $50,000 from the Bank of the Caribbean at 7% interest due in monthly installments over the next three years. Deposited these funds directly into the company's checking account.
4	7/18/08	Collected $5,000 from Raytheon via their MasterCard as a deposit on charter with Captain Jack Sparrow using the CAT 50 for 10 days. The company's policy for credit customers is to collect a deposit in advance and then bill customers when they return. Raytheon is given terms of net 15. Deposited this advance later in the week.
5	7/21/08	Rented the CAT 42 to a new customer, SBNEWS (Santa Barbara News-Press, located at 715 Anacapa Street, Santa Barbara, CA 93101) for one week, on terms of net 15. Collected a deposit of $2,500 (Check No. 0932), which was deposited into the bank the same day.
6	7/21/08	Rented the CAT 28 to Deckers for seven days using Sales Receipt No. 10005 and collected Visa payment for $1,663.20.
7	7/22/08	Deposited Raytheon and Deckers credit card payments.
8	7/25/08	Rented the CAT 32 to a new customer, Barry Cohen (located at 398 Alameda Padre Serra, Santa Barbara, CA 93105, Terms: Due on receipt) for 14 days using Sales Receipt No. 10006 and collected MasterCard payment for $4,158.00.
9	7/27/08	Captain Jack returns in the evening with the Raytheon charter and records his 10 days of work at eight hours per day from 7/18/08 to 7/27/08.
10	7/28/08	Paid utilities expenses of $1,500 to Edison using Check No. 107.
11	7/28/08	Paid computer and Internet expenses of $1,200 to Verizon using Check No. 108.
12	7/28/08	Paid repairs and maintenance expenses of $3,000 to Harbor Marineworks (located at 122 Harbor Way, Santa Barbara, CA 93109) using Check No. 109.
13	7/29/08	The company bills Raytheon for 10 days of Charter Boat Captain and 10 days of CAT 50 (Terms: net 15) using Invoice No. 7002. Applied the deposit already received to this invoice. (Be sure to combine hours into one line item on the invoice.)

Event #	Date	Business Event
14	7/30/08	Made a payment of $2,940.93 to Bank of Caribbean, using Check No. 110, as an installment on the long-term note. ($1,324.50 of this amount is interest expense.)
15	7/31/08	Received a $3,400 bill from Creative Resource Group (a new vendor) for advertising services provided in July. Terms: net 30. (**Hint:** Use QuickBooks Enter Bills to record this transaction. Payment is not made until the following month.)
16	7/31/08	Paid employees for the period 7/16/08–7/31/08. Nathan and Jeanne worked 33 and 42 hours, respectively, during that period. Jack Sparrow has already recorded his time sheet. Start with Check No. 111. Payroll withholding information is shown in Table 8.3.

Table 8.3

Payroll and Withholding Information for Santa Barbara Sailing

Item	Rob	Jeanne	Nathan	Jack
Earnings	2,708.33	756.00	264.00	2,000.00
Federal Withholding	–514.58	–143.64	–50.16	–380.00
Social Security Employee	–167.92	–46.87	–16.37	–124.00
Medicare Employee	–39.27	–10.96	–3.83	–29.00
CA Income tax	–216.67	–60.48	–21.12	–160.00
CA Disability	–16.25	–4.54	–1.58	–12.00
CA Employee Training Tax	2.71	0.76	0.26	2.00
Social Security Employer	167.92	46.87	16.37	124.00
Medicare Employer	39.27	10.96	3.83	29.00
Federal Unemployment	21.67	6.05	2.11	16.00
CA Unemployment	92.08	25.70	8.98	68.00
Check Amount	1,753.64	489.51	170.94	1,295.00

Print the following as of 7/31/08.

a.   Profit & Loss Standard

b.   Balance Sheet Standard

c.   Statement of Cash Flows

d.   Transaction List by Date

Chapter 8 Cases

Chapter 8 Case 1:
FOREVER YOUNG

service

sole proprietorship

In Chapter 7, you added some transactions to your QuickBooks file for Forever Young. Make a copy of that file, and use that copy to enter the following transactions.

Event #	Date	Business Event
1	1/16/08	Sebastian ran into an old friend, Larry Rice, at one of his speaking engagements and decided to hire Larry to speak with him at selected events. Larry agreed to work on an hourly basis at $500 per hour, and Sebastian planned to bill Larry's time to customers at $750 per hour to cover overhead costs. Larry's Social Security number is 133-20-7357; he's married with one income and is subject to all California taxes. He'll constitute a new payroll item called Professional Hourly and will be paid semi-monthly like other employees. Be sure to set up a new service item named 004, description: Professional Services, rate: $750, to account Consulting Income.
2	1/17/08	Signed a contract with Microsoft (Terms: net 30) to provide a full-day seminar on 1/25/08 at their sales convention with Mr. Rice speaking for two hours. Received a $2,000 deposit via Microsoft's Check No. 09380991 which was deposited that day.
3	1/19/08	Spoke at the Adobe officer's retreat (a full-day seminar), prepared Invoice No. 503, applied the previous credit, and received the remaining $5,000 due via Adobe's Check No. 698903, which was immediately deposited into the company's checking account.
4	1/21/08	Borrowed $50,000 on a three-year 7% note payable from Wells Fargo Bank. The funds were deposited into the company's checking account that day.
5	1/22/08	Wrote Check No. 7 in the amount of $6,000 to Westwood Design and Production for the purchase of brochures to promote future speaking engagements. Sebastian expects these brochures to last throughout 2008 and treated them as Prepaid Advertising.
6	1/25/08	Provided a full-day seminar at Microsoft's sales convention, where Mr. Rice spoke for two hours. (**Hint:** Record his time on a time sheet.)
7	1/28/08	Prepared Invoice No. 504 to Microsoft (billing it for the full-day seminar and Mr. Rice's time), applied the previous credit, and mailed the invoice to Microsoft's accounting department.
8	1/30/08	Wrote Check No. 8 to Global Travel for $5,600 in travel expenses.
9	1/30/08	Wrote Check No. 9 to Hertz for $800 in automobile expenses.
10	1/30/08	Wrote Check No. 10 to Cingular Wireless for $500 of telephone expenses.
11	1/31/08	Paid semi-monthly payroll starting with Check No. 11 for the period 1/16/08 to 1/31/08. Payroll tax information is shown in Table 8.4. Anne worked 45 hours during this period.

Item	Cory	Anne	Larry
Earnings	3,333.33	900.00	1,000.00
Federal Withholding	−633.33	−171.00	−190.00
Social Security Employee	−206.67	−55.80	−62.00
Medicare Employee	−48.33	−13.05	−14.50
CA Income Tax	−266.67	−72.00	−80.00
CA Disability	−20.00	−5.40	−6.00
CA Employee Training Tax	3.33	0.90	1.00
Social Security Employer	206.67	55.80	62.00
Medicare Employer	48.33	13.05	14.50
Federal Unemployment	26.67	7.20	8.00
CA Unemployment	113.33	30.60	34.00
Check Amount	2,158.33	582.75	647.50

Table 8.4

Payroll and Withholding Information for Forever Young

Event #	Date	Business Event
12	1/31/08	Signed a contract with ITP Thomson (Terms: net 30) to provide a full-day seminar on 2/12/08 at their sales convention with Mr. Rice speaking for three hours. Received a $3,000 deposit via ITP's Check No. 15474, which was deposited the next day.
13	1/31/08	Wrote Check No. 14 to Sebastian Young for $5,000 as an owner's draw.

Requirements:

Print the following as of 1/31/08.

1 Profit & Loss Standard

2 Balance Sheet Standard

3 Statement of Cash Flows

4 Transaction List by Date (from 1/16/08 to 1/31/08)

5 Customer Balance Summary

6 Item Listing

Chapter 8 Case 2:
OCEAN VIEW FLOWERS

corporation   merchandising

In Chapter 7 you created a new QuickBooks file for Ocean View Flowers, a wholesale flower distributor. Make a copy of that file and use that copy to enter the following transactions,

Event #	Date	Business Event
1	2/1/08	The company repaid a portion of the long-term debt it borrowed from Santa Barbara Bank & Trust with Union Bank Check No. 119 in the amount of $1,000. (All of this payment was principal and none was interest.)
2	2/4/08	The company prepaid a one-year liability insurance policy to State Farm Insurance with Union Bank Check No. 120 in the amount of $2,500. (The transaction was recorded to Prepaid Insurance, an other current asset account.)
3	2/5/08	The company created Purchase Order No. 5002 to Vordale Farms for the following items to be purchased on terms of net 30. (Use QuickBooks Help to add terms to the purchase order form.) All anthuriums are recorded as Sales.

Flower	Quantity Ordered	Cost	Sales Price
Bright Red Anthuriums	700	$20.00	$35.00
Peach Anthuriums	800	$22.00	$40.00
White Anthuriums	600	$27.00	$50.00

Item	Edward	Kelly	Margie	Marie	Stan
Federal Withholding	−667.00	−123.00	−113.00	−402.00	−286.00
Social Security Employee	−180.83	−57.66	−53.57	−155.00	−129.17
Medicare Employee	−42.30	−13.48	−12.53	−36.25	−30.20
CA Withholding	−192.30	−20.93	−8.60	−153.55	−61.86
CA Disability Employee	−14.58	−4.65	−4.32	−12.50	−10.42
CA Employee Training Tax	1.17	0.93	0.86	2.00	2.08
Social Security Company	180.83	57.66	53.57	155.00	129.17
Medicare Company	42.30	13.48	12.53	36.25	30.20
Federal Unemployment	9.33	7.44	6.91	16.00	16.67
CA Unemployment	0.58	0.46	0.43	1.00	1.05
Check Amount	1,819.66	710.28	671.98	1,740.70	1,565.68

Table 8.5

Payroll Taxes and Withholding for Employees from February 1, 2008, through February 15, 2008

Event #	Date	Business Event
4	2/8/08	The company cashed in $5,000 of its $25,000 short-term investment early and received $5,200, which was deposited into the Union Bank account. The $200 difference represents Interest Income, a new other income account.
5	2/12/08	The company received the following bills. (Accept any changes in terms and add new vendors as necessary.)

Vendor	Amount	Terms	Expense
GTE	$250	Net 15	Telephone
Edison	$300	Net 15	Utilities
FlowerMart	$ 60	Net 30	Subscriptions

Event #	Date	Business Event
6	2/15/08	The company paid payroll. All employees worked the entire period; Kelly Gusland worked 62 hours and Margie Cruz worked 72 hours. Checks were written using the Union Bank account starting with Check No. 121. Payroll taxes and withholding for employees are shown in Table 8.5.
7	2/18/08	The company received items and entered the bill from Purchase Order No. 5002 to Vordale Farms on terms of net 30.
8	2/22/08	The company created invoices to customers as follows: (If terms change, accept them as permanent; also, apply any available credits to these invoices.)

Customer	Invoice #	Item Sold	Quantity	Terms	Invoice
Latin Ladies	10001	Calistoga Sun	400	Net 15	$ 9,000
		Caribbean Pink Sands	100		
California Beauties	10002	White Anthuriums	500	2/10 Net 30	$25,000
FTD	10003	Bright Red Anthuriums	300	Net 30	$10,500

Event #	Date	Business Event
9	2/25/08	The company paid its GTE and Edison bills using Union Bank Checks Nos. 126 and 127, respectively.
10	2/25/08	The company received $9,000 as payment on account from Latin Ladies. The amount was held for deposit at a later time.

Event #	Date	Business Event
11	2/26/08	The company purchased a warehouse and land for $300,000 ($50,000 of the purchase price is attributable to the land). A cash payment using Check No. 128 for $30,000 was made to Hawaiian Farms. The remaining balance of $270,000 was satisfied by signing a long-term note payable to the Bank of California. *Hint:* Use the check to record this entire transaction. (Be sure to create two new accounts: a land account and a building fixed asset account. Also make sure the land account appears in the chart of accounts before all other fixed assets and that the accumulated depreciation account is the last fixed asset account.)
12	2/29/08	The company paid payroll for the period ending February 29, 2008. All employees worked the entire period; Kelly Gusland worked 50 hours and Margie Cruz worked 45 hours. Checks were written using the Union Bank account starting with Check No. 129. Payroll taxes and withholding for employees are shown in Table 8.6.

Requirements:

Record business transactions in chronological order (remember, dates are in the month of February 2008). After recording the transactions, create and print the following for February 2008.

1   Standard Balance Sheet

2   Profit & Loss Standard

3   Statement of Cash Flows

4   Transaction List by Date

Table 8.6

Payroll Taxes and Withholding for Employees from February 16, 2008, through February 29, 2008

Item	Edward	Kelly	Margie	Marie	Stan
Federal Withholding	−667.00	−96.00	−64.00	−402.00	−286.00
Social Security Employee	−180.83	−46.50	−33.48	−155.00	−129.17
Medicare Employee	−42.29	−10.88	−7.83	−36.25	−30.21
CA Withholding	−192.30	−13.32	0.00	−153.55	−61.86
CA Disability Employee	−14.58	−3.75	−2.70	−12.50	−10.42
CA Employee Training Tax	0.00	0.75	0.54	0.00	0.75
Social Security Company	180.83	46.50	33.48	155.00	129.17
Medicare Company	42.29	10.88	7.83	36.25	30.21
Federal Unemployment	0.00	6.00	4.32	0.00	6.00
CA Unemployment	0.00	0.38	0.27	0.00	0.37
Check Amount	1,819.67	579.55	431.99	1,740.70	1,565.67

Chapter 8 Case 3:
ALOHA PROPERTIES

corporation   service

In Chapter 7, you created a new QuickBooks file for Aloha Properties. Make a copy of that file and use that copy to enter the following transactions.

Event #	Date	Business Event
1	2/1/08	Wrote Check No. 994 for $31,000 to GMAC Mortgage (a new vendor) as an installment payment on a 7% note payable. (Interest expense, $22,604; note payable, $8,396.)
2	2/1/08	Recorded Invoice No. 7511 for rental of Moana Units #1, #3, and #4 and Villa Kailiana Units #1 and #4 for one week to Pixar. Applied $14,000 of their advance payment to this invoice, noted terms due on receipt, and recorded receipt of balance owed of $14,080 in the form of Check No. 87275. (When you apply credits, type 14000 in the column Amt. To Use and then click Done.)
3	2/1/08	Deposited Pixar check for $14,080 into checking account.
4	2/4/08	Received payment on account from Apple Computer of $25,000 (their Check No. 987426).
5	2/4/08	Received a bill from Reilly Custodial for cleaning expenses of $3,500.
6	2/5/08	Collected a $15,000 deposit from a new customer, American Airlines.
7	2/6/08	Deposited $40,000 from Apple Computer and American Airlines into the Bank of Hawaii checking account.
8	2/7/08	Received a bill from Blue Sky Pools for maintenance expenses of $1,800.
9	2/8/08	Recorded Invoice No. 7512 for rental of Moana Unit #4 and Villa Kailiana Units #1 and #4 for one week to Pixar. Applied $10,000 of their advance payment to this invoice, noted terms due on receipt, and recorded receipt of balance owed of $11,840 in the form of Check No. 87351.
10	2/8/08	Deposited Pixar check for $11,840 into checking account.
11	2/8/08	Recorded Sales Receipt No. 5119 for rent of Moana Units #1, #2, and #3 for one week each. Collected American Express payment in full of $8,840 from new customer Accenture.
12	2/8/08	Deposited Accenture's American Express credit card payment of $8,840 into the checking account.
13	2/11/08	Received a bill from Pacific Electric for utilities expenses of $2,600 with terms of net 15.
14	2/15/08	Recorded Invoice No. 7513 for rental of Moana Unit #3 and Villa Kailiana Unit #4 for one week to ExxonMobil. Applied their advance payment to this invoice, noted terms due on receipt, and recorded receipt of balance owed of $5,275 from ExxonMobil's Check No. 943098.
15	2/15/08	Deposited ExxonMobil's check for $5,275 into checking account.
16	2/18/08	Received a bill from Service Connection (a new vendor) for repairs of $5,200. Terms are net 15.
17	2/20/08	Received a bill from Sunset Media for advertising of $1,450. Terms are net 30.
18	2/22/08	Recorded Invoice No. 7514 for rental of all units for one week to Boeing. Terms are net 30; invoice total is $39,728.
19	2/25/08	Collected a $3,250 deposit from new customer UCLA with their Check No. 1025575.

Table 8.7

Earnings Information

Item	Fran	Daniele
Hours	n/a	160
Rate	75,000	20.00
Earnings	6,250.00	3,200.00
Federal Withholding	−856.25	−438.40
Social Security Employee	−387.50	−198.40
Medicare Employee	−90.63	−46.40
HI Withholding	−442.33	−210.53
HI Disability	−1.25	−0.64
HI E&T	0.63	0.32
Social Security Employer	387.50	198.40
Medicare Company	90.63	46.40
Federal Unemployment	50.00	25.60
HI Unemployment	187.50	96.00
Check Amount	4,472.04	2,305.63

Event #	Date	Business Event
20	2/26/08	Collected a $7,500 deposit from new customer UCB with their Check No. 7031223.
21	2/26/08	Deposited both checks (items 19 and 20) into checking account.
22	2/27/08	Paid all bills due on or before 2/28/08 for a total of $9,700 using Check Nos. 995–997. Note that even though there are four bills requiring payment, two are to the same vendor (Blue Sky Pools) and thus only three checks are required.
23	2/28/08	Paid sales tax of $2,128 due on 1/31/08 with Check No. 998.
24	2/28/08	Paid payroll tax liabilities due on 1/31/08. Federal taxes are paid to the U.S. Treasury (Check Nos. 999 and 1000). State taxes are all paid to the State of Hawaii Department of Taxation using ID 84325184.
25	2/29/08	Process payroll per the information provided in Table 8.7, starting with Check No. 1001.

Requirements:

Record business transactions in chronological order (remember that dates are in the month of February 2008). After recording the transactions, create and print the following for February 2008.

1   Standard Balance Sheet

2   Profit & Loss Standard

3   Statement of Cash Flows

4   Transaction List by Date

Adjusting Entries

Case: **Wild Water Sports, Inc.**

Karen has recorded the majority of Wild Water's financing, investing, and operating activities for January through April 2009. To help her prepare financial statements for the first quarter, she asks you to prepare any necessary adjusting entries for the period January 1 through March 31, 2009.

"Some people have trouble with adjusting entries," you remark, "but I'm not one of them. I was always helping my classmates understand these types of journal entries. Why don't I give them a try?"

"Okay with me," Karen responds. "Traditional journal entries are available in QuickBooks, but you don't have to use them." Karen explains that in QuickBooks the most common adjusting entries—accruing expenses, accruing revenue, recording asset expirations, and recording liability reductions—can be made by using the Make Journal Entry menu item in the Company menu or by using account registers. You decide to use the traditional journal entry process.

Accruing Expenses

Wild Water Sports had a long-term liability of $383,800 when Karen and Donna made their initial investment. That loan was paid off along with accrued interest on March 6, 2009. The remaining balance in the Loan Payable account represents three different loans. The first—a $250,000, five-year, 5% loan from the Bank of Florida—was made on January 4, 2009. The second was a $50,000, three-year, 6% loan from Citibank made on February 5, 2009. The third was just recently

Video Demonstration

DEMO 9A - Accruing Expenses

acquired when the company purchased a computer from Staples for $5,000. Since then the company has made two payments on the Bank of Florida loan.

According to the loan amortization schedule (see Figure 8.1), a payment of $4,717.81 is due to be made at the beginning of April on the $250,000 loan; $1,010.97 of this payment represents interest owed. As of March 31, 2009, that interest should be included in interest expense for March. Payments are due annually on the $50,000 loan. Thus, as of March 31, 2009, the company owes $750 of interest ($50,000 × 6% × 3/12). The Staples loan bears no interest.

"QuickBooks automatically assigns journal entry numbers for reference," Karen points out. "Thus, the journal numbers we'll use for March 31 adjustments may follow journal entries used for April business events. What's important is the date specified in the journal."

"Okay," you respond. "I'll take the information you've provided and create the adjustment necessary for interest expense as of March 31."

To accrue interest expense:

1 Restore the Wild Water Sports Ch 9 (Backup) file from your Data Files CD or download it from the Internet.

2 Click **Company**, and then click **Make General Journal Entries.** If a message pops up about assigning numbers to journal entries, check the **Do not display this message in the future** check box and then click **OK.**

3 Type **3/31/09** as the journal entry date.

4 Type **8** as the Entry No.

5 Select **Interest Expense** as the first account.

6 Type **1010.97** as the amount in the Debit column. This will increase Interest Expense (an expense account).

7 Type **Accrued Expenses** as the second account and then press **[Tab].**

8 Click **Setup** in the Account Not Found window and create a new account called Accrued Expenses, an other current liability account.

9 Type **1010.97** as the amount in the Credit column. This will increase Accrued Expenses. The resulting journal entry should look like Figure 9.1.

10 Click **Save & New.**

11 Type **3/31/09** as the journal entry date.

12 Type **9** as the Entry No.

13 Select **Interest Expense** as the first account.

14 Type **750** as the amount in the Debit column.

15 Select **Accrued Expenses** as the second account, and then press **[Tab].**

16 Type **750** as the amount in the Credit column.

17 Click **Save & New.**

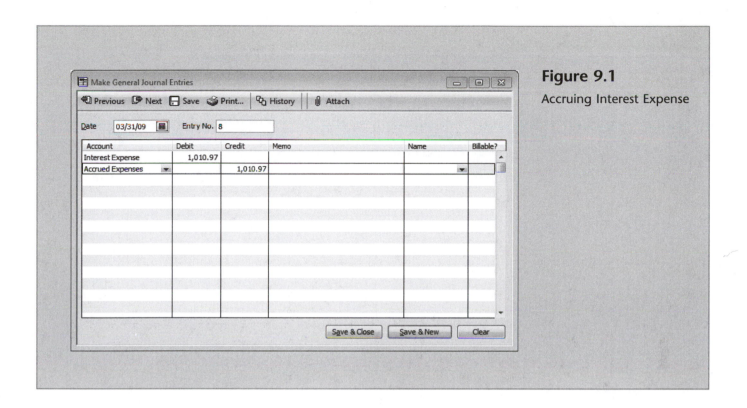

Figure 9.1

Accruing Interest Expense

Karen explains that this process reflects interest expenses in the correct accounting period (first quarter of 2009) and establishes the liability as of March 31, 2009. However, when the company pays the next installment on the $250,000 loan in April, it will have to remember that the interest has already been accrued.

"Either that, or we can reverse the adjustment as of April 1 and then just record the next payment as we've done in the past, with a portion of the payment going to interest expense and a portion going to reduce the loan principal," you suggest.

"I like that idea," Karen answers. "Do we do the same for the $50,000 loan?"

"Not necessarily," you respond. "The $50,000 loan is on an annual payment plan, so if we reverse the journal entry as of April 1 then we'll have to reestablish it again as of March 31 and accrue more interest for the second quarter. I suggest we reverse all accrual entries to be consistent."

To reverse all accrued expense entries:

1 Type **4/1/09** as the journal entry date.

2 Type **10** as the Entry No.

3 Select **Accrued Expenses** as the first account.

4 Type **1010.97** as the amount in the Debit column.

5 Select **Interest Expense** as the second account.

6 Type **1010.97** as the amount in the Credit column. Your journal entry should look like Figure 9.2.

Figure 9.2

Reversing Entry

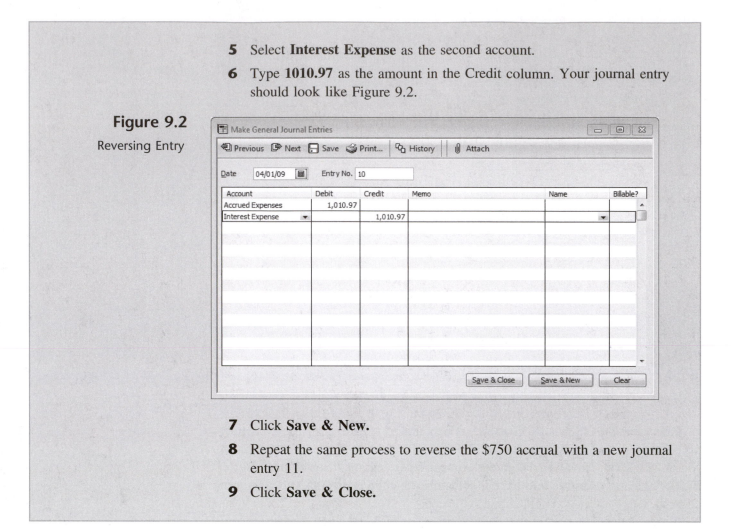

7 Click **Save & New.**

8 Repeat the same process to reverse the $750 accrual with a new journal entry 11.

9 Click **Save & Close.**

"After these entries were recorded on April 1, the accrued expense balance was 0 and interest expense for April has a credit balance of $1,760.97. Now," you explain, "when we record the next payment on this loan, we can use the amortization schedule to record the interest paid and reduction of principal. The payment will reduce cash and increase interest expense by $1,010.97, creating a balance of 0 in interest expense for April. If we need to provide GAAP-based financial statements in April, we'll need to accrue interest owed at April 30 for both loans."

Accruing Revenue

Video Demonstration

DEMO 9B - Accruing revenues

Karen tells you that she can also use journal entries to record revenue earned on investments. She points out that, during the quarter, the company had some short-term investments with ETrade that earned money market interest, which is paid quarterly. Since no interest was paid during the quarter, no interest income has been recorded. After checking with their investment advisor, Karen learns that $1,890.41 of interest income was earned but unpaid as of March 31, 2009.

To accrue interest income:

1 Click **Company**, and then click **Make General Journal Entries.**

2 Type **3/31/09** as the journal entry date.

3 Type **12** as the Entry No.

4 Select **Short-Term Investments** as the first account.

5 Type **1890.41** as the amount in the Debit column.

6 Type **Interest Income** as the second account.

7 Click **Setup** in the Account Not Found window and create a new account called Interest Income, an other income account.

8 Type **1890.41** as the amount in the Credit column.

9 Click **Save & New.**

"Aren't we going to record more interest income?" you ask. "Why did we choose to record this as interest income?"

"QuickBooks doesn't follow the accounting convention of recording interest revenue," you point out. "QuickBooks was originally created as a tool for businesses preparing tax returns, and the Internal Revenue Service uses the income reference for interest instead of revenue. Rather than changing the account title, we'll just use Interest Income."

Karen reminds you that you should reverse the interest income accrual, as you did with interest expense, on the first day of the following month. That way, when the interest income is actually received, it can be recorded and will be offset by the previous accrual.

To reverse the interest income accrual:

1 Type **4/1/09** as the journal entry date.

2 Type **13** as the Entry No.

3 Select **Interest Income** as the first account.

4 Type **1890.41** as the amount in the Debit column.

5 Select **Short-Term Investments** as the second account.

6 Type **1890.41** as the amount in the Credit column.

7 Click **Save & New.**

"Another issue we have to address is whether any products were delivered to customers but not recorded as sales at the end of the month," Karen comments. "For example, our records show that we delivered a boat to Spirit Adventures on March 31 but didn't invoice them until April 2. Thus, as of March 31, 2009, we need to accrue that additional revenue, sales tax, and cost of goods sold."

"Don't you also have to reduce inventory, since our records show that boat in inventory March 31?" you ask.

To adjust for sales occurring in March but not invoiced until April:

1 Type **3/31/09** as the journal entry date.

2 Type **14** as the Entry No.

3 Select **Accounts Receivable** as the first account.

4 Type **69225** as the amount in the Debit column.

5 Select **Spirit Adventures** as the Name in this row.

6 Select **Boat Sales** as the second account.

7 Type **65000** as the amount in the Credit column.

8 Select **Spirit Adventures** as the Name in this row.

9 Select **Sales Tax Payable** as the third account (a new account).

10 Type **4225** as the amount in the Credit column.

11 Select **Florida Department of Revenue** as the Name in this row.

12 Select **Cost of Goods Sold** as the fourth account.

13 Type **52000** as the amount in the Debit column.

14 Select **Spirit Adventures** as the Name in this row.

15 Select **Inventory Boats** as the fifth account.

16 Type **52000** as the amount in the Credit column.

17 Select **Spirit Adventures** as the Name in this row.

Figure 9.3

Accruing Sales Revenue

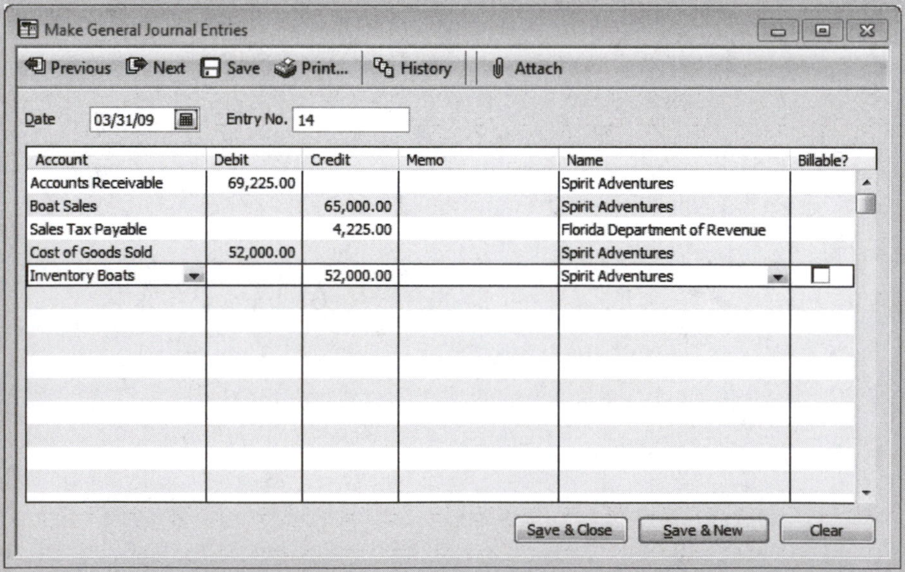

Make General Journal Entries					
Previous Next Save Print... History Attach					

Account	Debit	Credit	Memo	Name	Billable?
Accounts Receivable	69,225.00			Spirit Adventures	
Boat Sales		65,000.00		Spirit Adventures	
Sales Tax Payable		4,225.00		Florida Department of Revenue	
Cost of Goods Sold	52,000.00			Spirit Adventures	
Inventory Boats		52,000.00		Spirit Adventures	

Date 03/31/09   Entry No. 14

Save & Close   Save & New   Clear

18 Mark this item as unbillable by clicking the **Billable?** icon so the check box is unchecked. Your journal entry should look like Figure 9.3.

19 Click **Save & New.**

"Exactly," Karen answers, "plus, since this transaction is recorded as an invoice in April, we'll need to reverse this accrual entry on April 1."

"Where did you get the Cost of Goods Sold and Inventory Boat information?" you ask.

"I got it from our list of items, which provides the sales price, income account, and cost," Karen answers. "When we accrue the sales revenue, we must also accrue the related cost of goods sold."

Karen explains that this is another case where it is best to reverse this accrual the first of the next month so that, when the actual invoice is recorded in April, it will be offset by the previous accrual.

"This accrual accounting process is a lot of work!" you comment.

"Yes," Karen agrees. "But at least we get a picture of our performance and financial position based on when events occur, not just when we get around to recording them."

To reverse the sales accrual:

1 Type **4/1/09** as the journal entry date.

2 Type **15** as the Entry No.

3 Select **Accounts Receivable** as the first account.

4 Type **69225** as the amount in the Credit column.

5 Select **Spirit Adventures** as the Name in this row.

6 Select **Boat Sales** as the second account.

7 Type **65000** as the amount in the Debit column.

8 Select **Spirit Adventures** as the Name in this row.

9 Select **Sales Tax Payable** as the third account.

10 Type **4225** as the amount in the Debit column.

11 Select **Florida Department of Revenue** as the Name in this row.

12 Select **Cost of Goods Sold** as the fourth account.

13 Type **52000** as the amount in the Credit column.

14 Select **Spirit Adventures** as the Name in this row.

15 Select **Inventory Boats** as the fifth account.

16 Type **52000** as the amount in the Debit column.

17 Select **Spirit Adventures** as the Name in this row.

18 Mark this item as unbillable by clicking the **Billable?** icon so the check box is unchecked. Your journal entry should look like Figure 9.4.

Figure 9.4

Reversing the Sales Accrual April 1

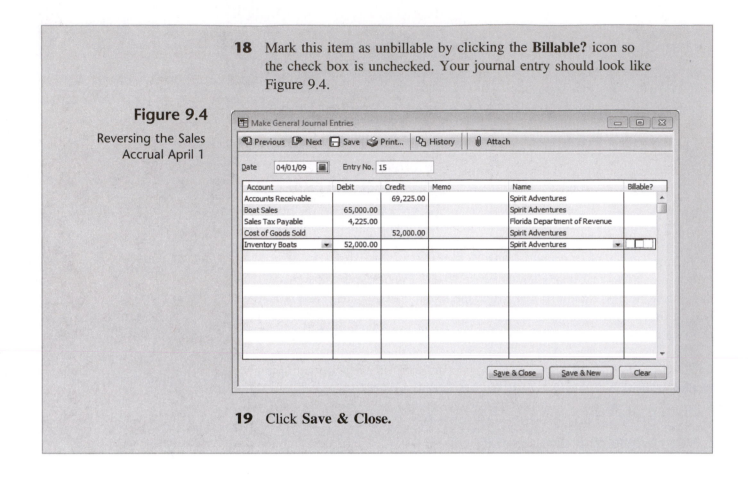

19 Click **Save & Close.**

Recording Expenses Incurred but Previously Deferred

Video Demonstration

DEMO 9C - Recording expenses previously deferred

The adjustments that you and Karen have recorded account for previously unrecorded transactions. Now Karen wants to demonstrate how to record adjustments that affect previously recorded business activity, such as the prepayment of expenses and the purchase of fixed assets.

On February 7, 2009, Wild Water Sports paid $24,000 to Coe Marketing for a one-year advertising campaign. Since this payment represented an expenditure that benefited more than the one accounting period, it was correctly recorded to Prepaid Advertising, an asset account.

On March 31, 2009, two months of the time period covered by the ad campaign had expired. Thus, two-twelfths of the cost ($4,000) should be recorded as Advertising and Promotion Expense with the Prepaid Advertising account reduced accordingly. Each month thereafter, one-twelfth of the cost ($2,000) should be recorded as Advertising and Promotion Expense with the Prepaid Advertising account reduced accordingly.

To adjust prepaid advertising:

1 Click **Company**, and then click **Make General Journal Entries.**

2 Type **3/31/09** as the journal entry date.

3 Type **16** as the Entry No.

4 Select **Advertising and Promotion** as the first account.

5 Type **4000** as the amount in the Debit column.

6 Select **Prepaid Advertising** as the second account.

7 Type **4000** as the amount in the Credit column.

8 Click **Save & New.**

On January 31, 2009, Wild Water Sports paid $22,000 to Manchester Insurance for a one-year liability insurance policy covering it for the calendar year 2009. Once again, since this payment represented an expenditure that benefited more than one accounting period, it was correctly recorded to Prepaid Insurance, an asset account.

On March 31, 2009, three months of the time period covered by the insurance policy had expired. Thus, three-twelfths of the cost ($5,500) should be recorded as insurance expense and the Prepaid Insurance account reduced accordingly. Each month thereafter, one-twelfth of the cost ($1,833.33) should be recorded as insurance expense and the Prepaid Insurance account reduced accordingly.

To adjust prepaid insurance:

1 Type **3/31/09** as the journal entry date.

2 Type **17** as the Entry No.

3 Select **Insurance Expense** as the first account.

4 Type **5500** as the amount in the Debit column.

5 Select **Prepaid Insurance** as the second account.

6 Type **5500** as the amount in the Credit column.

7 Click **Save & New.**

A similar adjustment called *depreciation* is needed to allocate the cost of previously recorded depreciable fixed assets. Depreciation on fixed assets is usually accumulated in a contra-asset account on the balance sheet for control purposes.

Although QuickBooks does have a separate module available to track fixed assets and calculate depreciation, Karen has chosen not to purchase this feature. Instead, she maintains a separate spreadsheet to track when fixed assets were purchased, how much depreciation should be recorded, and when fixed assets are sold. Her analysis indicates that $10,333 of depreciation should be recorded as of March 31, 2009, to reflect depreciation for the first quarter of 2009.

To record depreciation expense:

1 Type **3/31/09** as the journal entry date.

2 Type **18** as the Entry No.

3 Select **Depreciation Expense** as the first account.

4 Type **10333** as the amount in the Debit column.

5 Select **Accumulated Depreciation** as the second account.

6 Type **10333** as the amount in the Credit column. Your journal entry should look like Figure 9.5.

Figure 9.5

Depreciation Adjustment

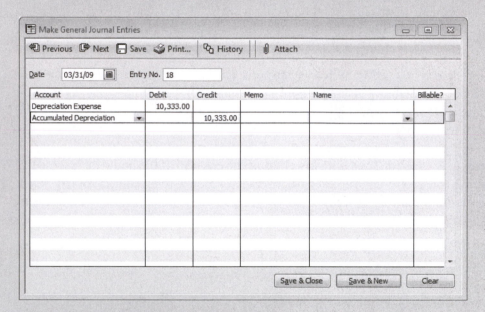

7 Click **Save & Close.**

8 If the Tracking Fixed Assets on Journal Entries window appears, check the box **Do not display this message in the future** and then click **OK.**

You ask Karen about reversing the prepaid advertising, insurance, and depreciation adjusting entries. She explains that accruals of income and expense need reversal entries but that adjustments of deferrals like prepaids and depreciation do not.

"They won't have subsequent events that we need to offset," she explains. "These adjustments are permanent."

You find these procedures to be very straightforward but are curious about the financial statement impact of these adjusting entries so far. You wonder if QuickBooks provides a way to view financial statements so you can see what effect these adjustments have had. Karen tells you that QuickBooks does have such a feature—you can view financial statements at any time without having to post entries. She suggests that you look at the balance sheet as of March 31, 2009, to see the effect of this adjustment on the balance sheet.

To view the fixed assets portion of the balance sheet as of March 31, 2009:

1 From the Reports Center create a Standard Balance Sheet.

2 Enter **3/31/09** in the As of text box, and then click **Refresh.**

3 Follow Karen's analysis (next paragraph) while referring to Figure 9.6.

Figure 9.6

Balance Sheet after Adjusting Entries So Far

Wild Water Sports Ch 9
Balance Sheet

	Mar 31, 09
ASSETS	
Current Assets	
Checking/Savings	
Bank of Florida	47,392.42
Short-Term Investments	39,890.41
Total Checking/Savings	87,282.83
Accounts Receivable	
Accounts Receivable	389,932.73
Total Accounts Receivable	389,932.73
Other Current Assets	
Prepaid Advertising	20,000.00
Inventory Boats	243,600.00
Inventory Parts	2,112.00
Prepaid Insurance	16,500.00
Total Other Current Assets	282,212.00
Total Current Assets	759,427.56
Fixed Assets	
Furniture and Equipment	295,000.00
Accumulated Depreciation	-17,833.00
Total Fixed Assets	277,167.00
TOTAL ASSETS	1,036,594.56
LIABILITIES & EQUITY	
Liabilities	
Current Liabilities	
Accounts Payable	
Accounts Payable	216,200.00
Total Accounts Payable	216,200.00
Other Current Liabilities	
Accrued Expenses	1,760.97
Payroll Liabilities	2,934.66
Sales Tax Payable	28,457.66
Total Other Current Liabilities	33,153.29
Total Current Liabilities	249,353.29
Long Term Liabilities	
Loans Payable	297,632.40
Total Long Term Liabilities	297,632.40
Total Liabilities	546,985.69
Equity	
Capital Stock	400,000.00
Net Income	89,608.87
Total Equity	489,608.87
TOTAL LIABILITIES & EQUITY	1,036,594.56

4 Close all windows.

Karen remarks that the ending balance in Prepaid Advertising as of March 31, 2009, makes sense given that Wild Water has 10 months left of the ad campaign (10 months × $2,000 per month = $20,000). She also says that the ending balance in Prepaid Insurance as of March 31, 2009, also makes sense because Wild Water has 9 months left of insurance coverage (9 months × $1,833.33 per month = $16,500). Finally, she notes the new balances in the Accumulated Depreciation accounts.

Having tackled the adjustments for prepaid and for depreciable assets, you and Karen are now ready to move on to the last category—adjusting unearned revenue.

Adjusting for Unearned Revenues

Video Demonstration

DEMO 9D - Recording revenues previously deferred

On March 31, 2009, Wild Water Sports received $10,000 from its customer Performance Rentals as a deposit on a boat in stock. On this date, Performance Rentals had an existing balance outstanding, but you and Karen chose to account for this as a separate transaction and not to apply this payment to the amount due. As described in Chapter 8, Karen recorded this transaction by increasing the checking account and decreasing Performance Rental's Accounts Receivable. Karen has decided to reclassify it as Unearned Revenue, a liability, on March 31, 2009. Here's why. Cash has been received, but the boat has not been delivered. Thus, on March 31, you need to reclassify the $10,000 to an unearned revenue account (a liability). When the company actually sells the boat to Performance Rentals in a future period, Wild Water will create an invoice, record the sale, and apply the credit remaining.

The effect of this adjusting journal entry is to increase accounts receivable and increase unearned revenue, reflecting the fact that Wild Water still has a balance owed by Performance Rentals of $1,293.98 and owes Performance Rentals $10,000 if it doesn't deliver the boat on which Performance placed the deposit. This entry is then reversed on 4/1/09 so that, when the sale takes place later, the credit can be applied.

To reclassify the $10,000 as unearned revenue at 3/31/09 and then reverse the reclassification on 4/1/09:

1 Click **Company**, and then click **Make General Journal Entries.**

2 Type **3/31/09** as the journal entry date.

3 Type **19** as the Entry No.

4 Select **Accounts Receivable** as the first account.

5 Type **10000** as the amount in the Debit column.

6 Select **Performance Rentals** as the Name of the customer to which this journal entry applies.

7 Type **Unearned Revenue** as the second account, and then press **[Tab].**

8 Click **Setup** to create a new account.

9 Select **Other Current Liability** from the drop-down list of other account types.

10 Verify **Unearned Revenue** as the Name.

11 Click **Save & Close** to create this new account.

12 Type **10000** as the amount in the Credit column.

13 Select **Performance Rentals** as the Name of the customer to which this journal entry applies. Your screen should look like Figure 9.7.

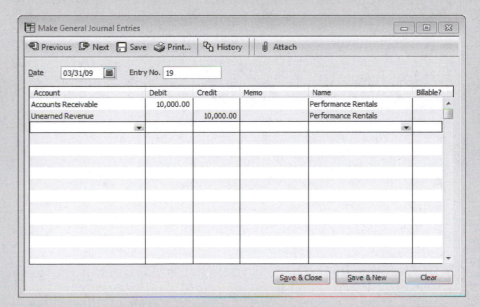

Figure 9.7

Adjusting for Unearned Revenue

14 Click **Save & New.**

15 Type **4/1/09** as the journal entry date.

16 Type **20** as the Entry No.

17 Select **Unearned Revenue** as the first account.

18 Type **10000** as the amount in the Debit column.

19 Select **Performance Rentals** as the Name.

20 Select **Accounts Receivable** as the second account.

21 Type **10000** as the amount in the Credit column.

22 Select **Performance Rentals** as the Name.

23 Click **Save & Close.**

"I always like to print out a copy of my adjustments to make sure everything was recorded correctly," Karen comments. "QuickBooks has a journal feature that we can use to print just those transactions occurring on March 31 and April 1 so we can see the effects of our adjustments."

To print the journal for March 31 and April 1:

1 Click **Reports** from the menu bar, click **Accountant & Taxes**, and then click **Journal.**

2 Click the **Modify Report** button.

3 Click the **Display** tab and then uncheck the **Memo** and **Trans #** fields so they do not show up in the Journal report.

4 Click the **Header/Footer** tab and then uncheck the **Date Prepared** and **Time Prepared** check boxes.

5 Click the **Filters** tab.

6 Select **Transaction Type** from the Choose Filter list and then select **Journal** from the drop-down list of Transaction Type.

7 Click **OK.**

Wild Water Sports Ch 9
Journal
March 31, 2009

Type	Date	Num	Name	Account	Debit	Credit
General Journal	3/31/09	6	Staples Staples	Furniture and Equipment Loans Payable	5,000.00	 5,000.00
					5,000.00	5,000.00
General Journal	3/31/09	8		Interest Expense Accrued Expenses	1,010.97	 1,010.97
					1,010.97	1,010.97
General Journal	3/31/09	9		Interest Expense Accrued Expenses	750.00	 750.00
					750.00	750.00
General Journal	3/31/09	12		Short-Term Investments Interest Income	1,890.41	 1,890.41
					1,890.41	1,890.41
General Journal	3/31/09	14	Spirit Adventures Spirit Adventures Florida Department of Revenue Spirit Adventures Spirit Adventures	Accounts Receivable Boat Sales Sales Tax Payable Cost of Goods Sold Inventory Boats	69,225.00 52,000.00	 65,000.00 4,225.00 52,000.00
					121,225.00	121,225.00
General Journal	3/31/09	16		Advertising and Promotion Prepaid Advertising	4,000.00	 4,000.00
					4,000.00	4,000.00
General Journal	3/31/09	17		Insurance Expense Prepaid Insurance	5,500.00	 5,500.00
					5,500.00	5,500.00
General Journal	3/31/09	18		Depreciation Expense Accumulated Depreciation	10,333.00	 10,333.00
					10,333.00	10,333.00
General Journal	3/31/09	19	Performance Rentals Performance Rentals	Accounts Receivable Unearned Revenue	10,000.00	 10,000.00
					10,000.00	10,000.00
TOTAL					159,709.38	159,709.38

Figure 9.8

Journal Entries on 3/31/09

8 Type **3/31/09** in both the From and To text boxes and then click **Refresh.**

9 Click **Print** in the report toolbar, choose **Landscape** orientation, and then **Print** in the Print Reports window. Your report should look like Figure 9.8.

10 Type **4/1/09** in both the From and To text boxes and then click **Refresh.**

11 Click **Print** in the report toolbar, choose **Landscape** orientation, and then **Print** in the Print Reports window. Your report should look like Figure 9.9.

12 Close all windows and return to the home page.

Wild Water Sports Ch 9
Journal
April 1, 2009

Type	Date	Num	Name	Account	Debit	Credit
General Journal	4/1/09	10		Accrued Expenses	1,010.97	
				Interest Expense		1,010.97
					1,010.97	1,010.97
General Journal	4/1/09	11		Accrued Expenses	750.00	
				Interest Expense		750.00
					750.00	750.00
General Journal	4/1/09	13		Interest Income	1,890.41	
				Short-Term Investm...		1,890.41
					1,890.41	1,890.41
General Journal	4/1/09	15	Spirit Adventures	Accounts Receivable		69,225.00
			Spirit Adventures	Boat Sales	65,000.00	
			Florida Department ...	Sales Tax Payable	4,225.00	
			Spirit Adventures	Cost of Goods Sold		52,000.00
			Spirit Adventures	Inventory Boats	52,000.00	
					121,225.00	121,225.00
General Journal	4/1/09	20	Performance Rentals	Unearned Revenue	10,000.00	
			Performance Rentals	Accounts Receivable		10,000.00
					10,000.00	10,000.00
TOTAL					134,876.38	134,876.38

Figure 9.9

Journal Entries on 4/1/09

Karen explains that most of these journals reflect the adjustments you just made and seem to be in order. She points out that each transaction has a transaction number, a type, a date, and a journal number (if applicable) as well as names, accounts, debits, and credits.

Preparing a Bank Reconciliation and Recording Related Adjustments

Video Demonstration

DEMO 9E - Preparing a bank reconciliation

Every month, the Bank of Florida sends Wild Water Sports a bank account statement that lists all deposits received by the bank and all checks and payments that have cleared the bank as of the date of the statement. You and Karen examine the bank statements for the months of January, February, and March; the latter shows an ending balance of $47,172.23 as of March 31, 2009. You would normally reconcile your statement each month, but you've been a little busy these last couple of months. You now turn your attention toward reconciling that balance with the balance reported by QuickBooks. You note that QuickBooks indicates an ending checking account balance of $47,392.42 at that same date. You believe that most of the difference between these two amounts is probably attributable to "outstanding checks" that Wild Water Sports has written but that the bank hasn't yet paid, deposits it has recorded but have not been received by the bank, bank service charges, and interest income.

A review of all three statements shows that all checks recorded by Wild Water Sports have been paid by the bank except payroll checks written on 3/30/09, totaling $6,994.74. All deposits recorded by the company have been received by the bank except one dated 3/29/09 for $7,264.93. Bank charges per the bank statement total $75, which has not yet been recorded by the company. Interest income credited to the company's bank account in the amount of $125 also has not yet been recorded by the company.

To reconcile the bank statement as of 3/31/09:

1 Click **Reconcile** in the Banking section of the home page.

2 Select **Bank of Florida** as the account to be reconciled.

3 Type **3/31/09** as the Statement Date.

4 Type **47,172.23** as the Ending Balance.

5 Type **75** as the Service Charge, **3/31/09** as the Date, and **Bank Service Charges** as the Account.

Figure 9.10

Beginning a Bank Reconciliation

Begin Reconciliation		☒
Select an account to reconcile, and then enter the ending balance from your account statement.		

Account: Bank of Florida

Statement Date: 03/31/09

Beginning Balance: 25,000.00   *What if my beginning balance doesn't match my statement?*

Ending Balance: 47,172.23

Enter any service charge or interest earned.

Service Charge	Date	Account
75.00	03/31/09	Bank Service Charges
Interest Earned	**Date**	**Account**
125.00	03/31/09	Interest Income

Locate Discrepancies   Undo Last Reconciliation   Continue   Cancel   Help

6   Type **125** as the Interest Earned, **3/31/09** as the Date, and **Interest Income** as the Account. Your screen should look like Figure 9.10.

7   Click **Continue.**

8   When the Reconcile – Bank of Florida window appears, click in the check box at the top of the page that says **Hide transactions after the statement's end date.**

9   Place a check mark next to all of the checks, payments, and service charges in January, February, and March of 2009 except Check Nos. 1038, 1039, and 1040. (These are the payroll checks issued 3/31/09 that have not yet cleared the bank.)

10 Place a check mark next to all of the Deposits, Interest, and Other Credits in January, February, and March of 2009 except the deposit of $7,264.93 dated 3/27/09. Your screen should look like Figure 9.11.

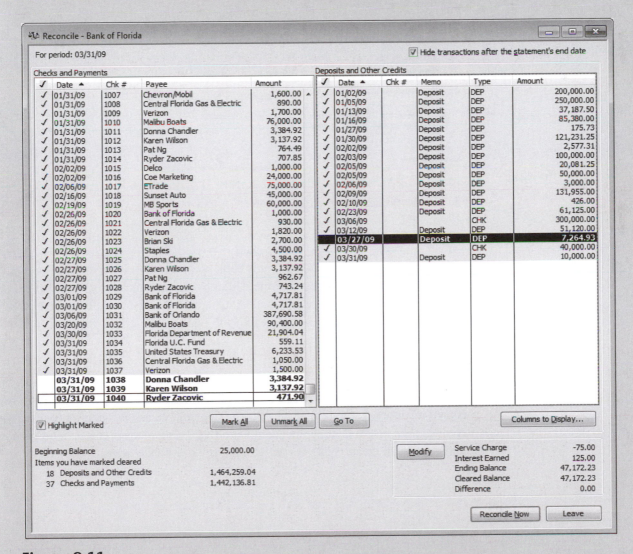

Figure 9.11

Bank Reconciliation Process

11 Note the difference of 0.00 in the lower right corner of the window.

12 Click **Reconcile Now.**

13 Click the **Summary** button.

14 Click the **Print** button and then click Print again to print this report. Your printout should look like Figure 9.12. Click **OK** in the Reconciliation Report window.

Figure 9.12

Summary Bank Reconciliation Report

Wild Water Sports Ch 9
Reconciliation Summary
Bank of Florida, Period Ending 03/31/09

	Mar 31, 09
Beginning Balance		25,000.00
Cleared Transactions	
Checks and Payments - 38 items	-1,442,211.81
Deposits and Credits - 19 items	1,464,384.04
Total Cleared Transactions	22,172.23
Cleared Balance		47,172.23
Uncleared Transactions	
Checks and Payments - 3 items	-6,994.74
Deposits and Credits - 1 item	7,264.93
Total Uncleared Transactions	270.19
Register Balance as of 03/31/09		47,442.42
New Transactions	
Checks and Payments - 13 items	-262,890.05
Deposits and Credits - 6 items	291,675.08
Total New Transactions	28,785.03
Ending Balance		76,227.45

15 Close the Reconciliation Summary window.

The only adjustments created in this bank reconciliation were the recognition of bank service fees and interest income. QuickBooks automatically records these in the checking account. Once reconciled, QuickBooks also inserts a check mark next to each transaction that has cleared the bank in the check register.

End Note

You've now helped Karen record various adjustments including accrued expenses, accrued revenues, expiration of prepaid and depreciable assets, creation of unearned revenue, and one reflecting the completion of bank reconciliation. You're now almost ready to create Wild Water Sports's financial statements.

Business Events Summary

Business Event	Process Steps	Page
Accruing expenses	Use make journal entries from Company menu	261
Reversing accrued expenses	Use make journal entries from Company menu	263
Accruing revenues	Use make journal entries from Company menu	264
Reversing accrued revenues	Use make journal entries from Company menu	265
Adjusting prepaid expenses	Use make journal entries from Company menu	268
Recording depreciation	Use make journal entries from Company menu	270
Adjusting unearned revenue	Use make journal entries from Company menu	272
Reconcile bank accounts	Use reconcile from Banking section of home page	276

Chapter 9 Questions

1 Explain the journal entry method of recording end-of-period adjustments.

2 Give an example of accrued revenue other than the examples given in this chapter. Explain how your example of accrued revenue would be adjusted using journal entries.

3 Give an example of an accrued expense other than the example given in this chapter. Explain how your example of accrued expense would be adjusted using journal entries.

4 Give an example of asset expiration other than the example given in this chapter. Explain how your example would be adjusted using journal entries.

5 Give an example of unearned revenue, and explain the process for end-of-period adjustments involving unearned revenue.

6 Explain how to access general journal entries.

7 What menu item do you use to start bank reconciliations?

8 What account is typically used to record service charges?

9 When you've finished reconciling a bank account, what should be the difference between the ending balance and the cleared balance?

10 What information is included in the Reconciliation Summary report?

Chapter 9 Matching

Select the letter of the item below that best matches the definitions that follow. Use the text or QuickBooks Help to complete this assignment.

a. Adjusting entries   _____ A liability for expenses created with adjusting journal entries.

b. Accrued expenses   _____ An asset for expenses paid but not yet incurred.

c. Prepaid expenses   _____ Entries made on the first of the following month that offset adjusting entries recorded in the previous period.

d. Accumulated depreciation   _____ Deposits/checks that the bank has received/paid and have been recorded in the accounting records.

e. General journal entries   _____ A liability for amounts received from customers before a company delivers a product or service.

f.   Unearned revenues   _____ Deposits/checks that the bank has not received/paid but have been recorded in the accounting records.

g.   Reversing entries   _____ Entries made to record the correct amount of revenue earned or expenses incurred that are not correctly recorded in the accounting records.

h.   Reconciliation   _____ Used to record business events made without the use of a source document like an invoice, bill, or check.

i.   Cleared transactions   _____ A contra-asset account used to amass the effects of a fixed asset's depreciation.

j.   Uncleared transactions   _____ A comparison made between the bank's records and a business's accounting records.

Chapter 9 Exercises

Chapter 9 Exercise 1
ACCRUING EXPENSES

Restore the file Boston Catering Ch 9 (Backup) found on the text CD or download it from the text Web site. Make the following adjustments and then print an income statement and balance sheet for the period 7/1/10 through 9/30/10 setting the columns to Month so that you view an income statement for July, August, and September 2010 and a balance sheet as of 7/31/10, 8/31/10, and 9/30/10.

a.   Accrue interest expense (a new other expense type account) and the related accrued expense liability as of 7/31/10 and 8/31/10 based on the following schedules (note that on 8/2/10 the company made the July payments of 926.29 and 610.32):

Month	Payment	Interest	Principle	Balance
				$ 50,000.00
Jul 2010	$926.29	$ 416.67	$509.63	$ 49,490.37
Aug 2010	$926.29	$ 412.42	$513.87	$ 48,976.50
Sep 2010	$926.29	$ 408.14	$518.15	$ 48,458.35

Month	Payment	Interest	Principle	Balance
				$ 25,000.00
Jul 2010	$610.32	$ 166.67	$443.66	$ 24,556.34
Aug 2010	$610.32	$ 163.71	$446.61	$ 24,109.73
Sep 2010	$610.32	$ 160.73	$449.59	$ 23,660.14

Month	Payment	Interest	Principle	Balance
				$ 10,000.00
Jul 2010	$0	$ 50.00	$0	$ 10,000.00
Aug 2010	$0	$ 50.00	$0	$ 10,000.00
Sep 2010	$0	$ 50.00	$0	$ 10,000.00

b. Reverse accrued interest expense for the first two loans on 8/1/10 and 9/1/10 as appropriate. Do not reverse accrued interest expense on the $10,000 loan.

Chapter 9 Exercise 2
ACCRUING REVENUE

Restore the file Boston Catering Ch 9 (Backup) found on the text CD or download it from the text Web site. Do not use the file created in Exercise 1 above. Make the following adjustments and then print an income statement and balance sheet for the period 7/1/10 through 9/30/10 setting the columns to Month so that you view an income statement for July, August, and September 2010 and a balance sheet as of 7/31/10, 8/31/10, and 9/30/10.

a. Accrue interest income (a new other income type account) as of 7/31/10 of $11 to the short-term investments account. Interest is paid at the end of every calendar quarter.

b. On 8/1/10 reverse the interest income accrual you made above.

c. Accrue interest income as of 8/31/10 of $115 to the short-term investments account.

d. On 9/1/10 reverse the interest income accrual you made above.

e. On 9/1/10 the company billed Fidelity Investments on invoice 1125 for a catering engagement held on 8/31/10 for 200 Fall Suppers (Item Code S300) resulting in $13,000 in catering sales and $650 in sales tax, which were billed on account (total $13,650). Sales tax is paid to Mass. Dept. of Revenue. The food purchases of $4,000 were set up as accounts payable to US Food Service. Accrue this revenue and expense as of 8/31/10.

f. On 9/1/10 reverse the revenue and expense accrual made above.

g. On 9/1/10 record the invoice described in (e) above.

h. On 9/1/10 record check 1512 to US Food Service for $4,000 in food purchases.

Chapter 9 Exercise 3
RECORDING EXPENSES INCURRED BUT PREVIOUSLY DEFERRED

Restore the file Boston Catering Ch 9 (Backup) found on the text CD or download it from the text Web site. Do not use the file created in the exercises above. Make the following adjustments and then print an income statement and balance sheet for the period 7/1/10 through 9/30/10 setting the columns to Month so that you view an income statement for July, August, and September 2010 and a balance sheet as of 7/31/10, 8/31/10, and 9/30/10.

a. The $3,000 prepaid insurance balance recorded as of 6/30/10 represented 3 months of insurance premiums, which expire equally in July, August, and September.

b. Depreciation expense was $1,000, $1,075, and $1,350 for the months of July, August, and September.

Chapter 9 Exercise 4
PREPARING BANK RECONCILIATION

Restore the file Boston Catering Ch 9 (Backup) found on the text CD or download it from the text Web site. Do not use the file created in the exercises above. Reconcile the Bank of America checking account and then print a summary bank reconciliation for each month.

a. The 7/31/10 Bank of America bank statement shows an ending balance of $78,881 with service charges of $39. All deposits made in July were received by the bank except that made on 7/31/10, which was received by the bank on 8/1/10. All checks written in July were cashed by the bank except check numbers 1505 through 1508, which cleared the bank in August.

b. The 8/31/10 Bank of America bank statement shows an ending balance of $54,036.64 with service charges of $45. All deposits made in August were received by the bank. All checks written in August were cashed by the bank except check numbers 1517 through 1522.

Chapter 9 Assignments

Chapter 9 Assignment 1
ADDING MORE INFORMATION: WILD WATER SPORTS

corporation

merchandising

Restore the file Wild Water Sports Ch 9A (Backup) found on the text CD or download it from the text Web site. Then add the following adjustments and perform bank reconciliation on the checking account as of April 30, 2009.

Event #	Date	Business Event
1	5/1/09	Invoice No. 10014 was recorded on this date for the sale of an MS LX to Alisa Hay for $52,000 plus tax. (Even though this isn't an adjusting entry, record this invoice on 5/1/09 in QuickBooks to illustrate how the accrual and reversal works.)
2	4/30/09	Accrue interest expense of $995.52 on the $250,000 loan as per the amortization schedule in Figure 8.1 with journal entry no. 21.
3	5/1/09	Prepare reversing entry of the preceding interest accrual with journal entry no. 22.

Event #	Date	Business Event
4	4/30/09	Accrue interest expense of $1,000 on the $50,000 loan and record related reversing entry on 5/1/09 with journal entry nos. 23 and 24.
5	4/30/09	Accrue interest income of $3,600 on short-term investments and record related reversing entry on 5/1/09 with journal entry nos. 25 and 26.
6	4/30/09	Records show that the company delivered an MS LX to Alisa Hay on April 30 but did not invoice her until May 1. The boat was sold for $52,000 and cost $41,600. Sales tax in the amount of $3,380 was collected on May 1 from the sale. Sales tax is paid to the Florida Dept. of Revenue. Prepare the appropriate adjusting entry no. 27.
7	5/1/09	Reverse the preceding sales revenue accrual with journal entry no. 28.
8	4/30/09	Adjust prepaid advertising $2,000 for April with journal entry no. 29.
9	4/30/09	Adjust prepaid insurance $1,833 for April with journal entry no. 30.
10	4/30/09	Record depreciation expense of $3,870 for the month of April with journal entry no. 31.
11	4/30/09	Reclassify the deposit of $16,250 received from Buena Vista Water Sports on 4/30/09 a to unearned revenue and record the related reversing entry on 5/1/09 with journal entry nos. 32 and 33.
12	4/30/09	The Bank of Florida bank statement as of 4/30 has an ending balance of $54,475.02. All checks cleared the bank account except Check Nos. 1050 to 1053. All deposits cleared the bank account except the $30,517.35 deposit made 4/30. The bank statement shows interest income of $35 and bank charges of $25.

a. Perform a reconciliation on the checking account and then print a summary bank reconciliation as of April 30, 2009.

b. Print a Profit & Loss Standard report for the month of April 2009.

c. Print a Balance Sheet Standard report as of April 30, 2009.

d. Print journal entries recorded on April 30, 2009 (no memo field, and make sure that you filter the transaction type for journal items only).

e. Print journal entries recorded on May 1, 2009 (no memo field, and make sure that you filter the transaction type for journal items only).

f. Print a standard income statement for the month of May 2009.

sole proprietorship

merchandising

Chapter 9 Assignment 2
ADDING MORE INFORMATION: CENTRAL COAST CELLULAR

Restore the file Central Coast Cellular Ch 9 (Backup) found on the text CD or download it from the text Web site. Then add the following adjustments and perform bank reconciliation on the checking account as of January 31, 2009.

Event #	Date	Business Event
1	1/31/09	Record depreciation expense of $1,500 for equipment and office furniture.
2	1/31/09	Accrue interest expense of $950.
3	1/31/09	Reclassify the credit balance of $10,000 in the City of San Luis Obispo account to unearned revenue.
4	1/31/09	The bank statement dated January 31, 2009, indicated a bank balance of $133,640.49, with all checks clearing except numbers 3010, 3011, and 3012. All deposits cleared. A bank service charge of $80 was reported.
5	2/1/09	Make all appropriate reversing entries.

a. Perform a reconciliation on the checking account and then print a summary bank reconciliation as of January 31, 2009.

b. Print a Profit & Loss Standard report for the month of January 2009.

c. Print a Balance Sheet Standard report as of January 31, 2009.

d. Print journal entries recorded from January 31, 2009, to February 1, 2009 (no memo field, and make sure that you filter the transaction type for journal items only).

Chapter 9 Assignment 3
ADDING MORE INFORMATION: SANTA BARBARA SAILING

corporation

service

Restore the file Santa Barbara Sailing Ch 9 (Backup) found on the text CD or download it from the text Web site, and use that copy to record the following events.

Event #	Date	Business Event
1	7/31/08	Adjust prepaid rent for $2,000 to rent expense with journal entry no. 5.
2	7/31/08	Accrue interest expense on the $50,000 Bank of Caribbean loan for $134.25 with journal entry no. 6.
3	7/31/08	Record depreciation for the month of $5,750 with journal entry no. 7.
4	7/31/08	The boat rented to Barry Cohen for 14 days was paid in advance and recorded in full. Of this amount, $2,079 was unearned as of 7/31/08. Reduce rental income accordingly and create unearned revenue with journal entry no. 8.
5	8/1/08	Make all appropriate reversing journal entries.
6	7/31/08	The bank statement dated 7/31/08 indicated a bank balance of $122,206.74, with all checks clearing except numbers 111–114. The bank charged a fee of $43 and provided interest income (other income account) of $70. All deposits were accounted for.

    a. Perform a reconciliation on the checking account, and then print a summary bank reconciliation as of July 31, 2008.

    b. Print a Profit & Loss Standard report for the month of July 2008.

    c. Print a Balance Sheet Standard report as of July 31, 2008.

    d. Print journal entries recorded from July 31, 2008, to August 1, 2008 (no memo field, and make sure that you filter the transaction type for journal items only).

Chapter 9 Cases

Chapter 9 Case 1:
FOREVER YOUNG

sole proprietorship   *service*

In Chapter 8, you added some transactions to your QuickBooks file for Forever Young. Make a copy of that file, and use that copy to record the following transactions.

Event #	Date	Business Event
1	1/31/08	Record the use of office supplies for January with journal entry no. 1 (assume that supplies are used evenly throughout the period for which they were purchased).
2	1/31/08	Accrue interest expense on Wells Fargo note payable of $96 with journal entry no. 2.
3	1/31/08	Record the use of brochures for January with journal entry no. 3 (assume that brochures are used equally each month).
4	1/31/08	Reclassify ITP's deposit to unearned revenue with journal entry no. 4.
5	1/31/08	Record depreciation of $67 for the month with journal entry no. 5.
6	2/1/08	Make all appropriate reversing journal entries.
7	1/31/08	The bank statement dated 1/31/08 indicated a bank balance of $63,233.82, with all checks clearing except numbers 11–14. The bank charged a fee of $25 and provided interest income (other income account) of $115. All deposits were accounted for.

Requirements:

1 Perform reconciliation on the checking account and then print a summary bank reconciliation as of January 31, 2008.

2 Print a Profit & Loss Standard report for the month of January 2008.

3 Print a Balance Sheet Standard report as of January 31, 2008.

4 Print journal entries recorded from January 31, 2008, to February 1, 2008 (no memo field, and make sure that you filter the transaction type for journal items only).

corporation   merchandising

Chapter 9 Case 2:
OCEAN VIEW FLOWERS

In Chapter 8, you modified your QuickBooks file for Ocean View Flowers. Make a copy of that file, and use that copy to record the following transactions.

Event #	Date	Business Event
1	1/31/08	The January bank statement reported an ending balance of $76,340.30, bank service charges of $45, and interest revenue of $100 as of January 31, 2008. Deposits for $100,000, $50,000, $6,600, and $22,200 were received by the bank. Checks 101–110 were paid by the bank.
2	2/29/08	Accrue interest expense of $3,190 on the $319,000 loan with journal entry no. 1.
3	3/1/08	Prepare reversing entry of the preceding interest expense accrual with journal entry no. 2.
4	2/29/08	Accrue interest income of $800 on short-term investments with journal entry no. 3.
5	3/1/08	Prepare reversing entry for the preceding interest income accrual with journal entry no. 4.
6	2/29/08	Record expired prepaid insurance of $100 for the months of January and February 2008 with journal entry no. 5.
7	2/29/08	Record depreciation expense of $3,100 with journal entry no. 6.
8	2/29/08	Reclassify the deposit of $5,000 received from FTD on 1/28/08 to unearned revenue with journal entry no. 7.
9	3/1/08	Prepare reversing entry for the preceding unearned revenue reclassification with journal entry no. 8.
10	2/29/08	A review of the shipping records indicates that a shipment of 2/28 was not invoiced until 3/3. Invoice No. 10004, recorded in the next accounting period, billed California Beauties $16,000 for 800 Calistoga Sun Daylilies, $7,200 for 300 Almond Puff Daylilies, and $20,000 for 500 Peach Anthuriums (cost: $22,600). Accrue this event with journal entry no. 9.
11	3/1/08	Prepare reversing entry for Invoice No. 10004 with journal entry no. 10.
12	2/29/08	The February bank statement reported an ending balance of $65,579.64, bank service charges of $55, and interest income of $75 as of February 29, 2008. Deposits for $5,000 and $5,200 were received by the bank. Checks 111–127 were paid by the bank.

Requirements:

1 Perform a reconciliation on the checking account, and then print a summary bank reconciliation as of January 31, 2008.

2 Perform a reconciliation on the checking account and then print a summary bank reconciliation as of February 29, 2008.

3 Print a Profit & Loss Standard report for the two months ended February 29, 2008.

4 Print a Balance Sheet Standard report as of February 29, 2008.

5 Print journal entries recorded from February 29 to March 1, 2008 (no memo field, and make sure that you filter the transaction type for journal items only).

Chapter 9 Case 3:
ALOHA PROPERTIES

In Chapter 8, you modified your QuickBooks file for Aloha Properties. Make a copy of that file and use that copy to record the following transactions.

Event #	Date	Business Event
1	2/29/08	Accrue interest expense of $22,555 on the $3,875,000 loan to a new account: Accrued Expenses.
2	3/1/08	Prepare reversing entry of the preceding interest accrual.
3	2/29/08	Accrue interest income of $210 on short-term investments.
4	2/29/08	Adjust prepaid insurance for January and February 2008 to insurance expense.
5	2/29/08	Record depreciation expense of $34,612 for the months of January and February 2008.
6	2/29/08	Reclassify the deposits received from American Airlines, UCLA, and UCB on 2/5/08, 2/25/08, and 2/26/08, respectively, to unearned revenue (a new other current liability account).
7	2/29/08	Prepare a reversing entry for the unearned reclassification.
8	2/29/08	The Bank of Hawaii bank statement as of 2/29 shows an ending balance of $115,292.39. All checks cleared the bank account except Checks 998–1002. All deposits cleared the bank account except for the 2/26 deposit of $10,750. The bank statement reports interest income of $175 and bank charges of $35.

Requirements:

1 Perform a reconciliation on the checking account, and then print a summary bank reconciliation as of February 29, 2008.

2 Print a Profit & Loss Standard report for the month of February 2008.

3 Print a Balance Sheet Standard report as of February 29, 2008.

4 Print journal entries recorded February 29 through March 1, 2008 (no memo field, and make sure that you filter the transaction type for journal items only).

Budgeting

Learning Objectives

In this chapter, you will:

- Create budgets for revenues
- Create budgets for expenses
- Create a budget for assets, liabilities, and equities
- Create a budgeted income statement
- Create a budgeted balance sheet

Case: **Wild Water Sports, Inc.**

Today Donna asks you and Karen to prepare financial statements for the first quarter of the year. She reminds you that you have already recorded all of the transactions for January through April, so you're ready to prepare the statements as of the end of the first quarter, March 31.

"But preparing the statements is only half the job," Karen points out. "We must be able to interpret these statements. How will we know if the company is doing well?"

Donna is quick to respond, "At the beginning of the year, I used a spreadsheet program to establish budgets for the year. I can compare the actual results shown in the statements you prepare with these budgets."

"Doesn't QuickBooks have a budgeting feature?" you ask.

"You're right!" exclaims Donna, "I didn't use that feature, but now that you mention it, I should have. Would the two of you mind entering my budget estimates into QuickBooks as well?"

"Not at all," you respond.

After Donna leaves, Karen explains to you that QuickBooks allows you to set up a budget for an account or for a customer within an account. To do this, you enter budget amounts for the income statement accounts or balance sheet accounts that you wish to track.

"Are you able to track actual versus budgeted amounts?" you ask.

"Yes," Karen replies. "I'll show you how to use QuickBooks's budget reports to examine the budget by itself as well as how to compare Wild Water Sports's actual results to its budgeted amounts."

You have another question. "Can we create different budgets based on different assumptions in QuickBooks?"

"No," Karen answers. "QuickBooks allows you to have a different budget for different fiscal years, but you may have only one budget per fiscal year."

Karen explains that QuickBooks allows you to set up budgets for specific accounts within financial statements or for all specific financial statements. It is easier to budget for specific accounts, but it might be more useful to prepare a budgeted income statement or budgeted balance sheet.

To begin, Karen suggests that you print Donna's spreadsheet budget. Then the two of you can establish the monthly budget for revenues.

Video Demonstration

DEMO 10A - Budgeting revenues

Budgeting Revenues

QuickBooks provides a setup window to enter budget information. In this window you specify fiscal year, account, customer and/or class, and the corresponding amounts for each month. As you fill in this information, you are setting up a budget for a single account, such as a balance sheet or an income statement account. If you also choose a customer:job or a class, you can set up a budget for that account and for that customer:job or class.

"I remember entering customer:job information in QuickBooks, but what are classes?" you ask.

"Classes are categories QuickBooks provides to help you group data into departments, product lines, locations, and the like," Karen responds.

"Do we need to set up budgets for customers or classes?" you ask.

"Donna's budget isn't that detailed," Karen responds. "We'll enter information for accounts only."

You also ask about QuickBooks's use of the term "income" instead of "revenues" for products and services. Karen reminds you that although "revenues" is the traditional accounting term for these items, QuickBooks has chosen to classify them as "income" in the type section of the chart of accounts.

Donna's budget predicts merchandise revenue of $200,000 in January 2009 and increasing by $50,000 each month throughout the year. Service and parts revenue is expected to remain constant, at $3,000 and $500 per month throughout the year.

To create a budget for specific revenues:

1   Restore the Wild Water Sports Ch 10 (Backup) file from your Data Files CD or download it from the Web site. See "Data Files CD" in Chapter 1 if you need more information.

2   Click **Company**, click **Planning & Budgeting**, and then click **Setup Budgets.**

3   Select **2009** as the budget year and **Profit and Loss** as the budget type in the Create New Budgets window, and then click **Next** twice.

4   Select the **Create budget from scratch** option, and click **Finish.**

5   The resulting Setup Budgets window is shown in Figure 10.1.

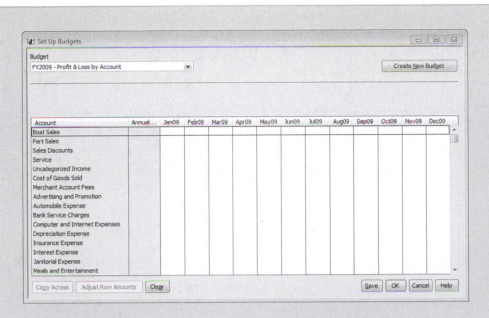

Figure 10.1

Setting Up Budgets

Trouble? Your screen may show the budget split into two 6-month periods based on your screen size. If that occurs, then you will need to press the **Show Next 6 Months** or **Show Prev 6 Months** button in order to enter information in the other 6-month period. Screen shots displayed in this chapter presume that your screen size will accommodate all 12 months.

6   Click in the cell at the intersection of the Jan09 column and the Boat Sales row. Type **200000.**

7   Click the **Adjust Row Amounts** button.

8   Select **Currently selected month** from the Start at drop-down list.

9   Select the first option button and type **50000** as the amount you want to increase each remaining month.

10   Select the **Enable compounding** check box. Your screen should look like Figure 10.2.

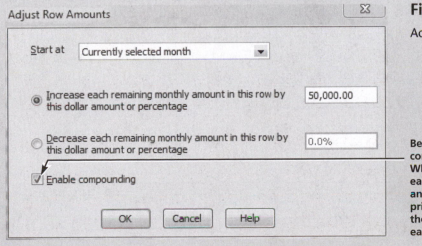

Figure 10.2

Adjusting Row Amounts

Be sure to check the Enable compounding check box. When this box is checked, each month is increased by an amount or % based on the prior month. In other words, the effect is compounded each month.

11 Click **OK.**

12 Click in between the Annual Total column title and the Jan09 title. Hold the mouse button down and increase the column width so that the amounts are completely visible.

13 Use the same method to increase the column width of the Jan09, Feb09, Mar09, and Apr09 columns.

14 Click on the **Part Sales** title of the next row so you can see the Boat Sales row amounts more clearly. Your screen should look like Figure 10.3.

Figure 10.3

Increased Column Widths

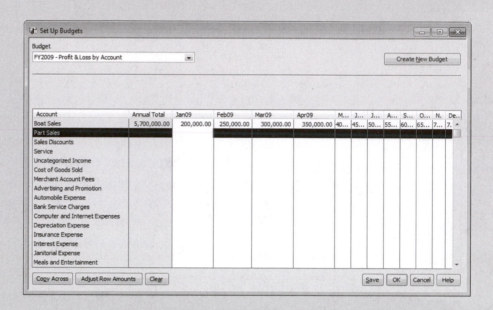

15 Click in the cell at the intersection of the Jan09 column and the Part Sales row. Type **500.**

16 Click the **Copy Across** button.

17 Click in the cell at the intersection of the Jan09 column and the Service row. Type **3000.**

18 Click the **Copy Across** button. The income portion of your budget for January through April 2009 should look like Figure 10.4.

Figure 10.4

Budgeted Revenue

Account	Annual Total	Jan09	Feb09	Mar09	Apr09
Boat Sales	5,700,000.00	200,000.00	250,000.00	300,000.00	350,000.00
Part Sales	6,000.00	500.00	500.00	500.00	500.00
Sales Discounts					
Service	36,000.00	3,000.00	3,000.00	3,000.00	3,000.00

Now you're ready to set up budget revenue amounts for expenses.

Budgeting Expenses

Video Demonstration

DEMO 10B - Budgeting expenses

The budget for Wild Water Sports cost of goods sold depends on product sales. Donna estimated that product cost should amount to approximately 80% of sales, since they mark up the boats 25% above their cost. Thus, as budgeted sales increase, so should budgeted cost of sales. Karen recalls that in January you set up the budget to include merchandise sales of $200,000. Thus, expected cost of sales should be 80% of the total January sales of $200,000, or $160,000. Each month thereafter, Donna expects sales of merchandise to increase by $50,000. Accordingly, the related costs of goods sold should increase monthly by 80% of $50,000, or $40,000.

Karen expects payroll expenses, the largest budgeted expense item for Wild Water Sports, to remain constant at $12,000 per month throughout the year. Depreciation expenses are expected to be $3,500 per month, insurance expenses $2,000 per month, office supplies $1,000 per month, advertising and promotion $2,500 per month, interest expense $2,800 per month, telephone expenses $2,100 per month, and utilities $900 per month.

To create a budget for specific expenses:

1 Click in the cell at the intersection of the Jan09 column and the Cost of Goods Sold row. Type **200000*.80** and then press the [**Enter**] key. This illustrates how to use the calculator function of the Budget process. The result should be 160,000.00.

2 Click the **Adjust Row Amounts** button.

3 Select **Currently selected month** from the Start at drop-down list.

4 Select the first option button, and type **40000** as the amount you want to increase each remaining month.

5 Select the **Enable compounding** check box.

6 Click **OK.**

7 Click in the cell at the intersection of the Jan09 column and the Advertising and Promotion row. Type **2500.**

8 Click the **Copy Across** button.

9 Click in the cell at the intersection of the Jan09 column and the Depreciation Expense row. Type **3500.**

10 Click the **Copy Across** button.

11 Click in the cell at the intersection of the Jan09 column and the Insurance Expense row. Type **2000.**

12 Click the **Copy Across** button.

13 Click in the cell at the intersection of the Jan09 column and the Interest Expense row. Type **2800.**

14 Click the **Copy Across** button.

15 Click in the cell at the intersection of the Jan09 column and the Office Supplies row. Type **1000.**

16 Click the **Copy Across** button.

17 Click in the cell at the intersection of the Jan09 column and the Payroll Expenses row. Type **12000.**

18 Click the **Copy Across** button.

19 Click in the cell at the intersection of the Jan09 column and the Telephone Expense row. Type **2100.**

20 Click the **Copy Across** button.

21 Click in the cell at the intersection of the Jan09 column and the Utilities row. Type **900.**

22 Click the **Copy Across** button.

23 Click **Save** to save your newly created budget, and then click **OK** to close the window.

Now that all of the detailed income and expense amounts have been created for our budget, you can create a budgeted income statement.

Budgeted Income Statement

Karen has entered budgetary information for several specific Profit & Loss report accounts, and she is curious to see a complete budget. To do this, she will create and print a budgeted Profit & Loss report for the first quarter of 2009.

To create and print a budget overview report:

1 From the **Report Center**, select **Budgets** and then double-click **Budget Overview.**

2 Select **FY2009—Profit & Loss by Account**, and then click **Next.**

3 Select **Account by Month**, and then click **Next.**

4 Click **Finish.**

5 Enter **1/1/09** and **3/31/09** as the From date and To date, respectively, in the Profit & Loss Budget Overview window. (Alternatively, you could use the calendar icons and choose specific dates.)

6 Click the **Refresh** button, and then modify the report to exclude the date prepared, time prepared, and report basis fields.

7 Click the **Print** button in the Report window.

8 Click **Portrait**, click the **Fit Report to 1 Page Wide** check box, and then click **Print** to print the report. Your report should look like Figure 10.5.

Wild Water Sports Ch 10
Profit & Loss Budget Overview
January through March 2009

	Jan 09	Feb 09	Mar 09	TOTAL Jan - Mar 09
Ordinary Income/Expense				
Income				
Boat Sales	200,000.00	250,000.00	300,000.00	750,000.00
Part Sales	500.00	500.00	500.00	1,500.00
Service	3,000.00	3,000.00	3,000.00	9,000.00
Total Income	203,500.00	253,500.00	303,500.00	760,500.00
Cost of Goods Sold				
Cost of Goods Sold	160,000.00	200,000.00	240,000.00	600,000.00
Total COGS	160,000.00	200,000.00	240,000.00	600,000.00
Gross Profit	43,500.00	53,500.00	63,500.00	160,500.00
Expense				
Advertising and Promotion	2,500.00	2,500.00	2,500.00	7,500.00
Depreciation Expense	3,500.00	3,500.00	3,500.00	10,500.00
Insurance Expense	2,000.00	2,000.00	2,000.00	6,000.00
Interest Expense	2,800.00	2,800.00	2,800.00	8,400.00
Office Supplies	1,000.00	1,000.00	1,000.00	3,000.00
Payroll Expenses	12,000.00	12,000.00	12,000.00	36,000.00
Telephone Expense	2,100.00	2,100.00	2,100.00	6,300.00
Utilities	900.00	900.00	900.00	2,700.00
Total Expense	26,800.00	26,800.00	26,800.00	80,400.00
Net Ordinary Income	16,700.00	26,700.00	36,700.00	80,100.00
Net Income	16,700.00	26,700.00	36,700.00	80,100.00

Figure 10.5

Budget Overview Report

9 Review the revised report, and then close its window.

Karen explains that this report simply describes the current budget but does not compare that budget with actual results from the quarter ended March 31, 2009. She suggests that you create a Budget vs. Actual report for the quarter ended March 31, 2009, showing only quarterly amounts.

"Why not monthly?" you ask.

"Remember, we made our adjusting entries only at the end of March," Karen reminds you. "We didn't make adjusting entries at the end of January and February. As a result, a monthly analysis of budget versus actual would reveal all sorts of discrepancies. Take insurance, for example. We budgeted insurance expense of $2,000 per month for January, February, and March. Our actual insurance expense will not be recorded until March, when we made an adjusting entry for prepaid insurance. Thus, we'll be under budget in January and February and over budget in March just because of when we recorded our adjustments."

"Then why don't we make adjusting entries every month?" you ask.

"Good question," Karen answers. "We could, but it would take lots of time. Instead, we'll just produce financial statements every quarter, since that's when the bank wants to see how we're doing."

To create and print a Budget vs. Actual report for the first quarter of 2009:

1 From the **Report Center**, select **Budgets** and then double-click **Budget vs. Actual.**

2 Select **FY2009—Profit & Loss by Account** then click **Next.**

3 Select **Account by Month**, and then click **Next.**

4 Click **Finish.**

5 Enter **1/1/09** and **3/31/09** as the From date and To date, respectively, in the Profit & Loss Budget vs. Actual window.

6 Select **Quarter** from the drop-down list of Columns.

7 Click the **Refresh** button, and then modify the report to exclude the date prepared, time prepared, and report basis fields.

8 Click the **Print** button in the report window.

9 Click **Portrait**, click the **Fit Report to 1 Page Wide** check box, and then click **Print** to print the report. Your report should look like Figure 10.6.

Figure 10.6

Budget vs. Actual Report

Wild Water Sports Ch 10
Profit & Loss Budget vs. Actual
January through March 2009

	Jan - Mar 09	Budget	$ Over Budget	% of Budget
Ordinary Income/Expense				
Income				
Boat Sales	767,500.00	750,000.00	17,500.00	102.3%
Part Sales	610.00	1,500.00	-890.00	40.7%
Service	6,685.00	9,000.00	-2,315.00	74.3%
Total Income	774,795.00	760,500.00	14,295.00	101.9%
Cost of Goods Sold				
Cost of Goods Sold	614,488.00	600,000.00	14,488.00	102.4%
Total COGS	614,488.00	600,000.00	14,488.00	102.4%
Gross Profit	160,307.00	160,500.00	-193.00	99.9%
Expense				
Advertising and Promotion	6,700.00	7,500.00	-800.00	89.3%
Bank Service Charges	75.00			
Depreciation Expense	10,333.00	10,500.00	-167.00	98.4%
Insurance Expense	5,500.00	6,000.00	-500.00	91.7%
Interest Expense	7,719.57	8,400.00	-680.43	91.9%
Office Supplies	4,500.00	3,000.00	1,500.00	150.0%
Payroll Expenses	32,945.97	36,000.00	-3,054.03	91.5%
Telephone Expense	5,020.00	6,300.00	-1,280.00	79.7%
Utilities	2,870.00	2,700.00	170.00	106.3%
Total Expense	75,663.54	80,400.00	-4,736.46	94.1%
Net Ordinary Income	84,643.46	80,100.00	4,543.46	105.7%
Other Income/Expense				
Other Income				
Interest Income	2,015.41			
Other Income	3,000.00			
Total Other Income	5,015.41			
Net Other Income	5,015.41			
Net Income	89,658.87	80,100.00	9,558.87	111.9%

Karen points out that, based on the Budget vs. Actual report, the company is doing pretty well. She'll ask Donna about budgeting for bank service charges and other income, since neither was included in the budget. She also wants to investigate the actual office supplies, which the report indicates were 50% over budget.

Budgeting Assets, Liabilities, and Equities

Video Demonstration

DEMO 10C - Budgeting assets, liabilities, and equities

Karen explains why creating specific budgets for assets, liabilities, and stockholders' equity accounts is not a simple task. First, you cannot complete this task until the budget for revenues and expenses has been established. This is due to the relationship that exists between net income and retained earnings. Budgeted retained earnings are dependent on net income/net loss. That is, budgeted retained earnings must be increased by monthly net income and decreased by monthly net losses, if any.

Second, budgets for accounts receivable are dependent on sales, whereas budgets for inventory and accounts payable are dependent on cost of sales and projected sales. Budgeted accumulated depreciation accounts are increased by monthly depreciation expenses. Fortunately for you and Karen, Donna has already created this budget in her spreadsheet program.

Donna's budget for assets had forecast the cash financing activities of issuing more stock, offering credit terms to their customers, buying more inventory for the showroom, temporarily investing some cash, and then eventually paying down some debt. She also planned to increase accounts payable by getting suppliers to offer credit terms.

Karen suggests that you complete this task one step at a time—first entering the budget for assets, then the budget for liabilities and for stockholders' equity. You agree and remind her that the budget amounts for these accounts are the ending balance expected for each quarter. For now, you'll just be creating budgeted balances for assets at the end of March 2009.

To create a budget for assets:

1 Click **Company**, then click **Planning & Budgeting**, and then click **Setup Budgets.**

2 Click the **Create New Budget** button.

3 Select **2009** as the budget year and **Balance Sheet** as the budget type in the Create New Budgets window, click **Next**, and then click **Finish.**

4 Click in the cell at the intersection of the Mar09 column and the Bank of Florida row. Type **34250.**

5 Click in the cell at the intersection of the Mar09 column and the Short-Term Investments row. Type **50000.**

6 Click in the cell at the intersection of the Mar09 column and the Accounts Receivable row. Type **400000.**

7 Click in the cell at the intersection of the Mar09 column and the Prepaid Advertising row. Type **20000.**

8 Click in the cell at the intersection of the Mar09 column and the Inventory Boats row. Type **200000.**

9 Click in the cell at the intersection of the Mar09 column and the Inventory Parts row. Type **2000.**

10 Click in the cell at the intersection of the Mar09 column and the Prepaid Insurance row. Type **16500.**

11 Click in the cell at the intersection of the Mar09 column and the Furniture and Equipment row. Type **295000.**

12 Click in the cell at the intersection of the Mar09 column and the Accumulated Depreciation row. Type **–17750.**

13 Click **Save.** Your screen should look like Figure 10.7.

Figure 10.7

Entering Asset Information into the Budget

Account	Annual Total	Jan09	Feb09	Mar09
Bank of Florida	34,250.00			34,250.00
Short-Term Investments	50,000.00			50,000.00
Accounts Receivable	400,000.00			400,000.00
Prepaid Advertising	20,000.00			20,000.00
Inventory Boats	200,000.00			200,000.00
Inventory Parts	2,000.00			2,000.00
Prepaid Insurance	16,500.00			16,500.00
Undeposited Funds				
Furniture and Equipment	295,000.00			295,000.00
Accumulated Depreciation	-17,750.00			-17,750.00

The liabilities and stockholders' equity items are less numerous, but they include (among others) accounts payable, loans payable, capital stock, and retained earnings. Loans payable was relatively easy to predict because the owners planned to borrow funds when they first opened up and then to pay down some of that debt when they took on another investor and sold some inventory. Capital stock was also easy, since Donna and Karen knew what they were going to invest and had already planned on a fourth investor. Retained earnings were linked to Donna's estimate for net income; because the company started the year with no retained earnings, ending retained earnings as of March 31 had to equal their budgeted net income, given that they hadn't planned to distribute any earnings via dividends.

To create a budget for liabilities and stockholders' equity:

1 Click in the cell at the intersection of the Mar09 column and the Accounts Payable row. Type **200000.**

2 Click in the cell at the intersection of the Mar09 column and the Accrued Expenses row. Type **1500.**

3 Click in the cell at the intersection of the Mar09 column and the Payroll Liabilities row. Type **3000.**

4 Click in the cell at the intersection of the Mar09 column and the Sales Tax Payable row. Type **15400.**

5 Click in the cell at the intersection of the Mar09 column and the Loans Payable row. Type **300000.**

6 Click in the cell at the intersection of the Mar09 column and the Capital Stock row. Type **400000.**

7 Click in the cell at the intersection of the Mar09 column and the Retained Earnings row. Type **80100.**

8 Click **Save.** The lower portion of your screen should look like Figure 10.8.

Accounts Payable	200,000.00		200,000.00
MasterCard			
Unearned Revenue			
Accrued Expenses	1,500.00		1,500.00
Payroll Liabilities	3,000.00		3,000.00
Sales Tax Payable	15,400.00		15,400.00
Loans Payable	300,000.00		300,000.00
Capital Stock	400,000.00		400,000.00
Dividends Paid			
Opening Balance Equity			
Retained Earnings	80,100.00		80,100.00

Figure 10.8

Entering Liability and Equity Information into the Budget

9 Click **OK** to close the budget window.

Now that all of the detail asset, liability, and stockholders' equity amounts have been created for our budget, you can create a budgeted balance sheet.

Budgeted Balance Sheet

Karen has entered budgetary information for several specific balance sheet accounts, and she'd now like to see a complete budget. Thus, she will create and print a budgeted balance sheet for the quarter ended March 31, 2009.

To create and print a budget overview report:

1 From the **Report Center**, select **Budgets** and then double-click **Budget Overview.**

2 Select **FY2009—Balance Sheet by Account**, and then click **Next**.

3 Click **Finish** and then change the From date to 1/1/09 and the To date to 3/31/09 and the Columns to Quarter only.

Figure 10.9

Balance Sheet Budget Overview

Wild Water Sports Ch 10
Balance Sheet Budget Overview
As of March 31, 2009

	Mar 31, 09
ASSETS	
Current Assets	
Checking/Savings	
Bank of Florida	34,250.00
Short-Term Investments	50,000.00
Total Checking/Savings	84,250.00
Accounts Receivable	
Accounts Receivable	400,000.00
Total Accounts Receivable	400,000.00
Other Current Assets	
Prepaid Advertising	20,000.00
Inventory Boats	200,000.00
Inventory Parts	2,000.00
Prepaid Insurance	16,500.00
Total Other Current Assets	238,500.00
Total Current Assets	722,750.00
Fixed Assets	
Furniture and Equipment	295,000.00
Accumulated Depreciation	-17,750.00
Total Fixed Assets	277,250.00
TOTAL ASSETS	1,000,000.00
LIABILITIES & EQUITY	
Liabilities	
Current Liabilities	
Accounts Payable	
Accounts Payable	200,000.00
Total Accounts Payable	200,000.00
Other Current Liabilities	
Accrued Expenses	1,500.00
Payroll Liabilities	3,000.00
Sales Tax Payable	15,400.00
Total Other Current Liabilities	19,900.00
Total Current Liabilities	219,900.00
Long Term Liabilities	
Loans Payable	300,000.00
Total Long Term Liabilities	300,000.00
Total Liabilities	519,900.00
Equity	
Capital Stock	400,000.00
Retained Earnings	80,100.00
Total Equity	480,100.00
TOTAL LIABILITIES & EQUITY	1,000,000.00

4 Enter **1/1/09** and **3/31/09** as the From date and To date, respectively, in the Balance Sheet Budget Overview window. Click the **Refresh** button.

5 Select **Quarter** from the Columns drop-down list and then modify the report to exclude the date prepared, time prepared, and report basis fields.

6 Click the **Print** button in the Report window.

7 Click **Portrait**, click the **Fit Report to 1 Page Wide** check box, and then click **Print** to print the report, which should look like Figure 10.9.

Karen explains that, once again, the report describes only the current budget and does not compare that budget with actual results. She suggests that you create a Budget vs. Actual report for the quarter ended March 31, 2009.

To create and print a Budget vs. Actual report for the first quarter of 2009:

1 From the Report Center, select **Budgets**, and then double-click **Budget vs. Actual.**

2 Select **FY2009—Balance Sheet by Account**, and then click **Next.**

3 Click **Finish.**

4 Enter **1/1/09** and **3/31/09** as the From date and To date, respectively, in the Balance Sheet Budget vs. Actual window.

5 Select **Quarter** from the drop-down list of Columns.

6 Click the **Refresh** button, and then modify the report to exclude the date prepared, time prepared, and report basis fields.

7 Click the **Print** button in the Report window.

8 Click **Portrait**, click the **Fit Report to 1 Page Wide** check box, and then click **Print** to print the report. Your report should look like Figure 10.10.

9 Close the Balance Sheet Budget vs. Actual window.

Figure 10.10

Balance Sheet Budget
vs. Actual Report

Wild Water Sports Ch 10
Balance Sheet Budget vs. Actual
As of March 31, 2009

	Mar 31, 09	Budget	$ Over Budget	% of Budget
ASSETS				
Current Assets				
Checking/Savings				
Bank of Florida	47,442.42	34,250.00	13,192.42	138.5%
Short-Term Investments	39,890.41	50,000.00	-10,109.59	79.8%
Total Checking/Savings	87,332.83	84,250.00	3,082.83	103.7%
Accounts Receivable				
Accounts Receivable	399,932.73	400,000.00	-67.27	100.0%
Total Accounts Receivable	399,932.73	400,000.00	-67.27	100.0%
Other Current Assets				
Prepaid Advertising	20,000.00	20,000.00	0.00	100.0%
Inventory Boats	243,600.00	200,000.00	43,600.00	121.8%
Inventory Parts	2,112.00	2,000.00	112.00	105.6%
Prepaid Insurance	16,500.00	16,500.00	0.00	100.0%
Undeposited Funds	0.00			
Total Other Current Assets	282,212.00	238,500.00	43,712.00	118.3%
Total Current Assets	769,477.56	722,750.00	46,727.56	106.5%
Fixed Assets				
Furniture and Equipment	295,000.00	295,000.00	0.00	100.0%
Accumulated Depreciation	-17,833.00	-17,750.00	-83.00	100.5%
Total Fixed Assets	277,167.00	277,250.00	-83.00	100.0%
TOTAL ASSETS	1,046,644.56	1,000,000.00	46,644.56	104.7%
LIABILITIES & EQUITY				
Liabilities				
Current Liabilities				
Accounts Payable				
Accounts Payable	216,200.00	200,000.00	16,200.00	108.1%
Total Accounts Payable	216,200.00	200,000.00	16,200.00	108.1%
Credit Cards				
MasterCard	0.00			
Total Credit Cards	0.00			
Other Current Liabilities				
Unearned Revenue	10,000.00			
Accrued Expenses	1,760.97	1,500.00	260.97	117.4%
Payroll Liabilities	2,934.66	3,000.00	-65.34	97.8%
Sales Tax Payable	28,457.66	15,400.00	13,057.66	184.8%
Total Other Current Liabilities	43,153.29	19,900.00	23,253.29	216.9%
Total Current Liabilities	259,353.29	219,900.00	39,453.29	117.9%
Long Term Liabilities				
Loans Payable	297,632.40	300,000.00	-2,367.60	99.2%
Total Long Term Liabilities	297,632.40	300,000.00	-2,367.60	99.2%
Total Liabilities	556,985.69	519,900.00	37,085.69	107.1%
Equity				
Capital Stock	400,000.00	400,000.00	0.00	100.0%
Opening Balance Equity	0.00			
Retained Earnings	0.00	80,100.00	-80,100.00	0.0%
Net Income	89,658.87	0.00	89,658.87	100.0%
Total Equity	489,658.87	480,100.00	9,558.87	102.0%
TOTAL LIABILITIES & EQUITY	1,046,644.56	1,000,000.00	46,644.56	104.7%

Karen points out that, based on the Budget vs. Actual report, the company is right on target. She'll ask Donna about budgeting for the MasterCard and Unearned Revenue accounts, since neither was included in the budget. She does want to investigate the Inventory Asset account, which was 21% over budget, and Sales Tax Payable, which—when you consider the accrued sales tax ($4,225) and sales tax payable ($24,233)—exceed the budgeted sales tax payable ($15,400) by 84%.

End Note

You and Karen have now entered all budgetary information for the first quarter of 2009. Donna can make changes to the budget at any time if additional information becomes available, and QuickBooks will automatically update any related budget report.

Business Events Summary

Business Event	Process Steps	Page
Create budgets for revenues and expenses	Planning and budgeting from Company menu	290
Create budgets for assets, liabilities, and equities	Planning and budgeting from Company menu	297
Create budgeted income statement	Budgets from Reports Center	294
Create budgeted balance sheet	Budgets from Reports Center	299

Chapter 10 Questions

1 Explain how the budgeting process is accomplished in QuickBooks.

2 Can multiple budgets be created in QuickBooks? Explain.

3 Explain how the Copy Across feature helps in creating QuickBooks budgets.

4 Explain how the Adjust Row Amounts feature helps in creating QuickBooks budgets.

5 Explain the typical relationship between sales and cost of goods sold, and describe how this information is included in the QuickBooks budgeting process.

6 Compare the process of budgeting revenues and expenses with the process of budgeting assets, liabilities, and owners' equity, and explain how this information is included in the QuickBooks budgeting process.

7 Describe the typical relationship between accumulated depreciation and depreciation expense and how this information is included in the QuickBooks budgeting process.

8 Which menus are used to create budget reports in QuickBooks?

9 Describe how you use the calculator feature that is built into QuickBooks.

10 Explain the typical relationship between retained earnings and net income/loss, and describe how this information is included in the QuickBooks budgeting process.

Chapter 10 Matching

Select the letter of the item below that best matches the definitions that follow. Use the text or QuickBooks Help to complete this assignment.

a. Copy Across button   _____ Budgeted revenues are compared with actual revenues.

b. Adjust Row Amounts button   _____ Allow amounts that are copied across different months in a budget to compound.

c. Enable compounding   _____ Copies amounts from one month to many months in a budget without modification.

d. Budget types   _____ Budgeted accounts receivable are compared with actual accounts receivable.

e. Fit Report to 1 Page Wide   _____ Must be account based.

f.   Balance Sheet Budget
Overview   _____ A budget can be in a profit & loss format or balance sheet format.

g.   Profit & Loss Budget
Overview   _____ Provides information about budgeted assets, liabilities, and equities only.

h.   Balance Sheet Budget
vs. Actual   _____ Copies amounts from one month to many months in a budget that has been increased or decreased by an amount or a percentage.

i.   Profit & Loss Budget
vs. Actual   _____ Provides information about budgeted revenue and expenses only.

j.   Budgets   _____ Forces a report to print in a defined amount of space.

Chapter 10 Exercises

Chapter 10 Exercise 1
BUDGETING REVENUES AND EXPENSES

Restore the file Boston Catering Ch 10 (Backup) found on the text CD or download it from the text Web site. Enter budgeted revenues and expenses described below and then print the profit & loss budget overview and profit & loss budget vs. actual reports for the month ended July 2010.

    a.   Budgeted revenues for July include bar sales of $2,000 and catering sales of $20,000.

    b.   Budgeted expenses for July include bar purchases of $1,400, food purchases of $2,500, interest expense of $600, depreciation expense of $1,000, insurance expense of $1,000, payroll expenses of $6,000, and rent expense of $3,000.

Chapter 10 Exercise 2
BUDGETING ASSETS, LIABILITIES, AND EQUITIES

Restore the file Boston Catering Ch 10 (Backup) found on the text CD or download it from the text Web site. Do not use the file created in the exercises above. Enter budgeted assets, liabilities, and equities described below and then print the balance sheet budget overview and balance sheet budget vs. actual reports.

    a.   Budgeted assets as of July 31, 2010 include cash in bank (Bank of America) $80,000, short-term investments $5,000, accounts receivable $20,000, food inventory $5,000, furniture and equipment $76,500, and accumulated depreciation $3,000.

    b.   Budgeted liabilities as of July 31,2010 include accounts payable $10,000, payroll liabilities $2,000, notes payable (Bank of America) $25,000, and notes payable (CitiBank) $50,000,

    c.   Budgeted equities as of July 31, 2010 include capital stock $90,000 and retained earnings $6,500.

Chapter 10 Assignments

Chapter 10 Assignment 1
ADDING MORE INFORMATION: WILD WATER SPORTS

corporation

merchandising

Restore the file Wild Water Sports Ch 10A (Backup) file found on the text CD or download it from the text Web site, and then modify the existing budget for 2009 as follows:

Boat sales for April are expected to be 10% higher than in March.

Cost of goods sold for April is still estimated at 80% of boat sales.

Payroll expenses for April are expected to be $15,000.

Assets, liabilities, and equities are as follows.

Bank of Florida	60,000	Accounts Payable	345,200
Short-Term Investments	30,000	Accrued Expenses	2,000
Accounts Receivable	500,000	Payroll Liabilities	3,000
Prepaid Advertising	18,000	Sales Tax Payable	30,000
Inventory Boats	290,000	Loan Payable	300,000
Inventory Parts	2,000	Capital Stock	400,000
Prepaid Insurance	14,250	Retained Earnings	?
Furniture and Equipment	307,000		
Accumulated Depreciation	−21,250		

You'll need to compute ending retained earnings based on the previous month's budget and your budget of April net income.

    a. Print a Profit & Loss Budget Overview report for the month of April 2009.

    b. Print a Profit & Loss Budget vs. Actual report for the month of April 2009.

    c. Print a Balance Sheet Budget Overview report as of 4/30/09.

    d. Print a Balance Sheet Budget vs. Actual report as of 4/30/09.

Chapter 10 Assignment 2
ADDING MORE INFORMATION: CENTRAL COAST CELLULAR

sole proprietorship

merchandising

Restore the file Central Coast Cellular Ch 10 (Backup) found on the text CD or download it from the text Web site, and use that copy to record the following events in 2009.

    Commissions of $2,000 are expected each month. Consulting income of $8,000 is expected in January, increasing 10% each month thereafter. Product sales of

$10,000 are expected in January, increasing by $5,000 each month thereafter. Cost of goods sold is estimated at 50% of product sales. Bank service charges of $80 and depreciation of $1,500 are expected each month. Interest expense of $1,000 and rent of $3,000 are expected each month. Payroll expenses of $10,000 are expected in January, increasing by $2,000
each month thereafter. Telephone expenses of $500 are expected in January, increasing $100 each month thereafter. Utilities of $300 are expected in January, increasing 5% each month thereafter. Assets, liabilities, and equities as of January 31, 2009, are as follows.

Checking	130,000	Accounts payable	24,380
Short-Term Investments	68,500	Accrued Expenses	1,000
Accounts Receivable	14,000	Payroll Liabilities	4,000
Inventory Asset	18,000	Sales Tax Payable	2,000
Supplies	3,000	Loan Payable	120,000
Furniture and Equipment	115,000	Owners Equity	198,620
Accumulated Depreciation	–1,500		
Security Deposit	3,000		

a. Print a Profit & Loss Budget Overview report by month for the quarter ending March 2009.

b. Print a Profit & Loss Budget vs. Actual report for the month of January 2009.

c. Print a Balance Sheet Budget Overview report as of January 31, 2009.

d. Print a Balance Sheet Budget vs. Actual report as of January 31, 2009.

Chapter 10 Assignment 3
ADDING MORE INFORMATION: SANTA BARBARA SAILING

corporation

service

Restore the file Santa Barbara Sailing Ch 10 (Backup) found on the text CD or download it from the text Web site, and use that copy to record the following budget information for 2008.

Charter income is expected to be $5,000 in July, increasing $1,000 per month thereafter. Rental income is expected to be $30,000 in July, increasing 10% each month throughout the year. Expenses are budgeted as follows and are expected to remain constant for the year. (Move the Rent Expense account down in the chart of accounts so that all expenses are listed
in alphabetical order.)

Advertising and Promotion	3,500
Computer and Internet Expenses	1,300
Depreciation Expense	5,750
Interest Expense	1,000
Payroll Expenses	10,000
Rent Expense	2,000
Repairs and Maintenance	2,500
Utilities	1,200

Budgeted assets, liabilities, and equities as of July 31, 2008, are as follows.

Checking	115,000
Accounts Receivable	4,000
Prepaid Rent	22,000
Boats	350,000
Furniture and Equipment	2,500
Accumulated Depreciation	−5,750
Accounts Payable	4,000
Payroll Liabilities	4,500
Sales Tax Payable	4,000
Loan Payable	317,500
Capital Stock	150,000
Retained Earnings	7,750

a. Print a Profit & Loss Budget Overview report for the quarter ended September 30, 2008.

b. Print a Profit & Loss Budget vs. Actual report for the month ended July 31, 2008.

c. Print a Balance Sheet Budget Overview report as of July 31, 2008.

d. Print a Balance Sheet Budget vs. Actual report as of July 31, 2008.

Chapter 10 Cases

Chapter 10 Case 1:
FOREVER YOUNG

sole proprietorship   service

In Chapter 9, you added some transactions to your QuickBooks file for Forever Young. Make a copy of that file, and use that copy to record the following budget information.

Consulting income is expected to be $40,000 in January, increasing $5,000 per month thereafter. Expenses are budgeted as follows and are expected to remain constant for the next three months.

Advertising and Promotion	500
Automobile Expense	1,000
Depreciation Expense	100
Interest Expense	100
Payroll Expenses	10,000
Professional Fees	4,000
Rent Expense	3,800
Telephone Expense	500
Travel Expense	7,000

Budgeted assets, liabilities, and equities as of January 31, 2008, are as follows.

Checking	50,000
Accounts Receivable	15,000
Prepaid Advertising	5,000
Supplies	2,100
Furniture and Equipment	4,000
Accumulated Depreciation	–100
Security Deposits Asset	4,000
Payroll Liabilities	5,000
Notes Payable	50,000
Owners Equity	25,000

Requirements:

1 Print a Profit & Loss Budget Overview report for the quarter ended March 31, 2008.

2 Print a Profit & Loss Budget vs. Actual report for the month ended January 31, 2008.

3 Print a Balance Sheet Budget Overview report as of January 31, 2008.

4 Print a Balance Sheet Budget vs. Actual report as of January 31, 2008.

Chapter 10 Case 2:
OCEAN VIEW FLOWERS

corporation

merchandising

In Chapter 9 you modified your QuickBooks file for Ocean View Flowers, a wholesale flower distributor. Make a copy of that file, and use that copy to enter the following transactions for 2008. Budgeted revenues and expenses are as follows.

Account	January	February
Sales	$35,000	$80,000
Cost of Goods Sold	16,000	42,000
Depreciation Expense	1,500	1,500
Insurance Expense	100	100
Interest Expense	1,600	1,600
Payroll Expenses	20,000	20,000
Professional Fees	500	500
Rent Expense	1,400	1,400
Telephone Expense	400	400
Utilities	300	300
Interest Income	500	1,000

Budgeted balances as of February 29, 2008, for assets, liabilities, and equity accounts follow.

Union Checking	46,300	Accounts Payable	52,800
Accounts Receivable	62,200	Payroll Liabilities	14,000
Inventory Asset	30,000	Long-Term Note Payable	320,000
Prepaid Insurance	1,000	Capital Stock	100,000
Short-Term Investments	25,000	Retained Earnings	13,200
Supplies	1,500		
Land	50,000		
Building	250,000		
Furniture and Equipment	37,000		
Accumulated Depreciation	−3,000		

Requirements:

1   Print a Profit & Loss Budget Overview report by month for the two months ended February 2008.

2   Print a Profit & Loss Budget vs. Actual report in total for the two months ended February 2008.

3   Print a Balance Sheet Budget Overview report as of February 29, 2008.

4   Print a Balance Sheet Budget vs. Actual report as of February 29, 2008.

Chapter 10 Case 3:
ALOHA PROPERTIES

In Chapter 9, you modified your QuickBooks file for Aloha Properties. Make a copy of that file, and use that copy to enter the following budget information for 2008.

Rental income is expected to be $60,000 in January and $100,000 in February, and it is expected to increase 18% per month thereafter through 2008. Advertising and promotion is expected to be $12,500 in January (for an initial advertising campaign) and then $1,500 per month thereafter. Cleaning costs vary with the number of units rented (these costs should average about 5% of rental income). Depreciation should be about $17,000 per month. Insurance, interest, repairs and maintenance, telephone, utilities, and payroll expenses are expected to be $2,000, $23,000, $3,400, $4,000, $3,000, and $10,000, respectively each month throughout the year. Expected assets, liabilities, and equities as of February 29, 2008, are as follows.

Checking	101,000	Accounts Payable	10,000
Accounts Receivable	50,000	Accrued Expenses	23,000
Prepaid Insurance	20,000	Payroll Liabilities	4,000
Short-Term Investments	40,000	Sales Tax Payable	5,000
Buildings	5,000,000	Notes Payable	3,859,600
Furniture and Equipment	23,000	Capital Stock	60,000
Accumulated Depreciation	−1,234,000	Retained Earnings	38,400

Requirements:

1   Print a Profit & Loss Budget Overview report for the two-month period ending February 2008.

2   Print a Profit & Loss Budget vs. Actual report for the two-month period ending February 2008.

3   Print a Balance Sheet Budget Overview report as of February 29, 2008.

4   Print a Balance Sheet Budget vs. Actual report as of February 29, 2008.

Reporting Business Activities

Learning Objectives

In this chapter, you will:

- Create and memorize a customized income statement
- Create and memorize a customized balance sheet
- Create graphs to illustrate financial information
- Create additional detail reports
- Export reports to Excel

Case: Wild Water Sports, Inc.

Now that you have entered the budget information for Wild Water Sports's first year and have entered the first four months of operating, investing, and financing transactions as well as adjustments, you are finally ready to prepare financial statements to send to the bank for Wild Water Sports's first three months. Donna has asked you and Karen to prepare these statements and to provide any additional information that will help her better understand Wild Water's financial performance. You and Karen would like to create more customized financial statements than you've printed so far and to give Donna the related supporting schedules and graphs that QuickBooks can so easily create.

You decide to prepare a customized income statement, a customized balance sheet, an accounts receivable and accounts payable schedule, and an inventory status report. To further enhance Donna's financial analysis of the business, you also decide to prepare one graph showing income and expenses and another graph showing the aging of accounts receivable and payable.

"The report and graph features of QuickBooks are quite extensive," Karen explains. "You can customize each report by adding percentages, hiding cents, changing report titles, and modifying the page layout."

"Can we graphically compare the current quarter's results with the budget we just created?" you ask.

"Absolutely!" Karen confirms. "Now that we have created the budget in QuickBooks, we can use the report information we created when comparing our budgeted activity with our actual results and produce a graphic illustration. This will help Donna or other users of this information to visually evaluate the financial results."

"Sounds like QuickBooks saves hours of work," you remark. "Let's get started."

Creating and Memorizing a Customized Income Statement

Karen decides to create one customized income statement for the three-month period ended March 31 without examining each month separately, because adjustments were made only as of March 31.

Karen explains that QuickBooks enables you to create reports for any period you desire. It also lets you create separate columns for a time segment—such as a day, a week, four weeks, a month, a quarter, and so on—within each period. At the end of the fiscal year, Karen will create an income statement report for the year with separate columns for each quarter.

Karen decides to print two customized versions of the income statement. One will be a "left page" layout alignment without cents and will include a % of Income column; it will be titled Income Statement for the three months ended March 31, 2009, and will be in an expanded format. The other will be a collapsed version of the same report but sorted by total from largest to smallest amounts.

"Do we have to go through this customization effort every time?" Karen asks.

"No," you reply. "QuickBooks has a Memorize feature that can 'memorize' or retain the customization—what columns we want, what period, what layout, and so on. That way, the next time we want a similar report, it will be available from a memorized report list."

To create and memorize a customized Income Statement:

1 Restore the Wild Water Sports Ch 11.qbb file from your Data Files CD or download it from the Internet site. See "Data Files CD" in Chapter 1 if you need more information.

2 From the Report Center, click **Company & Financial** and then double-click **Profit & Loss Standard.**

3 Click the **Modify Report** button, and then click the **Display** tab.

4 Change the report dates to read from **1/1/09** to **3/31/09** in the Modify Report window, and then click the **% of Income** check box.

5 Click the **Fonts & Numbers** tab, and then click the **Without Cents** check box.

6 Click the **Header/Footer** tab. Change the Report Title to **Income Statement.** Select **Left** from the Page Layout alignment drop-down edit box, and alter the Subtitle to read **for the three months ended March 31, 2009.**

7 Uncheck the **Date Prepared, Time Prepared**, and **Report Basis** check boxes and then click **OK.**

8 Click the **Print** button.

9 Click **Portrait** in the Orientation box. (If the Print Features window appears, click **OK.**) Then click **Print** in the Print Reports window to print the report shown in Figure 11.1.

Wild Water Sports Ch 11
Income Statement
for the three months ended March 31, 2009

	Jan – Mar 09	% of Income
Ordinary Income/Expense		
Income		
Boat Sales	767,500	99%
Part Sales	610	0%
Service	6,685	1%
Total Income	774,795	100%
Cost of Goods Sold		
Cost of Goods Sold	614,488	79%
Total COGS	614,488	79%
Gross Profit	160,307	21%
Expense		
Advertising and Promotion	6,700	1%
Bank Service Charges	75	0%
Depreciation Expense	10,333	1%
Insurance Expense	5,500	1%
Interest Expense	7,720	1%
Office Supplies	4,500	1%
Payroll Expenses	32,946	4%
Telephone Expense	5,020	1%
Utilities	2,870	0%
Total Expense	75,664	10%
Net Ordinary Income	84,643	11%
Other Income/Expense		
Other Income		
Interest Income	2,015	0%
Other Income	3,000	0%
Total Other Income	5,015	1%
Net Other Income	5,015	1%
Net Income	89,659	12%

Figure 11.1

Customized Income Statement

10 Change the sorting by selecting **Total** from the Sort By drop-down list and clicking the **Sort** button next to the Sort By drop-down list so that it reads Z to A (meaning largest to smallest).

11 Click the **Print** button.

12 Click **Portrait** in the Orientation box. (If the Print Features window appears, click **OK.**) Then click **Print** in the Print Reports window to print the report shown in Figure 11.2.

Wild Water Sports Ch 11
Income Statement
for the three months ended March 31, 2009

	Jan – Mar 09	% of Income
Ordinary Income/Expense		
Income		
Boat Sales	767,500	99%
Service	6,685	1%
Part Sales	610	0%
Total Income	774,795	100%
Cost of Goods Sold		
Cost of Goods Sold	614,488	79%
Total COGS	614,488	79%
Gross Profit	160,307	21%
Expense		
Payroll Expenses	32,946	4%
Depreciation Expense	10,333	1%
Interest Expense	7,720	1%
Advertising and Promotion	6,700	1%
Insurance Expense	5,500	1%
Telephone Expense	5,020	1%
Office Supplies	4,500	1%
Utilities	2,870	0%
Bank Service Charges	75	0%
Total Expense	75,664	10%
Net Ordinary Income	84,643	11%
Other Income/Expense		
Other Income		
Other Income	3,000	0%
Interest Income	2,015	0%
Total Other Income	5,015	1%
Net Other Income	5,015	1%
Net Income	89,659	12%

Figure 11.2

Variation on the Customized Income Statement

13 From the Report Center (not the report you just created), click the **Memorized** tab located at the top of the window.

14 Click the **Edit Memorized List** button at the top of the window and then click the **Memorized Report** button at the bottom of the Memorized Report List and then click **New Group** from the menu shown.

15 Type **Customized Reports** in the Name text box and then click **OK.**

16 Close the Memorized Report List window.

17 Activate the Profit & Loss report window you created earlier.

18 Click the **Memorize** button.

19 Type **Customized Income Statement** in the Name text box, click in the **Save in Memorized Report Group** check box and select **Customized Reports** from the drop-down list as shown in Figure 11.3.

20 Click **OK** to retain this customized report as Customized Income Statement.

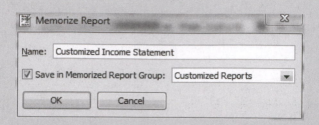

Figure 11.3

Memorizing Reports

21 Close the Customized Income Statement window.

22 From the Report Center, click the **Memorized** tab and then click **Customized Reports** from the list of Groups shown in the left hand column as shown in Figure 11.4.

Figure 11.4

Retrieving a Memorized Report

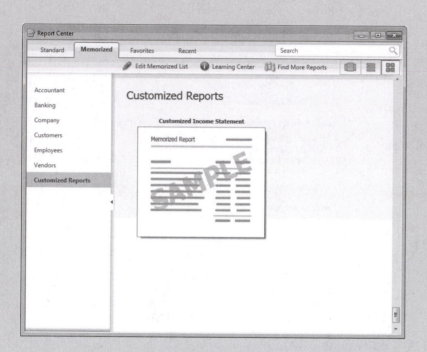

23 Close all windows.

Karen suggests that you take note of the % of Income column. She explains how this column reports each item's percentage of total revenue (what QuickBooks calls total income). Cost of goods sold at 79% and payroll expenses at 4% are the company's largest costs as a percentage of total revenue. Notice also that Wild Water's profit margin ratio (net income divided by total revenue) is 12%. You suggest a cup of coffee before you come back to customize a balance sheet.

Creating and Memorizing a Customized Balance Sheet

Video Demonstration

DEMO 11B - Create and memorize a custom balance sheet

You return to your office to create the balance sheet Donna needs as of 3/31/09. Karen explains to you that QuickBooks can prepare balance sheets for any accounting period you specify. Since Donna needs balance results as of 3/31/09, the two of you start by preparing a standard balance sheet. You want to keep the report simple—you'll include the main accounts from the chart of accounts and collapse the subaccounts into their main accounts. You decide to customize the balance sheet to include a percentage column.

To create and memorize a customized balance sheet:

1 From the Report Center, click the **Standard** tab and then **Company & Financial.** Scroll down the list of reports and then double-click Balance Sheet Standard under Balance Sheet & Net Worth.

2 Click the **Modify Report** button.

3 Change the report dates to read from **1/1/09** to **3/31/09**, and then click in the **% of Column** check box.

4 Click the **Fonts & Numbers** tab, and then click the **Without Cents** check box.

5 Click the **Header/Footer** tab. Select **Left** from the Page Layout alignment drop-down edit box.

6 Uncheck the **Date Prepared, Time Prepared**, and **Report Basis** check boxes and then click **OK.**

7 Click the **Print** button.

8 Click **Portrait** in the Orientation box, and then click **Print** in the Print Reports window to print the report shown in Figure 11.5.

9 Click the **Memorize** button.

10 Type **Customized Balance Sheet** in the Name text box and save this new report in the Customized Reports report group like you did before.

11 Click **OK** to memorize this customized report.

Wild Water Sports Ch 11
Balance Sheet
As of March 31, 2009

	Mar 31, 09	% of Column
ASSETS		
Current Assets		
Checking/Savings		
Bank of Florida	47,442	5%
Short-Term Investments	39,890	4%
Total Checking/Savings	87,333	8%
Accounts Receivable		
Accounts Receivable	399,933	38%
Total Accounts Receivable	399,933	38%
Other Current Assets		
Prepaid Advertising	20,000	2%
Inventory Boats	243,600	23%
Inventory Parts	2,112	0%
Prepaid Insurance	16,500	2%
Total Other Current Assets	282,212	27%
Total Current Assets	769,478	74%
Fixed Assets		
Furniture and Equipment	295,000	28%
Accumulated Depreciation	-17,833	-2%
Total Fixed Assets	277,167	26%
TOTAL ASSETS	1,046,645	100%
LIABILITIES & EQUITY		
Liabilities		
Current Liabilities		
Accounts Payable		
Accounts Payable	216,200	21%
Total Accounts Payable	216,200	21%
Other Current Liabilities		
Unearned Revenue	10,000	1%
Accrued Expenses	1,761	0%
Payroll Liabilities	2,935	0%
Sales Tax Payable	28,458	3%
Total Other Current Liabilities	43,153	4%
Total Current Liabilities	259,353	25%
Long Term Liabilities		
Loans Payable	297,632	28%
Total Long Term Liabilities	297,632	28%
Total Liabilities	556,986	53%
Equity		
Capital Stock	400,000	38%
Net Income	89,659	9%
Total Equity	489,659	47%
TOTAL LIABILITIES & EQUITY	1,046,645	100%

Figure 11.5
Customized Balance Sheet

12   Close all windows.

Trouble? Notice that QuickBooks includes a line item called "Net Income" in the (Owners') Equity section. Standard accounting practice does not allow inclusion of such an income statement category in a balance sheet. Usually, this net income is included in the Retained Earnings account.

Karen comments that at first she thought the percentage column was the same as the one shown in the income statement: each item's percentage of the total revenue (what QuickBooks calls "income"). But now she sees that this column actually shows the percentage of total assets. For example, total cash (i.e., the total amount in checking and savings) is 8% of Wild Water Sports's total assets, and accounts receivable is 38% of total assets. She comments that it looks like a large portion of those assets came from accounts payable (21%) and loans payable (28%) and that most of the balance is from equity (47%).

Creating Graphs to Illustrate Financial Information

"This is very helpful information," Donna comments as she quickly skims the customized income statement, balance sheet, and budget versus actual reports you previously created. "I can see Wild Water's financial position and how we stand in relation to where I thought we'd be. Can I see this information expressed in graphical form?" she asks. "I'm afraid I might miss something when I look at this detailed report. A graph would help me see things I might miss when I look at just numbers."

Both you and Karen agree that some graphs would be helpful. In particular, Donna is anxious to know more about product sales and expenses. It is clear that graphic representations of sales, revenue, and expenses will be helpful.

To create a Sales Graph:

1 From the Report Center, click **Sales** and then double-click **Sales Graph** located under Sales by Customer.

2 Click the **Dates** button and change the dates to read from **1/1/09** to **3/31/09** in the Change Graph Dates window. Then click **OK.**

3 Click the **By Item** button in the QuickInsight: Sales Graph window, if it is not already selected. Selecting this button causes QuickBooks to display sales in the graph by item, in this case by the boats and the services that Wild Water sells.

4 QuickBooks generates two graphs—a bar chart and a pie chart.

5 Click **Print** from the button bar, and then click **Print** from the Print Graphs window. Your printed graph should look like Figure 11.6.

Figure 11.6

Sales Graph by Item

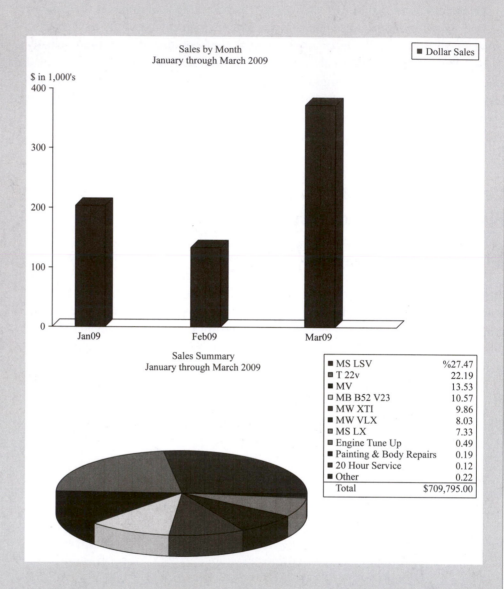

6 Click the **By Customer** button in the QuickInsight: Sales Graph window to create a graph that illustrates sales for the quarter by customer.

7 Click **Print** from the button bar, and then click **Print** from the Print Graphs window. Your printed graph should look like Figure 11.7.

8 Close the Sales Graph window.

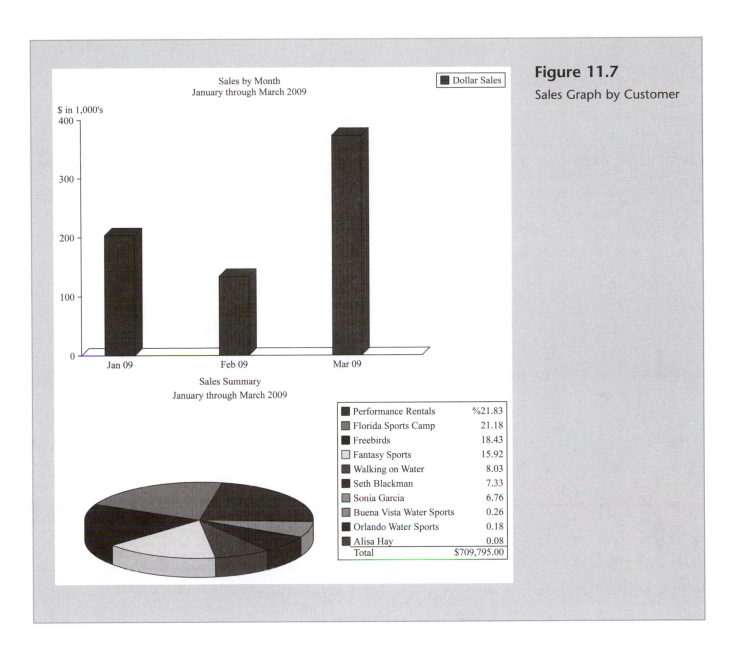

Figure 11.7

Sales Graph by Customer

Graphs such as these help managers interpret financial information, because they often reveal important relationships not obvious from the financial statements. For example, in Figure 11.7, sales growth by month is illustrated and the source of sales by customer is revealed. In this case, customer Performance Rentals represents almost 22% of sales for the three months.

Next, you decide to produce a graph that illustrates Wild Water Sports's revenues (or "income," as QuickBooks calls it) and expenses.

To create an Income and Expense Graph:

1 From the Report Center, click **Company & Financial** and then double-click **Income & Expense Graph** located under Income & Expenses.

2 Click the **Dates** button and change the dates to read from **1/1/09** to **3/31/09** in the Change Graph Dates window. Then click **OK.**

3 Click the **By Account** button at the top of the screen and the **Expense** button at the bottom of the QuickInsight: Income and Expense Graph window, if they are not already selected.

4 Click **Print** from the button bar, and then click **Print** from the Print Graphs window. Your printed graph should look like Figure 11.8.

Figure 11.8

Income and Expense by Account Graph

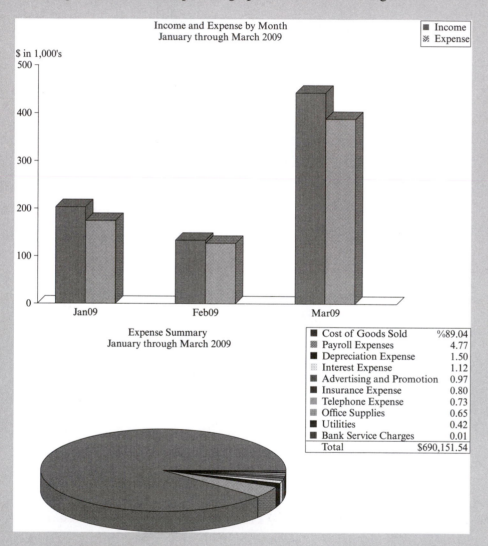

Trouble? Your vertical axis scale might be different, depending on the size of the figure you choose to view.

5 Close all windows.

These two graphs help to explain revenues and expenses, but they do not provide insight into the financial position of the company as of March 31.

"Does QuickBooks have similar graphing capabilities for items such as accounts receivable and accounts payable?" you ask.

"Yes," Karen responds. "In fact, we should probably create a graph for both accounts to demonstrate how current or noncurrent our receivables and payables are. QuickBooks can create a bar chart that illustrates aging for accounts receivable and then another for accounts payable, and it can simultaneously identify who owes us (and whom we owe) at any given time, such as March 31, 2009."

To create an Accounts Receivable Graph and an Accounts Payable Graph:

1 From the Report Center, click **Customers & Receivables**, and then double-click **Accounts Receivable Graph.**

2 Click the **Dates** button, and change the date to **3/31/09** in the Change Graph Dates window. Then click **OK.**

3 Click **Print** from the button bar, and then click **Print** from the Print Graphs window. Your printed graph should look like Figure 11.9.

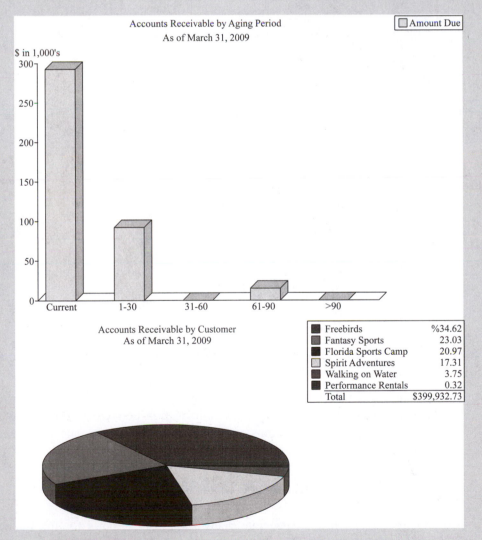

Figure 11.9

Accounts Receivable Graph

4 From the Report Center, click **Vendors & Payables**, and then double-click **Accounts Payable Graph.**

5 Click the **Dates** button, and change the date to **3/31/09** in the Change Graph Dates window. Then click **OK.**

6 Click **Print** from the button bar, and then click **Print** from the Print Graphs window. Your printed graph should look like Figure 11.10.

Figure 11.10

Accounts Payable Graph

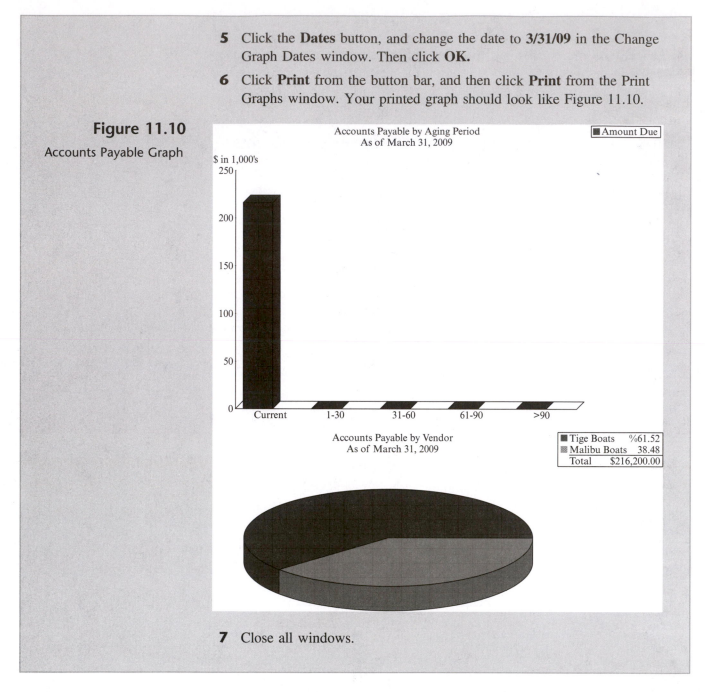

7 Close all windows.

When you show Donna these graphs, she comments that they will be very helpful. But she wants to see even more information derived from the financial statements—specifically, she wants to see detailed reports on sales, purchases, accounts receivable, accounts payable, and inventory.

Create Additional Detail Reports

With QuickBooks, you can generate many supporting reports for the financial statements—what accountants consider traditional support in the form of schedules. Karen reads through QuickBooks Help and discovers two reports that

QuickBooks generates that will help Donna: the Sales by Customer Summary and the Summary Sales by Item. Together, you decide that the Sales by Customer Summary should identify sales for each month of the quarter so you can identify the customer to which you sold products or services. The Summary Sales by Item reports on the number of items sold, the average price of each item sold, and each item's related average cost. This report also identifies the gross margin (sales revenue minus cost of goods sold) for each item and summarizes the gross margin for all items sold during the period. Karen suggests that you produce this report on a monthly basis.

To create the Sales by Customer Summary and the Summary Sales by Item reports:

1 From the Report Center, click **Sales**, and then double-click **Sales by Customer Summary** located under Sales by Customer.

2 Change the report dates to read from **1/1/09** to **3/31/09**.

3 Click the **Collapse** button.

4 Select **Total** in the Sort By drop-down list, and then click the sort button to read Z – A so that the report lists sales to customers from largest to smallest.

5 Select **Month** from the Columns drop-down edit box and then click **OK**.

6 Remove the date prepared, time prepared, and report basis from the report.

7 Click **Print** from the button bar, and then click **Print** from the Print Reports window. Your printed report should look like Figure 11.11.

Wild Water Sports Ch 11
Sales by Customer Summary
January through March 2009

	Jan 09	Feb 09	Mar 09	TOTAL
Performance Rentals	78,750.00	75,000.00	1,215.00	154,965.00
Florida Sports Camp	71,575.00	0.00	78,750.00	150,325.00
Freebirds	845.00	0.00	130,000.00	130,845.00
Fantasy Sports	0.00	0.00	113,000.00	113,000.00
Walking on Water	0.00	57,000.00	0.00	57,000.00
Seth Blackman	52,000.00	0.00	0.00	52,000.00
Sonia Garcia	0.00	0.00	48,000.00	48,000.00
Buena Vista Water Sports	0.00	0.00	1,845.00	1,845.00
Orlando Water Sports	0.00	1,250.00	0.00	1,250.00
Alisa Hay	165.00	400.00	0.00	565.00
TOTAL	203,335.00	133,650.00	372,810.00	709,795.00

Figure 11.11

Sales by Customer Summary

8 Click **Memorize**.

9 Type **Customized Sales by Customer Summary** in the Name text box and save it in the Customized Reports Group; then click **OK**.

10 Close the Sales by Customer Summary window.

11 From the Report Center, double-click **Sales by Item Summary** located under Sales by Item.

12 Change the report dates to read from **1/1/09** to **3/31/09**.

13 Select **Total Only** from the Columns drop-down edit box.

14 Adjust the column width to view more of the report on your screen. You may need to scroll down the report to view items sold and total sales.

15 Remove the date prepared, time prepared, and report basis from the report.

16 Click **Print** from the button bar, and then click **Print** from the Print Reports window. Your printed report should look like Figure 11.12.

Figure 11.12

Sales by Item Summary

Wild Water Sports Ch 11
Sales by Item Summary
January through March 2009

				Jan - Mar 09				
	Qty	Amount	% of Sales	Avg Price	COGS	Avg COGS	Gross Ma...	Gross Ma...
Inventory								
Air Filter	1	35.00	0.0%	35.00	28.00	28.00	7.00	20.0%
Engine Oil	9	45.00	0.0%	5.00	36.00	4.00	9.00	20.0%
MB B52 V23	1	75,000.00	10.6%	75,000.00	60,000.00	60,000.00	15,000.00	20.0%
MS LSV	3	195,000.00	27.5%	65,000.00	156,000.00	52,000.00	39,000.00	20.0%
MS LX	1	52,000.00	7.3%	52,000.00	41,600.00	41,600.00	10,400.00	20.0%
MV	2	96,000.00	13.5%	48,000.00	76,800.00	38,400.00	19,200.00	20.0%
MW VLX	1	57,000.00	8.0%	57,000.00	45,600.00	45,600.00	11,400.00	20.0%
MW XTI	1	70,000.00	9.9%	70,000.00	56,000.00	56,000.00	14,000.00	20.0%
Oil Filter	2	30.00	0.0%	15.00	24.00	12.00	6.00	20.0%
T 22v	2	157,500.00	22.2%	78,750.00	126,000.00	63,000.00	31,500.00	20.0%
Tune Up Parts	2	500.00	0.1%	250.00	400.00	200.00	100.00	20.0%
Total Inventory		703,110.00	99.1%		562,488.00		140,622.00	20.0%
Service								
20 Hour Service	5	875.00	0.1%	175.00				
Cleaning	6	450.00	0.1%	75.00				
Engine Service	4	500.00	0.1%	125.00				
Engine Tune Up	14	3,500.00	0.5%	250.00				
Painting & Body Repairs	17	1,360.00	0.2%	80.00				
Total Service		6,685.00	0.9%					
TOTAL		709,795.00	100.0%					

17 Click **Memorize.**

18 Type **Customized Sales by Item Summary** in the Name text box, save it in the Customized Reports Group, and then click **OK.**

19 Close the Sales by Item Summary window.

Karen tells you that two additional reports are commonly prepared to support the balance sheet: Accounts Receivable Aging and Accounts Payable Aging. QuickBooks can easily generate these reports.

To create Accounts Receivable and Accounts Payable Aging reports:

1 From the Report Center, click **Customers & Receivables** and then double-click **A/R Aging Summary** located under A/R Aging.

2 Change the report date to read **3/31/09** and then click **Refresh.**

3 Click the **Collapse** button.

4 Remove the date prepared and time prepared fields.

5 Click the **Print** button in the button bar, and then click **Print** in the Print Reports window.

6 Choose a **Portrait** orientation.

7 The report shown in Figure 11.13 appears. Examine this report.

Wild Water Sports Ch 11
A/R Aging Summary
As of March 31, 2009

	Current	1 - 30	31 - 60	61 - 90	> 90	TOTAL
Fantasy Sports	0.00	92,095.00	0.00	0.00	0.00	92,095.00
Florida Sports Camp	83,868.75	0.00	0.00	0.00	0.00	83,868.75
Freebirds	138,450.00	0.00	0.00	0.00	0.00	138,450.00
Performance Rentals	1,293.98	0.00	0.00	0.00	0.00	1,293.98
Spirit Adventures	69,225.00	0.00	0.00	0.00	0.00	69,225.00
Walking on Water	0.00	0.00	0.00	15,000.00	0.00	15,000.00
TOTAL	292,837.73	92,095.00	0.00	15,000.00	0.00	399,932.73

Figure 11.13

A/R Aging Summary

8 Click **Memorize.**

9 Type **Customized A/R Aging Summary** in the Name text box and save it in the Customized Report Group; then click **OK.**

10 Close the A/R Aging Summary window.

11 From the Report Center, click **Vendors & Payables** and then double-click **A/P Aging Summary** located under A/P Aging Summary.

12 Change the report date to read **3/31/09** and then click **Refresh.**

13 Click the **Print** button in the button bar, and then click **Print** in the Print Reports window.

14 Choose a **Portrait** orientation.

15 The report shown in Figure 11.14 appears. Examine this report.

Wild Water Sports Ch 11
A/P Aging Summary
As of March 31, 2009

	Current	1 - 30	31 - 60	61 - 90	> 90	TOTAL
Malibu Boats	83,200.00	0.00	0.00	0.00	0.00	83,200.00
Tige Boats	133,000.00	0.00	0.00	0.00	0.00	133,000.00
TOTAL	216,200.00	0.00	0.00	0.00	0.00	216,200.00

Figure 11.14

A/P Aging Summary

16 Click **Memorize.**

> **17** Type **Customized A/P Aging Summary** in the Name text box, save it in the Customized Report Group, and then click **OK.**
>
> **18** Close the A/P Aging Summary window.

Karen forwards these detail reports to Donna, who can now follow up on the Walking on Water outstanding accounts receivable of $15,000 that she believes is left over from when they bought the company January 1. She also plans to follow up on the Fantasy Sports receivable and to pay the Malibu Boats accounts payable soon.

Video Demonstration

DEMO 11C - Exporting reports to Excel

Exporting Reports to Excel

Karen explains that in QuickBooks you can export any reports you create to Microsoft's Excel spreadsheet program.

"Why export to Microsoft Excel when QuickBooks gives us so many report options?" you ask.

Karen explains that she may occasionally need to change a report's appearance or contents in ways that are not available within QuickBooks. Since the changes you make in Excel do not affect your QuickBooks data, you can freely customize a report as needed or even change report data in order to run "what if" scenarios.

Karen reads through QuickBooks Help and discovers that exporting a report to Excel is as simple as clicking a new button on the report's button bar. She suggests that the two of you experiment with this feature by exporting an income statement you have already memorized.

> ## To export a previously memorized report:
>
> **1** Open the Customized Income Statement that you previously memorized.
>
> **2** Click the **Export** button on the report button bar to display the Export Report window as shown in Figure 11.15.
>
> **3** Uncheck the box that adds a new worksheet with Excel tips on worksheet linking.
>
> **4** Click the **Advanced** tab in the Export Report window to view advanced options such as formatting and printing, as shown in Figure 11.16.
>
> **5** Make sure the options checked in the Advanced Options window are the same as those shown in Figure 11.16.

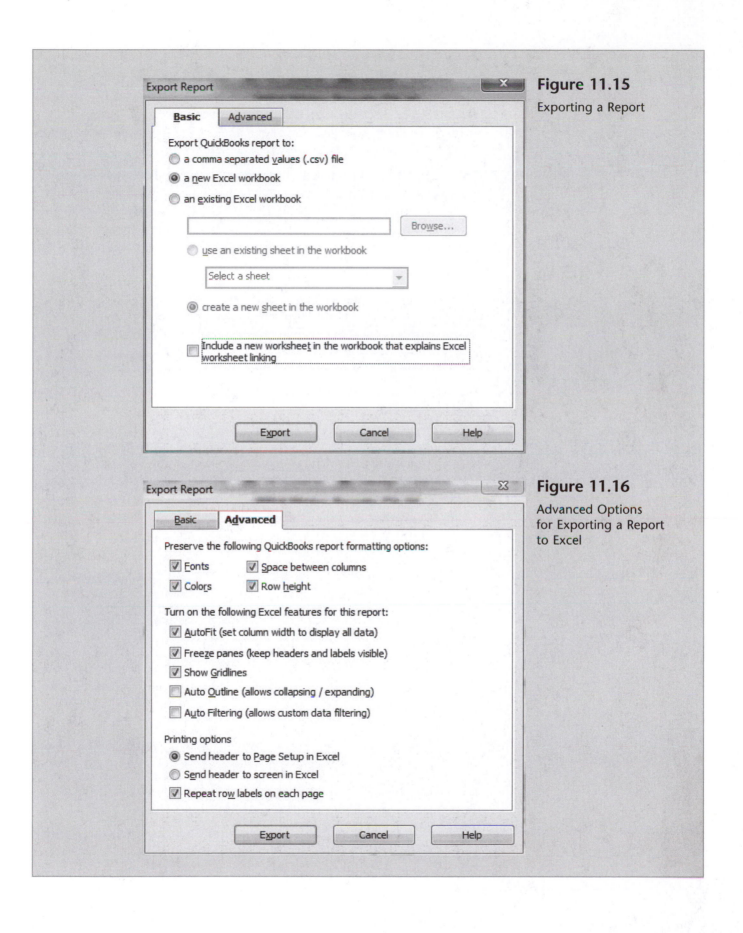

Figure 11.15

Exporting a Report

Figure 11.16

Advanced Options
for Exporting a Report
to Excel

6 Now click **Export** in the Export Report window. Your Excel program will now be opened and the report exported into Excel.

Trouble? To export reports to Excel, you must have Microsoft Excel 97 or higher installed on your computer. The figure shown below was created in Excel 2007. Your window may be different.

7 Select cell **F12** in the report just exported. Note that the export process has created a spreadsheet that has both numerical values and formulas, as shown in Figure 11.17.

Figure 11.17

Exported Excel Report

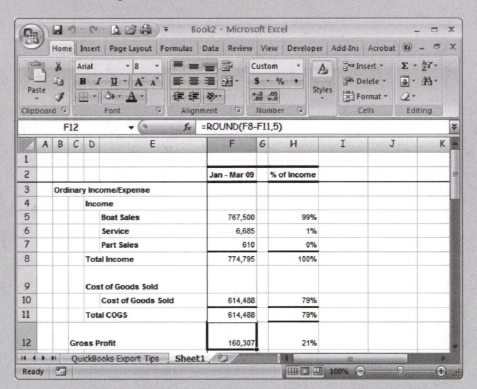

8 Click **Print** in Excel, and then click **Print Preview.** Note the header information reflects your previous modifications in QuickBooks.

9 Click **Page Setup** and then click the **Sheet** tab in the Page Setup window. Place a check mark in the **Gridlines** and **Row and column headings** check boxes. (This will enable the printing of gridlines and row and column headings.)

10 Click the **Page** tab, click the **Fit to:** option button to scale printing to one page wide and one page tall, and then click **OK.**

11 Click **Print** in the Excel Print Preview window, and then click **OK** in the Print window to print the Excel document you just created. Your spreadsheet should look like Figure 11.18.

Figure 11.18

Printed Excel Report

Wild Water Sports Ch 11
Income Statement
for the three months ended March 31, 2009

	A	B	C	D	E	F	G	H
1								
2						Jan - Mar 09		% of Income
3		Ordinary Income/Expense						
4				Income				
5					Boat Sales	767,500		99%
6					Service	6,685		1%
7					Part Sales	610		0%
8				Total Income		774,795		100%
9			Cost of Goods Sold					
10					Cost of Goods Sold	614,488		79%
11				Total COGS		614,488		79%
12			Gross Profit			160,307		21%
13				Expense				
14					Payroll Expenses	32,946		4%
15					Depreciation Expense	10,333		1%
16					Interest Expense	7,720		1%
17					Advertising and Promotion	6,700		1%
18					Insurance Expense	5,500		1%
19					Telephone Expense	5,020		1%
20					Office Supplies	4,500		1%
21					Utilities	2,870		0%
22					Bank Service Charges	75		0%
23				Total Expense		75,664		10%
24			Net Ordinary Income			84,643		11%
25		Other Income/Expense						
26			Other Income					
27				Other Income		3,000		0%
28				Interest Income		2,015		0%
29			Total Other Income			5,015		1%
30		Net Other Income				5,015		1%
31	Net Income					89,658		12%

12 Click **File** in Excel and then **Exit** to quit the Excel program.

13 Click **No** to not save the spreadsheet, since it will no longer be used.

14 Close all windows in QuickBooks.

End Note

You've completed the reports for Donna and decide to deliver them to her office. After quickly skimming each report, she compliments both you and Karen on your fine work. Walking back to your office, you comment, "That's the first time I've ever created financial statements without using debits and credits. How is that possible?"

"All the debits and credits are done for you," Karen explains. "Tomorrow I'll show you that QuickBooks, in fact, still keeps data in a debit and credit format and can provide the traditional general ledger, journal entries, and trial balance procedures you are more familiar with."

Business Events Summary

Business Event	Process Steps	Page
Create and memorize a report	Company and financial from Reports Center	313
Create graphs	Various sections from the Reports Center	319
Create additional detail reports	Various sections from the Reports Center	324
Exporting reports to Excel	Export from individual reports	328

Chapter 11 Questions

1   Explain how you can use QuickBooks to modify any report.

2   What are the optional columns available in the Modify Report window when you create a balance sheet?

3   What time periods are available for the columns of a balance sheet?

4   What options are available in the Fonts & Numbers tab for a balance sheet?

5   How do you resize a report that would normally print on two pages so that it will fit on one page?

6   When you create a balance sheet, what is the result of clicking the Collapse button?

7   What different graphs are available in QuickBooks?

8   Discuss why percentage changes identified in the budgeted vs. actual reports need to be interpreted carefully.

9   Describe the information available in the accounts receivable and accounts payable aging reports.

10 Describe the information available in the inventory stocks status report by item.

Chapter 11 Matching

Select the letter of the item below that best matches the definitions that follow. Use the text or QuickBooks Help to complete this assignment.

a. Memorized reports

b. Sales Graph by Item

c. Sales Graph by Customer

d. Income and Expense Graph

e. Accounts Receivable Graph

f. Accounts Payable Graph

g. Sales by Customer Summary

h. Sales by Item Report

i. A/R Aging Summary

j. A/P Aging Summary

_____ A report listing amounts owed by customers and organized by date due.

_____ A report illustrating income and expense by month.

_____ A report listing amounts owed to vendors and organized by date due.

_____ A process to keep customized versions of various reports.

_____ A report illustrating amounts owed to vendors by aging period.

_____ A report illustrating sales by month and by item.

_____ A report listing sales by item for a period.

_____ A report illustrating sales by month and by customer.

_____ A report listing sales by customer for a period.

_____ A report illustrating amounts owed by customers by aging period.

Chapter 11 Exercises

Chapter 11 Exercise 1
GRAPHS

Restore the file Boston Catering Ch 11 (Backup) found on the text CD or download it from the text Web site and create the following graphs for the period 7/1/10 through 8/31/10 unless otherwise specified.

a. Income and expense graph by month by account.

b. Income and expense graph by month by customer.

c. Sales graph by item.

d. Sales graph by customer.

e. Accounts receivable graph as of 8/31/10.

f. Accounts payable graph as of 8/31/10.

Chapter 11 Exercise 2
ADDITIONAL REPORTS

Restore the file Boston Catering Ch 11 (Backup) found on the text CD or download it from the text Web site and create the following reports for the period 7/1/10 through 8/31/10 (unless otherwise specified) in a manner similar to that used in the chapter.

a. Sales by customer summary.

b. Sales by item summary.

c. Accounts receivable aging summary as of 8/31/10.

d. Accounts payable aging summary as of 8/31/10.

Chapter 11 Exercise 3
EXPORT TO EXCEL

Restore the file Boston Catering Ch 11 (Backup) found on the text CD or download it from the text Web site.

a. Create a standard profit and loss report for the month of August 2010 removing the date prepared, time prepared, and report basis from the header.

b. Export the report created in (a) above to Excel in a manner similar to that used in the chapter.

c. Print the resulting Excel worksheet with gridlines and row and column headlines.

Chapter 11 Assignments

Chapter 11 Assignment 1
ADDING MORE INFORMATION: WILD WATER SPORTS

Restore the file Wild Water Sports Ch 11A (Backup) found on the text CD or download it from the text Web site, and then create and print the following reports, graphs, or spreadsheets. (**Hint:** Be sure to use the memorized reports you created before, where applicable, and just change the dates as appropriate.) As with all reports, remove the date prepared, time prepared, and report basis.

  a. Income Statement for the four months ended 4/30/09 that includes a % of Income column, prepared with a left page layout and without cents, titled "Income Statement" and subtitled "for the four months ended April 30, 2009," and sorted by total from largest to smallest amount.

  b. Balance Sheet as of 4/30/09 with a % of Column, without cents, and with a left page layout.

  c. Sales Graph by Item for the four-month period ended 4/30/09.

  d. Sales Graph by Customer for the four-month period ended 4/30/09.

  e. Income and Expense by Account graph for the four-month period ended 4/30/09.

  f. Acounts Receivable graph as of 4/30/09.

  g. Acounts Payable graph as of 4/30/09.

  h. Collapsed Sales by Customer Summary Report for the four-month period ended 4/30/09, sorted by total from largest to smallest amount with month columns.

  i. Sales by Item Summary Report for the four-month period ended 4/30/09, where columns display total only.

  j. Collapsed Accounts Receivable Aging Summary Report as of 4/30/09.

  k. Collapsed Accounts Payable Aging Summary Report as of 4/30/09.

  l. Export item (a) to Excel, and then print the Excel worksheet with gridlines and row and column headers.

Chapter 11 Assignment 2
ADDING MORE INFORMATION: CENTRAL COAST CELLULAR

Restore the file Central Coast Cellular Ch 11 (Backup) found on the text CD or download it from the text Web site, and use that copy to create and print the following. Be sure to remove the date prepared, time prepared, and report basis fields where appropriate, and memorize where possible in a report group called Solutions.

a. Income Statement for the month ended 1/31/09 with a left page layout and without cents, including a % of Income column. Use the title "Income Statement" and the subtitle "January 2009," and sort by total from largest to smallest amount.

b. Balance Sheet as of 1/31/09 with a % of Column, without cents, and with a left page layout.

c. Sales Graph by Item for the month ended 1/31/09.

d. Sales Graph by Customer for the month ended 1/31/09.

e. Income and Expense by Account graph for the month ended 1/31/09.

f. Accounts Receivable graph as of 1/31/09.

g. Accounts Payable graph as of 1/31/09.

h. Sales by Customer Summary Report for the month ended 1/31/09, sorted by total from largest to smallest amount with month columns.

i. Sales by Item Summary Report for the month ended 1/31/09, where columns display total only.

j. Accounts Receivable Aging Summary Report as of 1/31/09.

k. Accounts Payable Aging Summary Report as of 1/31/09.

l. Export item (a) to Excel, and then print the Excel worksheet with gridlines and row and column headers.

Chapter 11 Assignment 3
ADDING MORE INFORMATION: SANTA BARBARA SAILING

corporation   service

Restore the file Santa Barbara Sailing Ch 11 (Backup) found on the text CD or download it from the text Web site, and use that copy to create and print the following. As before, be sure to remove the date prepared, time prepared, and report basis fields where appropriate, and memorize where possible in a report group called Solutions.

a. Income Statement for the month ended 7/31/08 with a left page layout and without cents, including a % of Income column, titled "Income Statement," and sorted by total from largest to smallest amount.

b. Balance Sheet as of 7/31/08, with a % of Column, without cents, and with a left page layout.

c. Sales Graph by Item for the month ended 7/31/08.

d. Income and Expense Graph by Account for the month ended 7/31/08.

    e.   Sales by Customer Summary Report for the month ended 7/31/08.

    f.   A/R Aging Summary Report as of 7/31/08.

    g.   A/P Aging Summary Report as of 7/31/08.

    h.   Export item (a) to Excel, and then print the Excel worksheet with gridlines and row and column headers.

Chapter 11 Cases

Chapter 11 Case 1:
FOREVER YOUNG

sole proprietorship   service

In Chapter 10 you added some transactions to your QuickBooks file for Forever Young. Make a copy of that file, and use that copy to create and print the following. Be sure to remove the date prepared, time prepared, and report basis fields where appropriate, and memorize where possible in a report group called Solutions.

Requirements:

1   Income Statement for the month ended 1/31/08 with a left page layout without cents, including a % of Income column, titled "Income Statement," and sorted by total from largest to smallest amount.

2   Balance Sheet as of 1/31/08, with a % of Column, without cents, and with a left page layout.

3   Sales Graph by Item for the month ended 1/31/08.

4   Income and Expense Graph by Account for the month ended 1/31/08.

5   Sales by Customer Summary Report for the month ended 1/31/08.

6   A/R Aging Summary Report as of 1/31/08.

7   A/P Aging Summary Report as of 1/31/08.

8   Export item (1) to Excel, and then print the Excel worksheet with gridlines and row and column headers.

Chapter 11 Case 2:
OCEAN VIEW FLOWERS

corporation   merchandising

In Chapter 10 you added some transactions to your QuickBooks file for Ocean View Flowers. Make a copy of that file, and use that copy to create and print the following. Be sure to remove the date prepared, time prepared, and report basis fields where appropriate, and memorize where possible in a report group called Solutions.

Requirements:

1 Income Statement for the two months ended 2/29/08 with a left page layout and without cents, including a % of Income column, titled "Income Statement" and subtitled "for the two months ended February 29, 2008," and sorted by total from largest to smallest amount.

2 Balance Sheet as of 2/29/08 with a % of Column, without cents, and with a left page layout.

3 Sales Graph by Item for the two-month period ended 2/29/08.

4 Sales Graph by Customer for the two-month period ended 2/29/08.

5 Income and Expense by Account graph for the two-month period ended 2/29/08.

6 Accounts Receivable graph as of 2/29/08.

7 Accounts Payable graph as of 2/29/08.

8 Sales by Customer Summary Report for the two-month period ended 2/29/08, sorted by total from largest to smallest amount with month columns.

9 Sales by Item Summary Report for the two-month period ended 2/29/08, where columns display total only.

10 Accounts Receivable Aging Summary Report as of 2/29/08.

11 Accounts Payable Aging Summary Report as of 2/29/08.

12 Export item (1) to Excel, and then print the Excel worksheet with gridlines and row and column headers.

Chapter 11 Case 3:
ALOHA PROPERTIES

corporation   service

In Chapter 10 you added some transactions to your QuickBooks file for Aloha Properties. Make a copy of that file, and use that copy to create and print the following. Be sure to remove the date prepared, time prepared, and report basis fields where appropriate, and memorize where possible in a report group called Solutions.

Requirements:

1 Income Statement for the two months ended 2/29/08 with a left page layout and without cents, including a % of Income column, titled "Income Statement" and subtitled "for the two months ended February 29, 2008," and sorted by total from largest to smallest amount.

2 Balance Sheet as of 2/29/08 with a % of Column, without cents, and with a left page layout.

3 Sales Graph by Item for the two-month period ended 2/29/08.

4 Sales Graph by Customer for the two-month period ended 2/29/08.

5 Income and Expense by Account graph for the two-month period ended 2/29/08.

6 Accounts Receivable graph as of 2/29/08.

7 Accounts Payable graph as of 2/29/08.

8 Sales by Customer Summary Report for the two-month period ended 2/29/08, sorted by total from largest to smallest amount with month columns.

9 Sales by Item Summary Report for the two-month period ended 2/29/08, where columns display total only.

10 Accounts Receivable Aging Summary Report as of 2/29/08.

11 Accounts Payable Aging Summary Report as of 2/29/08.

12 Export item (1) to Excel, and then print the Excel worksheet with gridlines and row and column headers.

Comprehensive Problems

corporation   *merchandising*

Comprehensive Problem 1: SPORTS CITY

Restore the Sports City (Backup) file found on the text CD or download it from the text Web site. Record the following business events in chronological order (remember, dates are in the month of April 2009).

Chronological List of Business Events

Event #	Date	Business Event
1	4/16/09	Received a bill for $250 from Office Max for supplies purchased on account (record as Supplies, an expense; terms: due on receipt).
2	4/17/09	Received items and entered a bill from Nike for previously recorded Purchase Order No. 1 (terms: due on receipt).
3	4/20/09	Received items and entered a bill from Wilson Sporting Goods for previously recorded Purchase Order No. 2 (terms: due on receipt).
4	4/20/09	Hired a new employee, Anne Franks (112 East Fir #3, Lompoc, CA 93436), a single woman with Social Security number 233-89-4232. She will earn an hourly wage of $8.00, will be paid semi-monthly like all employees, and is subject to all payroll taxes including the training tax.
5	4/20/09	Received on account from Cabrillo High School a $400 payment, which is grouped with other undeposited funds.

Item	Anne	Kelly	Sam
Table 11.1			
Earnings Information for Sports City			
Earnings	600.00	1,250.00	1,458.33
Federal Withholding	−73.00	−147.00	−244.00
Social Security Employee	−37.20	−77.50	−90.41
Medicare Employee	−8.70	−18.12	−21.14
CA Withholding	−7.66	−40.72	−57.39
CA Disability Employee	−3.00	−6.25	−7.29
CA Employee Training Tax	0.60	1.25	1.46
Social Security Employer	37.20	77.50	90.41
Medicare Employer	8.70	18.12	21.14
Federal Unemployment	4.80	10.00	11.66
CA Unemployment	0.30	0.62	0.73
Check Amount	470.44	960.41	1,038.10

Event #	Date	Business Event
6	4/21/09	Invoiced Buena Vista Elementary (a new customer) for 100 shirts and 5 footballs.
7	4/22/09	Received on account from Lompoc High School a $600 payment, which is also grouped with other undeposited funds.
8	4/24/09	Borrowed $10,000 from Mid-State Bank with a short-term note payable.
9	4/24/09	Paid all bills due by 4/30/09 starting with Check No. 6.
10	4/27/09	Invoiced Cabrillo High School for 75 basketball shoes, 75 shirts, 75 shorts, 50 running shoes, 150 soccer balls, and 20 sports bags (terms: net 15).
11	4/29/09	Deposited by mail all previously received but undeposited payments, totaling $1,000, to Mid-State Bank.
12	4/30/09	Paid all employees for the pay period 4/16–4/30. Ms. Franks worked 75 hours during this period. Start with Check No. 12. (See tax information in Table 11.1.)
13	4/30/09	Recorded depreciation of $2,000 on furniture & fixtures.
14	4/30/09	Recorded the expiration of $3,000 in prepaid rent.
15	4/30/09	Reclassified the advance payment of $1,000 made by Arroyo Grande High School to Unearned Revenue (a new account).
16	4/30/09	Reconciled the bank account. The ending bank balance shown on the statement was $5,333.52. The bank charged a $40 service charge. Checks for the April 30 payroll do not appear on the statement, nor does the $1,000 deposited by mail on April 29. (Print a reconciliation summary report.)
17	4/30/09	Budget information for April through June 2009 is given in Table 11.2.

Create, memorize, and print the following reports with no date prepared, time prepared, or report basis fields.

a.   Transaction List by Date for April 2009 in landscape orientation.

b.   Profit & Loss Standard for April 2009 with a % of Income column.

c.   Balance Sheet Standard as of 4/30/09 with a % of Column.

Account	April 09	Following		Table 11.2
Sales	$30,000	15% increase each month thereafter		Budget Information for Sports City
Cost of Sales	18,000	60% of sales		
Depreciation Expense	2,000	Constant each month thereafter		
Payroll Expenses	6,500	$500 increase each month thereafter		
Rent	3,000	Constant each month thereafter		
Telephone	100	5% increase each month thereafter		
Utilities	200	5% increase each month thereafter		

d. Statement of Cash Flows for April 2009.

e. Profit & Loss Budget vs. Actual for April 2009.

f. Profit & Loss Budget Overview for April 2009 through June 2009.

g. Sales by Customer Summary Report for the month ended 4/30/09, sorted by total from largest to smallest amount with month columns.

h. Sales by Item Summary Report for the month ended 4/30/09, sorted by total from largest to smallest amount with total only columns in landscape orientation.

i. Accounts Receivable Aging Summary Report as of 4/30/09.

j. Income and Expense by Account graph for the month ended 4/30/09.

k. Export the Balance Sheet created in (c) to Excel, and then print the Excel worksheet with gridlines and row and column headers.

l. Reconciliation Summary as of 4/30/09.

Comprehensive Problem 2: PACIFIC BREW

This is a continuation of the Pacific Brew comprehensive problem from Chapter 7. Make a copy of the QuickBooks file you created for Pacific Brew in that chapter. Record the following business events in chronological order (remember, dates are in the month of January 2009).

corporation

merchandising

Chronological List of Business Events

Event #	Date	Business Event
1	1/17/09	Received items and entered a bill from Purchase Order No. 1003 to Lost Coast.
2	1/17/09	Received a bill for $2,500 from Staples (a new vendor) for supplies purchased on account (terms: net 15). These supplies will be used over the next six months; thus, you will need to create a Supplies (other current asset) account.

Event #	Date	Business Event
3	1/17/09	Using Purchase Order No. 1004, ordered from Lost Coast 1,000 of item #402, 1,500 of item #403, and 2,000 of item #404 for immediate delivery (terms: net 15).
4	1/17/09	Using Purchase Order No. 1005, ordered from Mad River 750 each of items #302, #303, #304, and #305 for immediate delivery (terms: net 30).
5	1/18/09	The manager believes that the company charges too little for its products and therefore increases all product prices 50%. (Search QuickBooks Help on prices to find out how to increase sales prices of items by a percentage. Be sure your new prices are 50% higher and not $50 higher!)
6	1/19/09	Using Purchase Order No. 1006, ordered from Humboldt 500 each of items #502, #506, and #507 for immediate delivery (terms: net 15).
7	1/20/09	Received and shipped an order to Bon Jovi's for 200 units of item #302, 150 units of item #303, and 100 units of item #507. Invoice No. 7001 was generated to bill the customer on terms of net 15.
8	1/20/09	Received and shipped an order to Ocean Grove for 100 units each of items #302, #304, and #305. Invoice No. 7002 was generated to bill the customer (terms: net 15).
9	1/23/09	Received and shipped an order to Avalon Bistro for 150 units each of items #502, #506, and #507. Invoice No. 7003 was generated to bill the customer (terms: net 30).
10	1/24/09	Received items and entered a bill from Purchase Order No. 1004 to Lost Coast.
11	1/24/09	Received a bill for $500 from Verizon (a new vendor) for January telephone expenses (terms: due on receipt).
12	1/24/09	Received a bill for $1,500 from the City of Arcata (a new vendor) for January utilities (terms: due on receipt).
13	1/26/09	Received a $4,575 check from Bon Jovi's on account (Invoice No. 7001), which will be deposited later in the week.
14	1/26/09	Received an advance on future orders from River House in the amount of $1,200, a check that will be deposited later in the week.
15	1/27/09	Deposit checks received earlier in the week to checking account.
16	1/30/09	Received items and entered a bill from Purchase Order No. 1005 to Mad River.
17	1/30/09	Paid bills from Verizon, City of Arcata, and Staples for a total of $4,500, using Check Nos. 110, 111, and 112, respectively.
18	1/30/09	Received and shipped an order (5007) to Hole in the Wall for 250 units each of items #303, #305, and #404. Payment of $7,032.50 was deposited and mailed to the checking account that same day.
19	1/31/09	Paid employees starting with Check No. 113. During the period, Duarte worked 83 hours and Lopez worked 79 hours. See tax information in Table 11.3.

Item	Emilio	Michael	Shawn	**Table 11.3**
Earnings	913.00	2,083.33	948.00	Earnings Information
Federal Withholding	−125.08	−285.42	−129.88	for Pacific
Social Security Employee	−56.61	−129.17	−58.78	
Medicare Employee	−13.24	−30.21	−13.75	
CA Withholding	−50.22	−114.58	−52.14	
CA Disability	−4.57	−10.42	−4.74	
CA Employee Training Tax	0.91	2.08	0.95	
Social Security Employer	56.61	129.17	58.78	
Medicare Company	13.24	30.21	13.75	
Federal Unemployment	7.30	16.67	7.58	
CA Company Unemployment	27.39	62.50	28.44	
Check Amount	663.28	1,513.53	688.71	

20	1/31/09	Recorded depreciation of $800 for the month with journal entry no. 1.
21	1/31/09	Recorded supplies expense (a new expense account) of $400 with journal entry no. 2.
22	1/31/09	Reclassified payment of $1,000 from River House to Unearned Revenue (a new other current liability account) with journal entry no. 3.
23	1/31/09	Accrued interest income (a new other income account) on Short-Term Investments of $2,000 with journal entry no. 4.
24	1/31/09	Accrued interest expense of $2,600 to Accrued Expenses (a new other current liability account) with journal entry no. 5.
25	1/31/09	Reconciled the Wells Fargo bank account. No bank service charges were noted on the bank statement. The ending bank balance was $31,173.30. All deposits were recorded by the bank except the $7,032.50 deposit of 1/30/09. All checks cleared the bank except those issued for payroll on 1/31/09.
26	1/31/09	Budget information for January through March is as follows. Consulting revenue is expected to remain constant at $15,000 per month. Sales of $20,000 are expected in January, increasing $5,000 each month thereafter. Cost of goods sold of $15,000 is expected in January, increasing $2,500 each month thereafter. Depreciation, interest, rent, and office supplies expenses are expected to remain constant at $1,000, $2,000, $2,500, and $500, respectively. Telephone expenses of $450 are budgeted for January and are expected to increase $50 each month thereafter. Payroll expenses are budgeted at $8,500 for January and February and then at $10,000 for March. Utilities expenses are budgeted at $1,200 for January and are expected to increase by 5% each month thereafter. Interest income of $1,500 is expected each month.

Create, memorize, and print the following reports with no date prepared, time prepared, or report basis fields:

a. Transaction List by Date for January 2009 in landscape orientation.

b. Profit & Loss Statement for January 2009 with a % of Income column using a right layout and without cents. Sort by total, largest to smallest.

c. Balance Sheet as of 1/31/09 with a % of Column with a right layout and without cents.

d. Statement of Cash Flows for January 2009 with a right layout and without cents.

e. Profit & Loss Budget vs. Actual for January 2009, without cents, sorted by total (largest to smallest).

f. Profit & Loss Budget Overview for January 2009 through March 2009, without cents, sorted by total (largest to smallest).

g. Sales by Customer Summary Report for the month ended 1/31/09, sorted by total (from largest to smallest amount) with month columns.

h. Sales by Item Summary Report for the month ended 1/31/09, without cents, sorted by total (from largest to smallest amount) with total only columns and in landscape orientation.

i. Income and Expense by Account graph for the month of January 2009.

j. Inventory Stock Status by Item report for January 2009.

k. Export the Profit & Loss Statement created in (b) to Excel, and then print the Excel worksheet with gridlines and row and column headers.

l. Reconciliation Summary as of 1/31/09.

Comprehensive Problem 3: SUNSET SPAS

corporation

merchandising

This is a continuation of the Sunset Spas comprehensive problem from Chapter 7. Make a copy of the QuickBooks file you created for Sunset in that chapter. Record the following business events in chronological order (remember, dates are in the month of January 2008).

Chronological List of Business Events

Event #	Date	Business Event
1	1/17/08	Paid $18,000 in liability insurance for the year to Hartford Insurance (a new vendor) using Check No. 111. (**Hint:** Record this in a new other current asset account called Prepaid Insurance.)
2	1/17/08	Received a bill for $500 from Staples (a new vendor) for office supplies purchased on account. Terms are net 30. (All supplies are expected to be consumed this month.)
3	1/17/08	Using Purchase Order No. 5003, ordered from Cal Spas one each of items #301, #302, and #303 for immediate delivery (terms: net 30).
4	1/18/08	Sold two of item #302 to Landmark Landscaping (a new customer, located at 8500 Ridgefield Place, San Diego, CA 92129) with six hours of installation (item #100) on sales Invoice No. 6004 (terms: net 15).

Event #	Date	Business Event
5	1/18/08	Sold two of item #202 and one of item #302 to Marriott Hotels with 15 hours of installation on sales Invoice No. 6005 (terms: net 15). Marriott Hotels had paid an advance toward future sales on 1/16/08; apply any remaining credit to this invoice when prompted.
6	1/20/08	Hired a new employee, Walton Perez (530 Miramar Rd. Apt. 230, San Diego, CA 92145), who is a single man with Social Security number 323-99-2394. He will earn an hourly wage of $9.00, will be paid semi-monthly, and is subject to all payroll taxes. He will start work 2/1/08.
7	1/21/08	Received a bill for $25,000 from Outlet Tool Supply for tools and equipment used for installation and support of spa services; terms of net 30. (Record as furniture and equipment.)
8	1/22/08	Deposited a $3,500 check from a new customer, Kristen's Spa Resort, for work to be performed next month. (Record this as a customer payment.)
9	1/23/08	Received a $23,000 bill from the City of San Diego for licenses and permits (a new expense account), payable with terms of net 15.
10	1/24/08	Sold three of item #203 to Pam's Designs with 18 hours of installation on sales Invoice No. 6006 (terms: net 15).
11	1/25/08	Received a $1,400 bill from Verizon for telephone installation and services; terms of net 15. (Record as telephone expense.)
12	1/28/08	Took delivery of a shipment from Cal Spas (our Purchase Order No. 5003). All items were received (terms: net 30).
13	1/28/08	Received $5,000 payment on account from Landmark Landscaping; this payment was deposited into the checking account.
14	1/30/08	Paid in full two bills (from City of San Diego and from Verizon) with Check Nos. 112 and 113, respectively.
15	1/31/08	Paid employees. During the period, Sanchez worked 84 hours and Lee worked 67 hours. Checks are to be handwritten starting with Check No. 114. See tax information in Table 11.4.
16	1/31/08	Sold four of item #201, three of item #202, two of item #301, and two of item #303 to a new customer, Hilton Hotels (Invoice No. 6007). Collected payment of $90,510, which was deposited the same day.
17	1/31/08	Recorded the expiration of $1,500 in prepaid insurance costs to the Insurance Expense account with journal entry no. 3.
18	1/31/08	Recorded depreciation expense of $1,750 with journal entry no. 4.
19	1/31/08	Accrued interest expense on note payable for $1,000 with journal entry no. 5. (**Hint:** Create a new other current liability account titled "Accrued Expenses.")
20	1/31/08	Accrued interest income on Short-Term Investments (a new account) for $75 with journal entry no. 6.
21	1/31/08	Reconciled the bank account. There were no bank service charges. The bank statement balance was $63,803.08 at 1/31/08, and Check Nos. 104, 114, 115, and 116 had not yet been paid. One deposit, made on 1/28/08 for $5,000, was not reflected on the bank statement.

Table 11.4	Item	Bryan	Loriel	Sharon
Earnings Information for Sunset	Hours	n/a	84	67
	Rate	$60,000.00	$13.00	$12.00
	Earnings	2,500.00	1,092.00	804.00
	Federal Withholding	−342.50	−149.60	−110.15
	Social Security Employee	−155.00	−67.70	−49.85
	Medicare Employee	−36.25	−15.83	−11.66
	CA Withholding	−137.50	−60.06	−44.22
	CA Disability	−12.50	−5.46	−4.02
	CA Employee Training Tax	2.50	1.09	0.80
	Social Security Employer	155.00	67.70	49.85
	Medicare Company	36.25	15.83	11.66
	Federal Unemployment	20.00	8.74	6.43
	CA Unemployment	6.25	2.73	2.01
	Check Amount	1,816.25	793.35	584.10

Event #	Date	Business Event
22	1/31/08	Budget information for January through March is as follows. Merchandise sales of $170,000 are expected in January, increasing $10,000 per month thereafter. Service sales of $10,000 are expected in January, increasing $1,000 per month thereafter. Cost of goods sold are expected to be 75% of merchandise sales. Depreciation, insurance, interest, office supplies, rent, and telephone are expected to remain constant at $1,800, $1,500, $1,000, $500, $3,000, and $1,500, respectively. A one-time license and permit fee of $20,000 was expected for January. Payroll expenses are estimated at $10,000 per month.

Create, memorize, and print the following reports with no date prepared, time prepared, or report basis fields.

a. Transaction List by Date for the period 1/17/08–1/31/08 in landscape orientation.

b. Profit & Loss Statement for January 2008 with a % of Income column, without cents, and centered.

c. Balance Sheet as of 1/31/08 with a % of Column, without cents, and centered.

d. Statement of Cash Flows for January 2008 without cents and centered.

e. Reconciliation Summary for January 2008 without cents and centered.

f. Profit & Loss Budget vs. Actual for January 2008 without cents and centered.

g. Profit & Loss Budget Overview for January 2008 through March 2008 without cents and centered.

h. Collapsed Sales by Customer Summary Report for the month ended 1/31/08, sorted by total (from largest to smallest amount) with total only columns, centered and without cents.

i. Sales by Item Summary Report for the month ended 1/31/08, sorted by total (from largest to smallest amount) with total only columns, centered, without cents, and in landscape orientation.

j. Accounts Receivable Aging Summary Report as of 1/31/08.

k. Accounts Payable Aging Summary Report as of 1/31/08.

l. Export the Profit & Loss Statement created in (b) to Excel, and then print the Excel worksheet with gridlines and row and column headers.

Payroll Taxes

Overview

Throughout this text, you have been provided information for employee payroll tax withholding and employer payroll tax expenses. QuickBooks has the ability to calculate each of these for you; however, they charge you an annual fee to do so. Some businesses will find this service very valuable and worth the cost, and some will not. Payroll tax computations are not straightforward. They are, in fact, quite convoluted and depend on all sorts of exceptions and rules. For example, federal income tax withholding depends on an employee's income; on how often he or she is paid (e.g., weekly, biweekly, semi-monthly, monthly); the number of exemptions claimed; and filing status: married, single, head of household, et cetera.

This appendix is designed to provide you with a basic overview of the payroll tax conundrum and is focused on federal taxes only. Each state has its own rules for income tax withholding, unemployment, and so forth.

Federal Income Tax Withholding

As previously mentioned, federal income tax withholding depends on a number of factors. Guiding employers in this regard is Circular E (Employer's Tax Guide), which can be found online at the Internal Revenue Service Web site: **http://www. irs.gov/pub/irs-pdf/p15.pdf**.

The IRS provides tables in this document for computing the specific amount to be withheld from each employee. It also provides a percentage method, which is much easier to produce for our purposes. Employees must supply employers with payroll tax information each year, such as their filing status (married, single, head of household) and the number of exemptions they are claiming.

To compute an employee's federal income tax withholding:

1 Determine the frequency of wage payments (weekly, biweekly, semi-monthly, monthly, etc.).

2 Determine the employee's filing status.

3 Based on the above, choose the appropriate table for Percentage Method of Withholding found in Figure A1.1.

Tables for Percentage Method of Withholding
(For Wages Paid in 2009)

TABLE 1—WEEKLY Payroll Period

(a) SINGLE person (including head of household)—

If the amount of wages (after subtracting withholding allowances) is: Not over $51 . . . . $0

Over—	But not over—	The amount of income tax to withhold is:	of excess over—
$51	—$200	10%	—$51
$200	—$681	$14.90 plus 15%	—$200
$681	—$1,621	$87.05 plus 25%	—$681
$1,621	—$3,338	$322.05 plus 28%	—$1,621
$3,338	—$7,212	$802.81 plus 33%	—$3,338
$7,212		$2,081.23 plus 35%	—$7,212

(b) MARRIED person—

If the amount of wages (after subtracting withholding allowances) is: Not over $154 . . . . $0

Over—	But not over—	The amount of income tax to withhold is:	of excess over—
$154	—$461	10%	—$154
$461	—$1,455	$30.70 plus 15%	—$461
$1,455	—$2,785	$179.80 plus 25%	—$1,455
$2,785	—$4,165	$512.30 plus 28%	—$2,785
$4,165	—$7,321	$898.70 plus 33%	—$4,165
$7,321		$1,940.18 plus 35%	—$7,321

TABLE 2—BIWEEKLY Payroll Period

(a) SINGLE person (including head of household)—

Not over $102 . . . . $0

Over—	But not over—	The amount of income tax to withhold is:	of excess over—
$102	—$400	10%	—$102
$400	—$1,362	$29.80 plus 15%	—$400
$1,362	—$3,242	$174.10 plus 25%	—$1,362
$3,242	—$6,677	$644.10 plus 28%	—$3,242
$6,677	—$14,423	$1,605.90 plus 33%	—$6,677
$14,423		$4,162.08 plus 35%	—$14,423

(b) MARRIED person—

Not over $308 . . . . $0

Over—	But not over—	The amount of income tax to withhold is:	of excess over—
$308	—$921	10%	—$308
$921	—$2,910	$61.30 plus 15%	—$921
$2,910	—$5,569	$359.65 plus 25%	—$2,910
$5,569	—$8,331	$1,024.40 plus 28%	—$5,569
$8,331	—$14,642	$1,797.76 plus 33%	—$8,331
$14,642		$3,880.39 plus 35%	—$14,642

TABLE 3—SEMIMONTHLY Payroll Period

(a) SINGLE person (including head of household)—

Not over $110 . . . . $0

Over—	But not over—	The amount of income tax to withhold is:	of excess over—
$110	—$433	10%	—$110
$433	—$1,475	$32.30 plus 15%	—$433
$1,475	—$3,513	$188.60 plus 25%	—$1,475
$3,513	—$7,233	$698.10 plus 28%	—$3,513
$7,233	—$15,625	$1,739.70 plus 33%	—$7,233
$15,625		$4,509.06 plus 35%	—$15,625

(b) MARRIED person—

Not over $333 . . . . $0

Over—	But not over—	The amount of income tax to withhold is:	of excess over—
$333	—$998	10%	—$333
$998	—$3,152	$66.50 plus 15%	—$998
$3,152	—$6,033	$389.60 plus 25%	—$3,152
$6,033	—$9,025	$1,109.85 plus 28%	—$6,033
$9,025	—$15,863	$1,947.61 plus 33%	—$9,025
$15,863		$4,204.15 plus 35%	—$15,863

TABLE 4—MONTHLY Payroll Period

(a) SINGLE person (including head of household)—

Not over $221 . . . . $0

Over—	But not over—	The amount of income tax to withhold is:	of excess over—
$221	—$867	10%	—$221
$867	—$2,950	$64.60 plus 15%	—$867
$2,950	—$7,025	$377.05 plus 25%	—$2,950
$7,025	—$14,467	$1,395.80 plus 28%	—$7,025
$14,467	—$31,250	$3,479.56 plus 33%	—$14,467
$31,250		$9,017.95 plus 35%	—$31,250

(b) MARRIED person—

Not over $667 . . . . $0

Over—	But not over—	The amount of income tax to withhold is:	of excess over—
$667	—$1,996	10%	—$667
$1,996	—$6,304	$132.90 plus 15%	—$1,996
$6,304	—$12,067	$779.10 plus 25%	—$6,304
$12,067	—$18,050	$2,219.85 plus 28%	—$12,067
$18,050	—$31,725	$3,895.09 plus 33%	—$18,050
$31,725		$8,407.84 plus 35%	—$31,725

Figure A1.1

Tables for Percentage Method of Withholding

4 Determine the amount of wage payment.

5 Determine the number of employee withholding allowances.

6 Use Figure A1.2 to calculate the value of a single withholding allowance.

Figure A1.2

One Withholding Allowance

Table 5. Percentage Method—2009 Amount for One Withholding Allowance

Payroll Period	One Withholding Allowance
Weekly	$ 70.19
Biweekly	140.38
Semimonthly	152.08
Monthly	304.17
Quarterly	912.50
Semiannually	1,825.00
Annually	3,650.00
Daily or miscellaneous (each day of the payroll period)	14.04

7 Compute the employee's withholding amount by multiplying his or her withholding allowances by the value of a single withholding allowance just calculated.

8 Calculate net wages by subtracting the employee's withholding amount determined above from his or her wage payment.

9 Using net wages determined above, calculate the required federal income tax withholding using the table you selected from Figure A1.1.

Example 1: A single employee claiming two withholding allowances is paid $600 weekly.

To calculate the federal income tax withholding:

1 Frequency of wage payments: weekly.

2 Employee's filing status: single.

3 Appropriate table for Percentage Method of Withholding: Table 1.

4 Amount of wage payment: 600.

5 Number of employee withholding allowances: 2.

6 Value of a single withholding allowance: 70.19.

7 Employee's withholding amount: $2 \times 70.19 = 140.38$.

8 Net wages: $600.00 - 140.38 = 459.62$.

9 Required federal income tax withholding:
$14.90 + [15\% \times (459.62 - 200.00)] = 53.84$.

Example 2: A married employee claiming three withholding allowances is paid $1,500 semi-monthly.

To calculate the federal income tax withholding:

1 Frequency of wage payments: semi-monthly.

2 Employee's filing status: married.

3 Appropriate table for Percentage Method of Withholding: Table 3.

4 Amount of wage payment: 1,500.

5 Number of employee withholding allowances: 3.

6 Value of one withholding allowance: 152.08.

7 Employee's withholding amount: $3 \times 152.08 = 456.24$.

8 Net wages: $1,500.00 - 456.24 = 1,043.76$.

9 Required federal income tax withholding:
$66.50 + [15\% \times (1,043.76 - 998.00)] = 73.36$.

Example 3: A married employee claiming five withholding allowances is paid $8,000 monthly.

To calculate the federal income tax withholding:

1 Frequency of wage payments: monthly.

2 Employee's filing status: married.

3 Appropriate table for Percentage Method of Withholding: Table 4.

4 Amount of wage payment: 8,000.

5 Number of employee withholding allowances: 5.

6 Value of one withholding allowance: 304.17.

7 Employee's withholding amount: $5 \times 304.17 = 1,520.85$.

8 Net wages: $8,000.00 - 1,520.85 = 6,479.15$.

9 Required federal income tax withholding:
$779.10 + [25\% \times (6,479.15 - 6,304.00)] = 822.89$.

Social Security and Medicare Taxes

The Federal Insurance Contributions Act (FICA) provides for a federal system of old-age, survivors, disability, and hospital insurance. The old-age, survivors, and disability insurance part is financed by the Social Security tax. The hospital insurance part is financed by the Medicare tax. Each of these taxes is reported separately. Generally, you are required to withhold Social Security and Medicare taxes from your employees' wages, and you must also pay a matching amount of these taxes. Certain types of wages and compensation are not subject to Social Security taxes. Generally, employee wages are subject to Social Security and Medicare taxes regardless of the employee's age or whether he or she is receiving Social Security benefits.

Social Security and Medicare taxes have different rates, and only the Social Security tax has a wage base limit. The wage base limit is the maximum wage that is subject to the tax for the year. Determine the amount of withholding for Social Security and Medicare taxes by multiplying each payment by the employee tax rate. There are no withholding allowances for Social Security and Medicare taxes. The current employee tax rate for Social Security is 6.2% (amount withheld). The employer tax rate for Social Security is also 6.2% (12.4% total). The 2009 wage base limit is $106,800. The current employee tax rate for Medicare is 1.45% (amount withheld). The employer tax rate for Medicare tax is also 1.45% (2.9% total). There is no wage base limit for Medicare tax; all covered wages are subject to Medicare tax. Guiding employers in this regard is Circular E (Employer's Tax Guide), which can be found online at the Internal Revenue Service Web site: **http://www.irs.gov/pub/irs-pdf/p15.pdf**.

To compute an employee's withholding and the employer's computation of Social Security and Medicare taxes:

1 Determine the employee's cumulative earnings (year to date) prior to this paycheck.

2 Determine the amount of wage payment for the current period.

3 Determine whether the employee's cumulative earnings exceed (or are close to) the Social Security wage base limit.

4 Calculate the Social Security tax by multiplying the appropriate wage payment by 6.2%.

5 Calculate the appropriate Medicare tax by multiplying the wage payment by 1.45%.

Example 1: In 2009, a single employee claiming two withholding allowances is paid $600 in the current week. Cumulative earnings to date are $3,000.

To calculate the Social Security and Medicare tax:

1 Cumulative year-to-date earnings: 3,000.

2 Wage payment: 600.

3 Cumulative earnings compared to the Social Security wage base limit: 3,000 is less than 106,800.

4 Social Security tax: $600 \times 6.2\% = 37.20$.

5 Medicare tax: $600 \times 1.45\% = 8.70$.

Example 2: In 2009, a married employee claiming three withholding allowances is paid $1,500 semi-monthly. Cumulative earnings to date are $6,000.

To calculate the Social Security and Medicare tax:

1 Cumulative year-to-date earnings: 6,000.

2 Wage payment: 1,500.

3 Cumulative earnings compared to the Social Security wage base limit: 6,000 is less than 106,800.

4 Social Security tax: $1,500 \times 6.2\% = 93.00$.

5 Medicare tax: $1,500 \times 1.45\% = 21.75$.

Example 3: In 2009, a married employee claiming five withholding allowances is paid $8,000 monthly. Cumulative earnings to date are $95,000.

To calculate the Social Security and Medicare tax:

1 Cumulative year-to-date earnings: 100,000.

2 Wage payment: 8,000.

3 Cumulative earnings compared to the Social Security wage base limit: 100,000 is less than 106,800 but close; difference is 6,800.

4 Social Security tax: $6,800 \times 6.2\% = 421.60$ (since this will bring the employee up to the wage limit).

5 Medicare tax: $8,000 \times 1.45\% = 116.00$.

Federal Unemployment Taxes

Use Form 940 (or Form 940-EZ) to report your annual Federal Unemployment Tax Act (FUTA) tax. This FUTA tax, together with state unemployment systems, provides for payments of unemployment compensation to workers who have lost their jobs. Most employers pay both federal and state unemployment taxes. Only the employer pays FUTA tax—do not collect or deduct it from your employees' wages. The FUTA tax rate for 2009 is 6.2% less state unemployment taxes paid up to 5.4%. Thus, the net tax (0.8%) applies to the first $7,000 you pay each employee in a year after subtracting any exempt payments. The $7,000 amount is the federal wage base. Your state wage base may be different. Instructions can currently be found at **http://www.irs.gov/pub/irs-pdf/i940.pdf**.

To compute an employee's federal income tax withholding:

1 Determine the employee's cumulative year-to-date earnings prior to this paycheck.

2 Determine the amount of wage payment for the current period.

3 Determine whether the employee's cumulative earnings exceed (or are close to) the FUTA wage base limit.

4 Calculate the FUTA tax by multiplying the appropriate wage payment by 0.8%.

Example 1: In 2009, a single employee claiming two withholding allowances is paid $600 in the current week. Cumulative earnings to date are $3,000.

To calculate the FUTA tax:

1 Cumulative year-to-date earnings: 3,000.

2 Wage payment: 600.

3 Cumulative earnings compared to the FUTA wage base limit: 3,000 is less than 7,000.

4 FUTA tax: 600 × 0.8% = 4.80.

Example 2: In 2009, a married employee claiming three withholding allowances is paid $1,500 semi-monthly. Cumulative earnings to date are $6,000.

To calculate the FUTA tax:

1 Cumulative year-to-date earnings: 6,000.

2 Wage payment: 1,500.

3 Cumulative earnings compared to the FUTA wage base limit: 6,000 is less than 7,000 but close; difference is 1,000.

4 FUTA tax: 1,000 × 0.8% = 8.00.

Example 3: In 2009, a married employee claiming five withholding allowances is paid $8,000 monthly. Cumulative earnings to date are $95,000.

To calculate the FUTA tax:

1 Cumulative year-to-date earnings: 95,000.

2 Wage payment: 8,000.

3 Cumulative earnings compared to the FUTA wage base limit: 95,000 is more than 7,000.

4 FUTA tax: $0 \times 0.8\% = 0.00$.

State Income Tax Withholding and Unemployment Taxes

Each state has its own rules for withholding state income taxes and computing the employer's cost for unemployment. Some states, Florida and Nevada for instance, do not have a state income tax. Other states, such as California and Hawaii, have not only state income taxes but also training taxes.

Most of the state income tax computations are similar to the federal computations in that they have different tables for different filing status as well as tables for exemption allowances. This book cannot explain how to calculate taxes for each state in the union, so you should visit your local state tax agency to determine income tax and unemployment tax rates and requirements. Sample Web site references are listed below, but the URLs will work only if the state has not since moved them or reconfigured their Web site.

California   **http://www.edd.ca.gov/Payroll_Taxes/**

Florida   **http://www.myflorida.com/dor/taxes/**

Hawaii   **http://hawaii.gov/tax/**

Appendix 1 Questions

1 What factors affect an employee's federal income tax withholding?

2 Where can employers obtain guidance on federal income tax withholding?

3 How do withholding allowances affect the computation of federal income tax withholding?

4 What does the Social Security tax finance?

5 What does the Medicare tax finance?

6 What is the Social Security tax rate?

7 Is there a wage base limit to the Social Security tax? If so, what is it for 2009?

8 What is the Medicare tax rate?

9 Is there a wage base limit to the Medicare tax? If so, what is it for 2009?

10 Who pays FUTA, and what is the current rate and computational structure?

Appendix 1 Assignments

1 In 2009, a married employee claiming one withholding allowance is paid $800 in the current week. Cumulative earnings to date are $4,000. Calculate the following:

   a. Federal income tax withholding.

   b. Employee Social Security taxes to be withheld.

   c. Employee Medicare taxes to be withheld.

   d. Employer Social Security tax.

   e. Employer Medicare tax.

   f. FUTA.

2 In 2009, a single employee claiming three withholding allowances is paid $2,000 semi-monthly. Cumulative earnings to date are $6,500. Calculate the following:

   a. Federal income tax withholding.

b.   Employee Social Security taxes to be withheld.

c.   Employee Medicare taxes to be withheld.

d.   Employer Social Security tax.

e.   Employer Medicare tax.

f.   FUTA.

3 In 2009, a single employee claiming no withholding allowances is paid $10,000 monthly. Cumulative earnings to date are $102,000. Calculate the following:

a.   Federal income tax withholding.

b.   Employee Social Security taxes to be withheld.

c.   Employee Medicare taxes to be withheld.

d.   Employer Social Security tax.

e.   Employer Medicare tax.

f.   FUTA.

Traditional Accounting: Debits and Credits

Learning Objectives

In this chapter, you will:

- Examine a trial balance and view underlying source documents
- Examine a general ledger and view underlying source documents
- Examine a journal and view underlying source documents

Case: Wild Water Sports

You and Karen have been recording basic business transactions for Wild Water Sports without using journal entries or mentioning the terms "debit" and "credit" even once. This is another one of the benefits of using QuickBooks: It enables businesspeople who were not accounting majors to "do accounting." Moreover, accountants appreciate QuickBooks because they can use it with clients who want to have more control over their finances yet do not have formal training in accounting.

As a user of QuickBooks you should know that, although you haven't actually used debits and credits in this book other than for adjusting journal entries, QuickBooks is based on a dual-entry (also known as double-entry) accounting system. Every transaction that you entered in Chapters 6 through 11 had an effect on two or more accounts in the chart of accounts. For example, every sales invoice increased Sales Revenue and Accounts Receivable. Every time you initiated a QuickBooks activity such as "receive payments," Cash was increased and Accounts Receivable was decreased.

QuickBooks actually provides three equivalent ways for you to record transactions using the double-entry system: You can record transactions by using business documents (what QuickBooks refers to as Forms), by using registers, or by making journal entries. So far in this textbook, you have used all three. Recall that using a document involves recording a transaction by completing a business document, such as a sales invoice or a check. When you correctly complete the document, the effect(s) of the transaction on the financial statements are automatically entered. For example, when Wild Water paid its yearly insurance premium of $22,000 on 1/31/07, the dual effects of this transaction on the Prepaid Insurance account (increased) and the Bank of Florida account (decreased) were processed by filling out a business document—specifically, a check. In contrast, using registers involves accessing a particular account's register and inputting the effects of the transaction. For example, you could choose either the Prepaid Insurance register or the Bank of Florida (cash) register and enter the changes (increase/ decrease) as needed.

You ask if it is still possible to use debits and credits in QuickBooks, because your formal accounting training focused primarily on journal entries as the source of every transaction. Karen explains that, yes, it is indeed possible, and she offers to demonstrate QuickBooks's ability to prepare a trial balance, a general ledger, and a journal entry. You point out that, under normal circumstances, you would begin the accounting process with a journal entry. However, in this case you will view the steps with her in reverse order, because the process has already been completed.

Trial Balance

The trial balance is a two-column listing of all asset, liability, owners' equity, revenue, and expense accounts. Accounts that have debit balances are listed in the debit column, and accounts that have credit balances are listed in the credit column. Although not foolproof, an equality between debits and credits generally indicates that the accounting process has been followed correctly.

With QuickBooks, you can quickly create a trial balance. All you need is the date as of which you want the trial balance. Then you can use QuickBooks's QuickZoom feature to view supporting accounts and supporting journals or business documents.

To create the trial balance and examine supporting detail:

1 Open the Wild Water Sports file you used in Chapter 11.

2 From the Reports Center, click **Accountant & Taxes** and then click **Trial Balance**.

3 Change the report dates to read from **1/1/09** to **3/31/09**; then click **Refresh** to view the trial balance you have prepared, as shown in Figure A2.1.

4 Double-click the **16,500.00** Prepaid Insurance amount to view the Prepaid Insurance account shown in Figure A2.2.

5 Double-click on the **5,500.00** amount to view the prepaid insurance adjusting journal entry in the Make General Journal Entries window, as shown in Figure A2.3. Recall that this adjusting journal entry increases an expense and decreases an asset.

6 Close all windows.

Figure A2.1

Trial Balance

Wild Water Sports Ch 11A
Trial Balance
As of March 31, 2009

	Mar 31, 09	
	Debit	**Credit**
Bank of Florida	47,442.42	
Short-Term Investments	39,890.41	
Accounts Receivable	399,932.73	
Prepaid Advertising	20,000.00	
Inventory Boats	243,600.00	
Inventory Parts	2,112.00	
Prepaid Insurance	16,500.00	
Undeposited Funds	0.00	
Furniture and Equipment	295,000.00	
Accumulated Depreciation		17,833.00
Accounts Payable		216,200.00
MasterCard	0.00	
Unearned Revenue		10,000.00
Accrued Expenses		1,760.97
Payroll Liabilities		2,934.66
Sales Tax Payable		28,457.66
Loans Payable		297,632.40
Capital Stock		400,000.00
Opening Balance Equity	0.00	
Retained Earnings	0.00	
Boat Sales		767,500.00
Part Sales		610.00
Service		6,685.00
Cost of Goods Sold	614,488.00	
Advertising and Promotion	6,700.00	
Bank Service Charges	75.00	
Depreciation Expense	10,333.00	
Insurance Expense	5,500.00	
Interest Expense	7,719.57	
Office Supplies	4,500.00	
Payroll Expenses	32,945.97	
Telephone Expense	5,020.00	
Utilities	2,870.00	
Interest Income		2,015.41
Other Income		3,000.00
TOTAL	**1,754,629.10**	**1,754,629.10**

Figure A2.2

Prepaid Insurance

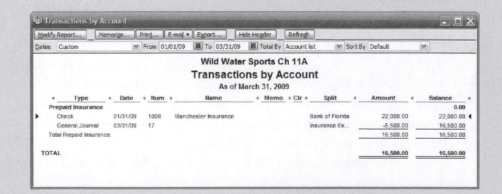

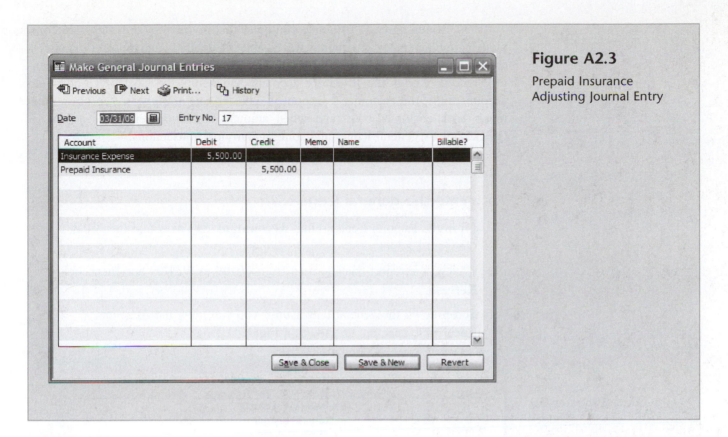

Figure A2.3

Prepaid Insurance Adjusting Journal Entry

The Prepaid Insurance register actually reflects the entering of an adjustment via a journal entry. The adjustment itself was an adjusting entry prompted by the existence of a business source document, such as a check, an invoice, or a bill.

General Ledger

The general ledger is used in accounting information systems to store the effects of individual asset, liability, owners' equity, revenue, and expense accounts. In manual accounting systems, journals are used to record business transactions, the effects of which are then posted or transferred to a general ledger. This recording and posting is compressed into one step in QuickBooks as the transactions are recorded. Karen decides to use a sales invoice to demonstrate how the effects of a transaction are stored in the general ledger.

She explains that the invoice itself is used as a source business document. Information is entered into the invoice; then, when you click OK, the invoice is stored and the consequence of that invoice is immediately recorded. In accounting jargon: once you enter the invoice, a debit is posted to the Accounts Receivable account in the general ledger and a credit is posted to the Sales Revenue account in the general ledger.

"In my accounting classes, we usually posted all the sales for a month with one journal entry," you comment. "In this case, it looks like each sale is recorded individually. Doesn't that take a lot of time?"

"Yes," Karen agrees. "But once you enter this invoice, several steps are completed simultaneously. Accounts Receivable is debited, and Sales Revenue is credited. If we're selling inventory, the same invoice updates the perpetual inventory record, credits the Inventory account, and debits the Cost of Goods Sold account. Plus, the customer's account is adjusted accordingly, so we know how much each customer owes and when amounts are due. Let's take a look at QuickBooks's general ledger and some underlying transactions."

To create the general ledger:

1 From the Reports Center, click **Accountant & Taxes** and then click **General Ledger**.

2 Change the report dates to read from **1/1/09** to **3/31/09** and then click **Refresh**.

3 Scroll down the general ledger until you can view the Accounts Receivable account, as shown in Figure A2.4.

Figure A2.4

Accounts Receivable Portion of the General Ledger

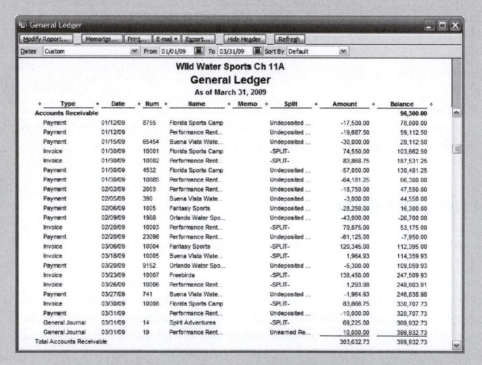

4 Double-click Invoice No. **10001** dated 1/30/09 to Florida Sports Camp in order to view the underlying source document: the specific sales invoice that increased accounts receivable by $74,550, as shown in Figure A2.5.

5 Close the Create Invoices window. Double-click the payment dated 1/30/09 from Florida Sports Camp via their Check No. **4532** to view the underlying source document: the specific payment that decreased accounts receivable by $57,050, as shown in Figure A2.6.

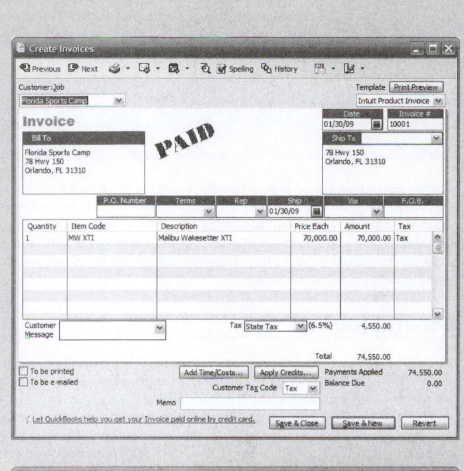

Figure A2.5
Invoice

Figure A2.6
Receive Payment

6 Print the first page of the General Ledger by clicking the **Print** button on the General Ledger window.

7 Click the **Pages** option button in the Page Range: section of the Print Reports window.

8 Type **1** in the To: text box and then click **Print**.

9 Close all windows.

After seeing how easy this is, you might wonder why QuickBooks—or some other similar program—isn't used all the time in business. The reason is that many companies often have their own accounting software that has been customized to their specifications. But many smaller businesses, which often can't afford the luxury of customized software, have found QuickBooks to be an inexpensive yet powerful and easy-to-use alternative.

General Journal

"I'm still not convinced that QuickBooks follows the debit and credit convention," you comment. "Most times you drill down from the general ledger or trial balance you get to a source document, not to a journal entry."

"That's true," Karen responds. "Remember, we entered most of these transactions from source documents, not from journal entries as you did in your accounting classes. However, I can still show you that, if needed, QuickBooks can provide you with the underlying debits and credits for all business transactions recorded."

To view journal entry support for business transactions:

1 From the Reports Center, click **Accountant & Taxes** and then click **Journal**.

2 Change the report dates to read from **2/1/09** to **2/28/09** and then click **Refresh**.

3 The first four transactions for the month of February are shown in Figure A2.7.

4 The first transaction shown debits the Inventory Parts account and credits the Bank of Florida account by $1,000. Double-click the transaction with **Delco** to reveal the check (source document) that was used to pay Delco for the parts purchased.

5 Close the check window. Scroll down the Journal window until you come to Sales Receipt 6005 recorded on 2/3/09, as shown in Figure A2.8.

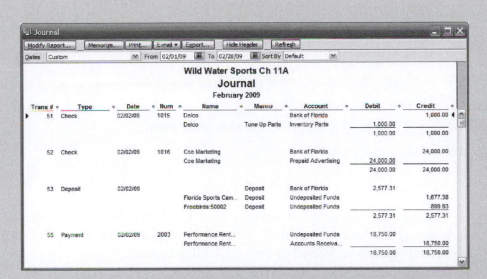

Figure A2.7

Journal Showing the First Four Transactions for the Month of February

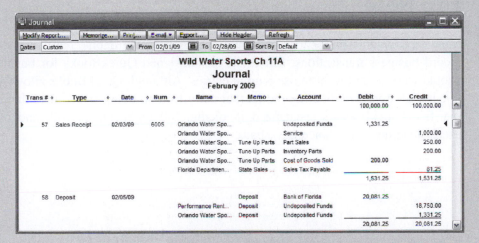

Figure A2.8

Journal Containing Showing Receipt 6005

6 The sales receipt transaction shows debits to Undeposited Funds (an asset) and Cost of Goods Sold (an expense) as well as credits to Service (an income account), Parts (an income account), Inventory Parts (an asset), and Sales Tax Payable (a liability).

7 Double-click **Sales Receipt 6005** to view the underlying source document that created this journal entry.

8 Close the sales receipt window.

9 The transaction below Sales Receipt 6005 should be the deposit made on 2/5/09. This transaction shows a debit to the Bank of Florida account and two credits to the Undeposited Funds account. (Recall that the previous transaction recorded the collection of cash as an increase in Undeposited Funds because they were not immediately deposited into the company's bank account.)

10 Double-click the **Deposit** journal entry to view the underlying source document that created this journal entry.

11 Close the deposit window.

12 Print the first page of the Journal by clicking the **Print** button on the Journal window.

13 Click the **Pages** option button in the Page Range: section of the Print Reports window.

14 Type **1** in the To: text box, and then click **Print**.

15 Close all windows.

You can now see why accountants want to see the Journal information. It validates QuickBooks as a "real" accounting program with underlying debits and credits like those learned in their accounting courses.

End Note

Many accountants prefer to use journal entries (i.e., the debit–credit format) to record business transactions. But Intuit Inc. designed QuickBooks for business-people who did not want to use journal entries. Although QuickBooks allows you to enter all transactions using the journal entry format, doing so requires that you sacrifice QuickBooks's specialized invoicing, bill payment, payroll, and other useful features. The choice is yours!

Appendix 2 Questions

1 In what order does QuickBooks list accounts in the trial balance report?

2 What QuickBooks feature allows you to access supporting accounts or journals when viewing the trial balance?

3 What happens when you double-click an amount on the trial balance?

4 Explain how a transaction recorded through an account register also creates a general journal entry.

5 Why does QuickBooks have a general ledger?

6 What advantages does QuickBooks's document-initiated recording method have over the standard journal entry method?

7 What happens when you double-click on an amount in the general ledger?

8 How do you print one page of the General Ledger?

9 What information about business transactions is shown in the Journal?

10 Why would someone want to look at a QuickBooks Journal?

Appendix 2 Assignments

1 *Creating a Trial Balance, General Ledger, and Journal for Wild Water Sports*

Use the Wild Water Sports file you completed in Chapter 11 for the following tasks.

corporation

merchandising

a. Create and print a Trial Balance for the period January 1 to April 30, 2009.

b. View the General Ledger for the period April 1 to April 30, 2009. Print Page 1 in landscape view.

c. View the Journal for the period April 1 to April 30, 2009. Print Page 1 in landscape view.

2 *Creating a Trial Balance, General Ledger, and Journal for Central Coast Cellular*

Use the Central Coast Cellular file you completed in Chapter 11 to perform the following tasks.

sole proprietorship

merchandising

a. Create and print a Trial Balance for the period January 1 to January 31, 2009.

b. View the General Ledger for the period January 1 to January 31, 2009. Print Page 1 in landscape view.

c. View the Journal for the period January 1 to January 31, 2009. Print Page 1 in landscape view.

Appendix 2 Case Problems

1 *Creating a Trial Balance, General Ledger, and Journal for Aloha Properties*

Requirements:

Use the file you completed for the Aloha Properties case in Chapter 11 to perform the following tasks.

a. Create and print a Trial Balance for the period January 1 to February 29, 2008.

b. View the General Ledger for the period February 1 to February 29, 2008. Print Page 1 in landscape view.

c. View the Journal for the period February 1 to February 29, 2008. Print Page 1 in landscape view.

2 *Creating a Trial Balance, General Ledger, and Journal for Ocean View Flowers*

Requirements:

Use the file you completed for the Ocean View Flowers case in Chapter 11 to perform the following tasks.

a. Create and print a Trial Balance for the period January 1 to February 29, 2008.

b. View the General Ledger for the period February 1 to February 29, 2008. Print Page 1 in landscape view.

c. View the Journal for the period February 1 to February 29, 2008. Print Page 1 in landscape view.

Index

A

Accounts
  handling opening balances, 117–120
  printing chart of, 120
  setting up, 115–116
  using names vs. using numbers for, 103–104
Accounts payables
  aging, 83–85, 327–328
  graphing, 323–324
  recategorizing opening balances, 117–119
  on statements of cash flows, 71–72
  vendor balances, 85–89, 114
Accounts receivables. *See also* Customer balances
  aging detail, 12–14
  aging summary, 77–80, 326–327
  graphing, 323
  investigating, 77–80
  recategorizing opening balances, 117–119
Accruing
  expenses, 261–264
  revenues, 264–268
Accumulated depreciation
  entering opening balance for, 116
  on statements of cash flows, 68–70
Active window, 10–11
Actual (Budget vs.) reports, 295–297, 301–303
Adjusting entries
  accruing expenses, 261–264
  accruing revenues, 264–268
  bank reconciliation, 276–278
  expenses incurred but previously deferred, 268–272
  overview, 261
  unearned revenues, 272–275
Advanced deposits
  applying, 166–169
  as credit balances, 155
  recording, 158–160, 233

B

Advertising, adjusting prepaid, 268–269
Alignment option, 37, 56
Assets
  assigned numbers for, 104
  budgeting, 297–298

Backup files
  creating, 11, 127–128
  restoring, 8–9, 129
Balance sheets
  budgeted, 299–303
  comparative, 30–31
  customized, 35–39, 317–319
  identifying owner of, 37
  printing, 40
  standard, 28–29, 185–186, 242–243
  summary, 31–32
  using QuickZoom with, 32–35
  viewing effect of adjustments on, 270–272
Balances
  credit, 155. *See also* Advanced deposits
  customer. *See* Customer balances
  opening, 117–120
  vendor, 85–89, 114
Banking. *See also* Loans
  on home page, 18
  reconciling statements, 276–278
  recording cash deposits, 163–164, 230–231, 235
  recording payment for sales, 169–170
Bar chart example, 6, 7
Bill payments
  recording checks written for, 174–175, 233–234
  viewing from transaction history, 88
Bills. *See also* Invoices; Sales receipts
  entering, 19
  upon receipt of inventory, 225–227

C

Cash, classifying, 69–70
Cash-oriented activities
  financing, 150–151
  investing, 152–155
  operating. *See* Cash-oriented operating activities
Cash-oriented operating activities. *See also* Deposits; Payroll; Recording
  creating invoice for inventory sale, 166–169
  creating purchase orders, 155–158
  overview, 155
CDs, installation and data file, 3–4
Centers, accessing from home page, 18
Century Kitchens, introduction, 2–3. *See also specific topics*
Chart examples, 6, 7
Chart of accounts, printing, 120
Checking register example, 6
Checks
  assigning to bills, 174–175, 233–234
  writing. *See* Writing checks
Classes, defined, 290
Classifying cash, 69–70
Coach, 21–23
Command menus, 9–10

Budgeting
  assets, liabilities, equities, 297–299
  creating/printing balance sheets, 299–303
  creating/printing income statements, 294–297
  expenses, 293–294
  overview, 289–290
  revenues, 290–292
Business activities, types overview, 149–150. *See also* Cash-oriented activities; Financing activities; Investing activities; Operating activities; Reports

Company
    creating new file, 97–101
    on home page, 18
Comparative balance sheets, 30–31.
    See also Balance sheets
Comparative income statements,
    50–51, 241–242. *See also* Income
    statements
Compensation setup, 124
Compounding in revenue budgets,
    291
Contact lists
    customers, 112–113
    employees, 127
    vendors, 115
Creating. *See also* Setting up
    accounts payable aging
        summary, 84
    accounts receivable aging
        summary, 77
    balance sheets. *See* Balance
        sheets
    budgets. *See* Budgeting
    company file, 97–101
    customer balance summary, 80
    graphs, 319–324
    income statements. *See* Income
        statements
    inventory valuation summary,
        81–82
    invoices. *See* Invoices
    jobs for existing customers, 175,
        227–228
    purchase orders, 155–158,
        224–225
    sales receipts, 161–162
    statements of cash flows,
        67–69
    Transaction List by Date reports,
        187–188, 242–244
    vendor balance summary, 85–86
Credit balances, 155. *See also*
    Advanced deposits
Credit card accounts, setting up
    example, 115–116
Credit cards, recording deposits
    using, 159
Credit terms, defined, 231
Customer balances. *See also*
    Accounts receivables
    detail, 14–16
    summary, 80, 111–112, 113

Customers
    adding new during PO creation,
        157–158
    adding new during sales receipt
        creation, 161–162
    creating jobs for existing, 175
    on home page, 17–18
    menu, 10
    printing contact list, 112–113
    sales summary report, 325
    setting up, 110–113
Customizing
    balance sheets, 35–38, 317–319
    income statements, 47–50,
        53–57, 313–317
    statements of cash flows, 69–71

D

Data files CD, 3–4. *See also* Files
Date format, changing, 45–46
Debts. *See* Loans
Deferred expenses, adjusting/
    recording, 268–272
Deposits
    into bank accounts, 163–164,
        169–170, 230–231, 235
    on future sales. *See* Advanced
        deposits
    for purchase of stock in
        company, 150–151
    as unearned revenue, 272–275
Depreciation expense
    recording, 269–270
    on statements of cash flows,
        68–70
Discount items, defined, 104
Display tab, balance sheets, 35–36
Divided by 1000 option, 36, 38

E

EasyStep Interview, 97–101
Editing items, 108–110. *See also*
    Modifying
Electronic transfers, 221, 236
Employee Center, 18, 20
Employees. *See also* Payroll
    on home page, 18
    hourly, on payroll, 180, 181, 182
    printing contact list, 127
    setting up, 123–127

End-of-month expenses, recording,
    239
Enter Bills example, 19
Equipment
    recording purchase of with cash,
        154–155
    recording purchase of with long-
        term debt, 240–241
Equities
    assigned numbers for, 104
    on balance sheets, 29
    budgeting stockholder's,
        298–299
    opening balance, 117–119
Evaluating firm's performance and
    financial position, 184–188,
    241–244
Excel, exporting reports to, 328–331
Expenses. *See also* Depreciation
    expense
    accruing, 261–264
    assigned numbers for, 104
    budgeting, 293–294
    graphing, 321–322
    incurred but previously deferred,
        268–272
    recording end-of-month, 239
Expenses tab on Write Checks
    window, 152, 153
Exporting reports to Excel, 328–331

F

Federal tax. *See* Payroll taxes
Files. *See also* Backup files
    automatic saving of, 12, 110
    creating new company, 97–101
Financial position, evaluating,
    184–188, 241–244
Financing activities. *See also*
    Writing checks
    cash-oriented, 150–151
    noncash, 240–241
    overview, 150
Fit report to *n* page(s) wide option,
    60, 61
Fonts & Numbers tab
    balance sheets, 36
    income statements, 58–60
Footer/Header tab. *See* Header/Footer
    tab
Forecast, defined, 67

Forms, overview, 4–6
Furniture, recording purchase of, 154–155

G

General journal. *See also* Adjusting entries
    opening balances adjustments on, 118–119
    printing entries, 273–275
General ledger, creating new account, 152–153
Graphs
    creating, 319–324
    overview, 6–7
Gross margin, on Sales by Item report, 325–326

H

Header/Footer tab
    balance sheets, 37
    income statements, 46, 48, 49, 54, 56
    statements of cash flows, 68
Help
    manual payroll setup using, 120–122
    menu, 10, 16
    using, 16–17
Home page, 17–20
Hourly employees, on payroll, 180, 181, 182

I

Icon bar, 10
Inactive windows, 10–11
Income and expense graphs, 321–322
Income statements
    budgeted, 294–297
    comparative, 50–51, 241–242
    customized, 47–50, 53–57, 313–317
    example, 6, 7
    identifying owner of, 48, 49
    printing, 57–61
    standard, 46–47, 185
    using QuickZoom with, 52–53
"Income" vs. "revenue," 46, 290

Installation CD, 3
Insurance
    adjusting prepaid, 269
    writing checks for prepaid, 171
Interest expense, accruing, 261–264
Interest income, accruing, 264–265
Inventory
    receipt of and billing for, 225–227
    receipt of and payment for, 164–166
    valuation, 81–83
Inventory part items. *See also* Items
    defined, 104
    writing checks for, 172
Investing activities
    cash-oriented, 152–155
    depreciation expense as, 68–69
    noncash, 240–241
    overview, 150
    short-term, 222–223
Invoices
    inputs for, 17–18
    for inventory sales, 166–169
    for sales on account, 231–233
    sales receipts vs., 182
    sample form, 4–5
    for service-related activities, 228–230
    viewing from accounts payable aging reports, 84–85
    viewing from accounts receivable aging reports, 78–79
    viewing from balance sheets, 33–34
    viewing from income statements, 52, 53
    viewing from inventory valuation detail reports, 82–83
    viewing from vendor balance detail reports, 86–87
Items. *See also* Inventory part items; Service items; *specific items*
    defined, 104
    editing, 108–110
    printing list of, 109
    sales summary report, 325–326
    setting up, 104–108
Items tab on Write Checks window, 152

J

Jobs
    creating, 175, 227–228
    overview, 175
Journal. *See* General journal

L

Landscape orientation, 60, 61
Ledger. *See* General ledger
Liabilities. *See also* Unearned revenues
    assigned numbers for, 104
    budgeting, 298–299
    credit balances and, 155
    payroll tax. *See* Payroll taxes
    sales tax, 235–237
Lists
    menu, 10
    overview, 4, 5
Loans
    accruing interest on, 261–264
    recording, 151
    recording equipment purchase in exchange for, 240–241
    recording payments on, 219–220, 221–222
Long-term liability accounts, setting up example, 116

M

Memorizing
    customized balance sheets, 38–39, 317–319
    customized income statements, 313–317
    other customized reports, 325–328
Menu bar, 9, 10
Menus, dynamic nature of, 12
Modifying items, 108–110. *See also* Customizing
Money market funds, recording purchase of, 152–153

N

Net income
    accumulated depreciation and, 68–69
    on balance sheets, 29, 319

retained earnings and, 297, 298–299, 319
Noncash investing/financing activities, 240–241
Number assignments, 104

O

Opening balance equity, recategorizing, 117–119
Operating activities. *See also* Cash-oriented operating activities; Deposits; Invoices; Purchase orders; Recording
  depreciation expense as, 69–70
  overview, 150
  paying sales and payroll taxes, 235–238
  receiving and billing for inventory, 225–227
Orientation, 60, 61
Owner's equity on balance sheets, 29

P

Payables. *See* Accounts payables
Payments. *See* Bill payments; Receipt of Payments
Payroll. *See also* Employees; Payroll taxes
  completing time sheets, 177–179
  creating jobs for existing customers, 175
  creating paychecks, 239–240
  manual vs. using service, 175
  processing, 179–181
  recording end-of-month, 239–240
  setting up, 120–123
Payroll taxes
  entering during employee setup, 124–126
  entering during paycheck creation, 240
  paying liabilities, 235, 237–238
  sources of withholding amounts, 182
Percentages
  % Change, 50, 51
  % of Column, 35, 36, 38, 317, 318

% of Income, 54, 55, 313, 314, 317, 319
  on balance sheets vs. on income statements, 319
Performance, evaluating firm's, 184–188, 241–244
Pie chart example, 6, 7
Planning and Budgeting. *See* Budgeting
Portrait orientation, 60, 61
Preferences, setting up, 101–104
Prepaid advertising, adjusting, 268–269
Prepaid insurance
  adjusting, 269
  writing checks for, 171
Printing
  budgeted balance sheets, 299–303
  budgeted income statements, 294–297
  chart of accounts, 120
  comparative summary balance sheets, 40
  customer balances, 15–16, 112, 113
  customer contact list, 112–113
  customized income statements, 57–61, 314–315
  employee contact list, 127
  exported Excel report, 330–331
  graphs, 319–324
  help topics, 17
  item listing, 109
  journal entries, 273–275
  other customized reports, 325–328
  preview feature, 58, 60
  reconciliation summary, 278
  statements of cash flows, 72
  vendor balances, 114
  vendor contact list, 115
Processing payroll, 179–181
Profit & Loss reports. *See also* Income statements
  budget, 294–297
  example, 6, 7
Promotions, adjusting prepaid, 268–269
Purchase orders
  creating, 155–158, 224–225
  overview, 155

receiving and paying for inventory, 164–166
viewing from bills, 87

Q

QuickBooks. *See also* Files; Help; Setting up; *specific features*
  exiting, 24
  launching, 8
  overview, 4–7
  window components, 9–11
QuickZoom
  using with accounts payable aging reports, 84–85
  using with accounts receivable aging reports, 77–78
  using with balance sheets, 32–35
  using with income statements, 52–53
  using with inventory valuation detail reports, 82–83
  using with statements of cash flows, 71–72

R

Receipt of Payments. *See also* Cash-oriented operating activities
  example, 19–20
  viewing from balance sheets, 34
  viewing from accounts receivable aging summary reports, 79–80
Receivables. *See* Accounts receivables; Customer balances
Reclassifying deposits as unearned revenue, 272–273
Reconciling bank statements, 276–278
Recording. *See also* Adjusting entries; Deposits; Invoices; Writing checks
  cash collected on account, 160, 234–235
  cash sales, 161–162, 230–231
  cash-oriented financing activities, 150–151
  cash-oriented investing activities, 152–155
  electronic transfers, 221, 236
  end-of-month expenses, 239
  end-of-month payroll, 239–240

equipment purchase, 154–155
expenses incurred but previously deferred, 268–272
furniture purchase, 154–155
inventory receipt and payment, 164–166
inventory sales, 166–170
loan payments, 219–220, 221–222
loans, 151
money market funds purchase, 152–153
noncash investing/financing activities, 240–241
opening balances adjustments, 118–119
purchase orders, 155–158, 224–225
sales payments, 169–170
service-related activities, 227–230
short-term investing activities, 222–223
Reducing report size for printing, 58–61
Registers, overview, 6
Reports. *See also* Balance sheets; Graphs; Income statements; Statements of cash flows; Supporting schedules/reports; *specific reports*
exporting to Excel, 328–331
menu, 10
overview, 6–7
Restoring backup files, 8–9, 129
Retained earnings
budgeting, 297, 298
net income/loss and, 297, 319
recategorizing opening balances, 117–119
"Revenue" vs. "income," 46, 290
Revenues
accruing, 264–268
adjusting for unearned, 272–275
assigned numbers for, 104
budgeting, 290–292
graphing, 321–322
Reversing
expense accrual, 263–264
interest income accrual, 265

reclassification of deposits as unearned revenue, 272–273
sales accrual, 267–268
Rounding to whole dollar, 36, 55–56, 72, 313, 317

S

Sales accrual, 265–268
Sales by Customer Summary report, 325
Sales by Item Summary report, 325–326
Sales graphs, 319–321
Sales on account, recording invoices for, 231–233
Sales receipts
for cash sales, 161–162
invoices vs., 182
for time recorded via payroll system, 182–184
Sales tax liabilities, 235–237
Service items. *See also* Items
defined, 104
recording and billing for, 227–230
Setting up
accounts, 115–116
customers, 110–113
employees, 123–127
items, 104–108
payroll, 120–123
preferences, 101–104
vendors, 113–115
Short-term investment activities, recording, 222–223
Spelling check, 156
Spotlighting workflows, 22, 23
Spreadsheets, exporting to, 328–331
Standard balance sheets, 28–29, 185–186, 242–243. *See also* Balance sheets
Standard income statements, 46–47, 185. *See also* Income statements
State tax. *See* Payroll taxes
Statements of cash flows, 67–72
Stock purchase
opening balance equity and, 117–119
recording deposits for, 150–151

Stockholder's equity, budgeting, 298–299
Subtitles, automatic change of, 56
Subtotal items, defined, 104
Summary balance sheets, creating, 31–32. *See also* Balance sheets
Supporting schedules/reports
accounts payable aging, 83–85, 327–328
accounts receivable aging, 12–14, 77–80, 326–327
customer balance, 14–16, 80, 111–112, 113
defined, 76
inventory valuation, 81–83
vendor balance, 85–89, 114

T

Taxes, payroll. *See* Payroll taxes
Taxes, sales, 235–237
Thousands, showing amounts in, 36, 38
Time, billing for, 182–184, 227–228
Time sheets
completing, 177–179
overview, 175
payroll and, 181, 182
use of when creating jobs, 230
Title bar, 9, 10
Transaction List by Date report, 187–188, 242–244
Transfers, electronic, 221, 236
Trial balance, 117
Tutorials, 22–23

U

Unearned revenues
adjusting for, 272–275
advanced deposits and, 155
Utilities, writing checks for, 173–174

V

Vendors
balances, 85–89, 114. *See also* Accounts payables
on home page, 18
printing contact list, 115
setting up, 113–115

W

Wild Water Sports, Inc.,
  introduction, 96–97. *See also*
  specific topics
Window menu, 10
Windows, active/inactive, 10–11
Withholding amounts, sources of, 182
Without Cents option, 36, 55–56, 72,
  313, 317

Workflows
  on home page, 17–18
  spotlighting, 22, 23
Writing checks
  for bill payments, 174–175
  for end-of-month expenses, 241
  for expenses and parts, 170–174
  for inventory received, 164–166
  for loan payments, 219–220,
    221–222

for money market fund
  purchases, 152–155

Z

Zooming in/out during printing, 40.
  See also QuickZoom